HISTORY
AND
HISTORIOGRAPHY

A THIRTY-ONE-VOLUME FACSIMILE SERIES
OF CLASSIC BOOKS FOR BOTH HISTORIANS AND STUDENTS
ON THE NATURE OF HISTORY,
HOW HISTORY IS COMMUNICATED,
AND HOW TO DO HISTORICAL RESEARCH

EDITED BY
ROBIN WINKS
YALE UNIVERSITY

A GARLAND SERIES

THE HISTORIAN'S WORKSHOP

ORIGINAL ESSAYS BY SIXTEEN HISTORIANS

edited by
L. P. Curtis, Jr.

Garland Publishing, Inc., New York & London

1985

For a complete list of the titles in this
series see the final pages of this volume.

Library of Congress Cataloging in Publication Data
Main entry under title:

The Historian's workshop.

  (History and historiography)
  Reprint. Originally published:
1st ed. New York : Knopf, c1970.
    1. History—Methodology—Addresses, essays, lectures.
2. Historians—Addresses, essays, lectures. I. Curtis,
L. Perry (Lewis Perry), 1932–   . II. Series.
D16.H6736   1985   907.2   83-49172
ISBN 0-8240-6357-0 (alk. paper)

The volumes in this series are printed
on acid-free, 250-year-life paper.

Printed in the United States of America

THE HISTORIAN'S WORKSHOP

THE
HISTORIAN'S
WORKSHOP
Original Essays
by Sixteen
Historians

edited by

L. P. CURTIS, JR.

University of California, Berkeley

Alfred A. Knopf　　　*New York*

Copyright © 1970 by Alfred A. Knopf, Inc.

All rights reserved under International and Pan-American Copyright Conventions. Published in the United States by Alfred A. Knopf, Inc., New York, and simultaneously in Canada by Random House of Canada Limited, Toronto. Distributed by Random House, Inc., New York.

Library of Congress Catalog Card Number: 70–107456

Manufactured in the United States by Kingsport Press, Inc., Kingsport, Tenn.

First Edition
987654321

Design by J. M. Wall.

TO THE MEMORY OF
JOSEPH R. LEVENSON
(1920–1969)

"Thought" and "thinking," "truth" and "life" need not be identical. Living history is full of "error," and death and truth are far from incompatible. Something logically plausible may be psychologically uncongenial. Something theoretically defensible may be historically undefendable. That is what we mean when we say that history is not a morality tale, and when we feel the poignancy of a lost cause—the loss of objective mastery—not just coldly clock the passing, changing years.

From the Preface to *Confucian China and Its Modern Fate: A Trilogy*, 1968

Self-knowledge is a remarkably elusive thing, for the self is transformed in the knowing, and Liang, trapped like any man in his own present, could hardly reveal himself and remain himself.

From the Preface to *Liang Ch'i-ch'ao and the Mind of Modern China*, 1959

CONTENTS

Introduction

The notion or caprice behind this volume dates back to the winter of 1965–1966, when I was living near Oxford, on Cumnor Hill to be exact, enjoying my first leave of absence since starting to teach in 1959. Had it not been for that year of searching and researching in the British Isles—a year made possible by a fellowship from the American Council of Learned Societies—I might never have found the right time and place to think about the relationship of my immediate historical concerns to the diffuse and often elusive context which we sometimes call History with a capital H. One of the results of that musing about the meaning and existence of Clio is the present volume, which presumes to deal with the ways some professional historians go about their work.

The essays that follow illuminate with varying intensities of light and shadow some of the steps particular historians have taken in their pursuit of an idea, problem, pattern, image, metaphor, or myth. The focus, then, is on the "workshop" wherein historians conceive and reflect about their projects, search for evidence, "tool up" or "retool," haunt archives, pore over bibliographies and book catalogs, compile note cards, sort and re-sort notes, write and rewrite drafts, polish prose, and clean up the galleys of their books and articles. We offer here no manual for history without tears, no magic formula for writing "definitive" monographs, no sure-fire method for preventing maculate historical conceptualization. Instead of preaching to untutored congregations about how they should read and write history, each contributor tries to explain—as much to himself as to any imagined reader—how he came to write some of his works, while scattering a few clues here and there as to how and why he came to be a historian. The emphases of this workshop lie somewhere between self-understanding and historical understanding, and in some cases distinctions between the two cannot be easily drawn. Although we represent no single school of history and are as diverse in our interests, skills, and approaches to the past as any nonrandom sample of historians could possibly be, we prefer to think of this volume as something more than just sixteen historians "doing their own thing," to use Juvenal's now popular phrase (*rem suam agit*). Just what that "something more" amounts to must and will vary from reader to reader as he works his way through sixteen highly individual essays.

Historians have traditionally tended to be rather shy and close-guarded, if not downright secretive, about the ways they have gone about producing their books and articles. Some notable exceptions to the rule do, of course, exist; but on the whole, it is safe to say that historians would far rather write about the working habits and assumptions of other historians than expose their own methods to public scrutiny. Every monograph or work of history has its own private life which rarely, if ever, gets into print. It would be foolish to pretend that all those private lives are worth the cost of printer's ink. But a few "brief lives" of certain works of history might contain more intellectual substance or food for future historical thought than hundreds of conventional prefaces to scholarly monographs, which are laden with author's acknowledgments to those mentors or tormentors (not to be confused with wives and children) who had some hand in helping or hindering his book. Since these prefaces reveal little or nothing about the conception and gestation of the work in question, the "true life story" of the book is never told. In many cases this is just as well: There are historians for whom such revelations would be more than embarrassing. It is the hidden or inner life of the historical monograph that we seek to explore here, having no illusions about our ability to exhaust the subject, let alone to write the definitive history of our own works. It does not always follow that historians who understand their own working methods, not to mention themselves, have a better understanding of the past. In some cases, quite the opposite is true. But here, in this workshop, we have deliberately cultivated a certain self-awareness with the object of exploring some of the special influences that have left their mark on our work over the years.

There are, to be sure, a number of priestly or druidical historians who could not be persuaded in a month of sabbatical leaves to allow their congregations so much as a peek into their private workshops. For these men, what goes on behind the altar of History and in the historian's sacristy is not meant for the eyes of laymen, let alone skeptics and nonbelievers. The more secular and realistic members of the historical profession, on the other hand, prefer to practice rather than preach their methods, because that is where both the psychic and material rewards lie. This leaves a small group of historians with the necessary cheek, *chutzpa*, narcissism, or what have you, as well as time, to discuss in print their historical sensibilities, their methods and nonmethods, and their special ways of turning questions into answers, or hypotheses into conclusions.

It was not just curiosity, then, made morbid by the Oxford climate, that first prompted me to undertake a workshop study of "the historian's craft." Quite apart from my own readiness to learn from other historians, I was becoming increasingly disenchanted with the state of writing about the writing of history. Books, manuals, and published lectures about history, historicism, philosophy of history, historiography, historical method, meta-history, Clio, Cliometry, and so forth, were fetching a market price of something like $40 a dozen, and practically all of them dealt in optative terms—pointing the way, after a good deal of ax-grinding or bush-beating, to how History should or should not be done. Not that all such books and essays are wrong-headed or futile. We do have something to learn from periodic examinations of the collectivity to which we belong and the assumptions as well as methods which seem to hold it together, even if one historian's epistemology or methodology happens to be anathema to another. But times have changed since Lord Acton first envisaged the era of "ultimate history." Not only has the teaching and writing of history become a multimillion-dollar industry with countless fringe benefits, especially if one is in the "right" field, but more and more historians appear to be spurning Clio altogether, preferring instead to play with "scientific" models: the more mathematically or sociologically sophisticated, the better. For many younger historians, it is in the borderland or frontier zone between history and such disciplines as sociology, anthropology, demography, econometrics, economics, and psychology that "the real intellectual action" is now taking place. Much as it may offend the humanistic yearnings of some historians, Clio seems to be growing ever more remote from and undesirable to those professional historians who are attracted to the problems and problem-solving devices of various social and behavioral scientists. At the outset, therefore, this volume was prompted by some questions and curiosities not only about the newer directions of historical inquiry, but also about the content of the leading sectors of the historical economy in the later 1960s. Readers might as well be told now that many of those questions and curiosities still remain in the editor's mind three years and sixteen essays later.

Because I could think of no book that revealed just how historians went about choosing their subjects, doing their research, shaping their interpretations, and writing up the results, it seemed appropriate to put together an anthology in which some historians addressed themselves to these specific aspects of their careers and craft. E. H. Carr had, I thought, posed a rather tired and tiresome question, albeit in an urbane manner, when he published his Trevelyan Lectures in 1961 under the title *What Is History?* Even if one happened to subscribe to the author's ultimate answer to his own loaded question—and I did not—this popular work told us a good deal about Carr's relations with both Clio and Hegel, not to mention Isaiah Berlin and Hugh Trevor-Roper, but it effectively concealed Carr the working historian, author of *A History of Soviet Russia* and other important books. The questions that intrigued me were admittedly less cosmic and teleological, and because they were also less ideological, they were more difficult in some respects to answer. Among those questions were: "What is your kind of history?" "Why did you choose it?" and, above all, "How did you go about doing it?"—all very personal and distinctly empirical questions, and therefore likely to annoy or offend the more sacerdotal historians at home and abroad. Carr had, after all, given Freud some credit for "reinforcing the work of Marx" by encouraging "the historian to examine himself and his own position in history, the motives—perhaps hidden motives—which have guided his choice of theme or period and his selection and interpretation of the facts. . . ." Prompted by the assumption that he was living in "the age of self-consciousness," Carr concluded none too soon that the historian "can and should know what he is doing."[1]

The more personal and introspective questions so assiduously avoided by Carr in his Trevelyan Lectures seemed to me well worth asking during that sabbatical year in England, when problems of method, interpretation, and evidence loomed larger in my work than ever before. Every historian of my acquaintance had his own special way of dealing with comparable or analogous problems in his own field, and some of these ways or methods had to be more efficient and rewarding than others, assuming a roughly equal distribution of native ability or intelligence among the historians in question. Here, then, was the lame and somewhat naïve excuse of utility underlying part of the workshop. But even in my most sanguine moments, I had no illusions about the readiness of other historians to profit from the successes, not to mention the mistakes or reverses, of their fellow workers who dared to discuss them in print.

Once I had made up my mind to pursue this set of curiosities to the point of a workshop anthology, I drew up a memorandum explaining the "purpose" of such a volume and laying down some flexible guidelines for the convenience of prospective contributors. Each author was asked, in effect, to combine a degree of self-portraiture with a brief biography of his own work. The assignment did, it is true, require a certain amount of mirror-gazing, but the purpose of that operation was to explain, not admire, what one saw in the mirror. The prospectus sent out to each candidate contained the following counsel:

Each essay would or should seek to explore the relationship between methodology and interpretation, premises and conclusions, evidence and hypothesis—all set within the frame of what the author considered to be his most important or original piece of work. The essay would thus represent the history of a particular idea, hypothesis, or argument as it evolved into the form of an essay or book. Whether that frame of reference happens to be a book or article published some years ago or a research project currently under way makes little difference from the historiographical point of view. It would be up to each historian to explain his particular choice from among his works and to set forth, as honestly and incisively as possible, the road by which he traveled from the commencement to the completion of that research. What these essays ought to elucidate, in short, is the process by which some historians "make" or write history.

Although autobiography was not the main purpose of this undertaking, I was convinced from the start that historical research and writing could not and ought not to be completely separated from the personal history of the man engaged in that process. If any contributor chose to write in an autobiographical vein before settling down to explain the operations in his own workshop, so much the better. As it turned out, however, relatively few of the contributors showed much desire to step outside their workshops for long. The assignment to write about their own writings struck most of them as subjective enough to begin with. Anything more personal than that seemed to border on sheer narcissism or "true confession." There is, of course, a substantial difference between contemplating one's work and contemplating one's navel. If each of the contributors to this volume had agreed to write about the connections between his early-childhood experiences and his later interest in studying history, the results might be judged too prurient to print, even in this permissive era. After all, it was one of the most skilled craftsmen in the workshop who wrote to me at the end of December 1966: "It may be a relief to turn from China-watching to auto-analysis, though it reminds me of the wifflebird, who flew in ever-decreasing concentric circles until it—but you can follow the mystic course. Anyway, I'll be happy to take part, read between the lines of Narcissus' *oeuvre,* and try to catch the author out."

Drawing up the list of prospective contributors to the volume turned out to be the trickiest part of the whole operation. Who should be invited in the first round, and who should be named as substitutes for those who refused to take the time and the chance? The range of choice was formidable, judging merely from the number of professional historians at work in England and America in 1966. But the choice was limited somewhat by my early decision not to turn the workshop into an *omnium gatherum* of eminent historians recruited from all over the world.[2] The volume was not supposed to become either an arena for cronies and clients or the printed platform for any particular school or orthodoxy of history. The decision to confine the search for willing "hands" to America and England was a subjective one, reflecting my own greater familiarity with historians who worked within these two cultures. (It is almost, but not quite, superfluous to say that one could produce an enthralling volume by tapping the historical talent of Europe and the non-Western world.)

Those historians invited to take part in the workshop were, in the main, established scholars who had written books and articles that ventured beyond the conventional methods and interpretations of their fields.[3] To the editor, at least, the most eligible candidates for the volume were men who had worked on the frontiers and borders between and among disciplines, cultures, methods, and territorial units. Age, rank, institution, and the familiar paraphernalia of academic success mattered less than originality and vigor of mind. The workshop also needed men with a certain flair and adventurousness about their work. The original plan called for a relatively even distribution of authors across the recognized major fields or branches of history, but whole categories had to be abandoned in the face of refusals from many who were first approached.

Since the purpose of the volume, if that is not too strong a word, was to shed light on the ways some historians went about writing history, everything depended on finding "the RIGHT CHAPS," as Vivian Galbraith advised me in December 1966. "And the R.C.s," he added, "should be those who, by and large, do NOT tackle it too egotistically." What sound advice that proved to be, and how difficult it was at times to follow. It is important to note, however, that the "right chaps" in this workshop really chose themselves as much as they were chosen. Out of fifty-two formal invitations sent out over a two-year period, only fifteen recipients, or roughly 29 percent, not only agreed to take part, but actually fulfilled the terms of the contract. Since the declination rate proved especially high among historians in Ivy League universities and England, this volume became more of a Berkeley product than some might have wished.[4] But the obvious retort to charges of "inbreeding" would be that it is foolish to go far afield in search of the right chaps when they may occupy offices only a few doors down the corridor. Besides, six of the seven Berkeley contributors hold degrees from Eastern universities, and the seventh, Carlo Cipolla, divides his teaching year between Berkeley and Pavia, so our apparent provincialism or regionalism must be qualified.

Almost all those who spurned the invitation to join the workshop took the trouble to express their thoughts on the proposal with refreshing, if occasionally bruising, candor. Although it would be indiscreet, and just possibly libelous, to publish all the comments received from nonparticipants, there are some passages which ought to be quoted simply because they help to represent the vast constituency of historians that flourishes beyond the confines of this workshop. A few anonymous excerpts may illustrate the point. One English historian tried to evade my net with the following disclaimer: "Besides, I am a bad person to write about methods—I have none. I have only once written a book on my own, based on research, and decided never to do it again." An eminent American historian delivered the following judgment: "This is an intriguing idea, and I certainly would want to do some cogitating about it. The trouble is that one somehow recoils from looking too deeply into one's own soul. Who knows what one would find? One might be compelled to work as one's own demolition squad. It is ever so much more attractive to look to the future and leave the writing of one's obituaries to others." From an American intellectual historian came the following: "Your proposal is wonderful. If all the contributors complied really honestly with your request, the history profession would be shattered fore and aft. What we now merely suspect would be proved without question—that nobody proceeds as the research manuals say we should." Another historian high on my list declined in the following terms: "I think my writing, like my metabolism, is something which I do not understand anyway, and I will make you the discouraging prediction that you will find this true of a number of your contributors." Lastly, there came this screed from a good friend in an Eastern university: "This time I fear that we part company. Though I can see the fascination of your proposal I simply refuse to take myself all that seriously. I find this kind of self-consciousness, so characteristic of our psychoanalytic age, rather offensive, from both the scholarly and the aesthetic point of view. Besides, skeptical of oral history as well as of post-hoc remembrances, I should hope that scholars wouldn't give a dime for my musings." To say that the editor's job of finding some skilled hands for his workshop constituted a challenge would be an understatement. And yet some hardy souls, daring to risk the inevitable smirks and jibes about narcissism, egotism, and psychoanalytic self-absorption, came through with essays that deserve to be called calm, restrained, semidetached, as well as eminently readable.

Some of the special difficulties under which the workshop labored from the outset were anticipated by John Pocock, who wrote to the editor in the spring of 1967 as follows:

I foresee your main editorial problem as finding yourself confronted with a number of spacecraft, varying sharply in purpose and design, and all photographed at different distances from the launching pad. Some contributors, I imagine, will respond to the emphasis implicit in the term "workshop" and give a straight, professional ac-

count of the genesis of a particular piece of work. Others, whose productive lives have been organised around the discovery and pursuit of a particular class of problems, will be obliged—whether or not they enjoy the prospect as I do—to write what amount to professional autobiographies; and I imagine that some of your contributors—I won't guess at names—will turn out to be immense and brooding spirits who write considered statements of their personal philosophy of history, at which point Spinoza will be out of his workshop altogether. And I don't doubt that this threefold division I've suggested will prove to be altogether too tidy. What sort of editorial problems will you then face in grouping the different types of contribution together and displaying to the reader the nature of whatever unity the volume possesses?

In several respects this forecast proved uncannily accurate, especially with regard to the problem of diversity or untidy categories. To impose a single pattern upon a cluster of markedly different rockets would be to deny—willfully and wrongly—that those very differences, radical or moderate as the case may be, make history what it is by reflecting historians as they are. To continue the Pocock metaphor, it is the design of the rocket or spacecraft that tends to divide historians and the purpose of the space probe that unites most of them. The actual distance from the launching pad is governed by such variables as age, experience, intellectual weight, and the thrust of our "Clionauts" or "histronauts," not to mention the rate at which they produce prose fit for publication.

The heterogeneity of the essays that follow does indeed reflect the heterogeneity of the books and articles from which they derive. The very diversity of our contributors and their subjects, however, serves to underline the essential universality of history and the catholicity of historians' concerns. In the minds of some seekers after unity we may well deserve Burke's description of the Chatham ministry formed in 1766: ". . . a cabinet so variously inlaid; such a piece of diversified mosaic; such a tesselated pavement without cement; here a bit of black stone, and there a bit of white." Whatever the labels people choose to affix to this workshop, the volume should at least point up the folly of trying to place rigid boundary markers around the so-called discipline of history.

This workshop contains no partisan or dogmatic orthodoxy beyond the commitment of its members to the cause of historical heterodoxy. As a group we have no single ax to grind and no particular field or method to promote. Our ages vary almost as much as our subjects: We range from thirty-six to eighty with an average of 47.7 years and a median of 45. We range in residence, too, taking in not only the major regions of the United States, but Adelaide, Pavia, and Oxford. Our special fields vary so widely that we might be said to comprise the nucleus of a department of history.

Proceeding in roughly chronological order, that is, according to the periods represented in each essay, we begin with Vivian Galbraith discussing some of the classic problems as well as formidable students of English medieval history he has encountered along the way. Our next contributor, Robert Brentano, who once studied under Galbraith, epitomizes in his essay the intense involvement of the historian's senses and sensibilities in evoking the past—in this case English and Italian Church history during the thirteenth century. Lynn White, Jr., writes about his odyssey from California to Sicily and back to America in search of the connections between technology and society in Western Europe during the Middle Ages. Carlo Cipolla contributes a wise and witty discourse on the role of Chance in shifting his attention away from monetary problems in seventeenth-century Milan and toward the history of clocks, guns, ships, population trends, and literacy rates since the fourteenth century. Raymond Kent's account of the way he unraveled the myths surrounding the early history and ethnography of Madagascar reads like a detective story set in the historian's equivalent of a forensic laboratory. Donald Robertson's essay on devising methods for dating and analyzing pre-Columbian and European art in sixteenth- and seventeenth-century Mexico illuminates a creative and often overlooked form of historical inquiry.

The Tudor-Stuart historian Thomas Barnes then explains how a congeries of personal and familial experiences helped to steer him toward the central theme of his work in English political and legal history, namely the ways in which the substance of authority is vitally affected by the forms of its exercise. John Pocock recounts his long and rewarding quest for ways to "decode" English political thought and the language of politics from the age of Bodin to Burke. Robert R. Palmer next discusses the making of his classic work, *The Age of the Democratic Revolution*, and its reception among historians at home and abroad. George Rudé retraces his path from an early commitment to the French language and Marxism to his well-known work on riots, collective disturbances, and the revolutionary crowd in England and France.

Shifting our attention to America, John William Ward explains how he used Andrew Jackson as a symbol with which to discover patterns of popular culture and consciousness in the early nineteenth century. The African historian Jan Vansina then guides us past the obstacles he had to surmount in his ethnographic reconstruction of Tio life and culture spanning three centuries. From the Kingdom of the Great Makoko we move (some would say appropriately) to Ireland, or rather to the turbulent history of Anglo-Irish relations in the later Victorian period, as the editor relates his own pilgrimage toward an understanding of the Irish Question. The next essay takes us close to the heart and mind of Confucian China, as the late Joseph Levenson reveals in his intimate yet detached way how he came to use metaphor in order to understand the "death and transfiguration" of Chinese civilization. Rudolph Binion then plunges us into the heady, fantasy-ridden, abreacted world of Frau Lou Andreas-Salomé, as he explores the interaction of the psychoanalytic biographer with both his subject and the documentary materials at his disposal. Finally, Lawrence Levine discusses the way he bridged the culture gap between himself and William Jennings Bryan.

We are, then, a mixed bag, a potpourri. To force these essays into tight categories based on topical, regional, or methodological criteria would do too much violence to the very uniqueness and richness of each contribution. It might also touch off internecine war within the workshop. None of these essays can be neatly pigeonholed or stored in empty historical boxes labeled "cultural," "social," "political," "economic," "intellectual," or "technological" history. Such labels tend to compress the countless planes and angles of historical inquiry out of all recognition. Our decision to arrange the essays here according to the time span involved may seem both clumsy and arbitrary, but it is the least of various evils, and it does have the incidental attraction of allowing us to begin with the oldest and to end with the youngest member of our crew.

Since history is really nothing more nor less than what historians do or think and write, it ought to matter a good deal how historians go about their business of interpreting the past. E. H. Carr's first answer to his own rhetorical question "What Is History?" deserves to be quoted in this context: "It is a continuous process of interaction between the historian and his facts, an unending dialogue between the present and the past."[5] But no matter how attractive the idea of a "dialogue" may be, it must be added that the process in question often looks more like a monologue or soliloquy which takes place within each historian. If it is a dialogue, it is usually a one-sided affair in which only the historian is capable of answering himself and of revising his previous impressions and interpretations in the light of new evidence and changing moods.

Almost seventy years ago that great English historian F. W. Maitland singled out Bishop Stubbs as a paragon of historical understanding in the following terms:

No other historian has so completely displayed to the world the whole business of the historian from the winning of the raw material to the narrating and generalising. We are taken behind the scenes and shown the ropes and pulleys; we are taken into the laboratory and shown the unanalysed stuff, the retorts and test tubes;

or rather we are allowed to see the organic growth of history in an historian's mind and are encouraged to use the microscope.[6]

No one in the workshop would insist that he had given quite so fine a "practical demonstration . . . of the historian's art and science from the preliminary hunt for manuscripts, through the work of collation and filiation and minute criticism, onward to the perfected tale, the eloquence and the reflexions" as Bishop Stubbs. But taken together, these essays may prove to be, to quote Maitland again, "far more effective than any abstract discourse on methodology could be."[7] Both the kind of effect and the degree of effectiveness are bound to vary from one reader to another in much the same way as formal historical writing—not least the work of Stubbs—provokes widely differing responses.

There is, of course, some risk involved in leaving readers quite free to make this anthology of discrete essays fit their own preconceptions of what history is and ought to be all about. But if we ever want to get close to the core of historical thought and writing, then we should begin by inspecting some of those workshops wherein historians spend much of their professional lives in the hope of seeing what happens to the raw and semifinished materials as they move along the highly personal production line. Surely Marc Bloch had some such thoughts in mind when he wrote in his wise and eloquent introduction to *The Historian's Craft:* "The uncertainties of our science must not, I think, be hidden from the curiosity of the world. They are our excuse for being. They bring freshness to our studies." Whether or not we happen to share Bloch's belief that history is an imperfect as well as poetic science constituting "but a fragment of the universal march toward knowledge," those of us who make a life and something of a living out of history as well as those from other walks of life who read what historians write may find something worth remembering or challenging from a tour of this particular workshop.

It should be clear by now that this workshop is not a compendium of all that need be known about the state of historical research and writing in the 1960s. We represent neither a random nor an adequate sample of what historians have been doing in the English-speaking world since the end of World War II. Indeed, from a statistical point of view, we are only sixteen out of some ten thousand professional historians now at work in America and the United Kingdom. But it is just possible that these essays will diffuse some useful scraps of knowledge about what kinds of questions, materials, hunches, and techniques have yielded the best results for a handful of historians. We would not object if these essays encouraged some students of history to think that much harder about why they are historians and how they are going about writing history. We would be delighted if our very shortcomings or limitations spurred a few readers to devote more time and thought to the inner art and outer form as well as the substance of their next research project.

This volume is addressed, then, not just to graduate students and history buffs who are curious to see how some of the so-called experts have earned their reputations, and it is not aimed exclusively at those foundations which have generously supported our researches at some critical stage in the past and want to know how their money was spent. It is our hope that all students, friends, and patrons of history, regardless of age, occupation, experience, and expertise will find a few pointers and signals here which may help them to avoid a pitfall or to pose a better question in the course of their own work. But it is not necessary to our well-being that the volume have so utilitarian and mechanical a function. There are historical manuals and methodologues enough as things stand, and our "purpose" here, such as it is, comes closer to "telling it like it is," to use the current *patois*, than to telling people how it ought to be.

The catholic complexion of this workshop tends to reinforce or confirm the definition of history as whatever historians or members of departments of history choose to teach and write about. No doubt some latter day Historical Methodist who believes in the transforming power of the computer or someone who is wedded to an elegant mathematical model of human behavior will disagree. But if this volume is ever going to be used to "prove" anything—and most of us in the workshop shudder at the prospect—it should surely demonstrate the primacy of inquiry and searching in the lives of historians. All of us here are seekers rather than soothsayers, devoting our careers to the piecing together of those vital, however obscure, connections in the past which make our fields the challenge they seem to us to be. Whether or not we join with Lynn White, Jr., in seeking to "globalize history" or share Joseph Levenson's concern for discovering in his own field "ties that bind a world," whether we wish to use history to some purpose or prefer to be used by it, we still remain students of our subjects, susceptible to changing fashions, receptive to criticism, and ready to revise our thinking over time.

What we do have in common is an overriding concern, indeed an insatiable appetite, for the primary sources of history. These raw materials are indispensable to our entire operations, no matter how method-conscious or model-minded we may be. These materials vary as much in kind as do our contributors and their fields. Nothing, in fact, better illustrates the varieties of history and the vagaries of historians than the materials we have used in our monographs. The materials stored away in this workshop consist not only of numerous written sources: charters, chronicles, writs, rolls, Domesday Book, ecclesiastical records, state papers and public records, private correspondence, printed books and pamphlets, military documents, police reports, prison registers, convict lists, the legal records of central and local courts, the proceedings of local assemblies, provincial councils, and national parliaments, novels, poems, plays, songs, folklore, newspapers, diaries, autobiographies, funeral orations, political speeches, and reams of purely quantitative data. But equally and at times more important to some of our contributors are such nonverbal and non-written sources as equestrian harness, armor, weapons, bells, clocks, paintings, drawings, cartoons and caricatures, sculpture, architecture, ship design, naval and military tactics, agricultural tools, industrial machines, cattle markings, divination practices, foodstuffs, currency, and such ingredients of oral history as folklore, legends, loan words, and proper names. Even this abridged list of the primary sources scattered through the workshop gives some indication of what history is or at least of what goes into history, and it may help us to judge better whether the nets we cast over our individual fields are wide or narrow in comparison with some of the nets revealed herein.

As Jan Vansina rightly observes, "there really are no data without significance." Some data, however, are more significant than other data, and some historians are more skilled than others at extracting meaning from documents or nonverbal data. The type of evidence chosen by the historian has, of course, a decisive influence on the outcome of his researches: It usually determines the limits of what he can prove or disprove about the society or culture he has chosen to study, and it is bound to affect the number of readers who accept or reject his interpretation in whole or part.

What Vivian Galbraith describes as an "obsession with the original sources of history" does not in itself guarantee the production of a first-class piece of history. Every one of the sources in question requires the application of special skills and the perspective of certain disciplines to yield any meaning. Apart from the universally required procedure of careful scrutiny of all evidence, the historians here have relied on various methods and disciplines in order to extract precious metals from their historical ore. Among the ancillary tools represented here are archeology, art history, computerology, demography, diplomatics, epigraphy, ethnography (including such subdisciplines as ethnobotany and ethnolinguistics), etymology, genealogy, geography, iconography, oral history, paleography, and psychoanalytic biography. Judging by the techniques applied in this workshop, the historian who aspired to become "complete" and to write "total history" would have to spend most of his life in apprenticeship, learning the various specialized skills which historians have found indispensable to their work over the years.

The essays here also share in common a quality of intellectual movement or growth. Virtually every contributor has ventured some distance beyond the accepted or traditional limits of his field, and in so doing he has usually had to abandon the outlines and hypotheses which once seemed so neat, well-defined, plausible, and therefore irresistible. In a number of cases the really critical patterns and correlations began to appear only after months or years of reading, reflecting, and writing. Lord Acton once declared that every historical inquiry should begin with a problem or a question. But the truth is that many historians have started with an archive or a bundle of documents and have then proceeded to work out the problems inherent within them. Even if one is fortunate enough to begin with a good or significant problem, what really matters is the way that problem changes or evolves as the result of the historian's repeated exposure to the evidence. He must often refine his original questions repeatedly, as new information comes to light and as new or revised constructions are put on documents already read several times. It is the dynamic and chameleon nature of historical problems, the metamorphoses of both form and substance through which monographs should and must pass, that find expression in most of these essays. Such metamorphoses are indispensable to the historian who wishes to write a book or article that lasts beyond the immediate review by his co-workers and academic promotion committees.

About one feature of the workshop there should be no misunderstanding. From its inception this volume was supposed to deal first and foremost with the ways historians went about their research and writing. Nothing explicit was said in the editorial guidelines about teaching and the relationship between course work and book production. Only a few of the contributors, therefore, have discussed the role or significance of teaching in their careers. Every essay, on the other hand, implies a good deal about the importance of teaching to scholarly writing and vice versa. Whatever the individual views of our contributors may be about the connections between teaching and research, the locus of each essay here is the workshop where books and articles are put together; it is not the classroom or lecture hall. If most of us have chosen to separate teaching from writing in our essays, it would be quite wrong to assume that we see no ties or links between the two activities. In some cases the ties are not only constant but vital, and in all cases the intellectual nourishment flows both ways. The members of this workshop have not forgotten those teachers who helped them along the road to higher research and eventual publication, and they are aware of their obligation to pass on to succeeding generations what they have learned from those who taught them so wisely and so well.

Perhaps this volume will be remembered most, providing it is remembered at all, for what the contributors left out; for the thousand and one censored, repressed, or discarded thoughts and autobiographical fragments that might have revealed too much about what goes on inside the historian's psyche as distinct from his workshop. But the time for might-have-beens is past. We cannot pretend to have isolated and identified the double helix of the historical imagination in this volume. If the essays shed insufficient light on precisely how and why historians arrive at their interpretations and innovations, if we still know far too little about our intellectual metabolisms and next to nothing about the intrapsychic dynamics of historical creativity, we may take some comfort in the knowledge that historians are only human, and are therefore no more capable of having their minds "made as plain as the road from Charing Cross to St. Paul's"—*pace* James Mill—than the rest of mankind. It will require more than one workshop volume, in other words, to "shatter the profession fore and aft"; given the growing popularity of history as profession and avocation among recent graduates of our universities and colleges, it looks as though professional historians are going to be gainfully employed for many years to come.

Although it may sound frivolous or far-fetched at first, this volume should really be treated as a tray or table laden with antipasti. Each essay should be taken piecemeal and relished for its own special flavor, shape, and consistency. The analogy is not frivolous because each essay ought, in fact, to serve as an appetizer, hopefully whetting the reader's appetite for the books, articles, or essays on which it is based. To read only the workshop essay and to leave untouched the corpus of historical literature which lies behind it makes as much sense as gorging oneself on antipasti and then spurning the entrée.

It would be asking too much of the contributors here to agree upon a single purpose for a volume of this kind. Some of our authors would, no doubt, prefer to amuse rather than edify their readers; others believe that to amuse is to edify. Although as individuals we do have advice to give, lessons to impart, and warnings to post, the contents of each message do not add up to a single party platform. There is, however, one theme or precept that arises implicitly, even spontaneously, from the sum of all our contributions. That precept could be articulated at considerable length using yards of verbiage and garnishing every point with weighty quotations from Acton, Bloch, Collingwood, Croce, Freud, Marx, and other eminents. But the essence can be boiled down to the following deceptively simple lines: Historians should not only seek to understand themselves—in the fullest sense of "know thyself"—they should also *dare to be themselves*. They should, that is, engage their own sympathies and empathies in their scholarly investigations, use their special skills, hobbies, passions, yes, even their obsessions, whenever and wherever they are historically helpful or heuristic. They should enrich their writing and thinking with what Wordsworth once called "sensations sweet, felt in the blood, and felt along the heart." But they should do all these subjective things at the same time as they learn the languages, the methods and materials, the objective facts, and the parameters of their fields, taking great care, all the while, not to allow those sensations to warp or distort the documentation or primary sources which make up the common reservoir of historical data. However much they may aspire to the building of "scientific" models of past behavior, historians should not shrink from drawing upon the rich funds of personal experiences which have made them who and what they are. History without the stamp of a vital, sensitive, even volatile personality lacks not only luster but lasting meaning. The contributors to this workshop try to evoke, not just to explain, the past, and they seek to fill their pages with real people and ideas that matter rather than endless, mindless, and bloodless data.

There is nothing strikingly new about this exhortation to "be thyself." But it is extremely hard at times to act upon it honestly, in a manner that does justice to both the past and one's own moral and emotional imperatives. Perhaps the only safe generalization to be made about this workshop is that all of us in it write history because that is what we seem to do best or enjoy most. And the sooner we leave the glass house of this workshop and return to the familiar furnishings, the absorbing problems, and the comforting privacy of our own workshops the better.

L. P. C., Jr.
May 1969
Berkeley, California

NOTES

1. Edward Hallett Carr, *What Is History?* (London, 1962), pp. 134–35.
2. Consultation with several friends and advisers, who did not themselves take part in the venture, lengthened the list of prospective contributors and helped to prevent the workshop from becoming too parochial in terms of subject matter, method, and personnel. To those councilors I am more than indebted, no matter how skeptical of the undertaking they may be once they have read the results of their choices.

   Because my own qualms about contributing an essay were so pronounced, I resolved at the outset to do no more than assemble and edit the essays of the workshop historians. But the strong urgings of a colleague and contributor, who insisted that the captain had no choice but to suffer the same fate as his crew, finally lowered my resistance to the point where autobiographical impulses took command.
3. For obvious reasons, the editor must invoke editorial license at this point and emphatically exclude himself from all the qualitative categories mentioned in the following paragraphs.
4. The thirty-seven declinations include two who did not answer my invitation and six who accepted and then dropped out along the way. In the cases of both American history and European economic history, seven of the eight men asked decided not to take part.
5. Carr, *op. cit.*, p. 24.
6. H. A. L. Fisher, ed., *The Collected Papers of Frederic William Maitland* (Cambridge, England, 1911), vol. III, p. 498.
7. *Ibid.*

THE HISTORIAN'S WORKSHOP

Afterthoughts

VIVIAN H. GALBRAITH

VIVIAN HUNTER GALBRAITH was born on December 15, 1889, in Sheffield, Yorkshire. He received his B.A. from Manchester University in 1910 and in 1918 earned an Oxford M.A. After teaching history at Manchester University for a year (1920–1921), he joined the staff of the Public Record Office where he worked as an Assistant Keeper from 1921 to 1928. He then moved from London to Oxford where he became a tutor and fellow of Balliol College from 1928 to 1937. He left Oxford in 1937 to become Professor of History at Edinburgh University. From 1944 to 1947 he served as Director of the Institute of Historical Research in London. In 1947 he was named Regius Professor of Modern History at Oxford, a chair he held for ten years. Galbraith served on the Royal Commission on Historical Monuments for both England and Scotland. Since his official retirement in 1957, he has led an active life, delivering many guest lectures, writing articles and books, and appearing as a visiting professor at the University of California, Berkeley (1961–1962 and Summer School, 1965), Mount Holyoke College (1965–1966), Emory University (1957 and 1966), and Johns Hopkins University (1957).

Galbraith is a Fellow of the British Academy, member of the American Philosophical Society, and Fellow of the Royal Historical Society. In addition, he has received a number of honorary degrees. Among his monographs are the following: *An Introduction to the Use of the Public Records* (London, 1935), *The St. Albans Chronicle 1406–1420* (Oxford, 1937), *Studies in the Public Records* (London, 1948), *The Making of Domesday Book* (Oxford, 1964), and *An Introduction to the Study of History* (London, 1964). Galbraith's articles in various reviews and journals exceed in sheer volume the sum of his writing in book form. A list of his published work may be found in T. A. M. Bishop and Pierre Chaplais, eds., *Facsimiles of English Royal Writs Presented to V. H. Galbraith* (Oxford, 1957).

At present Galbraith is working with Dr. Pierre Chaplais on *Early English Charters, 1006–1135,* to be published by the Clarendon Press, Oxford.

P rofessor Richard Southern's inaugural lecture on "The Shape and Substance of Academic History" (1961) paid a just tribute to the massive achievement of German universities since the time of von Ranke, who first instilled into them "the atmosphere of the *workshop* in which everyone was collaborating in original creation." By and large, the same spirit and the same atmosphere—we like to think—inspires the world-wide study of history today, when every university has its own school or department of history. But there have been great changes, and in the same lecture Professor Southern reminds us that in the last century in England "the academic study of history has grown from nothing to the status of a considerable national industry occupying the full-time energies of several thousand persons of considerable skill and ability." A century ago it was the amateurish hobby of a few largely well-to-do people, inadequately paid, to teach the young. Today a large number of professional historians, highly trained and probably overpaid, are simultaneously and equally required both to teach history and to write it. Their claim to be heard and to be read depends upon their paid status as teachers in a large number of universities, while their prestige among their fellows springs not from their teaching, but from the quality and even the quantity of their publications. This industrialization of academic history is now assuming the proportions of a revolution, in the course of which, however unconsciously, the teaching function which should come first has been eclipsed by that of published research. For the young, professional aspirant, history is now a rat race for promotion, and its slogan—"publish or perish." In the world hunger for historical reading matter at every level, commercial publishers are flooding the market with books, all of which, as the work of professionals, fall within the category of "research"—and teachers and taught alike are hard put to it to keep abreast of this feverish activity.

This recent increase in reading matter and the reading public is rapidly becoming a factor in democratic politics, and Robert Lowe's (Lord Sherbrooke) apothegm, "we must educate our masters," is much more than a joke. The academic historian is not merely required to write books, but to write books which everyone can read, and the "blessed" word *Research* is invoked to describe the process by which this is done. This new development comes to us directly from America, which demands the Ph.D. or "thesis" qualification for all higher academic posts. The Americans took it from the nineteenth-century Germans, whose research was a function of renascent German nationalism, and theses the appropriate apprenticeship for the pupils of Mommsen, Von Sybel, and the other masters. The task of these young men was to develop or work out the patriotic conclusions of the school to which they belonged. Today, I believe there is a growing reaction against the system by which hundreds of professors ingeniously devise subjects for thousands of young people. These students, in turn, waste precious years in compiling "original" theses, most of which just have to be "passed" in the end. My own view, at any rate, is very different, for I see research not as a process of turning the "raw materials" of the past into the finished "product" of a popular book, but as the only and necessary path for all real students to follow, its purpose being to educate the man who does it. In short, the only way to understand the past is to study the sources at first hand.

For this present state of affairs some of the responsibility lies with the "dismal science" of economics, which has taught us to assess, if not to measure, the meaning and health of historical studies as of all else in crude terms of "productivity." For me, at the age of eighty, though my whole life has been spent as one of these paid professionals, this economic concept has little meaning, for across forty or fifty years I have been increasingly conscious of a conflict between the twin functions of teaching and writing. Not that I ever wanted to teach. My instincts and my training alike channeled me toward research. But one had to live; and in my very first job, I was struck by the fact that, while I had been elaborately trained in the method of research and the ancillary sciences of paleography and diplomatics, no one seemed to know or to care how a young man should set about teaching history, a far more difficult task than writing it. But the "hungry sheep looked up," and had to be fed; and common decency suggested that one was not paid a whole-time salary to do a half-time job. In this dilemma I found a working solution by making my research the handmaiden of my teaching, or in other words by lecturing as far as time permitted straight from the original sources, cutting out whenever possible the slick narrative of the textbooks. My vision of a *magnum opus*, with which, like all my generation, I began, insensibly faded, and looking back today I see that my modest publications—the epithet refers to their size—are grouped around the focal moments of the university history syllabus ranging from *Asser's Life of Alfred* to the reign of Richard II. No doubt this was not the way to make a reputation as a writer of history. Most of what I wrote, though by no means all, was too specialized and technical for that. But I insensibly thereby converted my "teaching load"—as it is so oddly called—into a process of lifelong research whereof my published works were no more than the occasional by-products. Others, I dare say, have done the same, and have the same grateful recollections of students at every level who, in my experience, welcome all deviations from orthodoxy, when supported by the evidence of the original sources.

This obsession with the original sources of history has for me been an expanding revelation over a long life, which took shape in an elementary book I wrote for the BBC a few years ago called *The Historian at Work.*[1] History, surely, is living knowledge in living minds, a common awareness of the past by teachers and taught, a search for truth ever changing as error is corrected and more is discovered. The past itself is dead, and the books we write tombs of learning, except insofar as they live in the consciousness of their readers. So conceived, we travel pleasantly, but by the nature of things we never arrive. The main job of the academic historian (with which alone I am concerned) is to convey this sense of kaleidoscopic change to his audiences; if so, his own views will never reach finality. Indeed, much of what I wrote and published thirty years ago now strikes me as *vieu jeu,* so swift is the process of discovery. In such a world, television, radio, and journalism are valuable mediums for the diffusion of new ideas, but only to those sufficiently initiated to understand how little we still know about the past. The history that reads like a romantic novel has just about the same value, and it takes the faith that moves mountains to believe that the Gibbons and Macaulays of today will still be read a hundred years hence. I speak as a medievalist, who has never come within five hundred years of the present. The writer who yearns for immortality should stick to contemporary history. Thucydides, the historian of the Peloponnesian War, has claims to have written the best of all histories—but his book is now among the "original" sources of history.

Nonetheless, large histories are being written today, and one suspects that the reason why men and women become professional historians is that they want to write, rather than to teach, history. And if so, there are and always have been two ways of doing it. History is either "a science, no more and no less," as J. B. Bury declared in 1904, or it is a branch of literature poetical in inspiration—something with a "message" and therefore taking sides, and showing bias, as set out in G. M. Trevelyan's *Clio, a Muse* (1913). From these alternatives there is no escape. You can't have it both ways, however much you try by dilution, not to say diffuseness, by "tarting up" the writing, eschewing statistics, and omitting the footnotes. It might be thought, indeed I used to think it myself, that this dilemma was first created by the introduction of history as a subject taught in our universities in the mid-nineteenth century. In fact, it goes back into the Middle Ages, and no doubt earlier still.

At the end of the twelfth century, Gervase, a monk of Canterbury Cathedral, wrote a history of his own times beginning with the reign of King Stephen (1135–1154). It was, like so many medieval histories, a huge discursive book, written in Latin, and its chief interest for us lies in his Prologue. Looking backwards, he says, he found that the Christian Fathers had left behind them glorious examples to be followed, both in their histories and their annals (sometimes called chronicles). He then explains that there is a great difference between the two forms, though both aim at the same goal—to tell the truth. The historian writes diffusely and elegantly, while the humble chronicler writes simply and briefly. Then, quoting Horace and Vergil, he praises the historian's splendid bombast (*ampullas*) and high-sounding phrases (*sesquipedalia verba*), his purpose being to soothe the reader by his fine writing and elegance, but sticking to the truth. The chronicler, on the other hand, is content to get his facts and dates right and to describe briefly the chief deeds of kings and princes, together with other noteworthy events, miracles or portents. Dr. R. L. Poole, who first brought this passage to light, took Gervase's remarks quite seriously, but I rather suspect he was satirizing his contemporaries in a period when, like today, history was enjoying a boom, for he then adds that "there are many Chroniclers today who make broad their phylacteries and enlarge their borders." A long account of Gervase's own new and revolutionary chronology, of which he is obviously very proud, follows, and he concludes—with conventional medieval humility—that he himself is unworthy to be numbered, even among the chroniclers, as his book is not intended for the "public library but simply for his friend Thomas and the rest of the Canterbury monks." The huge book that follows, need I add, chronology and all, is very much the same as the other chronicles of the time!

In this passage, Gervase, for a moment, bridges the gap of more than seven centuries. The distinction he draws between the historian and the chronicler is surely very like the one we draw today between the Gibbons and Macaulays, on the one hand, and contemporary writers seeking to be "creative," like the "great men," but hampered by the equal demands of methodology and scientific research. As long ago as 1888, F. W. Maitland, wondering why a great history of English law had never been written, echoed the sentiments of Gervase:

> *Perhaps our imaginary student is not he that should come, not the great man for the great book. To be frank with him, this is probable; great historians are at least as rare as great lawyers. But short of the very greatest work, there is good work to be done of many sorts and kinds, large provinces to be reclaimed from the waste, to be settled and cultivated for the use of man. . . . At least he can copy, at least he can arrange, digest, make serviceable. Not a very splendid occupation and we cannot promise him much money or much fame. . . . He may find his reward in the work itself—one cannot promise him even that; but the work ought to be done and the great man when he comes may fling a footnote of gratitude to those who have smoothed his way, who have saved his eyes and his time.[2]*

We can, in short, all be chroniclers by applying the principles, though hardly the practice, of Gervase. Maitland himself was the author of a "great book," indeed more than one; he also contributed a mass of detailed technical research to the Selden Society (which he founded). But even his "great books," though often praised and cited, were addressed to a smaller and more professional public than those of his later imitators.

I mention the Selden Society because of its salutary innovation by which all the old French or Latin texts printed in its publications were accompanied by English translations *en face*. I followed this example in the Medieval Texts Series, which has now published close to thirty medieval historical works, each edited, with English translations, by scholars of repute. One cannot really "get down" to medieval history without some Latin, and my own is none too good. Also, the Latin of the Middle Ages (of which there is still no adequate lexicon) differed materially from that of classical times. In this quandary I sought the aid, as fellow editors, first of Sir Roger Mynors and more recently of Professor C. N. L. Brooke. With such experts, we can claim to have given new and better texts than hitherto published, while the English translations can safely be allowed to be free renderings, as the reader has the Latin text before him.

From modest beginnings, the Series has now made its way in the world, and I like to think it has contributed far more to the advancement of learning than my own published researches. It has already filled gaps left by the sadly abandoned Rolls Series, and in the safe hands of the Clarendon Press at Oxford can confidently look forward to an indefinite future of usefulness. Its publications are equally valuable to intelligent undergraduates and to working professional historians. Certainly nothing has taught me more history than the Medieval Texts, and it should be added that this undertaking owes its existence to Dr. H. P. Morrison, a great patron of scholarship, who at its inception was managing director of Thomas Nelson & Sons, Edinburgh. These books are the very stuff of history which no substitute can replace.

An old Irish proverb says it is to please himself the cat wags his tail, and the rather highbrow line my studies have taken springs no doubt from innate personal inclination. However that may be, it was deepened by the seven years I spent as an Assistant Keeper in the Public Record Office. The sheer bulk of the records—hundreds of tons —was intimidating, and their keepers formed a sort of "college of historical pundits," whose collective learning far transcended that of the professors of all countries who flocked to study them. By and large, these *savants*—there is no English equivalent unless it is "pedants"— did not write history books. They knew too much at first hand, but they were very much at home among their materials, and spent a lot of their time teaching the teachers to write their books and articles.

When I left them, I was still no more than an apprentice, who *faute de mieux* succeeded Dr. Lane Poole as Reader in Diplomatic at Oxford in 1928. This discipline was virtually unknown in England, for Dr. Poole, who had German antecedents, had learned it in Germany. For the next ten years I spent half my time teaching graduates the history of the papal and national chanceries, the structure and formulas of charters, and the crucial problems of forgery, and the other half as a tutor at Balliol teaching undergraduates for the history school. This teaching simultaneously on two levels was rendered more difficult by the old-fashioned conception of historical study still current among the senior college tutors. They did not believe in all this diplomatic, which they were apt to confuse with the history of diplomacy, and their resistance to all change recalled the immortal words which Thomas Peacock, with 1832 in his mind, put into the mouth of the drunken Welshman, Seithenyn ap Seithyn Saidi:

> That the embankment [to keep out the sea in Gwaelod] is old, I am free to confess; that it is somewhat rotten in parts, I will not altogether deny; that it is any the worse for that, I do most sturdily gainsay. . . . Our ancestors were wiser than we: they built it in their wisdom; and if we should be so rash as to try to mend it, we should only mar it.

They regarded the syllabus as sacred, and when I later returned as professor, it was still not very different.

The vast extension of research during the last hundred years has so quickened public interest in the preservation and printing of the sources upon which it depends as to give rise to a new science, that of archives, and a new profession of archivists trained in their safekeeping. England is now served by a network of well-run county and city archives which powerfully assist researchers. In this great movement, the staff of the Public Record Office has played a prominent part in the selection of the best records to preserve in their safekeeping. It was a shock to discover in 1921 the existence of a "destruction committee" charged with the tricky problem of dividing the annually growing accretion of central records in every department of government into two unequal halves—the larger of which are systematically destroyed after a few years, the smaller perpetually preserved. At first sight this struck me as an alarming procedure, but in fact some such arbitrary decision has been followed from the very beginning, and poses great problems for the historians of administration. It was generally believed that, had the whole of the public records made in World War I been preserved, they would have filled the Crystal Palace. The necessity of selection is a saddening reminder to historians of the limitations inherent in all research in the future as well as in the past. Since 1838 when the central Public Record Office was first set up, the public records have been adequately, if sparingly, cared for by Acts of Parliament; hundreds of volumes of calendars, indexes, and, in some cases, full texts have been printed by the Stationery Office. But private records—the archives of our country houses—still have no adequate protection, although their immense riches have been very imperfectly explored. Indeed, in my view—which has been expressed in the report of a parliamentary committee—the sale or at any rate the export of these should in many cases be prohibited by law, instead of being lumped in with "works of art" with which they have basically no connection.[3]

Nor is the historian's interest limited to documents. Every town, village, church, and countryside abounds in visible evidences of the past, and these, too, though better protected by law than the contents of country houses, are everywhere disappearing before our eyes. For twenty years I served on the advisory committee appointed to advise the minister responsible for reconciling ancient monuments and modern town planning. All over the country buildings of "special architectural or historical importance" were classified and scheduled, and we had the melancholy task of weighing considerations of private gain or even public convenience against the claims of history and architecture. Closely connected with the work of the "civil service" experts are the publications of the Royal Commissions on the Ancient Monuments of England, Scotland, and Wales, which for more than half a century have published, county by county, inventories of monuments that extend from prehistoric earthworks to those of the Gothic revival. Their sumptuous volumes are the best examples we can show of the "historians' workshop" regarded as a collaborative exercise. As a commissioner, first in Scotland and later in England, I had the duty and privilege of reading the proofs of their admirable volumes and enjoyed, as I had earlier in the Public Record Office, the stimulus engendered by working as one of a group. The results obtained by these full-time experts, working in close collaboration, unencumbered by either teaching or administrative tasks, are likely to have greater permanence than any individual work. If only public money were available, their publications could be greatly speeded up.

The sureness of touch engendered by working as a community gives to the publications of the P.R.O., the British Museum, and the Royal Commissions an authority and a standing higher than that of most private research. These civil service historians, who take the cash and let the credit go, include some of the greatest medieval scholars of the last century: men like Sir George Warner, Sir Frederick Madden, J. P. Gilson, Sir Charles Peers, Robin Flower, Charles Johnson, A. W. Clapham, and many more. Their lives were spent in daily contact with the original sources, and their work, if not their names, is a guiding factor in the training of academic historians who hand on newly won knowledge of the past to that hypothetical entity, the general public. My own debt to these institutions is lifelong, and I have repeatedly sought their help in my own isolated research. Indeed, the most difficult publication of my life, "Who Wrote *Asser's Life of Alfred the Great*," has employed my leisure for many years, purely and simply owing to the destruction of the original manuscript, Otho.A.xii, which was burned in the Cottonian fire of 1731.[4] The question at issue is whether this, the earliest royal biography in English history, was written in 893 by Bishop Asser, one of Alfred's helpers, or in the eleventh century, when the lost manuscript was certainly written. It is a melancholy testimony to our abysmal ignorance of pre-Conquest history that we still cannot with certainty distinguish by internal evidence the date of any literary work within a century; and our Old English scholars cannot easily reconcile themselves to the loss of so vital a source for Alfred's life. But it makes a good detective novel, and I mention it here only because of the rubbish—for it is no less—written by its defenders regarding a "free-hand" copy of a page of the original manuscript prefaced to Wise's edition of the *Life* in 1722, and reproduced in that of W. H. Stevenson in 1904. To anyone whose life has been spent among original documents, this sketch is virtually useless, and to argue from a mere copy is the prostitution of paleography. No medieval manuscript can be *certainly* dated from its script within much, if any, less than half a century, and even so, it can easily be falsified if reproduced either smaller or larger than the original. And it is, of course, a blatant untruth to think of, let alone describe, a free-hand copy as a "facsimile." The Asser problem illustrates the inherent weakness of so much English scholarship, which still thinks in terms of the printed word, using the evidence of manuscripts only in an emergency to bolster wishful thinking.

In dealing with Asser, one worked in the twilight of historical and literary criticism without the sure guide of contemporary manuscripts. In *The Making of Domesday Book* (Clarendon Press, 1964), the circumstances were dramatically reversed. By almost incredible good luck we still have the original volumes written in 1086–1087. It is our first "public record," still safe in government custody after nearly 900 years. Yet strangely enough, the full testimony of the actual documents has only been sought in the last thirty years or so. Till then scholars preferred to work from the printed edition made in 1783. It has engaged my interest, as I have been one of its official custodians since I entered the Public Record Office in 1921. In those days the junior staff, working in dungarees because of the dirt and dust, were still sorting hundreds of bundles of legal writs, and I was offered many a dollar or its English equivalent by American tourists who wanted me to show them Domesday Book! For twenty years I was guided by my old teacher, Professor James Tait, who had made his name in 1897 as the author of the only critical review—in the true sense—of Maitland's *Domesday and Beyond* (1897). Together we published *in facsimile* an official copy of the text for Herefordshire, made (almost certainly) by Henry II's famous expert, Thomas Brown. Nothing less was adequate, for in the margins of the manuscript scribes had attempted to bring Domesday Book up to date by adding the names of the landowners a century after the survey. This discovery was a vital link in the chain of evidence that proved the continuous reliance of the Treasury on Domesday Book for several centuries after the survey, a fact as astonishing as it is significant, and in flat contradiction of a recent textbook which lays it down that "within a generation Domesday Book itself had become a historical monument, respected but unused."[5]

What is the explanation of the survival of Domesday Book as a live instrument of the royal *curia* across whole centuries? The classic answer of J. H. Round, swallowed more than whole by Maitland in his *Domesday Book and Beyond,* was that "one great purpose seems to mould both its form and its substance; it is a geld book," whose purpose was to make possible a new assessment of that ancient land tax. Reflecting that both Round and Maitland, like everyone else of their generation, learned about Domesday Book from Freeman's *Norman Conquest,* I traced this improbable hypothesis to its source, where, however, even Freeman admitted that other motives must have been at work. To reduce this vast survey to the Gladstonian concept of direct taxation was just another of those Victorian "anachronisms" that bedevil so much nineteenth-century medieval research. The eleventh century was not yet the age of the common man and "fair taxation," but of royal rights and a dominant military aristocracy. Perhaps the best clue to the purpose of the survey is afforded by the fourteenth clause of Magna Carta a century and a half later. This lays down that when the king wishes to have "deep speech" (*commune consilium*) with his people, he will summon archbishops, bishops, earls, and the more important laymen (*barones maiores*), by individual writ, and *all other tenants-in-chief* collectively through the sheriffs. It is all nonsense, of course, for such a gathering would have run to many hundreds, but at least it gives one the theory of the Norman state, evolved between 1066 and 1086; and it was this theory which guided the compilation of Domesday Book. There, in two handy volumes, can be seen the blueprint of the Norman state, that is, a record, county by county, of the royal demesne, and the lands of the tenants-in-chief listed one after the other, beginning with the lords of great "honours" and tailing off gradually to quite humble folk—chaplains, foresters, or pensioned nurses and such-like, whose holdings are fractional. The medial or "honorial" barons are, in general, mentioned in Domesday Book, but only incidentally under the names of the tenant-in-chief from whom they held their lands.

Such is Domesday Book, the simplicity of which for the last half century has been hidden by the extraordinary, yet misguided, ingenuity of J. H. Round. Intent upon his search for geld, he misjudged the administrative process by which it was compiled. He pictured the "original returns" made to the Treasury at Winchester as a huge muddle of geographical "Hundred Rolls," because geld was collected by hundreds. These he was then constrained to admit were, by immense toil and a complete reversal of policy, converted into a personal list of tenants-in-chief in Domesday Book. Misled by Round, many good scholars concluded, not without reason, that Domesday Book could only have been compiled as we have it, some or even many years after William's death in 1087, which in the then state of society was unthinkable. The actual process of taking the survey was both rapid and simple. Panels of commissioners were sent on seven or eight "circuits," each comprising a group of counties. Each circuit returned to Winchester a sort of local Domesday Book in the same form as the final record as printed—but with a difference that made all the difference, viz., that each local circuit return was several times larger than the final version, and some high official—who may have been Samson, later bishop of Worcester—was given the responsible task of preserving what he deemed essential and discarding the rest of the information recorded by the circuit. By this typical exercise of practical Norman genius, the gigantic detailed record of the survey was reduced to two large but still usable volumes.[6] Herein lies the secret of the survival of Domesday Book as a live record for centuries to come.

The Making of Domesday Book is the most elaborate and protracted reconstruction I have ever undertaken, and its full impact has hardly yet got down to the textbooks. The work that went into it stretches across forty years. It owes much to T. F. Tout's pioneer work on administrative history, and perhaps even more to R. L. Poole's teaching and expertise in paleography and diplomatic. Nor shall I live long enough to discover the inevitable flaws in its arguments or to see the results of the further research that it will evoke from younger men. Indeed, one of the trials of medieval research is the natural reluctance of scholars, each increasingly involved with his own specialty, to accept any major departure from orthodoxy on such central topics as the authenticity of Asser or the making of Domesday Book. Yet until a new view is either accepted or adequately refuted, further progress on these matters is indefinitely suspended. Reviewers (I have found) for the most part play safe, while one's contemporaries tend to adopt the policy of the Priest and the Levite in the parable, and so "to pass by on the other side." Not for them to emulate the Good Samaritan, more especially since to refute worthwhile conclusions involves a study as arduous as that entailed in putting them forward. This is a particularly relevant consideration in respect to Asser, a problem that cannot even be approached until one has mastered W. H. Stevenson's learned *apologia* in his exhaustive edition of 1904, which is many times as long as the *Life* itself. His monumental effort to defend the indefensible (as it seems to me) sprang simply from the destruction of the only manuscript in 1731. *The Making of Domesday Book* has had a better reception, since it rests upon the unshakable evidence of three *absolutely* contemporary manuscripts, viz., Domesday Book, Vols. I and II, and the "Exon Domesday" preserved in Exeter Cathedral. These three, taken in conjunction, and used properly, cannot mislead us.

No academic historian paid to teach the Middle Ages can very well escape writing about Magna Carta (1215), on which, as Bishop Stubbs remarked, all later medieval history is a commentary. Nor was I an exception. Indeed, since the publication of McKechnie's *Magna Carta* (1904); scholars have been continuously engaged in destroying the Victorian myth regarding this undoubted turning point in our history. My own part began many years ago when it was generally believed that King John *signed* Magna Carta. As Robin Flower wrote:

> With a grey goose quill he signed it,
> Signed it and underlined it

while Archbishop Langton (the "good man") and the papal legate (the "bad man") stood looking on. Such anachronisms were only the outward and visible signs of a total failure to see the crisis through the eyes of contemporaries, and the 750th anniversary of the charter in 1965 evoked a great outburst of writing both in England and in America. To this world-wide symposium the contributions of Professor C. R. Cheney and J. Holt were outstanding, and a year later I tried to assess the results of all this research in a lecture to the American Philosophical Society called *Runnymede Revisited*. Much of it came from Cheney and Holt, but—to my own surprise—I was constrained to suggest (I won't say to prove) a more far-reaching reappraisal than theirs of the part played by the papacy. Briefly, it now seems certain to me that we owe the *survival* of Magna Carta not to a "nation in arms" nor to English church leadership, but to the enlightened statesmanship of Pope Innocent III and his immediate successors.

Even today, English historians play down the significance of John's surrender of his kingdom and himself to the pope in 1213. From that moment, the papacy, however long the interval, was bound to triumph in the end, since, as Maitland long ago pointed out, the autonomous "Church of England" was as yet unborn and unthought of. So the papacy, now the King's ally, tried hard to bring about a compromise peace in 1215, and when this failed, saved the throne on John's death in 1216 for his son Henry; then reissued an amended charter in 1216 [7] and again in 1217. This charter, in turn, led to that of 1225, the Magna Carta of all later history. Without papal guidance, Magna Carta would have disappeared forever in the anarchy that would have followed King John's death. It is a conclusion not easily swallowed by English historians; but in the early thirteenth century, the universal Catholic Church had reached the highest point of its influence and in every dispute was bound to win in the end. In life, kings and princes could oppose it, but no man, high or low, could then afford to die outside its communion—its hopes of Heaven and its certainty of Hell. So Magna Carta survived the crucial fifty years of the pious Henry III's reign. By that time it had taken firm root, and neither the decline of papal influence nor the bitter opposition of Edward I could shake its authority.

All the radical work mentioned above, though most of it was slowly matured over the years, has been published since my retirement at the age of sixty-seven in 1957. At times I wonder whether this is a mere accident, or due to the escape from orthodoxy half-unconsciously imposed by the rat race of professional teaching.[8] All establishments frown upon heretics, who are quickly classed as wild men, and this attitude is perhaps most evident in medieval studies. Nearly all the scholars whose work I have most admired have been arch-conservatives, even to the point of voting Tory in elections. And most of them, I think, had "finalized" their reconstructions of the past by middle age. The single exception was my first teacher, Professor Tout, who, somewhat incongruously to me, combined a loathing for the *Manchester Guardian*, the Bible of my youth, with a unique readiness to revise his published work of thirty years by embarking upon a vast administrative history at the age of fifty-five. This is a source of comfort to me, for at eighty years of age, I have to confess that my views on the past are still hesitant, not to say fluid.

However that may be, the main field of my published research until I was fifty years of age lay in the fourteenth century, and more particularly in the reign of Richard II, which I taught for many years as a "special subject." It remains today the only century in which I have a reasonable grasp of the main sources. Much of this research was devoted to the tangled problems presented by the narrative sources, more especially those of St. Albans Abbey. Under a great abbot, Thomas de la Mare (1349–1396), it all but revived the glories of the *scriptorium* in the days of Matthew Paris, whose example inspired its most prolific historian, Thomas Walsingham. His manuscripts were scattered in many libraries, and years were spent in disentangling the incidents of his long life and his innumerable drafts. The result was published as the *St. Albans Chronicle 1406–1420*,[9] and the only thing to be said about it is that it would have been much better if Richard Vaughan's brilliant *Matthew Paris*[10] had been there to help me. I was also drawn inevitably to a study of Higden's *Polychronicon*, the most famous and widely diffused universal history of the later Middle Ages, which has since been examined in greater depth by Dr. John Taylor.[11]

Altogether, the work of these years was a sizable contribution to knowledge, and I can decently expect that when the "great man" comes to write *the* history of the period, he may fling me a footnote of gratitude for having saved his eyes and his time. But the time will not be yet, nor soon. The spadework still to be done is immeasurable, and whoever he is will require the full armament of the economic historians, whose rapid rise is such a feature of the work being done today. Even now the historian faced by the Peasants' Revolt of 1381 is led to wonder whether the historians of the earlier centuries have quite done their job. In its suddenness, as in its violence, it still remains unexplained; nor have the Marxists come up with a reasonable answer. Most baffling of all, perhaps, is the complete failure of our sources to provide convincing living pictures of our fourteenth-century worthies. No historian has succeeded in conveying to us the living identity of the Black Prince, of Edward III, or of John of Gaunt, although we have ample remains of their activities and their households. The men themselves remain inscrutable figures, immured forever in full plate armor on monuments and on brasses. Yet, medieval historians to a man conceived of history as the doings (*gesta*) of kings, great warriors, and great churchmen; and their inability to paint convincing portraits of their heroes is a permanent bar to the writing of a convincing history of medieval England. After years of preparatory toil intended to do just this, I abandoned the idea altogether, distrusting the validity of a task so subjective and so whimsical.

This instinct to substitute for my personal reactions to the past something rather more objective has much to do with my efforts to master diplomatic, the basic training for anyone concerned with medieval charters. It may be defined as the lore of official documents, as opposed to chronicles; that is, the narrative sources, at a period when society was still mainly guided by oral testimony and iron custom. It is, in fact, by the proper use of charters and like documents that we trace the transition to a more bureaucratic organization which occurred all over Europe in the late twelfth century. In England, for example, the practice of keeping copies of outgoing documents—that is, of chancery enrollment—underwent a startling enlargement on King John's accession in 1199. From that moment, the writing of our history becomes much more laborious, but vastly more rewarding. I still recall Professor Tout once saying to me that he had, owing to poverty, written many early saints' lives for Sir Sidney Lee's *Dictionary of National Biography,* and then turned his attention to a later period—the thirteenth century—"about which something was *known*"! From this century onward, our history reaches a higher plane of credibility, and thus reveals by contrast the deplorable habit of earlier times of filling the many gaps in our records by unproved hypotheses, if not by sheer wishful thinking. It was in this frame of mind that I published a tiny book called *An Introduction to the Use of the Public Records,*[12] which is unquestionably my most successful book. After nearly forty years it still sells, though much of it is quite out of date.

My "diplomatic" study of the Public Records was halted by my removal to Oxford in 1928. Since then my interest has increasingly turned to the large *corpus* of pre-1066 charters, of which—and it is a disgrace to our scholarship—the last complete edition was that done by John Kemble more than a century ago. To fill this vacuum, some preliminary steps have already been taken by the British Academy, for the job is far beyond the capacity of any individual. Meanwhile I have been employed, along with Dr. Pierre Chaplais, on a major book about one section of these early charters, which is almost ready for the press. It calls for mention here, only to put on record that whatever the title page says when the book does appear, most of the work and all the credit (or the reverse!) will lie with Dr. Chaplais, whose articles in this field are among the most truly dynamic publications I have read in my lifetime.

The *Historian's Workshop* involves a lapse into autobiography—of all kinds of history the most suspect. Too often the career on which one looks back, and then plots as a sort of graph, is no more than a chapter of accidents, arising largely from economic causes. There are no constants in history, not even human personality. There is nothing but change, however much we ignore it, and this factor increases steadily with the length of life. The trouble is not that "old men forget," but that they unconsciously reshape their memories. In my age group the difficulty is maximized, for I was well set on the career of a scholar, when at the age of twenty-five I was swept into the catastrophe of World War I and changed in a night from a "clerk" into a "man of blood" as a serving infantry officer for four years. Just what it did to me, I hardly know myself; but at least it is certain that I thereby forfeited for life all "benefit of clergy," emerging with my scholarly illusions—and much else—shattered, and a pessimism about the future which was only cured by marriage and raising a family. But I am at least correct in recollecting that I then turned from reading George Meredith to Thomas Hardy and have ever since been "full of strange oaths," as well as convinced, with Chaucer, that "the grettest clerkes be not the wisest men." The dedicated writer of large books, perhaps, perished in that ordeal. Yet it was in many ways a kind of enfranchisement, as I realized that there was nothing that really mattered in life except people. My scholarship had sprung, however unconsciously, from mere physical inferiority to my more athletic school fellows, with whom I had "cut no ice" at all. I had been compensating for youthful obscurity at the heavy cost of scholarly isolation from the general run of chaps. The war years ended for me this life apart, and actually made it more worth living—even raising the standard of my golf above the lowest of all categories, that of university professors. I have wondered, at times, whether the gentle scholars produced by our system of almost infant specialization really are the proper people to narrate "the crimes and follies of mankind" through the ages.

When the war was over, however, I had gone too far to turn back, and since no one offered me a better job, I persevered in scholarship, although acutely conscious of a different outlook on affairs from that of my teachers and elder contemporaries. It was at this moment, I recollect, that Reginald Lane Poole, extolling the virtues of the great Vinogradoff, remarked to me, "But when I turn to Vinogradoff for a *definite* answer to a *significant* question, he often fails to supply it." This criticism, which I only remember because I had myself suffered from his Russian incoherence, tallied exactly with my practical army life, which had more than once shown itself as "nasty, brutish and (probably) short." Indeed, my effort ever since to follow Poole's advice is my only justification for writing anything at all. It seems to me, to say in a phrase, exactly what Gervase of Canterbury was getting at in the twelfth century.

To sum up, then, a rambling narrative: The past is dead, and neither scholarship nor imagination nor a combination of both is ever likely to make exactly thinkable again the thoughts of men who lived centuries ago under a different dispensation. Yet it is this impossible goal we must strive to attain. In this unending process, I see the function of the paid, professional, academic historian as that of outlining to his pupils in conversation, classes, and lectures—the perfect medium—the best available opinion at the moment. This he can only do by a lifelong research upon the original sources, in the course of which he may hope to stumble on occasional new discoveries and perhaps upon hypotheses that can be verified by close, critical study of his material. These by-products of a way of life will form his publications. In this way, with rising standards of research, society will move to a more objective outlook on the past, an outlook independent of the changing fashions aired in popular journals and reviews. The "great man" who can synthesize whole fields of study may turn up in the future, as he has in the past. But then again, he may not; meanwhile, great dangers attend the growing industrialization of academic history by confusing the spheres of the arts and the natural sciences. Long ago a cynic described higher education in the arts as "casting false pearls before real swine." It was a naughty thing to say, but something of the kind happened long ago in Greece and Rome. There is no such thing as "history without tears"; historical study suffered a certain debasement from the very moment it became a subject taught, and therefore examined, in universities, its students being somewhat arbitrarily classified. This gave rise to the "crammer," who is still—indeed increasingly—with us, and who still defeats the ends of proper teaching. Real history has no commercial value for looking into the future, and only charlatans say it has. Its true study is purely and simply educative. It has no technological value, and in the wrong hands can be used to prove anything. Except by those whom it delights, it is better forgotten; and to speak of it in terms of productivity is nonsense. History has no other value—and who would wish it otherwise?—than in a hard world to make its devotees "less forlorn."

In this record of an octogenarian's life, it remains to speak of a debt, more pervasive and inspiring than all the rest put together—my marriage. I was more than thirty years of age when this vital accident occurred; but if my wife and I can only hold on until July 1, 1971, our children, grandchildren, and our great-grandchild—who are now "our life"—will, collectively, have to do something about our golden anniversary. We met in Sir Maurice Powicke's study in 1920, when, I recall, we differed radically on something to do with *The Constitution of the Dominican Order,*[13] the publication of which was the chief preoccupation of our early married life. I can never forget the first words of her friend, Priscilla (née Gladys) Conway, on hearing of our engagement. They were, "What am I to say, Vivian? I can't believe that you won't fight, for you will—but at least I can promise that you will never be *bored.*" She was dead right on both counts, and our equal union over almost half a century has admitted no impediments. What I was like in 1931 I can now only guess at; but what I have become is very relevant to *The Historian's Workshop.* The precise literary parallel to our marriage, which neither Homer nor Vergil nor Dante nor Shakespeare could supply, I owe to the genius of Charles Dickens. *Mutatis mutandis* —and there's a lot to change—our present relationship is as near as makes no matter the same as that of Mr. and Mrs. Bagnet in *Bleak House.* Mr. Bagnet was an ex-artilleryman, and Mrs. Bagnet "a soldierly looking woman"; their idyll will be found in Chapter XXVII. Here a single quotation must and does suffice. Mr. Bagnet is talking to his friend George Rouncewell, the trooper. " 'George,' says Mr. Bagnet, 'you know me. It's my old girl that advises. She has the head. But I never own to it before her. Discipline must be maintained. Wait till the greens is off her mind. Then, we'll consult. Whatever the old girl says, do—do it!' " and I do.

NOTES

1. Republished in my *An Introduction to the Study cf History* (London, 1964).
2. F. W. Maitland, *Collected Papers* (Cambridge, England, 1911), vol. I, p. 496.
3. This was the "Waverley" Committee appointed in October 1950 by Sir Stafford Cripps. The report was published by H.M. Stationery Office.
4. Published in my *An Introduction to the Study of History*, pp. 83–129.
5. H. G. Richardson and G. O. Sayles, *The Governance of Medieval England* (Edinburgh, 1964), p. 28.
6. The original intention was to compress the whole survey into a single volume, which is volume I of the printed edition. But the local return from the East Anglian circuit was never epitomized—perhaps because it arrived late—and was therefore not added to that volume. It became volume II of Domesday Book; thus Norfolk, Suffolk, and Essex are more extensively dealt with than the rest of England.
7. Papal control was exercised successively by the papal legates Guala and Panducy. The charter of 1216 was issued under the seals of Guala and of William the Marshal, a nonpolitical "father figure" of nearly eighty years of age. Sidney Painter, *William Marshall* (1933), pp. 257-259 shows clearly that Pope Honorius III regarded William Marshal as ruler of the Kingdom. See *Runnymede Revisited* (Proceedings of the American Philosophical Society, Vol. 110, No. 5, October 1966, p. 316).
8. Including, of course, the *burden* of departmental or administrative duties which Sir Frank Stenton used always to call "odd jobs."
9. Thomas Walsingham, *St. Albans Chronicle 1406-1420* (Oxford, 1947).
10. Richard Vaughan, *Matthew Paris* (Cambridge, England, 1958).
11. John Taylor, *The Universal Chronicle of Ranulf Higden* (Oxford, 1966). By pure chance I found an "author's MS" of this work in the Huntington Library, San Marino, California, in 1957.
12. *An Introduction to the Use of the Public Records* (Oxford, 1934).
13. *The Constitution of the Dominican Order* by G. R. Galbraith (Manchester, 1927). It was dedicated to me and our two elder children. This was resented by our third child (a later addition), to whom tardy justice was done in 1967 by the dedication of *The Journal of the Reverend William Bagshaw Stevens* (Oxford, 1967).

Bishops and Saints

ROBERT BRENTANO

ROBERT BRENTANO was born on May 19, 1926 in Evansville, Indiana. After earning his B.A. at Swarthmore College in 1949, he studied at Oriel College, Oxford, as a Rhodes Scholar. In 1952 he received the D.Phil. degree and then joined the Department of History at the University of California at Berkeley, where he is now Professor of History. Brentano returned to Swarthmore as a Professor during 1963–1964. His special field is medieval Church history in England and Italy.

Brentano belongs to the Royal Historical Society, the Mediaeval Academy of America, and the Society for Italian Historical Studies. He has won fellowships from the American Council of Learned Societies (1960–1961), the Fulbright-Hays Committee (1955–1957), and the John Simon Guggenheim Foundation (1965–1966).

Among his published works are *York Metropolitan Jurisdiction and Papal Judges Delegate (1279–1296)* (Berkeley, 1959), *The Early Middle Ages* (Glencoe, Ill., 1964), and *Two Churches: England and Italy in the Thirteenth Century* (Princeton, 1968). Brentano has also written articles for *Mediaeval Studies, Journal of British Studies, Speculum, Traditio, English Historical Review, Scottish Historical Review,* and *Quellen und Forschungen.*

He is presently at work on two books: *Papal Rome: Innocent III to Boniface VIII,* and a study of the Church of Rieti in the thirteenth century.

I wrote the third chapter ("Bishops and Saints") of *Two Churches* on the Via di Villa Ruffo in Rome during the summer of 1964. I wrote it at Eric Bercovici's big desk in a bay window looking out over the north flank of Santa Maria del Popolo and (like a barbarian on the Pincio) looking into the city. The room in which I wrote, a bedroom, was extraordinarily pleasant. Its other windows looked into the park of the Villa Borghese at the level of the trees' branches and beyond them of the internal roads of the park, so that the aspect was sometimes rural and sometimes very urban, with the urbanity of great nineteenth- and twentieth-century city parks. I hope that by the time this essay is finished it will be clear that this fact, the fact of the room on the Via di Villa Ruffo, is as important as any to the way in which the chapter was made.

What I wanted to do, I thought, as I began to write *Two Churches*, and particularly as I wrote its first chapter, was to break something. I wanted to protest against everything "vague and arranged and fine" on the dead surface of contemporary historical writing, to shout like Thomas Carlyle or Gertrude Stein, that life and truth, present or past, are rough, difficult, and to be felt. I tried to signal this point by quoting Carlyle, although Stein was probably more important in forming my attitudes. This sort of signal may not be much noticed. In my first book (*York Metropolitan Jurisdiction*), I echoed a line from *Sense and Sensibility* to make a point and perhaps even more to give simple pleasure by recalling the complicated but disciplined tone of Jane Austen's book. Most people did not, I think, see, so this time I used quotation marks.

Most particularly I wanted to object to the sugary good taste that seems to me to dominate historical writing, at least in America. Good taste, although one may recall it with simple longing sometimes, is and must be the deadliest enemy of anything creative. And it seems clear to me that if history is not creative, is not art, it is not worth the sustained effort of any serious man. Good taste protects the reader from experience and the writer from experiment. It gives them both an excuse for rejecting what they do not understand.

Beyond that, I felt that *Two Churches*, like all written history, had a right to be as difficult, intricate, hard to get at, even unintelligible, as I wanted to make it. I thought my job was to create something that would have its own existence, not to provide a simple, pretty, light guide to a classical countryside unconfusing in the convention of its imagery and arrangement. I think, and thought, that history should be allowed to be, should be made to be, as demanding (and always as complex) as a play or a novel. I cannot understand the chasm. Why should people who are willing in patience to listen through a play like *Waiting for Godot* in the hope that they will have some little understanding of it, some experience from it, turn to history and demand the slick prettiness and intelligibility of Trevelyan or, at the other extreme, the statistical, sociological firmness of clear answers in matters in which they must know there are no real answers. I cannot understand why, or at least I cannot accept the fact that, only history should be permitted to be, forced to be, unreal. (Perhaps both reader and writer are placated by history's "factual" texture; because it is "factual," it need not be real.) If history is worth writing at all, it must be written "real," with the violent and complex reality of serious fiction.

My talk of audience is something of a red herring. I am of a generation some of whom grew up believing those of its predecessor's poets who talked of creation rather than communication. I do not believe much in communication. At most, I think it should be a by-product. Again, it seems to me that my job is to make something, perhaps to make it for myself, not to keep thinking, "Will this get across to an audience?" Make does not, of course, mean to make from nothing or without rules. The particular niceness of medieval history is that it has unusually rigorous rules and that it demands rather peculiar skills; at best, the remaining, discoverable, hard-sought past (as it is seen, not, of course, as it existed) controls one's hand as much as the shape of a sonnet does. In the matter of audience, teaching seems different from writing. Teaching is like ballet—not that the connection with the audience is like the connection with the audience in ballet, the connection with the audience is like the movement of ballet (perhaps it could be so even in writing).

In the first chapter of *Two Churches* ("The Connection") I tried very hard to create something in which the convolution of prose and matter would make them inseparable so that the total shape of the whole chapter would express the active repulsiveness of the thirteenth-century papal curia and the feverish, greedy insecurity there. Although I had only fragments of people to work with (and more than fragments would probably have disturbed the text), I wanted the fragments to suggest real people in real places. Within the chapter I tried to show this in at least four ways. I tried to sharpen the presence of the fragment figures in the curia by presenting them with a blunt physiological-chemical mixed metaphor. I played with the figure of one curial proctor, Pietro of Assisi, at some length, so that I could show one fragment being slowly extended by additional evidence and then stopping with lack of evidence so that the remaining growth had to be imagined. I tried to expose the relatively full humanity of the English cardinal, Hugh of Evesham, by talking at length of his will. Wills are excellent documents, reservedly formal, but rehearsing much of the donors' experience and affection. Hugh's will makes little maps of university towns and of the locations of his livings. I also tried quickly to suggest a combined image of crowd-piazza-stage by using a real papal piazza, Orvieto (and I intended to include a plate of it), a suggestion of repeated figure line by mentioning Guardi crowds, and a nightmare image of a general council from Matthew Paris—all tied to a masque at a stage court. I wanted the small hard pieces of proctors that dominate the center of the chapter to be eased into large comprehensible pieces at the end, particularly with Hugh and the extravagant polygonal crowd-stage image. And I wanted Matthew Paris, who opens the book, to keep turning up, but not as a chorus, more perhaps as an inverted Polonius, with foolishness in a shrewd mouth.

The chapter is not so bold as I intended it to be. The brutal business of presentation of evidence and transition works hard against any imagined pattern. Besides, historians are timid by profession. We are all hiding among external, previously formed patterns. My most blatant timidity changed the first sentence of the chapter. The chapter begins with Matthew Paris's talk of heavy winds around a council in 1237. I meant the first sentence to be dizzying, to swing around, careeningly announcing the tone of the chapter. It had, originally, seventy-nine words in it. It should have stayed as it was. But, finding it more than my flesh could bear, I dropped a conjunction and cut the sentence in two. Too much time passed in writing the book for me to sustain the courage that the original chapter required. My taste changed. Even the chapter's title, "The Connection," which had seemed to me pleasingly to suspend the chapter between Marx and the then "scene," palled and grew dated. Still, even in its tamer form, the chapter seems to me a pretty violent expression of revolt, in a way that the third chapter, "Bishops and Saints," is not at all, or hardly at all.

Since this is true, it may seem odd that I have chosen to write about the third rather than the first chapter of the book (although the chapters are not really separable). There is a glaringly obvious reason for my selection. I enjoyed writing the third chapter a great deal more than the first. Writing it really gave me a great deal of pleasure, surprisingly, probably suspiciously, unalloyed with the usual pain of historical writing. I have only felt this sort of pleasure in writing an essay on Stubbs, the description of the character of William Wickwane in *York Metropolitan Jurisdiction*, some small parts of the *Early Middle Ages*, part of chapter five ("The Written Church") of *Two Churches*, and a couple of papers that I wrote for the American Historical Association. (I am better at writing things to speak.) It seems to me worth noting this obvious thing, that an historian, this historian at least, chooses to write about things because he likes them. I think the historian is all too often viewed as a sort of machine (a vacuum cleaner? a baler?), all too little as a man and a writer. I think that this view robs both the writing and reading of history of its proper resonance.

The pleasure I felt in writing "Bishops and Saints" was due in part to the Via di Villa Ruffo, but I wrote chapter four ("Fortresses of Prayer") at the same desk during the same summer, and I have written very painful chapters in very beautiful rooms. The summer in which I wrote "Bishops and Saints" was, in general, a particularly happy one for me. It followed a personally difficult period during which I had written the earlier chapters of the book. I remember with particular clarity the earlier joy I had felt when I wrote the Stubbs essay in a wonderful, primitive penthouse on the Via del Mattonato in 1960. I sat at a table by a large window and looked out into the yellowing leaves of the Gianicolo and the Fontana Paola, as the older children, then both under two, played in the sun on the terraces. Although personally painful things were happening in America, it was in lots of ways a golden autumn. The period between it and the summer of 1964 was for me much less golden. I can remember writing chapter two ("Provinces, Dioceses, and Paths of Appeal") through a whole Swarthmore winter, and surely part of its somber tone is due to my somber mood. (It seems to me that this is important, that the Roman senate looks bright or dull to the historian and his reader depending upon the one's mood when he writes as well as the other's while he reads.) But the summer of 1964, for some reason, largely I suppose intellectually inexplicable and connected with the passage of time, seemed fresh and bright and full of joy. In it, with the preliminary research already done, I sat down, as I have said, with pleasure to write "Bishops and Saints."

There is another reason for my choosing to write about "Bishops and Saints." In a book which calls itself an essay, "Bishops and Saints" is more truly an essay than any other chapter. It is less a hoard of faceted stones, of small pieces of examined evidence, painfully collected, to give in mass a general idea. It moves in relatively broad sweeps; it has relatively extended passages of continuous prose. It states most boldly the thesis (the wrong word, perhaps the "idea") of the book. It is the center of the book.

The book as a whole is meant to be a general comparison of the total styles of the English and Italian churches in the thirteenth century. Its first chapter talks about the connection between the two churches, particularly in the Roman curia. It spends a long time with curial proctors. The second chapter talks about the administrative and judicial structures of the two churches and their attempts at diocesan reform. It spends a long time with cases in courts of law. The third chapter compares the sorts of men who became bishops and who were considered saints in the two churches. The fourth chapter describes monasteries, particularly decayed ones, and deals at greatest length with the monastery of Fiastra and her daughter houses. Finally, the fifth chapter concerns itself with the ways in which records were kept in the two churches and the ways in which their histories were written —two aspects of the way in which each church wrote about itself.

It is hard to remember exactly when and how I first decided to write the book in its present form. It took a long time to work out and write, a long time for me or it to find its final shape. Some of its elements had been in my mind a long time. In the first place, I had never liked what seemed to me conventional history. "Conventional" is a dangerous and perhaps silly adjective, particularly in the mouths of rebels. We often rebel because we need the movement, not because there is something real and appreciated to rebel against. My "conventional" may not be anyone else's "conventional," and it may in fact not exist, or it may be a thing of straw. The pejorative "conventional" may seem particularly dubious from me since my first medievalist hero, the first writer of medieval history who tempted me to follow his field through the beauty of his work, was T. F. Tout in his *The Place of the Reign of Edward II in English History*. Tout is not normally considered inflammatory. He was for me. I had not known that his sort of written art could exist until, as a sophomore at Swarthmore, I read him.

Like most students, my first real connection with history had been through historians acting as teachers rather than writers—Jean Wilson, Mary Albertson, George Cuttino. They, like Tout, encouraged in me a taste for tough beauty created out of rigor. Certainly none of them ever suggested any killing kind of conventional, proper thought in history. They asked questions which were dry and sharp and provocative. One of them, George Cuttino, persuaded me that it was a normal and desirable thing to spend my junior summer on a raft with Johnson and Jenkinson (*Medieval English Court Hand*) and my senior winter reading microfilms of fourteenth-century pipe rolls. I learned from George Cuttino, or at least I learned when he taught me, to dislike finding things out from secondary sources and even to dislike using printed editions. There is something terribly boring, it still seems to me, about a printed edition of almost anything, and something very interesting about any unedited document, at least from the years between 1000 and 1400. This attitude is obvious in my work. I cannot help choosing, whenever possible, the unprinted rather than the printed source.

When I was at Swarthmore, I was equally committed to medieval history and Victorian poetry. In a way I am always trying to make the two things meet. It really is a sort of basic tension, and I think it explains, or is at least consistent with, the way I work.

At Oxford I was overwhelmed by Sir Maurice Powicke. Both he and his successor, V. H. Galbraith, seem to me explosive. Their existence encourages the throwing away of old patterns. They effect this, at least with me, in very different ways. I think, though, that a sensitive observer could look at *Two Churches* and tell pretty easily that I am an Oxford product of the Powicke-Galbraith period and that I was taught by Kathleen Major and W. A. Pantin.

Powicke's influence on me was direct and personal. I listened to him very intently, in scenes that are fixed in my mind, walking through wet bracken at Boot and thinking about Furness, listening to him read *Persuasion*. I could not, having known him, accept a lesser view of history than his. His Langton and his Winchelsey and his Henrician-Edwardian community are clearly my models, and his Maitland. I do not always like what he wrote. He is sometimes too softly Christian for me, and even, in his essays, particularly the rather popular ones, just too soft. (He himself was anything but soft.) Even his generally accepted masterpiece, *King Henry III and the Lord Edward*, sometimes seems a little loose and slack to me. But I think that the idea of *Stephen Langton* dominates, as it should, the most interesting—to me —medieval work of this century. *The Thirteenth Century*, with its tight, uncompromising execution of a fantastically elaborate but fully imagined pattern, just at the edge of human comprehension, never cheapened by labeling phrases, but expressed complexly in the reflecting arrangement of exact and exactly described particulars—this it seems to me is the real book of history, even surpassing *Domesday Book and Beyond*. Certainly *Two Churches* is written to *The Thirteenth Century*. It is, implicitly, always talking about Powicke's Langton, Powicke's Grosseteste, Powicke's Edward, and Powicke's Winchelsey. They are the model human structures for the men who live in my book, they and the great extended Grosseteste of Father Daniel Callus's collection of essays, particularly his own and Pantin's.[1] But the debt to Callus is very explicit in the *Two Churches*. The debt to Powicke is different. The *Two Churches* swims around in Powicke's mind. The world it believes in is the world he created. Its people and ideas try to touch each other in his way—or in his way cracked and spangled by an Italianate American who lives and teaches in Berkeley.

Powicke, however, was not deeply interested in documents. He was not really an archival historian. There is nowhere in his work the sort of fierce beauty that a single piece of parchment, perfectly exposed and understood, creates. This is Galbraith's sort of beauty. He combines it, in a way particularly seductive to me, and more so as I grow older, with the sweep of rash generalization, the nominalist's generalization, which pretends to be neither true nor false, but brilliantly enlightening.

I am directly involved with Galbraith's own thought and work, but at Oxford my closest contact with an historian who made beauty out of the perfect handling of a specific piece of parchment was with Kathleen Major. Her quiet classes in diplomatic within the miserable Maitland library in Schools were as satisfyingly and involvingly theatrical for me as any performance I have ever seen. I have never been able not to want to work in diplomatic since. The purest excitement I find in history is still, and from that time, looking at a new, strange document in a set of archives. The dismal, cold room at Farfa disappears when I see a document. This has obviously given me much pleasure. That it forms my work, the slightest glance at my footnotes should make apparent, particularly in a chapter like "Provinces, Dioceses, and Paths of Appeal" and, overwhelmingly, in "The Written Church." But it is also destructive to my work, because I am inherently incapable of being a decent diplomatist. I only like the initial step. I like to find, to puzzle, to read, to understand, to transcribe—and at all of these things I am competent enough. But I cannot take legible notes; I detest searching journals for references to related documents; I am incapable of proofreading perfectly. The edition of a single document like my own " 'Consolatio defuncte caritatis': a Celestine V letter at Cava" is valueless or at least unbeautiful if it is not perfect and perfectly introduced and annotated, and mine is not perfect.[2] I am, in diplomatic, hopelessly attracted to work for which I am unsuited. The edition of a papal letter should be like a haiku. But a haiku is written and created; the edition of a papal letter involves the patient use of tedious machinery. That the form of "Bishops and Saints" demanded my eschewing most diplomatic was probably one of its advantages.

The way I worked in *Two Churches* could not, I think, be understandable at all if it were separated from my background. But I should not like to imply, since it is the very opposite of what I believe, that significant background is essentially academic, or even that my pertinent academic training was limited to college and university, or history. The particular ways in which, at school, Brother Daniel taught Virgil, and Brother Jareth, Milton, were more important to me than much university history. As both teacher and historian I have been violently influenced by the way W. H. Auden taught a little course in Shakespeare's sonnets and the way Ethel Brewster taught Terence at college. Beyond that, my whole approach to history is very much formed by my own teaching and by my students at Berkeley. My work, I think, screams Berkeley—not the Berkeley of computers or even of learned colleagues (although it may indeed also scream them too, particularly George Guttridge), but the Berkeley of the freshman section of Western Civilization and the junior section of historiography, of the undergraduate course, the Berkeley of activist, morally directed, intelligent, eccentrically educated young people. I could never understand Gregory IX so well, or hate him so much, I think, if I had not taught at Berkeley. Texts from my teaching (a letter to Boniface, Walter Daniel) appear specifically in chapter three; they have become inseparable from me. Historians whom I teach, Bede, William of Malmesbury, Parkman, Carlyle, direct me.

But Berkeley like Oxford is academic, if in a different way. The real background that forms an historian can hardly be described to an historian's audience, to other historians. It would embarrass them. It is the background of sibling position (as one of my most brilliant students endlessly points out), of family, of class, of village. It is at the simplest level apparent to me that my strong sympathy with both Powicke and Honorius IV has much to do with my being a late child of old and unbelievably attractive parents. My sympathy for the Frangipane in the thirteenth but not in the twelfth century has everything to do with my growing up surrounded by gentle people living on smaller and smaller incomes and remembering the past. Most of all, my mind is equally expanded and imprisoned by the beauty of the small Indiana river town in which I spent summers and some winters as I grew up. What I always want to write is the way the white path above the hill meadow runs parallel to the blue river beneath it, the way a rotten, brown apple hangs on a bare, black branch in the November evening, Pyramus and Thisbe in the moonlight by the mulberry tree above the river, the mist in the southern cypresses. It seems to me that when I wrote of Federigo Visconti in Sardinia in "Bishops and Saints," I was coming as close as I dared to these real images in my mind. It seems to me worth embarrassing readers with these minor revelations, because in different ways they must be true of all historians. They are almost too obvious to mention; but things that are too obvious to mention are often forgotten. The historian is a man, a human being, and in his way an artist, and he is trying hard to express the images in his mind, his real and full mind, within the constricting, disciplining event of the past. In very different ways he sometimes succeeds—look at Maitland, look at Parkman, and above all look at Ranke.

My Oxford dissertation, which I finished in 1952 and published in a slightly revised version in 1959, was a study of the metropolitan jurisdiction of the archbishops of York, that is, their jurisdiction over the suffragan dioceses within their province in the later thirteenth century. In fact, the dissertation became also, because of what I found in the archives, a study of papal judges delegate. Most of my research was done at Durham, in the Dean and Chapter archives, and at the British

Museum, but I also came to Rome to do a little work. I had already come to Florence for a vacation and stayed, like most of my friends, at the Lanini near the Ognissanti and the Arno. Italy was just recovering from the war. It was quiet and poor, and parts of Florence were still broken. It did not occur to me in Florence that I might work on Florentine history, but it did become clear to me that I liked the winter sun, the air, the countryside, the buildings, the paintings, and, as much as anything else, the food.

When I finished my dissertation, I found that I had moved in a peculiar direction. Although I had intended to do at York, for a short time, part of what Irene Churchill had done at Canterbury, my results were very different from hers.[3] She had managed to control herself and present an outline; I had broken out into an untidy assortment of people and cases. And I was unhappy about working on York, on England, on the north of Europe in isolation. It had also become apparent to me, as it must to most Americans as they work, that it is almost impossible for an American to be, or be allowed to be, a local European historian. We are not from Cornwall or Wensleydale. Even before I had finished the dissertation, W. A. Pantin had suggested that I write to Evelyn Jamison to ask her, since I wanted southern comparisons, about the south of Italy. Miss Jamison suggested that I begin looking at Bari, and I myself was increasingly attracted to Salerno.

In the years between 1952 and 1956, when I arrived in Italy for a Fulbright year, I became more certain that I wanted to do a comparative study of English and Italian ecclesiastical institutions. My plan was not very well formed, but I thought that I wanted to work in the south, at some place like Catanzaro or Reggio Calabria (Gissing country). But, as always with archival historians, my plans were re-formed by archives. In those days the Fulbright Commission sent scholars to Perugia for an initial month to be taught Italian. I could not stand the idea of being near archives and not working in them. The archives of Umbria were not then catalogued as they are now, but I had looked at Paul Kehr's Umbria volume of *Italia pontificia*. Kehr did not profess an interest in documents after 1198 (when Innocent III and my real interests begin), but he, and his successor Walther Holtzmann, in their regional volumes, compiled by far the best guide to Italian local archives (although Mazzatinti is good on the things he covers).[4] Their work stands like a *faro* over the wastes of Italian medieval history. Kehr suggested that there might be interesting things at Città di Castello.

I went over from Perugia and found the bishops' books of Città di Castello, and I have been involved with them, and the extraordinarily active bishops they record, ever since, but never so profoundly as I then assumed I would be. The bishop's registry at Città di Castello was my first real introduction to Italian local archives, and I was lucky in it. I was treated kindly, allowed to read, and put next to the stove. I was allowed to find out what riches could exist in a local collection without having to face the rude, stupid hostility that guards the doors to so many Italian collections. I also went to the Archivio di Stato in Perugia and there found the records of Santa Maria di Valdiponte, and particularly its detailed chamberlain's accounts from the period between 1265 and 1288. I had, then, and meant not to lose, the monks of Valdiponte, as I had the bishops of Città di Castello, but I did not know exactly what I was going to do with them. I also went to Bologna and found the rich fond of the Dominican convent of Sant'Agnese so attractive in its litigiousness. I was also becoming interested in curial proctors (a few of whom had been important in my first book). I bought in November in Florence a small red leather notebook, and in it I copied the name of the proctor from the dorse of every papal letter that had one. I went about the Italian countryside, to Gubbio, to Verona (beginning as Pantin noted a sort of *iter Italicum*), demanding to see papal letters. I thought I would write something on proctors.

I was still bound for the south, although initial inquiries about archives had been discouraging. At the beginning of December I went with my wife to Salerno so that I could work there. It was hard to find a place to live. Amalfi, in winter, seemed a good place to find a flat or house, and a place from which I could commute to Salerno. Because I believed in looking for archives everywhere, I sent a note to the chancellor of Amalfi to ask if I could see his archives. After some time, the chancellor, Don Gabriele Vissicchio, wrote to say that I might work in the archives if I would sort them. Until May, on ferial days when there was no funeral, my wife and I worked together sorting and making a handlist. When there was feast or funeral, Don Gabriele played the organ, and so the chancellor's office and the archives remained closed. Don Gabriele, although his eyes were very poor and it was rather difficult for him even to get home to Atrani, also worked at a local orphanage. He was a very busy and a very good man. His archives were high above the cloisters of Paradise. Their documents stretched from the eleventh to the twentieth century. Our work (which was annoying to some Neapolitan archivists because it was done by foreigners) was done in a sort of vacuum without scholarly tools, but it was absorbing and informative. It was Pitt Rivers, the opposite of Collingwood. I immersed myself in the documents, and learned from them, let them form my questions. The cupboards in which the documents were stuffed were like a dig. From Amalfi I went to Monsignor Balducci's archives in Salerno and the Archivio di Stato, to Ravello, to Naples, to Palermo and Bari, and finally through Sardinia north again to Perugia, Assisi, Bologna, and Città di Castello. The year was an Amalfi-centered general *iter*.

Amalfi was like going to school again. The things I learned were various, but I was most interested in the documents issued by the archbishops of Amalfi, as late as 1490, over a lead seal. I was particularly pleased by a practical archival joke, a document with the wrong seal attached to it by shopkeepers' string, as if it were designed to point out the collection's diplomatic queerness. Through the winter, as I looked at these sealed documents, I became increasingly intent upon trying to define for myself the peculiarities of a society that could produce them, a society in which they would seem natural. This was pure Collingwood. The seals were my Albert Memorial. The curious artificiality with which Collingwood, in his *Autobiography*, presents his Albert Memorial experience (perhaps because it is an example, unlike the Bath Gorgon, so far from his professional interests) should not disguise its central validity, its real helpfulness in the understanding and explaining of the development of historical research. My friend and colleague Gunther Barth looking at and wondering about Victorian buildings in Oregon seems to me like me looking at and wondering about lead seals in Amalfi; we both seem to have been following the Collingwood pattern.

By the time I came back to Italy, to Rome, for a year in 1960–1961, the plan of a general book comparing the two churches had formed in my mind, although the patterns of its chapters had not. A group of ideas now moved in my mind around the Amalfi seals, the Bologna cases, the Valdiponte monks, and the Città di Castello books and bishops. I had already decided to compare bishops and saints and historians, and I already thought that the historians would be, as they are (in chapter five), Matthew Paris and Salimbene. I knew that I wanted to combine in the book the most minute local archival work with, at least by implication, the broadest generalization about two societies.

In Rome that fall I found the documents of the Cistercian monastery of Fiastra in the Marches. There are still, in the Archivio di Stato in Rome, about nineteen hundred thirteenth-century documents in the Fiastra collection. I went through them all. (No one who has not worked in the Archivio di Stato in Rome can know what that means. The Archivio collects archival absurdities in its beautiful building— della Porta—Borromini—whose porticos are stained by the oil slicks of the cars that use its *cortile* as a parking lot.) I became so interested in Fiastra that I almost deserted my general plans to work on it alone. Just as I finished reading, I discovered that Wolfgang Hagemann had been through the fond a short time before I started. The heart of his

findings was published in *Quellen und Forschungen* for 1961.[5] I was
kept from deserting my general book by work at the German Institute,
just as, earlier, Peter Herde's work had helped keep me from hiding
completely in proctors (and it should be known that work at the
German Institute, unlike much medieval work in Italy, has been consistently excellent). It became clear to me that I really could not
escape the general book, and I began more seriously to plan the shape
of its chapters.

I imagine that no historian can really remember the chronology of
this sort of planning. (It seems to me a fault in us that we do not use
more our own uncertainty about time and the difficulty of fixing it,
stopping it in imagination, as an historical tool.) I myself have a
particularly bad memory, except for scenes, patterns, conversations—a
difficult and unpleasant fault in an historian. I have notes that show
stages of composition and ideas, but they are, of course, not dated. As I
remember it, the general shape and function of my chapters at this
point formed themselves in my mind rather quickly. Increasingly I
thought of the chapters as five movements in some sort of musical
composition. My knowledge of music is too thin for the analogy to have
been very detailed, but it was helpful to me; it was the best way I could
think of for dealing with the structures I wanted. The first chapter,
ugly and discordant (and, as the book's preface says, about what the
book is not about—the connection between the two churches) was
meant to establish my tone and terms. Its themes are not the themes
of the book, but they were meant to prepare the listener's ear and to
separate him from his preconceptions. The second chapter was meant
to be a long slow movement, uningratiating and difficult, in which all
the themes of the book were to be stated, but in fragments not easily
to be grasped. It is the chapter of administration, visitation, lawsuits.
The third chapter was meant to be a fast movement, in which the
themes were to be restated in a relatively attractive, even pretty, and
obvious way, so that the reader-listener would be reassured about what
he thought he had read or heard in the previous chapter, and also
convinced of it because he had moved from difficult illustration to
bright statement. This is the first chapter about relatively whole people, bishops and saints, and, as I have said, of relatively extended ideas
and patches of prose. The fourth chapter, on monasteries, was again
meant to be slow, to recall earlier themes in difficult and relatively
unmelodic and inarticulate surroundings, to prepare the reader for
more difficulty. The fifth chapter was designed in two parts. The first of
its parts was meant to be the most difficult of the book, hard and very
discordant talk of diplomatic with even measurements in centimeters
in the text—a set of footnotes and a bibliography broken into the text,
a sort of kidnapping into prose of the mechanics of historical work.

Then in mid-chapter there was to be a switch to the fastest, brightest, hopefully most easily perceptible part of the whole book, in which all the themes would be restated in the comparison of Matthew Paris with Salimbene, and the movement would be back and forth, back and forth, like, almost, the sawing of violins. I liked this whole concept and, once having perceived it, I kept it in my mind.

But my perceptions are much more usually visual. Like Italo Svevo's Emilio Brentani (and probably for some of the same bad reasons), I have the "habit of always thinking in images" (and partly the images of whatever novel I happen to be reading). I always thought of chapter four as being square, like a box, a cloister, or just a square. Chapter three I thought of as a physical movement, a trip, a journey. My hardening of this image and deciding how to use it is one thing that I can date roughly, because I can remember the physical circumstances that surrounded it. I was walking home from the Vatican to the Via del Mattonato at noon on a sunny day in the winter of 1960–1961 and thinking of Federigo Visconti. (Walks are, I think, very helpful to historians; it seems to me in fact that the walk is the most readily convincing part of Collingwood and the Albert Memorial.) Just as I got to the Porta Settimiana I realized that I wanted Federigo's 1263 Easter visitation of Sardinia, his long trip, to be the central knot of my chapter, the thing that would tie it together. I wanted it not just because I was fascinated with Federigo, the things he said and did and wore, but also because I remembered traveling something of the same path, before I had paid any attention to Federigo, at about the same time in the spring of 1957. I wanted the green Sardinian spring (and it was still the old Sardinia) and the Pisan churches that I had seen, and particularly Santa Giusta, at the center of the book and chapter. Since then Federigo has been inextricably connected in my mind with the Porta Settimiana, and he probably really walks and rides, at least in part, there or on the roads of the Borghese or on a street in Indiana.

There is a long (for me, three and one-half years) and often very painful time between the arrival of that sort of general idea and the actual composition of a piece of history. Even with the material found and the more detailed pattern of the work established, the writer has to decide exactly what part of his discoveries he wants to use, and how. I have a full sheet of blue stationery divided into five parts on which I tried to separate my material, to decide what should be emphasized in each chapter. It is an odd-looking thing. The third chapter has pairs or groups of names in it like "Celestine V Winchelsey" and "Filippo Benizi. Grosseteste. Manasses of Volturara Oliver Sutton" (with Oliver Sutton circled in red). "Louis of Toulouse" is underlined; "Obizzo" written in red crayon; "Peter Lo." in pencil and in a pencil

square. There is a note reading "physica absorption in material/ rejection of/ Rainaldo of Rieti in S." In a series of ellipses are: "Francis
—Celestine," "Langton—Winchelsey," "E. of A." There is more, some
illegible. Around this scheme were piles of papers, notes, often illegible
in parts. I have never been able to keep my notes on file cards (although, ironically, for years I taught Berkeley juniors how to do it;
and I always intend to do it myself with the next book)—like the graduate student–professorial brief case, it is something I have not yet been
able to bring myself to. As a result, everything is harder and messier.
Working conditions have not changed much for me since at Oxford on
John's Street I used to get up each morning and spread out my great
sheets of foolscap all over the floor and gather them all up again in the
evening.

Now, some months after *Two Churches* has been published, I can
make myself look at "Bishops and Saints" coldly to see if I can tell
why I chose the people and examples I did. They were for the most
part not inevitable—lots of bishops and saints would seem to have
done much the same job.

First of all, two people dominate the chapter, Francis and Grosseteste. For me at least, they were inevitable. But they are treated very
differently in the chapter. Grosseteste, already wonderfully exposed by
the Callus collaborators, did not need to be completely exposed again;
but he is dealt with relatively straightforwardly and is, I think, normally introduced into the chapter. Francis is spiritually and biblio-
graphically very different from Grosseteste. I could not deal with him
straightforwardly for various reasons. His words and acts are surrounded by a great mass of uncertainty. They were hidden by his
successors, and they are argued over by our contemporaries. They are
not easy and clear. Moreover, I myself am too much in awe of Francis,
and something more than that, to reduce him to an illustrative character in a chapter. I tried in a way to make Francis shine above the
chapter ("like the sun out of Ganges"). In any case he and Grosseteste,
as the two ideals, were to dominate the chapter. I also found Winchelsey and Celestine V inescapable. I was intrigued by their meeting in the
Abruzzi. Powicke and Rose Graham had made me see how extremely
interesting Winchelsey was; Celestine V (on whose feast Malcolm X,
Ho Chi Minh, and I were born), I disliked with a particular intensity.

The chapter begins with a paragraph about Philip Benizi as a
pre-contrast with Grosseteste. I am not sure exactly why I chose him. I
like the story of his crying for his book, and I like looking at him on
San Marcello on the Corso. I think, though, that I chose him because
he makes my point about Italian saints and their anti-activist position
familiarly and respectably (and so he makes an easy beginning) and
also because I thought my first sentence about him ("Saint Philip

Benizi, flaming with love, wanted not to be a bishop"), which arrived at my mind whole, dove nicely into the matter. From Benizi I moved to Grosseteste and through him to Hugh of Lincoln, the last twelfth-century bishop of Grosseteste's see. I wanted to use Hugh because I wanted to stay in Lincoln, to use it in a way for itself and also to build up to a successor of Grosseteste's, Oliver Sutton. But also accidentally, I happened to be paying attention to Hugh because I had been review-ing an edition and translation of one of his lives, so his great change from "contemplative" to "active" was in my mind. It struck me that it would be very helpful to the book.

I wanted very much to use Oliver Sutton who comes next. For a long time before my actual writing, I had played with the idea of his "bursting mind" filled with the minutiae of an English bishop's job; I wanted it in a long bursting-pudding paragraph. I wanted physical things in the paragraph, like Ralph Paynel's swans and Robert of Wootton's copy of Gregory's *Moralia* on Job (partly because I had grown to love that book when I worked on the *Early Middle Ages*). But the reason why I had particularly chosen Sutton (besides his being from helpful, great Lincoln, to which good registrars and Kathleen Major had attracted me), rather than some other conscientious late thirteenth-century bishop, seems to me quite clear. It is obviously because Sutton was edited by Rosalind Hill. It is not just that it is an edition in which one has complete confidence, but also that Miss Hill has, in introductions and essays, made Sutton (and his companion Schalby) interesting and attractive in a way that his contemporary bishops are not. I suspect that if she had edited one of the others I would have been attracted to, and written about, him. There was, however, a catch in my having become so sure that I wanted to use Sutton. In Rome in the summertime it was impossible for me to find a full text of Hill, and my notes were impressionistic and a mess. My point was quite clear; but it would be no point without names, pages, dates—and these were inaccessible. This is the sort of headache that constantly troubles a scholar working on two countries in two coun-tries—the documents and the books are often not available at the same time. Nothing (except the perversity of Italian archivists and my own terrible handwriting) has made my work harder than the books missing from Italian libraries.

I moved from Oliver Sutton, so beautifully recorded, to Bishop Manasses of Volturara, from whom, insofar as I know, only one document, the grant of a house by Trajan's gate in Benevento, survives. The contrast is obviously a nice one; but there are lots of poorly recorded Italian bishops. I chose Manasses because I noticed the document when I was going through the Aldobrandini archives in the Vatican and liked it (in some part because of Trajan's gate, which is very beautiful, and because of the document's church bell). Manasses is followed by a quick juxtaposition of two clusters of tenants under trees, a cherry and an ash, near Genoa and Saint Albans, which I chose because I wanted a quick introduction of the property-holding Church with something memorably physical (I also got a misspelling), because I like things that happen under trees, because I like Miss Levett on Saint Albans, and in spite of the fact that I would if I could steer forever clear of Genoa—in spite of its editions.[6]

The point that I am trying to make is that the historian chooses his actual examples for complex and partly personal and, at least in my case, visual reasons. Louis of Toulouse, for example, obviously caught my attention because of Margaret Toynbee's book about him, and also, like everybody else's attention, because of Simone Martini's painting in Naples, but I also found irresistible a life (full of splendid rejection) that tied together the Castel dell'Ovo and the Ara Coeli.[7] I obviously am attracted to Margaret dedications because I have a young daughter named Margaret who looks for her name-saint. On the other hand, if I were writing "Bishops and Saints" now, I would write much more of Peter Martyr, because I now have thought more about him and have come to understand better his historical significance. Some of the people whom I chose when I did write, Rainaldo of Rieti, Rainaldo of Nocera Umbra, Pietro the Lombard, are figures meant to be more central in later work of mine. It should be clear that my chapter three, and I should think every historical essay, is caught in a web and connected with its author's earlier and later work.

At least for me, it is often very difficult to decide (although sometimes immediately obvious) how an idea or a figure should be presented in the text. I found a problem in deciding, for instance, in taking the figure of Rainaldo of Rieti from Salimbene, how much Salimbene to retain. I decided that I wanted Salimbene at least as much as Rainaldo and that I wanted to use the narrative of Rainaldo to illustrate Salimbene's techniques and persuasions, so I kept to a close paraphrase of his text. When I was writing about Federigo Visconti I was aware of something curious nagging at the back of my mind, an echo of some English visitation. I suddenly realized that this great Italian visitation, in some ways, in some lights, reminded me of the most notorious of thirteenth-century English visitations, of Boniface of Savoy at Saint Bartholomews. I decided to present my discovery as it occurred. The odd connection seemed to me useful, but only useful to the reader if he could discover it, going in the right direction, as I had. So I took a chance and stuck my own mind, observed, rather forcefully into the chapter. Again, in reading of Federigo, I was—perhaps partly for very superficial reasons (his name, for example)—reminded of Federigo Borromeo in Manzoni's *I promessi sposi*. I then read Dora Lucciardi's similar reaction.[8] I decided, for conviction, to try to preserve the sequence of discovery in my book.

To bishops and saints I needed to attach other things. I needed the tone, the realization of the existence of heretics, Greeks, and Saracens. I did not, in this book, at this time, want to explore any of them in depth. I had to talk about them just enough to get their sound or scent in the chapter's later pages. I also wanted relics, miracles, and dedications. The last are particularly hard. They are slippery and indistinct, and the work that has been done on them is not reassuring. But I felt that I needed so much to have their sort of evidence apparent, for the reader to be aware of it, that I decided to use a sampling of dedications and at the same time to make perfectly clear through my notes how provisional my use of them was. This obvious device has advantages. Footnotes (although all historians must hate the drudgery of writing them correctly) bring tension to the page of history. The real life of the page depends on that tension between footnote and text; and at best, I think, it is apparent, taut, and complicated.

In "Bishops and Saints" I was particularly anxious to press the connection between the sources of episcopal income and, also, episcopal backgrounds and the nature of episcopal reform. It seemed, and seems, to me very important to examine this provocative connection. I thought it was an opportune place to try to introduce a neat socioeconomic model and "quantification." At the very least, it would have seemed natural to count different types of bishops in economic-class categories. I was forced in the end to realize that even this gesture would be destructive and misleading. My categories were shaky, my information in crucial areas very light and, even more, uneven. About some aristocratic bishops, for example, I knew as much as one could hope to know from the thirteenth century. About some I had only an adjective, the suggestion of a name, a hint in Ughelli.[9] I knew specific incomes, but not total incomes; but I knew more than that alone would imply if I could express it in words rather than numbers. To put these people and incomes together in blocks would suggest completely unwarranted certitude. Numbers are very clear, hard-edged. They would be an absurdity for a country, Italy, in which I could not even count the bishops. (Even if one feels sure about which dioceses to include, one's actual count may be several hundred off due to defective lists based on defective evidence.) So, after much thought, with hands clean, in the service of exactitude, I gave up counting. Instead of avoiding selectivity and disguising the unevenness of my evidence, I decided to press them upon the attention of my reader. It was, in a way, fortunate for me. I find computerized history deeply boring. The things that it can discover can almost never be the things that I want very much to know. It eliminates the most exciting part (the uneven, jagged connection, the perceived individual) of historical investigation. Still, although I think that I was right to back away, there is always something disturbingly feeble about retreat.

About categories themselves I tried to be exact in example. I also, however, in perhaps a rather cowardly way, depended upon other people, for example on Gibbs and Lang, whose categories of elected bishops I used as an adjustable model. In a book that extends itself as mine does, one almost must rely on other people and move where they have moved. Because of Lazzeri I could talk of Arezzo; because of Russo, of Cosenza (although it would be wrong to imply that I depended equally upon these two books or that they were of the same quality).[10] In the other direction, just because so many people, particularly so many able Americans, work in and on Florence, I tried to avoid it. I wanted my book to complement rather than to use their work.

Like other historians, I imagine, I am concerned with the problem of morality in history. Why write about saints? Do they have specifically saintly values? Should the moral values of the subject and the historian move back and forth and touch each other? I follow Acton, and at a greater distance, the Spiritual Franciscans. I disagree with what I take to be Rosalind Brooke's and M. D. Lambert's forgiving understanding of the later conventional Franciscans.[11] I think their perversion, their ugliness, is part of their appearance. The historian's disapproval of them (if he has it) is a tool for reviving them, and making them live again. I do not suggest that it should replace understanding, but rather be a part of a more complex understanding. I do not disguise, I think, my feelings, but in "Bishops and Saints" they had to be expressed in a rather complicated way: I really believe that the English church was morally positive in a way that the Italian church was not, but that Grosseteste for all his greatness was morally pale and even inept beside Francis. Moral persuasions shape historical essays and books. The sharply observable difference in shape between my book and William Bouwsma's new book, *Venice and the Defense of Republican Liberty* (a book also different from almost all other contemporary books of history because of its incredibly sustained brilliance) is in some little part at least due to our, for the moment, different attitudes about judging historical figures.

All the historian's grandiose plans for the writing of history, at least all my plans, are threatened by error, by simple mistakes. They grow like lichens on a text. The quickly or carelessly written note is easily misread; one of many typing and typesetting fingers can be put on the wrong key and the mistake not noticed. Years of careful work come to look silly. Beyond that simplest and most plaguing sort of error is the kind that comes from ignorance. In a book as broad as

Two Churches (at least one written by me), there were bound to be errors of ignorance. Beyond them, there are errors of direction, errors that come when one looks at something the wrong way, in the wrong connection: an oath that comes from, and that I had read in, the *Corpus iuris canonici* looked to me, as I was writing *York Metropolitan Jurisdiction* and thinking of local things, local and feudal; and I said so. The structure of *Two Churches* begs for this sort of error (but, fortunately, also for the awareness of it).

All these levels of error eat away at the effectiveness of a piece of history and make it seem pretentious and foolish and hollow. But the only way, at least for me, to avoid them, if it is at all possible, is to write a little, narrow, closed piece of history. And I do not want to do that. Of course, not all histories that look subdued on the surface are dead. Edward Miller's *The Abbey and Bishopric of Ely,* for example, may seem a quiet, closed book to the superficial observer, but for some fortunate reason its conventional order seems, at least to me, to burst with life. The book does not parade its vivacity, but within the pattern of its good order, conventional prose, carefully examined evidence, persuasive logic, it simply lives.

Like many, perhaps all, historians, I assumed when I was young that I would grow old writing in verse. I am still much attracted to, perhaps incapable of avoiding, the poet's ordering of material. He need not, even in a narrative poem (think, for instance, of Arnold's *Tristram and Iseult*) worry with dull, soggy transitional passages, with tedious explanations. He can present his series of images and ideas whole, clear, bright, and let the transition occur, as it should, without the dullness of written words, in the reader's mind. Without words, transition becomes beautiful. If I ever have enough nerve, I shall write history completely without transition. "Bishops and Saints" is an easy start. Its pattern does not require, in many places, more than the juxtaposition of contrasting figures.

I also envy the poet sound, particularly as in Clough—crazy, daring, ugly sound. I have tried using it, but not, I think, very interestingly, except sometimes in the timing of phrases, in *Two Churches.* Three hundred and fifty pages of sounding history has to be pretty subtle to be bearable; it is not, unfortunately, like a song from *The Princess.*

I am also constantly bothered by being unable to reproduce visual things. The Princeton Press did an imaginative job in *Two Churches* with plates seven to twelve. These plates scramble thirteenth-century representations of bishops and some of the ecclesiastical buildings inhabited in the text: bishops and buildings move together. I like the arrangement very much, although I did not work it out. Still for years

I have lived in, intermittently, and written about Italy. The things that really interest me most in Italy, that stop me, hold me in one place, are things like the way folds of drapery cut the grilled rectangle of a church transom, the way the arches of a Tiber bridge cut into quay and river or frame a monastery. While I am absorbed by these patterns, I write of the way in which senators ruled—not uninteresting, but there seems an odd and somehow destructive distance between what I look at and what I do. This essay itself should more pleasingly be the description of enclosed and open spaces, the way my room moves toward the Mattei and Campitelli. Sometimes these things come together. As I wrote "Bishops and Saints," I stared day after day at Santa Maria del Popolo; and (as I discovered Roth's work at the same time) the Popolo's new order, the wild Augustinian hermits, pressed their way first into the chapter then to importance in it.[12]

If I wrote as I should like to write, this long essay would have been very Japanese, a little George Herbert, the length of a paragraph but not a paragraph, a series of sounds, pictures (or rather molds and mobiles—spacial relations) and phrases. The vapid, soggy words would be evaporated. Images (the piazza at Bologna, the castle at Wallingford, Pecham's three gold pins), hard, bare ideas, quotations, and noisemakers would be dispersed and three-dimensional in a complicated and sounding pattern (reflecting in some way the room on the Via di Villa Ruffo) on the page—and the footnotes would be exact and obvious, or completely absorbed.

NOTES

1. D. A. Callus, ed., *Robert Grosseteste* (Oxford, 1955).
2. *English Historical Review*, LXXVI (1961), 296–303.
3. Irene Churchill, *Canterbury Administration* (London, 1933).
4. For example, Mazzatinti on Rieti: Giuseppe Mazzatinti, *Gli archivi della storia d'Italia*, IV (Rocca San Casciano, 1906), pp. 208–68.
5. Wolfgang Hagemann, "Studien und Dokumente zur Geschichte der Marken im Zeitalter der Staufer, II: Chiaravalle di Fiastra," *Quellen und Forschungen aus italienischen Archiven und Bibliotheken*, XLI (1961), 48–136.
6. Ada Elizabeth Levett, *Studies in Manorial History* (Oxford, 1938).
7. Margaret R. Toynbee, *St. Louis of Toulouse* (Manchester, 1929).
8. Dora Lucciardi, "Federico Visconti arcivescovo di Pisa," *Bollettino storico pisano*, II, 1 (1933), 16.
9. Ferdinando Ughelli, *Italia sacra* (Venice, 1717–1722).
10. Marion Gibbs and Jane Lang, *Bishops and Reform, 1215–1272* (Oxford, 1934); Corrado Lazzeri, *Guglielmino Ubertini, vescovo di Arezzo (1248–*

1289) *e i suoi tempi* (Florence, 1920); Francesco Russo, *Storia dell'arcidiocesi di Cosenza* (Naples, 1957).

11. Rosalind B. Brooke, *Early Franciscan Government* (Cambridge, England, 1959); M. D. Lambert, *Franciscan Poverty* (London, 1961).

12. Francis Roth, "Cardinal Richard Annibaldi, First Protector of the Augustinian Order, 1243–1276," *Augustiniana*, II (1952), 26–60, 108–49, 230–47; III (1953), 21–34, 283–313; IV (1954), 5–24.

History
and
Horseshoe Nails

LYNN T. WHITE, JR.

LYNN T. WHITE, JR., was born on April 29, 1907, in San Francisco, California. He graduated from Stanford University in 1928, received an M.A. from Union Theological Seminary in 1929, and then studied at Harvard University from which he earned an M.A. in 1930 and a Ph.D. in 1934. From 1933 to 1937 he worked as an Instructor in History at Princeton University. He then moved to Stanford University where he taught for six years, becoming Professor of History in 1940. He was appointed President of Mills College, Oakland, California, in 1943, a position he held until 1958. Since that time he has been Professor of History at the University of California, Los Angeles.

Since 1964 White has been director of the UCLA Center for Medieval and Renaissance Studies. In the spring of 1965 he was a Fellow of the Institute for Advanced Study at Princeton. He spent the year 1968–1969 at Cornell University as Senior Visiting Fellow of the Society for the Humanities. In 1969 he was named Fellow of the Southeastern Institute for Medieval and Renaissance Studies. White holds honorary degrees from MacMurray College (LL.D. 1946), Lake Erie College (LL.D. 1957), and Mills College (LL.D. 1958). He was appointed an Officier d'Académie in 1948, received a Guggenheim Fellowship for 1958–1959, and won the Pfizer Award of the History of Science Society in 1963, as well as the Leonardo da Vinci Medal of the Society for the History of Technology in 1964. Among the many learned societies to which he belongs are: the Académie Internationale d'Histoire des Sciences (membre correspondant), American Academy of Arts and Sciences, American Association for the Advancement of Science, American Historical Association (member of the Council, 1968–1970), California Historical Society, American Philosophical Society, History of Science Society (Councillor, 1953–1958, 1962–1964, Vice-president, 1967–1969), Istituto Italiano per la Storia della Technica, Mediaeval Academy of America (Fellow, Vice-president, 1967–1970), Phi Beta Kappa, Newcomen Society, Renaissance Society of America, Royal Society of Arts, Society for the History of Technology (President, 1960–1962), Society for Medieval Archaeology, and the Society for Religion in Higher Education.

White is the author of *Latin Monasticism in Norman Sicily* (Cambridge, Mass.: 1938), *Educating Our Daughters: A Challenge to the Colleges* (New York, 1950), *Medieval Technology and Social Change* (Oxford, 1962), and *Machina Ex Deo: Essays on the Dynamism of Western Culture* (Cambridge, Mass., 1969). He is also editor of *Frontiers of Knowledge in the Study of Man* (New York, 1956) and *The Transformation of the Roman World* (Berkeley and Los Angeles, 1966).

He is editor of *Viator: Medieval and Renaissance Studies* and serves on the editorial boards of *Speculum* (1968–1971), *Isis, Manuscripta,* the *Smithsonian Journal of History,* and the *Journal of Developing Areas.* At present, White is working on India and medieval Europe and on the problem of psychological aggression in the Middle Ages and the Renaissance.

H istorians are suspicious of memoirs, having found them generally to be, often unconsciously, defenses of the writer's ego. To ask a historian to put himself under his own scalpel is to demand a candor which is hard to fulfill because it converts a habitual subject into an object.

Objectivity is the more difficult in my own case, because in the autumn of 1933 I was unhorsed on a road to Damascus and since then have had an evangelical zeal to propagate a kind of history which I am convinced is integral to the quality of our time and thus to understanding ourselves and our age. I am trying to globalize history not by studying simultaneities, but by tracing cultural debts between peoples normally treated separately; I am trying to democratize history by bringing into it a sense of the creativity of the groups who seldom left written records; I am trying to deepen history psychologically by verbalizing past movements and attitudes which contemporaries either could not, or felt no need to, put into words.

On the evening of February 28, 1933, I left the archive of St. Agatha's in Catania, bought a newspaper, and headed for the pension where I was staying. In shrieking headlines the paper announced the burning of the Reichstag, and the Fascist press of Italy chorused Hitler's accusation that the Communists had committed the crime.

I had arrived in Sicily by a winding road: San Francisco, Stanford, New York, the banks of the Charles. In Charles Haskins' seminars I had learned to find pleasure in the Normans. When tragic illness forced his retirement, I had transferred my academic allegiance to George LaPiana, a Sicilian who suggested a doctoral dissertation on the introduction and development of Latin monasticism in Sicily—an island which had been entirely Muslim and Greek—after the Norman conquest. Haskins approved: clearly, it was a significant topic which might well lead into other things. Harvard kindly provided the Bayard Cutting Fellowship. So there I was in Catania, hard at work with my nose among the parchments and much enjoying them.

The pension where I was living was chiefly inhabited by German tourists. An hour after I had read the news, as I sat alone at dinner listening to the neurotic passion in the talk at the little tables around me, I saw with absolute certainty that Europe was headed toward a second catastrophe which nothing could prevent. Like most Americans at that time, I was an isolationist; fifteen years earlier, we felt, the United States on bloody battlefields had won the "war to end war," and then at Versailles had lost the peace because of the vengefulness and imperialist ambitions of Lloyd George and Clemenceau. Next time Europe could pull its chestnuts out of the fire without our assistance. But as I sat at my table, I realized that it would be rash for an American scholar like me to plan a program of research which would require the use of European archives during the next decade or more. That night I decided to finish my current project as quickly as possible, and meanwhile to start hunting for a topic in medieval history so unexplored that useful work in it could be done on the basis of published materials.

Late in the spring I found a job at Princeton, thanks to the warm support of Harris Harbison: we had roomed together at Harvard. It paid me $1,800, but 1933 was the bottom of the Great Depression, work was hard to get, and a dollar bought more than it buys today. I was happy at Princeton. The Princeton faculty, however, was the most intellectually conservative in my experience, before or since. Despite student interest, it had no use for novelties like anthropology or human geography. One of the more adventurous spirits was John Pomfret, who eventually became director of the Huntington Library in San Marino. Just before I arrived in Princeton, he had finally persuaded the history department to let him teach a course that was a montage of some of the newer disciplines in the social sciences. He needed an assistant for discussion groups (a "preceptor," in the local dialect); I was the newest and most vulnerable member of the department. Despite my entire lack of preparation for such work, I was drafted to help him.

The first book the students read was Alfred Kroeber's masterly textbook *Anthropology*.[1] I knew nothing at all about anthropology, and what archeology I had encountered was the classical variety that had little of the earthiness and vividness I found in Kroeber. Suddenly, and with shock, I realized that my training as a historian had frightening limitations. I had been taught to read the texts critically, but Kroeber was a scholar who managed to reconstruct and interpret societies of great interest which had few or no written texts. He was eager to apply anthropological methods to literate cultures. And because a people's relation to its environment is so dependent on the state of its technology, Kroeber was greatly concerned with tools. Could Kroeber's approach be applied to the Middle Ages? I do not know how much the students learned in that autumn semester of 1933, but I have not been the same since.

By serendipity, I soon found Commandant Richard Lefebvre des Noëttes' amazing monograph on the history of the use of horsepower, which had been published less than two years earlier.[2] Lefebvre des Noëttes came of an old military family: one of his grandfathers had been a marshal of Napoleon. He graduated from the famous cavalry school at Saumur, lived the life of an officer, and about 1910 retired on a military pension to devote himself to his hobby, the history of the harness. He had no training as a historian, but he had spent decades with horses and knew them as no scholar ever had known them.

Hans Delbrück[8] had noticed that in antiquity horsemen always wielded the spear at the end of the arm, whereas in the Middle Ages the spear was normally held under the right armpit. But Delbrück had no real sense of the advantage of the new method or the reason for the change of posture. Lefebvre des Noëttes, trained as a hussar, understood that in the new method of fighting, the blow is struck not by the strength of human biceps, but by the impetus of a charging horse—an immense increase in violence. He also saw that the presupposition of the new style of mounted shock combat was the stirrup. So he started out to find the origin of the stirrup.

He looked at pictures of the Greco-Roman horse harness and saw that it was astonishingly inefficient as compared with either the breast-strap or the rigid-collar harness of later ages. He built some Roman harness and found experimentally that a team of horses equipped with modern harness could pull between three and four times as heavy a load as with ancient harness. Clearly, the new medieval method of tapping horsepower made the horse not only a military but also an economic animal, with vast consequences for production and transportation in Europe. So Lefebvre des Noëttes determined to find the beginnings of modern harness.

When I read his book, I could see at once that Lefebvre des Noëttes was a genius whose essential insights would survive all criticism. But it was also clear that his massive labors were not disciplined by adequate historical criticism. Since texts for such subjects are almost nonexistent, he had turned to iconography, but he had managed to misdate a considerable number of the representations which he considered. Moreover, he neglected large areas of archeological evidence, particularly burials of warriors with fully equipped horses. As a result, none of his specific conclusions could be trusted, much less his efforts to correlate the new uses of horsepower with the general cultural developments of the early Middle Ages.

I determined to see what could be done to amplify and tighten up the evidence he had assembled. By orthodox professional standards, the task (as several friends told me) was "impossible," since it ranged over all the horse-riding cultures of the Old World—from Japan to Ireland and Morocco. Obviously no one could command all the languages (living and dead) or all the subdisciplines of archeology, art history, and etymology needed for such a study. Fortunately, Lefebvre des Noëttes had not been intellectually sterilized by learning in seminars what it is not respectable for a scholar to do. He was wrong in many details, but superbly right in all fundamentals. I decided that if he could be a stallion, I was not going to be a gelding.

And indeed, even in the early 1930s it was becoming clear to more historians than were prepared to do anything concrete about it that history must be made global, even though this meant that the individual historian, outside his primary area of expertise, must henceforth depend far more on the skills of scholars in other fields than had been traditional when research could confine itself to small areas involving only a few tongues. Yet in the thirties there was still a hesitancy in such matters that seems curiously archaic from our stance a generation later. For example, as was inevitable from my early base of operations in Sicily, some of my first articles were related to Byzantium. This worried certain of my well-wishers, who urged me to stick to "the main line" and not to be drawn off into Byzantine studies, which, they assured me, "are a dead end." I had no intention of becoming a Byzantinist—my love has been the Latin West—but memory of that advice amuses me whenever I visit the superb "dead end" of Dumbarton Oaks.

In widening the pioneer track first cut through the historical jungle by Lefebvre des Noëttes, I found not merely magnificent but unique tools at Princeton. The library in archeology and art history was even then one of the best. But, above all, Charles Rufus Morey was in the midst of creating the Princeton Index of Christian Art, which was designed to gather and organize photographs of every published—and many an unpublished—item of Christian art from the first graffiti in the Catacombs to the year 1400. At that time the Index was available only at Princeton. Today, with its coverage still being expanded, copies are maintained in Europe at the Vatican and in Utrecht; in the United States, it is available at Dumbarton Oaks and (not by coincidence) at the University of California, Los Angeles.

In my opinion the Princeton Index is the greatest single research instrument for the history of Western civilization. It contains, carefully classified and indexed, everything that was pictured—from objects to symbols of ideas—during twelve immensely vital centuries out of which the modern West emerged. Indeed, its scope exceeds the West: it is filled with Byzantine, Slavic, Georgian, Syrian, Coptic, Christian Arabic, Armenian, and Ethiopian materials. Unfortunately, from my point of view, Morey was strictly an iconologist, a major entrepreneur in art history who had little notion that the materials he was collecting would be useful in other fields. In the interest of economy he made decisions which seemed legitimate for iconology but which handicap other sorts of research. For example, when eventually I became interested in ship construction, I found he had ordered that incidental pictures of ships after 1200 should not be indexed; there were simply too many of them. But it was only about 1200 that the great period of innovation in ship design, which three centuries later helped to make possible the feats of Columbus, Vasco da Gama, and Magellan, began.

So, for this crucial period one must look at the "set pieces" showing boats: Noah's ark, Jonah being cast to the whale, Jesus walking on the water, St. Paul's shipwreck, and a few events in lives of saints. But nowhere else can one find so much material on such topics as in the Index, and the stuff which is not indexed is hidden there to be found if one burns enough tapers at appropriate altars.

In 1933 only art historians were using the Index, and the exploration of its riches by scholars in other fields has scarcely begun even today. Recently I persuaded a learned Spencer specialist to dip into it. He reported that in half an hour he spotted six items not in the literature. Humanists pride themselves on their spiritual freedom; they seldom ponder their subjugation to tradition. Above all, they are word-bound. The texts are everything, and the other means by which men have left evidence of their thoughts and passions, achievements and failures, are disregarded. Humanism will not mature until all the sources of understanding are pondered and exploited.

Groping into the labyrinth of the Princeton Index and into the archeological record, I gradually found much material to rectify Lefebvre des Noëttes' datings of the arrival in Europe both of the stirrup and of modern horse harness. The dating of the stirrup ca. 730 enabled me to confirm the essence of Heinrich Brunner's classic theory of the origins of feudalism, published in 1887, which had been so vigorously debated over the decades.[4] Brunner traced the feudal system to a military revolution under Charles Martel. Martel, he believed, had defeated the horse-riding Muslim invaders at Poitiers in 732 with an infantry army, but had seen that for permanent superiority he must shift the focus of the Frankish host from footmen to horsemen. To that end, he confiscated vast amounts of Church lands and distributed them for the support of vassals sworn to fight on horseback at his bidding. These endowed, mounted warriors became the knights of the Middle Ages.

Brunner was wrong in some details. The invading Muslim army was not to any great extent mounted. The battle of Poitiers was fought in 733, not 732; yet the first confiscation of Church lands and their distribution to vassals occurred in 732. On two grounds, then, the action was not provoked by Muslim invasion. Brunner had not had the advantage of Lefebvre des Noëttes' insight, as a professional cavalryman, into the implications of the stirrup. Now that I could date the arrival of the stirrup in Gaul at about 730, the reason for Martel's drastic action was clear: he too was a professional fighter of great ability; he or his advisers saw that the stirrup gave a vast new advantage to the mounted warrior; the security of the realm demanded an immediate and costly translation of the Frankish army into the new style of military technology. The effects of this military revolution upon the later Middle Ages were obvious and almost beyond estimation.

The discovery in the Index of a crude but convincing representation of horse collars and lateral traces in the *Apocalypse* of Trier, ca. 800, enabled me to date modern harness in Europe a century earlier than Lefebvre des Noëttes had dated it. This got me into the history of agriculture and especially into the field so magnificently opened by Marc Bloch's Oslo lectures, published the same year as Lefebvre des Noëttes' great book.[5] To my eyes, Bloch was the most seminal medieval historian of his generation: his death by torture at the hands of the Germans a decade later was one of the most horrifying individual crimes of our century. Bloch saw that the history of the land had been written in terms of ownership, whereas it should have been written in terms of the agrarian technology that made land worth owning. In a period when at least nine-tenths of the people lived on the land, any increase in productivity would have had profound effects. Less by original basic research than by synthesizing the work of others, I have helped to crystallize the concept of a vast agricultural revolution in the early Middle Ages north of the Alps and the Loire which so greatly increased the surplus of food grown by the average peasant that population, urbanism, and commerce experienced an explosive expansion from the late tenth to the late thirteenth centuries. In 1937 there was published posthumously the final form [6] of Henri Pirenne's famous hypothesis that the Islamic conquests of the seventh and early eighth centuries, by smashing the unity of the Mediterranean, forced northern Europe into an isolation in which the Franks created a new type of culture out of which the later Middle Ages and the modern world emerged. During the intervening decades, Pirenne's theory has been largely destroyed, but his initial observation, that the Carolingian period marks the shift of Europe's focus from the shores of the Mediterranean to the great northern plains, stands intact. The fact is better explained by the agricultural revolution occurring in the north of Europe in that epoch.

It was also largely Bloch who led me into the mechanical and industrial technology of the Western Middle Ages through his basic study of the diffusion of the watermill.[7] From this I went on to look at the other novel sources of power discovered or elaborated in the Middle Ages.

Power machines pushed me into the problems of machine design, and I was particularly entranced by the study of rotary motion published in 1933–1934 by H. T. Horwitz,[8] another eventual victim of the Nazis. Horwitz made me aware of the mechanical crank as second in importance for machine design only to the wheel. I began looking for medieval cranks, since there were none in antiquity outside China. Ernest DeWald of Princeton had recently issued a superb facsimile edition of the Utrecht *Psalter* illuminated near Reims about 825. There, on plate 58,[9] I found the first European crank turning the first rotary grindstone anywhere. I well remember telling Ernest of my discovery. He was an excellent scholar and one of the most genteel of gentlemen. He was polite, but obviously to him these were matters of no importance. I tried to explain that, after the neolithic spindle and the potter's wheel, the rotary grindstone was the third instance of the flywheel principle; I tried also to explain that since the crank is the most common means of joining reciprocating with continuous rotary motion, this first European appearance of the crank in his beloved *Psalter* was a matter of moment. In vain: I was beginning to learn that the Greek contempt for the banausic is so deeply embedded in the tradition of humanistic education that humanists normally would consider my interests eccentric and a waste of time almost in proportion as they were well educated in that tradition. And Princeton was very humanistic.

That illumination in the Utrecht *Psalter* provided trauma of another sort for me thirty years later. In 1965 Bruce Spiegelberg of Colby College, then a graduate student in English at Berkeley, asked me whether I had ever looked at the total implication of the illumination showing the cranked grindstone. I had not; yet the message is clear. On the right stands King David, blest of God and protected by an angel. With him is a tiny band of the righteous eagerly shooting arrows at a larger group of the ungodly on the left. A major interest in the picture lies in the fact that in each camp a sword is being sharpened. The evil-doers are content with an old-fashioned whetstone. The elect, in contrast, are using the novel and more efficient grindstone. The artist is emphatically identifying moral virtue with technological advance. As Spiegelberg remarked, "This is sheer progressivism!" It is; moreover it fits the technological atmosphere of that age. But where had my eyes and perception been these past thirty years that I should have identified the gadgets but overlooked the much more important significance of that picture for the history of the West? Such humiliation may be good for the soul, but it should not happen too often in a lifetime.

People at Princeton were immensely kind to me, and for the reasons indicated, it was the best place in the world at that time to do research on medieval technology. Nevertheless, when Stanford offered me an assistant professorship early in 1937, I accepted without negotiating with Princeton. The reasons were several. Californians in exile have an incurable yearning to return. In the summer of 1936, while at home for a visit, I had met my future wife who, at sixteen, was entering Stanford that autumn as a freshman. She did not yet know that she was destined to be my wife, but I thought it would be simpler to inform her if I spoke with the authority of a member of the Stanford faculty. And I suspected that Stanford might be somewhat more open than Princeton to new ideas.

I was not disappointed, either personally or professionally, by the results of the move. Most of my spare time at Princeton had been spent not on medieval technology but rather on expanding and polishing my book on *Latin Monasticism in Norman Sicily*,[10] and before I left for Stanford the manuscript was in the hands of the Mediaeval Academy. It was good enough so that thirty years later, in 1968, it was worth reprinting. The inevitable conflict was clearly coming soon in Europe. I settled at Stanford with a new sense of freedom to follow my own concerns both in teaching and research.

The Stanford library was very bad for my purposes, but I started building it in my field and quickly discovered quite remarkable resources in the San Francisco region, especially at Berkeley. Moreover, I came to treasure the conversation of two remarkable historians in Berkeley. James Westphall Thompson was a man with a genius for making errors, but he possessed a gargantuan enthusiasm for the study of the Middle Ages which overrode all his defects. Ernst Kantorowicz had the sharpest intelligence, the widest range of learning, and the most ebullient wit of any medievalist in my experience. Two men more different can hardly be imagined, yet each was a good friend, and each in his own way helped my thinking.

By 1938 I had decided that I must make a study of the total bibliography for medieval technology, since no one had done so or knew how to get at it. As is the way with bibliographers, I was soon crushed by avalanches of little cards, but gradually the resources for study in the field began to take on a pattern. In 1940 I published a survey article, "Technology and Invention in the Middle Ages," [11] which was designed to attract others to this neglected field and which concluded with a bibliographical indication of how they might find materials. By then, however, no one in Europe was listening. And that autumn all American men of my age registered for the draft.

On December 7, 1941, the Japanese struck Pearl Harbor and destroyed the American Pacific fleet. It is difficult now to remember the national anxiety of the years that followed. I was not drafted, but the American higher educational system was almost entirely turned to military puposes. Late in 1942, I was offered the presidency of Mills College in Oakland. Mills was underendowed, deep in debt, and saddled with an inefficient campus. Its chief merit was a faculty of a quality far higher than the salaries they received. Mills was not then attractive.

However, my wife and I went up to Oakland by train one rainy day during the December vacation to let a senior member of the faculty show us about the place, which was dripping and deserted. When we returned, gloomily, to San Francisco on our way back to Stanford, we bought another newspaper that changed my life. In it Henry Stimson, Secretary of War, officially announced the adjournment of liberal education "for the duration": It was a luxury embattled America could not afford. My wife turned to me and said, "Well, I guess we're going to Mills." We both felt that, in a conflict which at that point threatened to be another Thirty Years' War, our country was in peril of destroying internally the values that globally we were claiming to defend. We thought that a small women's college like Mills might be more immune to the barbarizing pressures arising from war than any other sort of college or university. We hoped that in the raging storm we might help to preserve precious things for the long future. It was not a good bet, but it was one worth taking. Fortunately, the war ended far sooner than could have been foreseen at that time.

I told the trustees of Mills, in accepting their offer, that I wanted them to recognize that a certain amount of continuing historical research and publication was part of my job as president. On such a campus, the president must say "no" far more often than he can say "yes." If the faculty believes that he is himself a scholar, they will accept "no" from him with reasonable grace. If they are convinced that their president is no longer a scholar, faculty morale is eventually destroyed. So, for the fifteen years (1943–1958) of my presidency at Mills, I continued to keep my union card as a medieval historian, despite almost impossible pressures. Occasionally I found a Saturday afternoon for work in the Berkeley library. Whenever I traveled, I carried bibliographic cards in my pocket to be checked at the local libraries when I had an hour or so between appointments. It was hard, but I believe that it helped the temper of the Mills College community in years which always seemed filled with crisis, mostly financial. It helped me to find a new job when a new job was needed.

In February of 1957, thanks to Julian Bishko of the University of Virginia, who had been in Haskins' seminars with me, I gave the three James W. Richard Lectures in History at Charlottesville on "Medieval Technology and Social Change." I decided not to attempt a total coverage of the problem, but rather to concentrate on three major phases of medieval technology which were clearly related to social development. The first was the mutation in the art of war which occurred during the eighth century and the way in which its character shaped the secular aristocracy of Europe. The second was the agricultural revolution of the early Middle Ages in the North and its effect on the condition of the peasants. The third was the new medieval exploitation of sources of power and novel mechanical devices, which implemented late medieval industrialism and burgher capitalism. This sort of thing had not been done before, and some of the results were unexpected both in general and in detail. When the lectures were ended, Julian said to me with a twinkle, "Lynn, when you publish you must document lavishly; otherwise no one either will or should believe you."

He was correct: the book had to be a monograph for specialists simply because the bibliography for many of the topics had never been gathered and sifted. Over half of it, when it appeared, consisted of footnotes, some of them long and intricate.[12] The labor of constructing such mosaics was vindicated when Ernst Kantorowicz read the book and wrote to me registering his astonishment that "the very existence of the great mass of the literature which you cite was quite unknown to me." If "EKa" didn't know it, no one did: of this I was confident.

Quite apart from the defense of my theses, such documentation was essential for a related reason. In the autumn of 1933 I had deliberately chosen the study of medieval technology because it was a topic in embryo. The encouraging development of it in Europe in the 1930s was crushed by the war and the subsequent chaos. Inevitably, in so unexplored a subject, I would make errors. It was important that anyone filled either with enthusiasm for, or doubt of, my statements be given a bibliographic springboard for his own researches.

Yet I could not be content to make this volume simply an item for library shelves. Over the years I had developed a passion for the spreading of a new notion of how to write history: one which transcends the traditional barriers between the histories of the major world cultures; one which recognizes that every society—including our own—neglects to put many of its doings into the written record; one which, in the wisdom of the accomplished fact, searches not simply the unverbalized but even the subliminal elements of life in the past. For this sort of history I am an unabashed propagandist, less by exhortation than by offering concrete examples of how to write it. I wanted to infect students with my enthusiasms. To that end, in *Medieval Technology and Social Change* I decided to preserve the fluid form of the lecture rather than adopt the more granitic manner of the monograph. I feared that with such a contrast between text and notes I would fall between two stools, but evidently I did not. Both in America and in Britain the book has appeared in paperback; Italian and German translations are on the market; at this writing, the French version is said to be imminent; contracts have been let for Swedish and Spanish editions. Naturally I am pleased.

Not all reviewers were friendly; indeed, some were so hostile that it was clear I had violated their presuppositions about the writing of history. That the book contains blunders is not surprising, considering its relation to previous scholarship in the field. What troubles me is that I stupidly overlooked a few significant items which were staring me in the face. For example, I neglected the importance of the invention of the grubby whippletree and the use of the horse for heavy hauling. In my single reference to it (p. 66, n. 5), I dated its first appearance 1152–1154; in fact it was known in England by 1077, and probably in southern Germany by the middle of the eleventh century.[13] But all that any historian can do, since history is an infinite frontier between ignorance and understanding of the human record, is to work very hard and be happy when his mistakes and inadequacies are rectified either by his own further labors or by others.

My continuing interest is not to follow the line of thinking found in *Medieval Technology and Social Change,* but rather to explore three topics related to it.

When, in 1959, I finished the manuscript for that book, I was painfully aware that it contained a grave defect of omission. I had established that the Western Middle Ages, beginning very early, developed a technological thrust which quickly surpassed that of its more generally sophisticated sister cultures Byzantium and Islam, and which had outstripped even that of China by the middle of the fourteenth century. This is a conclusion of importance for the twentieth century, since our present global technology stems directly from that of the Middle Ages. But I had evaded the historian's responsibility to try to explain not merely what happened, but also why it happened. This dereliction of duty weighs on my conscience. To tell the truth, I am far more sure of the *what* than the *why,* and in 1959 I was unwilling —in print—even to send up a trial balloon of explanation.

This is the sort of problem that must be approached in stages usually consisting of unpublished—and unpublishable—addresses designed to evoke criticism and draw new kinds of evidence toward the core of the subject. The surging creativity of the Middle Ages in technology cannot be credited to any inherent economic necessity, since such necessity is common to all peoples but is not operational until it is felt as necessity. The historical question, then, is: What makes a given set of technological advances seem necessary in a certain time and place?

A very preliminary talk on "What Accelerated Technological Progress in the Western Middle Ages," presented in London in the summer of 1960, led Alistair Crombie to ask me to expand, polish, and repeat it at a conference in Oxford a year later.[14] Here I tried to draw up an inventory of various possible explanations, none of them mutually exclusive, and not all of equal cogency. For example, in Roman times the Celts showed themselves to be the most inventive population of the empire; perhaps the medieval West simply represents an amplification of indigenous talents. But this only transfers the enigma from the medieval to the Roman period. Another hypothesis: change leads to more change. The early medieval West was somewhat more deeply disturbed than were the Eastern regions once ruled by Rome. Perhaps the more thorough destruction of the old order produced a cultural climate in the West more open to innovation than in the East. But, if true, this does not explain why so much of that opportunity for innovation should have expressed itself in technology.

My own bent of mind leads me to put more weight on the conditioning power of the religious ambience. After all, I am the son of a liberal Calvinist professor of Christian ethics, and between graduating from Stanford in 1928 and going to Harvard in 1929, I studied in Union Theological Seminary at the feet of the most passionate neo-Augustinian of our times, Reinhold Niebuhr: I have a *mens naturaliter theologica*. To me it seems clear that the Christian destruction of animism—the notion that spirit exists in nature apart from man and angels, fallen or other—and the Christian conviction that the whole of nature was divinely designed solely for man's benefit, undercut the ancient pagan inhibitions about the rational exploitation of our environment. It seems equally evident that the monastic revival of the very nonclassical Jewish idea that manual labor is an essential part of the spiritual life helped to narrow the old gap between the practical and the speculative during the centuries in which the working monks were also the most highly educated men of their society. Such a combination could scarcely fail to encourage technological growth.

The trouble with this line of argument, however, is that during the Middle Ages the Greek East held the Christian faith as ardently as the Latin West, and Greek monks labored and studied as rigorously as their Benedictine contemporaries did; yet after the seventh century, the Byzantine realm produced little that was new in technology. If the sources of technological innovation are to be found in its religious context, the nature of those sources must be identified in the differences of tonality between the Latin and Greek forms of Christianity.

The survival of a literate laity in the East relieved the Greek monks of any large responsibility for the preservation of secular culture and encouraged their complete intellectual immersion in religious studies. In contrast, the tragic decay of secular institutions in the West demanded that the Benedictines preserve and develop not only the religious, but also the secular aspects of literate culture during the early Middle Ages. In the West spirit and flesh were more mutually involved than in the East. There is scattered but emphatic evidence that Western ascetics from the sixth century onward were concerned with technological advance. I know of no similar evidence from the Christian East.

Even more important, I believe, was the influence of Latin voluntarism as compared with Greek intellectualism. This contrast in religious "styles" has long been observed: the Greeks believe that sin is ignorance and that salvation comes by illumination; the Latins believe that sin is evil action and that salvation comes by doing the right thing. Greek saints are normally contemplatives; Western saints are normally activists. Technology naturally did better in the Latin than in the Greek atmosphere.

Historical rumination of this kind is a bit like making cheese: you shape it up, set it on a shelf in a cool place, and after a time come back to see whether it has matured properly. The causes of the epochal medieval adventure in technology demand much more prolonged discussion than they have received.

Perhaps not only new facts about technology, but new findings about attitudes toward technology will help such analysis. In 1963, I was attracted by a sixteenth-century woodcut showing the virtue Temperance wearing a mechanical clock as a hat. Since it was not very becoming, I wondered why she was so embellished. What emerged is presented as "The Iconography of *Temperantia* and the Virtuousness of Technology" in the volume in memory of "Jinks" Harbison of Princeton.[15] Harbison was my best friend. I wanted to lay a good wreath on his grave. This is, I think, the most profitable thing I have written, partly because it uses pictures alone to show the reemergence in the fifteenth century of the idea, first stated by the artist of the Utrecht *Psalter*, that technological progress is an aspect of high morality—an idea no contemporary seems to have put into words, despite the fact that it was then, and has remained, one of the major forces in Western civilization. I have no doubt that many similar studies remain to be done, and that when more have accumulated, we may know what we are talking about when we discuss the development of technology.

A second line of my present research has stemmed from *Medieval Technology and Social Change*. Scattered through it were indications of technological elements diffused to medieval Europe from the more distant parts of Asia. Joseph Needham's superb work [16] makes it redundant for most of us to underscore such borrowings from China; so long as his studies are in process, one can only offer an occasional new item or correction. But obviously medieval Europe was indebted to other far regions as well. I gathered the technological material in an essay entitled "Tibet, India and Malaya as Sources of Western Medieval Technology," [17] with results that seemed surprising to some. As I rethought the evidence, I came to realize that far more than technology traveled from India westward during the millennium before Vasco da Gama; yet there was no systematic study of these Indic intrusions and of their impact, if any, upon the Middle Ages. The matter interested me the more because such osmoses between cultures seem normally to occur below the level of the written record. It is a great consolation to a devout diffusionist to deal with Indian water buffaloes in fifteenth-century Italy in confidence that they cannot be the results of parallel invention. I hope eventually to bring some order into this topic.

A third area of study has also emerged in relation to my earlier work. The late tenth and eleventh centuries were a time of vast change in Europe: The agricultural revolution was beginning to push population upward very rapidly; increased productivity per peasant was permitting a higher proportion of that population to go to the cities; the cities, bursting with energy, were starting to develop the power machines and labor-saving devices that shortly initiated a style of industrial production unprecedented elsewhere, even in China. Whether technology was the "cause" of all this or simply a manifestation of deeper energies, we cannot yet say. But the new form of Europe in the eleventh century was intimately related to technological advances; of this there is no doubt.

Unfortunately, Hell also broke loose in the eleventh century. Its representations grew more cruel, the tortures more explicit. To calm the fears of the faithful, the Latin Church developed the expedient of granting indulgences—a practice quite unknown in the Greek Church, where it would have been unnecessary. Apocalyptic and messianic movements began to spread the violence of the next world to this. Jews had not been loved in the Latin West, but save for a period in Visigothic Spain which seems to have involved more confiscation and exile than slaughter, they were not physically assaulted until the proto-pogroms of 1010 in Rouen, Limoges, and Mainz. Thereafter, they were never safe. For six centuries, in the West heretics were excommunicated but not executed. Then, in 1022 at Orléans, the habitual burning of them began. When in the late thirteenth century, thanks to the newly established Inquisition, the supply of incinerable heretics ran low, the burning of witches began. There is no record in the West of the trial and execution of a witch between 584 at Paris and 1275 at Toulouse. Such fluctuations of aggression demand explanation.

In the summer of 1954, I had a three-hour conversation with a Navaho boy in the northern part of the Navaho reservation. It was mostly about witches. At that time there was a fearful resurgence both of witchcraft and of witch hunting among the mesa people; there were some ghastly executions about which the Indian Service could do nothing. Clyde Kluckhohn's pioneering *Navaho Witchcraft* [18] had studied an earlier plague of witches and witch persecutors following the conquest of the tribe by the American military. Now, in the 1950s, the many Navahos who during World War II had served in the armed forces or in factories and who had then returned to the very different context of the reservation were in profound psychic distress. Some clutched at supernatural power to solve their problems and became witches (incidentally they were nearly all male among the Navahos, as they were female in the European tradition); others needed to hunt witches on whom their anxieties could be blamed. It would seem that the level of violence in a society depends on its level of anxiety, and that the level of anxiety is related to the pressures for change.

I expect to dig deeper into such matters. No hypothesis, including the one suggested above, "saves" all the present evidence. For example, quite suddenly about the middle of the seventeenth century it was no longer necessary, except in peripheral areas like Poland and Massachusetts, to torture and slay identifiable deviant groups such as heretics, Jews, and witches. Certainly at that time the velocity of change, technological or other, did not decline in Western culture. Perhaps a new attitude toward change developed, and anxiety in the face of change was lessened. We do not know, but we may be able to solve the problem if many of us work hard at it.

NOTES

1. Alfred L. Kroeber, *Anthropology* (New York, 1923).
2. R. Lefebvre des Noëttes, *L'attellage, le cheval de selle à travers les âges,* 2 vols. (Paris, 1931).
3. H. Delbrück, *Geschichte der Kriegskunst* (Berlin, 1900), vol. I, p. 141.
4. H. Brunner, "Der Reiterdienst und die anfänge des Lehnwesens," *Zeitschrift der Savigny-Stiftung für Rechtsgeschichte, Germanistische Abteilung* (1887), vol. 8, pp. 1–38.
5. M. Bloch, *Les caractères originaux de l'histoire rurale française* (Oslo, 1931).
6. H. Pirenne, *Mahomet et Charlemagne* (Paris, 1937).
7. M. Bloch, "Avènement et conquêtes du moulin à eau," *Annales d'histoire économique et sociale,* vol. 7 (1935), 538–63.
8. H. T. Horwitz, "Die Drehbewegung in ihrer Bedeutung für die Entwicklung der materialen Kultur," *Anthropos,* vol. 28 (1933), 721–57; vol. 29 (1934), pp. 99–125.
9. E. DeWald, ed., *The Utrecht Psalter* (Princeton, 1932).
10. Lynn White, Jr., *Latin Monasticism in Norman Sicily* (Cambridge, Mass., 1938).
11. *Speculum,* vol. 15 (1940), 141–59. Today, to my delight, this is almost obsolete: the study of the subject has advanced notably.
12. Lynn White, Jr., *Medieval Technology and Social Change* (Oxford, 1962).
13. Lynn White, Jr., "The Life of the Silent Majority," in R. S. Hoyt, ed., *Life and Thought in the Early Middle Ages* (Minneapolis, 1967), p. 96.
14. Published in A. C. Crombie, ed., *Scientific Change* (New York, 1963), pp.

272-91. A German translation appeared in *Technikgeschichte*, vol. 32 (1965), 201-20.

15. T. K. Rabb and J. E. Seigel, eds., *Action and Conviction in Early Modern Europe: Essays in Memory of E. Harris Harbison* (Princeton, 1969).

16. J. Needham, *Science and Civilization in China*, to date 4 volumes in 5 parts (Cambridge, England, 1954-65).

17. *American Historical Review*, 65, 3 (April 1960), 515-26.

18. Clyde Kluckhohn, *Navaho Witchcraft* (Cambridge, Mass., 1944).

Fortuna Plus Homini Quam Consilium Valet

CARLO M. CIPOLLA

CARLO M. CIPOLLA was born on August 15, 1922, in Pavia, Italy. He took his *laurea cum laude* in political science at the University of Pavia in 1944, and after studying in Paris and London, he joined the faculty of economics at the University of Catania, where he taught from 1949 to 1953. Cipolla has also been a member of the faculty of the Universities of Venice (1953-1961), Turin (1961-1964), and Pavia (since 1964). Since 1959, he has also been Professor of Economic History at the University of California at Berkeley, where he teaches European economic history.

Cipolla is a corresponding member of the Academy of Sciences of Turin, as well as a review correspondent for *The Economic History Review*. He spent 1953-1954 in America as a Fulbright Fellow, and he has been invited to deliver lectures at many universities in both Europe and America.

Among his numerous books are *Money, Prices and Civilization in the Mediterranean World* (Princeton, 1956), *The Economic History of World Population* (Harmondsworth, England, 1962), *Guns and Sails in the Early Phase of European Expansion* (London, 1965), *Clocks and Culture, 1300-1700* (London, 1967), and *Literacy and Development* (Harmondsworth, England, 1969). He has also written many articles on European economic history for such journals as *Bollettino Storico Pavese, Annales, Giornale degli Economisti, Rivista Storica Italiana, Economic History Review,* and *Economia Internazionale.*

Cipolla is currently working on two books: a history of education and a history of medicine in relation to social and economic conditions.

I n the prefaces of my books and the footnotes of my articles I almost
always acknowledge my debts to those who in one way or another
contributed something to my work. But I must admit that I have
always failed to acknowledge my immense and incalculable debts to
the mysterious personage whom, for want of better knowledge and
more precise terminology, we call Fortuna or Chance. Now Chance,
disguised as my colleague and friend, Perry Curtis, has given me the
opportunity to pay my long-standing debt. And I am perfectly willing
to oblige: first, as a matter of good manners; second, because in a
highly probabilistic world, the last thing I would want to do is antago-
nize Chance.

From the very moment of our conception, our life is virtually
determined by Chance. But I do not intend to discuss here what led to
the chance of my being born in Pavia, or why I have blue eyes, a fragile
constitution, and so forth. These things are of interest only to me and
to the loving members of my family circle. Here I want instead to pay
tribute to the powerful influence of Chance on my academic and
scholarly activity over the years.

The first thing I owe to Chance is my being an economic historian.
When I left my lyceum, I had not the faintest idea of what economic
history was all about. As a matter of fact, I did not even know that
such a subject existed. Nevertheless, before I knew what was happening, I was being trained in economic history by an excellent teacher. It
all occurred in a rather curious way. At the age of seventeen my
greatest ambition was to become a teacher of history and philosophy
in the lyceum. The most reasonable thing for me to do, therefore, was
to enroll in the department of humanities in the local university. But in
those days departments of humanities in Italy accepted only those
students who came from the classical lyceum, and I had attended the
scientific lyceum. However, the University of Pavia had a department
of political science, and students graduating from such a department
were allowed to apply for the position of professor of history and
philosophy in the lyceum. The curriculum of political science did not
offer one course in philosophy, and the history courses were limited to
the modern and contemporary period. But the mysteries of Italian
academic bureaucracy need not detain us here.

Faut de mieux, I enrolled in the department of political science.
The year was 1940; Italy had entered World War II, and on the
wrong side. The professor who taught modern history in the department was a good one, but he lived in Naples. Normally the journey
from Naples to Pavia took fifteen hours or more by train. With the
war, the journey grew disproportionately long and tedious, either
because of air raids or because trains were busy moving troops and
war material. Over a two-year period, I saw the professor at no more

than a dozen lectures. There was, however, another historian closer to home. Although a professor at the University of Genoa, he actually lived in Pavia. All this should not surprise the innocent reader: French and Italian professors rarely live where they teach. When later in my life I became a professor at the University of Venice, I had a charming colleague who was born in Venice and had lived all his life there. The day he got his chair at Venice he moved to Rome. Of course, professors read avidly while on trains. At any rate, Professor Borlandi was professor of economic history at the University of Genoa and lived in Pavia. In order to supplement his income, he petitioned to give a special course at the University of Pavia. Alas, the university had no department of economics, and economic history was taught in no other department. Italians are skilled in the art of setting up complicated regulations, but they are also adroit at getting around those regulations. The faculty of the department of political science at Pavia, where Professor Borlandi had good friends, could not appoint him to teach a course in economic history, so they requested instead that he teach a course on colonial history and policy. Needless to say, such a course offered by such a department in Fascist Italy was compulsory. I had to take it; so it was in this way that I first met Professor Borlandi. Neither he nor I could have cared less about Italian colonial history and policy. He was an economic historian with a strong interest in medieval matters; I wanted to become a teacher of history and philosophy in the lyceum. But there we were, thrown together by Chance, one allegedly teaching and the other allegedly learning Italian colonial history and policy.

There were few students in the class: sometimes only two or three showed up. Those were terrible days; most young Italian males were in the army, and many of them were being killed in the field. I stayed at home because of my fragile constitution and my stubborn determination to avoid military service at all costs. So the professor and the faithful student who attended his lectures regularly became good friends. That bright, sunny day when Professor Borlandi asked me if I wanted to do research under his supervision is one of the most vivid and pleasant memories of my life. He was then and still is a marvelous teacher. He wrote very little, and most of the things he published scarcely give a fair idea of his qualities. There are scholars who are better in print than in person. And there are scholars who are better in person than in print. Borlandi belongs most emphatically to the second group. He had what I believe was an excellent method for introducing a young man into the field. He did not intimidate me with long lists of books and articles, and he did not force down my throat a dry, forbidding bibliography whose meaning in those days I could hardly grasp. Instead he suggested that I embark on a specific project which required original research in the local archives. *Faber fit in fabricando*. The topic was the history of the population of the town of Pavia. In this way he introduced me to the archives and to the pleasure of hunting for unpublished documents. My excitement at doing research gradually and unobtrusively aroused in me a curiosity about the related bibliography. The topic was nicely limited and circumscribed.[1] How many capable young men I saw later in my life getting a bad start because their imprudent teachers handed them big topics to deal with or topics that did not require the painful, detailed search for documents in local archives. One does not learn to be a historian by chewing the cud that has already been ruminated by other scholars. Nor does one learn how to think and write historically by wrestling with overwhelmingly big problems that can easily lead a young, uncritical mind to indulge in superficial generalizations. I remember with a warm sense of pleasure and gratitude those lovely afternoons spent at the home of my teacher, along the banks of the Ticino River, when all excited about what seemed to me important discoveries, I showed Professor Borlandi the new material I had found in the archives. With great patience he would discuss it with me, never forcing his ideas, but always helping me to find a viable interpretation. Professor Borlandi taught me to be thorough in research, to be critical with the evidence, and to be honest in the exposition of my findings. He devoted countless days over a number of years to these tutorials. And he never asked me to do any research for him; nor did he ever take advantage of my material for any of his own works. Although my earliest articles were totally rewritten by him, he did not want to be mentioned in a footnote. He taught me economic history, but more important, he gave me an unforgettable lesson in the ethics of teaching and scholarship.

Eventually, I graduated with a thesis on the history of agriculture in the "Bassa Lombarda," which I then revised in a painstaking way in order to make a book. Without fully realizing it, however, I was in the doldrums. A decent study on the history of agriculture in the "Bassa Lombarda" could hardly be contained in less than five hundred pages, and I knew I was constitutionally incapable of writing such a lengthy work. It is hard enough for me to write one hundred pages. When I start writing, I am devoured by a diabolic fire that compels me to say quickly and succinctly what I want to say. Besides, I like to play with one idea and put it forward forcefully; each one of my books is essentially centered around one, and only one, basic thesis. The kind of work that entails exhaustive description and the coverage of a number of related topics is not at all my cup of tea. Had I persevered in that endeavor, I would have come out with a boring, undistinguished book.

But Chance was vigilant. One day while I was working in the city archive at Pavia, I came across a sixteenth-century document filled with figures. This document contained the series of the average rates of exchange between the gold ducat and the Lombard pound, year by year, from the end of the fourteenth to the beginning of the sixteenth century. This long and unusual list of figures intrigued me. I went home full of excitement and plotted the data on a chart. The result was an interesting curve with a peculiar succession of alternating periods of rapidly increasing rates (corresponding to devaluation of the local currency) and relative or even absolute stability. This was more than enough to excite a neophyte. Only later did I learn that the document had already been published, although never properly studied. But at that moment I did not know it, and that was my good fortune, because the delusion of having discovered an unpublished document of obvious importance added fuel to my enthusiasm. Before long, the agrarian history of the "Bassa" was forgotten, and I was completely immersed in the study of medieval currency. This new research was infinitely better suited to my logical mind, and my reputation among economic historians was in fact to be established by my works on medieval monetary history. When I recall those events, I can never stop thinking that if at that moment I had been endowed by some foundation with money for my studies, I would probably have had a research assistant look at the peripheral material relating to my work, and a research assistant obviously would not have picked up that fateful document because it had nothing to do with the agrarian history I was studying. More often than not it pays to be "poor" and to have to do the "dirty work" oneself. Even the most routine calculation and analysis of the primary raw materials can suggest new ideas and often open up new avenues of thought and research.

At the end of the sixteenth century, the much traveled and urbane Fynes Moryson wrote:

> One thinge I cannot commend in the Germans, that for desyre of vayneglory, being yet without beardes and of smale knowledge, they make themselves knowne more than praysed, by untimely printing of bookes and very toyes, published in theire names. Young students who have scarce layd theire lipps to taste the sweete fountaynes of the sciences, if they can wrest an elegy out of theire empty brayne, it must presently be printed, yea if they can but make a wrangling disputation in the University, the questions they dispute upon, with the disputers names, must also be printed. Yea very grave men and docters of the liberall professions are so forward to rush into these Olimpick games, for gayning the prise of others, as they seeme rather to affect the writing of many and great than iudicious and succinct bookes, so as theire riper yeares and secound counsells (allwayes best) hardly suffice to correct the errours thereof, and change (as the Proverb is) quadrangles to round formes.

These wise words taken from Moryson's *Itinerary* do not apply only to sixteenth-century German scholars. They certainly applied to me in my green years—and not only then. A few months after having found the document in the Pavian archive, I hastily wrote an article on the devaluation of Lombard currency in the later Middle Ages which was accepted for publication by the *Giornale degli Economisti*—a journal with a glorious tradition, associated with names such as Pareto and Pantaleoni, although scarcely distinguished in our own days.

My interest in monetary matters had been awakened, and I began to look eagerly around for more material. I soon discovered that the document found in the Pavian archive was not an exceptional or isolated instance. Similar documents were available for a number of other areas, and where they were not available, it was comparatively easy to compile series of rates of exchanges, because such data were recorded both officially and privately during the later Middle Ages as well as in the early modern period. By plotting on charts the abundant material available, I soon discovered that there was a remarkable synchronism among the monetary movements in the different principalities of northern and central Italy. I realized, too, that there was a rough correlation between high levels of economic activity and devaluation of the currency both in the long as well as short run. These new discoveries convinced me that I had been most unwise to send the article on the Lombard currency to press: The curve of the devaluation of the currency was all right, but my interpretation explained everything in terms of local events, while it was now obvious to me that the monetary movements were of a general and not local nature. Thus, I wrote at once to the editorial board of the journal asking them not to publish my article. No answer to my letter came, but this is not unusual in Italy, so I put my mind at ease.

The next few months were spent in France on a scholarship from the French government, but my sojourn there was neither very profitable nor pleasant. Life was hard in Paris in the years immediately after the war. I soon fell ill, and illness turned to despair when I discovered that it was impossible to obtain even a cup of milk or tea, not to mention lemons, at the hospital of the Cité Universitaire. I returned to Italy in fairly bad shape, but I gradually recovered and resumed my study of monetary movements in the later Middle Ages. It was then that I discovered, to my astonishment, that the article on the Lombard currency had been published.[2] This was only the first of a series of surprises. When I went to the editorial office of the journal in Milan to ask for some explanation, I was told that my letter had never been received. The people in the office, moreover, insisted that I had not only corrected the proofs of the article, but that I had requested a large number of offprints. All this sounded very mysterious to me, but it did not take long to uncover the mystery. Somewhere in the southern part of the peninsula there lived an elderly gentleman whose name was also Carlo Cipolla. He had written two or three book reviews for the journal in the past, and the journal had a card in its files with his name and address. When the proofs of my article were ready, they were erroneously sent to him for correction. This other Cipolla had not returned the parcel and pointed out the editor's mistake. Instead, he had carefully corrected the proofs and sent them back with a request for numerous offprints. Of course, I could have taken legal measures against him. But I am too lazy in such matters. And my annoyance melted away when I thought of the pleasure he must have derived from handing out all those offprints among his friends at the coffeehouse in the piazza of his little village. What a *bella figura* he must have made by pretending that he had written about the monetary history of the great metropolis in the north. Why spoil such pleasure?

The coronation of my efforts came in 1948 when my first book on the monetary history of late medieval Italy was published.[3] The book secured me the appointment of professor of economic history at the University of Catania in Sicily. Here I must add that it was published only because my dear father generously paid for two-thirds of the cost of printing.

A few years later I published, in France, another essay on the history of coinage in the state of Milano under Spanish domination.[4] In 1953 the good offices of Professors R. S. Lopez of Yale, the late R. Reynolds of Madison, Wisconsin, and C. Krueger of Cincinnati helped me to obtain a Fulbright fellowship, and I sailed to the United States in the summer of that year. That was my first visit to America. I spent a few months in Madison, Wisconsin, one month in Baltimore at Johns Hopkins University, and one month in Cincinnati. Through Professor Krueger's recommendation I was invited to deliver the annual Taft Lectures at the University of Cincinnati. This was quite an honor because the Taft Lectures are a civic event, although they are not quite as mundane as the Taft Concerts. For the first time in my life I was interviewed by the press, and for the first and only time in my life I was paid a princely fee for the five lectures I delivered. Since the subject was left to me, I chose, of course, monetary history. Basically I knew only Italian monetary history, but I was wise enough to try to include some French and Spanish material as well. The lectures were subsequently published as a small book which was nicely received in the scholarly world.[5]

What impresses me now, as I look back on those events, is how little I was influenced in my interests and studies by my first visit to the United States. I had left Italy almost exclusively interested in the medieval monetary history of Italy. While in the States I spent most of my time preparing the Taft Lectures on the same subject. When I returned to Italy in January, 1954, and moved to the University of Venice, I was still firmly rooted in my own limited field. As a matter of fact, after two years or so, I published another book on monetary matters: an outline of the purchasing power of the lira from the age of Charlemagne to the present.[8] A good book, I think, but the trouble was that I had become one-track-minded. When a publisher asked me to edit a collection of essays by various authors on Italian economic history, the first plan I drew (which was fortunately discarded) included numerous articles on money and prices. I often think with horror at the kind of "specialist" I might have become had not Chance come once more to my rescue. This time Chance took the form of an American major.

God only knows how much I dislike military people. The mere sight of a general is enough to spoil my day. What on earth Major T. was doing in Italy I will never know. Officially he was the head of an agency that was supposed to help the Italians improve their economic productivity. However, the major's office was in a building guarded by a Marine, and in order to be admitted to the place one had to be cleared by various officials. Besides, why should a major be interested in economic productivity? At any rate, despite my instinctive revulsion against military uniforms and their content, I came to like Major T. First of all, I never saw him in uniform. Second, when I met him, he was in a state of utter confusion. He was trying to put together an Italian mission that would visit the departments of business administration in a number of American universities and would then advise the Italian government about establishing similar departments in Italian universities. The major was in his forties, frank and open as a good Yankee should be, and direct in the best military manner. In the rarefied world of the Italian universities of fifteen years ago—a world of relatively aged people, a world of ceremonious smiles and pompous formality—the poor major was totally lost. The sight of a young professor who knew English, who had been in America, and who did not look forbidding was obviously a great relief to him. He managed to invite me to Rome, where the Italian Ministry of Education promptly appointed me head of the mission that was to visit the United States. The other two members of the mission were a professor at the University of Naples and a chief inspector from the Ministry. It could not exactly be called the best of all possible missions. For myself, I had never had the slightest interest in business administration, and the inspector from the Ministry was even less interested than I, if that was possible. The only one really concerned about the success of our mission was the professor from Naples, who unfortunately suffered from some debilitating disease and was on the verge of retirement.

Our mission arrived in New York in May, 1956, and for a whole month we were rushed from one airport to another, from one university to another, and from one school of business administration to another—through all kinds of adventures which included my falling in love with an airline hostess, the inspector becoming sick, the professor from Naples almost being arrested, and the three of us getting drunk on the "Champagne Flight" from Los Angeles to San Francisco. Back in Washington we were given an award commemorating our "great accomplishment," and at the same time we were compelled to attend a session in which an expert in public-relations psychology indoctrinated us as well as members of other missions (mostly from underdeveloped countries) on how to go about selling our American experiences to our countrymen without offending them. The level of the talk was just what one expects to find in books called "How to Succeed with Women Without Really Trying." On one of the walls of the room there hung a huge board with the motto, "How to be sympaticho" (*sic*), with a small footnote explaining the meaning of the word "sympaticho." The results of our mission were obviously nil, but the fault did not lie entirely with us. For all our limitations, shortcomings, and lack of real interest, we actually did some work, but there was no follow up to the report on our mission, which the bureaucracy simply filed away and forgot.

Although totally useless in regard to the teaching of business administration in Italy, the mission did prove highly profitable to me. Wherever I went during that hectic month in the States, I tried as a matter of course to meet the resident economic historians. At the University of California, Berkeley, I met Dr. Riemersma, who was teaching European economic history in the department of economics. Over a cup of tea, Dr. Riemersma told me casually that he was returning to his native Holland and that the department was desperately looking for an economic historian: Would I be willing to take the position? That conversation did have a follow up. In 1957 I returned to Berkeley for one year as a visiting professor, and that was the beginning of a more permanent and long-standing affiliation with the University of California.

This appointment marked a turning point in my studies. Up to that time my outlook and interests had been essentially parochial not only in the sense that they were limited to one specific aspect of history, but also in the sense that they were confined geographically, because my intellectual concerns scarcely went beyond the borders of Italy and France. I was not entirely to blame for this condition. In general, a European historian tends to be more parochial than his American counterpart. His library facilities are very limited. The environment in which he teaches is not exactly conducive to a broader outlook. There are few if any other historians in his department with whom he can discuss his work. At Berkeley, on the other hand, I was confronted with students who cared little about Italy as such but cared a great deal about Europe as a whole. In addition, I could work in a magnificent library containing books and journals from and about all parts of the world. In most American universities one may enjoy stimulating daily contacts with colleagues, some of whom may be foreign-born or American citizens whose parents were immigrants, and this fact is still visible in their cultural interests and activities. Last but not least, there was the influence of San Francisco itself, a marvelous harbor city overlooking the Pacific and possessing a large Chinese community. For the first time in my life, I "felt" the reality of Asia.

All these environmental riches were enhanced by the personalities of such colleagues as Gregory Grossman, Harvey Leibenstein, and Woodrow Borah, who together deeply affected my scholarly activity. The net effect was a great cultural shock to my mind and in blew a fresh, westerly wind. New horizons loomed in the distance, beckoning me to embark on new journeys. The first product of my new activity was a little book on a big subject, *The Economic History of World Population*.[7] As the title no doubt suggests, I started it almost as a joke. But then the subject took hold of me, and the more I wrote, the more I liked it. This book enjoyed some success. It was followed by *Guns and Sails in the Early Phase of European Expansion*[8]—a work inspired by a conversation I had with Professor Woodrow Borah of the department of history over the famous book by K. M. Panikkar, *Asia and Western Dominance* (London, 1961). Next came *Clocks and Culture, 1300–1700*,[9] which was a complementary by-product of *Guns and Sails*. My latest book, *Literacy and Development*,[10] is in some respects a testimonial to my growing dissatisfaction with economic history as it is narrowly conceived and practiced these days, and it reflects my progressive drifting toward a broader kind of social history.

I often wonder why my second visit to the United States, rather than my first, gave me such a cultural shock. I think that the explanation lies in the kind of arrangement and the different responsibilities imposed on me. When I came to the States with a Fulbright fellowship in 1953, I was given a pleasant study where I could work. I was invited to parties in the houses of colleagues where we talked politely about politics and the weather. And my visit to Cincinnati culminated in the preparation and delivery of five lectures on the subject most familiar to me. When I came to California in 1957, on the other hand, I was asked to teach full courses to audiences that were expecting to hear from me not only what I knew but much more. Since I was no longer a mere "visiting professor," I found myself actively involved and increasingly interested in the doings of the academic community. It was a totally different challenge. And it inspired a different response.

Now I think it is time for Chance to help me out again. Will she?

NOTES

1. This study was published in 1943 while I was still a student at the University of Pavia.
2. Carlo M. Cipolla, "La svalutazione monetaria nel Ducato di Milano alla fine del medioevo," *Giornale degli Economisti e Annali di Economia,* N.S. Anno VI, 9–10 (September–October 1947), 540–45.
3. Carlo M. Cipolla, *Studi di storia della moneta* (Pavia, 1948).
4. Carlo M. Cipolla, *Mouvements monétaires dans l'Etat de Milan, 1580–1700* (Paris, 1952).
5. Carlo M. Cipolla, *Money, Prices and Civilization in the Mediterranean World* (Princeton, 1956).
6. Carlo M. Cipolla, *Le avventure della lira* (Milano, 1958).
7. Carlo M. Cipolla, *The Economic History of World Population* (Harmondsworth, England, 1962).
8. Carlo M. Cipolla, *Guns and Sails in the Early Phase of European Expansion* (London, 1965). The American edition of this work is entitled *Guns, Sails and Empires: Technological Innovation and the Early Phases of European Expansion, 1400–1700* (New York, 1965).
9. Carlo M. Cipolla, *Clocks and Culture, 1300–1700* (London, 1967).
10. Carlo M. Cipolla, *Literacy and Development* (Harmondsworth, England, 1969).

The Real Magnitude
of a
Small Historical Problem

RAYMOND K. KENT

RAYMOND K. KENT was born on June 14, 1929, in Belgrade, Yugoslavia. He completed his primary and secondary schooling in Trieste, Italy, Belgrade, and Beirut, Lebanon. After three years of service in both the Royal Air Force and the United States Army, he enrolled at Columbia University where he earned a B.S. degree in 1958 and the M.A. in 1960. He received his Ph.D. degree from the University of Wisconsin in 1967, having worked under Jan Vansina. In the summer of 1966 he joined the Department of History at the University of California at Berkeley, where he is now an Associate Professor, teaching courses in early and modern African and Brazilian history.

Fellow of the African Studies Association and corresponding member of the Académie Malgache, he has won the Tiro-a-Segno prize in Italian Literature and Language (Columbia University, 1957) and has received research grants from the Ford Foundation (1962–1963 and 1963–1964) as well as from the Foreign Area Fellowship Program in conjunction with the Social Science Research Council and the American Council of Learned Societies (1964–1966). He has also been awarded a Guggenheim Fellowship for 1969–1970.

Kent is the author of numerous works about the Island of Madagascar, including *From Madagascar to the Malagasy Republic* (New York, 1962), *Early Kingdoms in Madagascar, 1500–1700* (San Francisco, 1970), and such articles as "How France Acquired Madagascar, 1642–1896," *Tarikh*, II, 4 (April, 1969); three successive articles in the *Journal of African History* under the general heading of "Madagascar and Africa," subtitled "The Bara Problem" (IX, 3, 1968), "The Sakalava, Maroserana, Dady and Tromba Before 1700" (IX, 4, 1968), and "The Anteimoro, a Theocracy in Southeastern Madagascar" (X, 1, 1969). He has also published in local journals in Madagascar.

At present, Kent is preparing *A History of the Sakalava of Western Madagascar, 1650–1896.*

E arly in 1965, a French *bananier* disgorged me at the eastern Malagasy port of Tamatave, along with my wife, a taperecorder, two suitcases, and a pronounced sense of excitement. At last, after having had the audacity of inexperience to write a short general book and some articles about Madagascar,[1] my feet were on the soil of the Great Island.

As the small, narrow-gauge railroad took us in a long ascent from the coast up into the high plateau, we saw no habitations and no people. The landscape was one of lush vegetation with rows of trees standing far away at attention, like an army of perennially green men. At times, stretches of meandering river broke into our field of vision, the cascading dirty-gray water deflected by rocks varying infinitely in size and form. This still life gave us the instinctive feeling of entry into a land where the present and deep antiquity had somehow managed to interlock into a single point in time. Then, almost imperceptibly, we began to descend. The sight below was in sharp and unexpected contrast. Hundreds of neatly partitioned and almost equal plots, all under irrigation, reflected the setting sun like beautifully polished mirrors. Although no movement could be discerned from such a distance, we no longer felt the eerie, encapsulating presence of arrested time. The order in the valley was imposed by man, not by nature. As if by conditioned reflex, the purpose which brought us to Madagascar returned to my mind.

I was to prepare a dissertation in history devoted to one Malagasy society, the west-coast Sakalava. Historical concern for a little-known group of some 200,000 living in a distant island off the coast of south-east Africa did not seem even unusual by the mid-sixties. Two decades earlier, at a Yugoslav lycée in Belgrade, my birthplace, I had already concluded that the *study* of any given past was absolutely equal to that of any other. Logical in itself, this premise was both sired and sustained long afterward by passion—a sense of indignation against the continuous stress on *Western* Europe and the arrogant misconceptions about my own native land. Indeed, the "primitive" Balkans, eternal "powder keg" since the overblown incident of 1914, were invariably peopled by wolf-men, vampires, followers of Satan, dark-eyed anarchists, white slavers, political assassins, and other assorted characters of Amblerian fiction, none of whom could control the baser urges and sheer lust for power and profit. It has certainly not been difficult to perceive why a good deal of historical effort by foreign scholars has shown a nostalgia for the old Austro-Hungarian overrule.

In the mid-fifties, as an undergraduate at Columbia University, my thoughts turned toward Africa, hardly a surprising development. A few years later, it even became possible to advance some parallels in an article entitled "Africa and the Yugoslavs."[2] Involvement with Africa was becoming, however, progressively less individualistic. Rapidly, fields other than anthropology turned toward the huge continent; within the confines of a few American universities, historians began to study the past of Africa, putting into practice the universalism of their discipline. The large foundations, moreover, offered financial support, and in so doing adopted and implemented the basic idea of anthropology; namely, that field work *in* Africa was essential to any scholarly endeavor.

My choice of the Sakalava was not a random one. What makes them unique among the Malagasy is the fact that the Sakalava were builders of the first local empire, around the turn of the eighteenth century. It extended over most of the western littoral, from Tuléar in the south to Analalava in the north, reaching unevenly inland anywhere from 50 to 250 miles. It was controlled by rulers of the same dynasty; shared a particular religion; held a monopoly over trade in slaves, cattle, and firearms; incorporated different ethnicities into its political structure; and collected annual tribute from vassals deep in the interior of Madagascar. The task I had set for myself consisted of a number of clear steps: to find the essential antecedents of this major innovation, determine how it came into being, and then trace its growth, apex, decline, and, ultimately, loss of sovereignty.

In a purely emotional, intellectual, and opportunistic sense, it is relatively easy to decide to reconstruct the past of a preliterate society. But sooner or later, a historian's commitment to this decision will undergo the first basic test, one of source materials. When missionaries, explorers, and the early colonial administrators began to write about Madagascar, the Sakalava were no longer a political success story. A single work came close to my concerns, especially for the period around 1770–1840.[3] Two or three students of Madagascar had discussed the Sakalava in book chapters and individual monographs.[4] There were also some two dozen very uneven articles about the Sakalava scattered in as many unrelated periodicals. Beyond the printed word, I knew of a fair amount of unpublished materials composed on the whole during the last seven or eight decades. Many of these, however, were either in private hands (known and unknown) or else failed to show up in the repositories that were supposed to house them. In short, the patrimony of written sources for the Sakalava appeared far from promising. If only for a brief moment, I began to doubt the wisdom of dealing with three centuries of a past for which there was little documentary evidence.

One way out would have been to follow the lead of many other students writing about the past of Africa and to have restricted the time period to the "recent" past and stressed the impact of Europe on the island, for which an ampler documentation was and is available.

This approach would differ from the old "imperial history" mainly by minimizing the belief that Europe was the sole catalyst of local change. It was also possible to abandon the Sakalava and work instead on the more recent Merina Empire, which spanned the nineteenth century and was the focal point of Anglo-French political, commercial, and religious rivalry. Without question, the Merina are the most studied and best researched of all the Malagasy, while their precolonial archives *alone* constitute a rare source gift to the historian. Thus, a Sakalava history from 1860 to 1960 would demonstrate the presence of "scholarly apparatus," since many letters and memoranda would be cited in the footnotes. A Merina history from 1800 to 1900, on the other hand, seemed even safer, since English-speaking readers, including students of the African mainland, could hardly be aware of the extent to which my "own" ideas and data were in reality borrowed from a vast and often obscure literature, much of which was in French and Malagasy. While considering these options, moreover, I had to bear in mind that my grant would run out in a year and that I could not afford the luxury of uninterrupted devotion to art for the sake of art without some concern for the mundane problems of life.

Nonetheless, there was an intuitive refusal to be deflected from pursuing what I had set out to do. The mere opportunism of a predetermined "switch" would have taken away something decidedly precious and undefined—perhaps a piece of my "soul," for lack of a more precise term. Equally, I had no intention of becoming an archivist whose writing is informed strictly by the available unpublished sources, or yet of doing over what was already accomplished in another language. I could not simply by-pass most of the Sakalava precolonial history, nor was it possible to avoid trying to answer the most significant question of when, how, and why a group of Malagasy created an entity for which there was no discernible precedent in the island. The problem itself was seminal enough to warrant further effort; only another historical problem, of greater magnitude, could ever have forced me to modify it. Such a problem was nowhere in sight at the time.

Thus, a process of self-doubt led to an even firmer commitment. The relative paucity of written materials did not foster a second wave of "panic." After all, Madagascar is an island on the route to the Indies and was visited by Portuguese, Dutch, English, and French vessels. A host of primary accounts concerning Madagascar in general prior to 1800 could be found in a single nine-volume collection.[5] Many of the accounts were bound to contain data about the western section of Madagascar. Because of both an attempted settlement at Fort-Dauphin (1643–1674) and later, the continuous involvement of French Mascarenes with the Great Island, France had come to regard it as her overseas "possession" (at least since 1665).[6] Hence, archives in Paris also contained sources about the island, and the same could be said for the archives at Reunion and Mauritius. Although it was my misfortune to visit Reunion precisely when the local archives were closed for a long holiday, many copies and reproductions of documents were available in Tananarive. The Documentary and Archival Service of the Malagasy Republic owned as well microfilms of many Mauritius materials, secured through the British Museum. After 1960, its *Bulletin de Madagascar* began to publish them at the rate of one or two every month. The Académie Malgache, founded in 1902, the Bibliothèque Grandidier at the Scientific Research Institute of Madagascar (IRSM), and the University of Madagascar were also there to be tapped. Last but not least, a number of French and Malagasy families owned private collections well worth looking into if permission could be obtained. The *rat de bibliothèque* asserted itself as I tracked down hundreds of promising titles, storing them away like a true miser. Soon there were over six hundred references to the western coast of Madagascar alone. In short, I read everything and anything within reach.

It was, of course, too soon to tell if the sum total of what might eventually be culled from every scrap of paper would amount to much in the way of concrete evidence. I had, however, already learned not to regard the written source either as being mainly of chronological value or as the only "document" of use to historians. This attitude had begun to form in Yugoslavia and had come to fruition many years later at the feet of a most gifted and unusual historian. From Belgrade, I took with me a sentimental attachment to oral tradition and a high degree of respect for "folk" history based on it. A good deal of the Serbian past had filtered into print from traditions preserved orally by the once ubiquitous *guslari*.[7] One of them, the blind Filip Višnjić, became a personal hero for a period until displaced by Vuk Stefanović Karadžić (1787-1864), who had done much to codify the Serbian vernacular and reconstruct the Serbian past by questioning hundreds of informants. Indeed, the father of modern historiography, Leopold Von Ranke, wrote his *History of the Revolutions in Serbia* on the strength of oral accounts collected and set down on paper by Vuk (a fact acknowledged in the third edition of 1879). If any lesson emerged from these early encounters, it was that oral sources increase in value with greater detail, more onomastics, and toponymy. At the same time, I had no idea of the limitations to be set on the historical value of oral traditions, the importance of context, and the disparate nature of those elements that can be lumped under the general heading of "oral tradition."

In 1962, I began to study African history with Jan M. Vansina at the University of Wisconsin. His book, *De La Tradition Orale: Essai De*

Méthode Historique (1961), went beyond anything I had known or thought about, although it did not contain a single word about Serbia or any mention of Vuk and others whose work in Serbian oral litera-ture was a gold mine in its own right. Yet this omission detracted nothing from his study of the nature of oral tradition, the formulation of method, and the textual criticism needed to transform it into valid historical document. In his lectures and seminar, I was finally exposed to the uses of ethnographic data and linguistics in historical recon-struction. Above all, his humanism, insatiable curiosity, and determina-tion to go on exploring the little-known or unknown aspects of the African past made up those subtle yet powerful influences that come from inspiring teachers.

Thus, I had come to Madagascar armed with more than an ortho-doxy of unreconstructed narratives, skeletal footnotes, and written documents. Soon the taperecorder was whirling away in the Sakalava land as my wife and I collected directly from the "bush" both Sakalava art objects and notes about environment and custom. Malagasy was the eighth language I endeavored to learn, but my progress was mainly ideographical. With a dictionary, I could decode many a passage, even if numerous word formations eluded me. Interpreters, transcribers, rough translations of oral texts continued to be necessary. By the end of 1965, I was more or less ready to begin the written part of my work.

The first pages were supposed to state and define the historical problem to be resolved and outline whatever my predecessors had discovered about the early Sakalava past. Other materials were then to be added to confirm or revise their own conclusions in a substantial opening chapter more inclusive and richer in detail than anything done previously. No source I knew, written or oral, disputed that the found-ing of an initial Sakalava state—the kingdom of Menabé—coincided with the advent of the Maroserana dynasty which would produce all subsequent rulers, expand northward to build the second Sakalava kingdom of Boina, and remain in power well into the nineteenth century. The date of about 1650, given by Guillain for the founding of Menabé, did not seem unreasonable.[8]

Where did the Maroserana come from? The Sakalava texts were far from silent on this question, allowing for numerous versions, which can safely be reduced to two basic traditions. The prevalent one was that the Maroserana ancestors came from outside the island, landing among the Mahafaly who lived just to the south of Menabé. The other view, encountered less frequently, held that they arrived among the Mahafaly from the interior of Madagascar. It was, obviously, a matter of considerable importance to determine whether the Maroserana were from another part of the world or else local Malagasy migrating from one area of the island to another. If their origin was non-Malagasy, the Sakalava expansion and empire-building could then be explained by foreign innovators familiar with different political ideas and structures. Later, an ethnographic study of the ruling family could reveal connections with some overseas society and point to a possible Maroserana home.

It took little time to find out that the prevalent Sakalava tradition had been rejected as unsound by Alfred Grandidier, unquestionably the most important and intensive student of the Malagasy. From firsthand observation in the 1860s, when local institutions were still functioning, as well as from numerous oral traditions collected, Grandidier was able to establish that two other groups besides the Sakalava and Mahafaly had been ruled by the Maroserana kings. One, known as the Bara, occupied the vast southern interior with borders extending from the Sakalava in the west to the Mahafaly in the southwest and the Anteisaka in the east. Because the Anteisaka people of the southeastern littoral also had Maroserana rulers, it was clear to Grandidier that this dynastic family had created at least four kingdoms while crossing Madagascar in one steady migration from the southeastern to the southwestern coast. Grandidier was equally certain that the Anteisaka were the real ancestors of the Sakalava. Their name *Ante-I-Saka* * contained the root *Saka*, eventually adopted in compound form (*Sakalava*) on the western littoral.

Since the early European accounts failed to note a single powerful, large, or clearly defined Malagasy kingdom until *after* the 1650s, I was suddenly searching far beyond the immediate antecedents of the first Malagasy empire for the birth and spread of early kingdoms in Madagascar as a whole! The Maroserana could not now be discussed in an exclusively Sakalava setting, and it became essential to learn at once if they were the sole king-makers in the island or if other king-making families, contemporary or anterior, independent or related, might have been around. By process of gradual elimination, there remained only two other early dynastic families in Madagascar—the Andriana of Merina in the central highlands and the Anteony of the Anteimoro (northern neighbors of the Anteisaka), also on the eastern littoral. Mainly from internal traditions and king lists, it also emerged that all three of the families had started to form in three geographically unrelated sections of Madagascar roughly at the same time, ca. 1550. I now had to conceive an altogether new work, provisionally entitled *Early Kingdoms in Madagascar and the Birth of the Sakalava Empire.* Instead of considering only the Sakalava from about 1600 to

---

* *Ant/ante* is "people" in Malagasy. Given the infix *I* used for persons or places, *Anteisaka* could be translated either as the "people of *Saka*" or "people of *Isaka.*"

1896, when France annexed Madagascar, I had on hand a much broader subject with a narrower time span (from 1500 to 1700). To the Sakalava, I would add the Merina, Anteimoro, and also the Bara. Their extremely strategic position between the Sakalava and Anteisaka promised to hold a key to the early Maroserana formation. The Bara past, moreover, was one of the most obscure in Madagascar.

All this was surprising enough, but what really took me aback was the discovery that the Malgachisants considered the Maroserana Indians to be from the Indian subcontinent. This was not easy to digest, since neither Sakalava political and religious institutions nor their vocabulary contained a trace of anything "Indian." In a short article prepared at the end of 1965, I expressed for the first time a few doubts about the previous scholarship.[9] But, if that "problem of greater magnitude" did, after all, manage to surface and force me to modify the original project, the really monumental nature of what I had stumbled upon was yet to manifest itself. For a while, however, I nearly succumbed to a form of historical determinism in order to explain why the dynastic impulse began to radiate in separate parts of the island toward ca. 1550. The sixteenth century, it is worth noting, *was* a harbinger of new developments within Madagascar. Its coastal populations came into contact with Europe, represented mainly by the Portuguese. Certain domesticated plants were introduced, while the use of iron underwent both expansion and refinement. Some firearms passed into Malagasy hands, and the slave trade began to increase considerably. New food plants and the resultant "population pressure," iron weapons and firearms, slave trade and the related need for organization: did not all of these provide a natural stimulus for king-makers and kingdoms? Indeed, several historians working on the mainland of Africa were explaining the local state-building precisely in these terms. Why should Madagascar be any different? Although certainly "neat," this scheme of things seemed increasingly unworkable the closer I got to the sources for local history.

Since a "causation" theory could not be imposed on the many disparate and incongruous elements, I needed to determine next whether the Andriana and Anteony were non-Malagasy in origin, whether they were related to each other or to the Maroserana themselves. Was there a common ancestor for all three? Why not attribute all of the early kingdoms to the branches of a single king-making family? It was an attractive solution to both timing and innovation. Once more, I turned to the existing literature, especially statements in recent works of history. The answer was that the three families were not related. The Andriana had come from Indonesia, landed on the east coast of Madagascar, migrated into the central highlands among the indigenous Vazimba, and created the first local monarchy. The Anteony, on the other hand, were Arabs from the Arabian peninsula. The Anteimoro, who were ruled by the Anteony monarchs, represented a mixture of migrants from Arabia and the indigenous populations of the southeastern littoral.

The origin assigned to the Maroserana had already alerted me to the very distinct possibility of myth-making, and as my own innocence was coming to an end, I began to demand something more than dogmatic assertions. Working back from the more recent to older sources, I realized that all roads returned to Alfred Grandidier. Virtually the entire past of Madagascar rested on the shoulders of a single scholar, and if the subsequent researchers and students did in effect add greater detail to certain aspects of Malagasy history, the basic outlines, ideas, and interpretations retained his indelible stamp. It was a burden, I mused, no one should bear too long even under the most ideal historiographical conditions—a kind of Clio's garden dense with written documents, giving a daily account of the last two thousand years, together with dates and hours of the day. Lamentably, such conditions were not present in old Madagascar. Here was a huge island, third largest in the world if uninhabited Greenland is excluded, separated from Africa by some 300 miles of the Indian Ocean. Yet, despite a strong Negroid element, the Malagasy are generally considered to be Mongoloid. Their language does not derive from Africa, as one would expect from the factor of sheer proximity; it belongs instead to the Indonesian linguistic family spoken thousands of miles away.[10] The two "races" are now hopelessly intermixed, and although divergences of dialect do exist and can be considerable, all of some 6 million Malagasy speak basically the same language (syntax, grammar, morphology, phonetics).

Until Grandidier came along, very little work had been done to explain the unity of language in the face of somatic differences among the Malagasy—differences which suggested more than one origin. The answer given by him was a relatively simple one. The proto-Malagasy, represented by the now-extinct Vazimba of the central highlands, came from the general direction of Indonesia and were themselves Negroid and Indonesian-speaking. Later, other groups of non-Negroid settlers arrived. They, too, were from Indonesia and came in several migrations, which ended with the Malay-speaking Javanese, who became the Andriana. Thus, there could be nothing peculiar either about the biracial nature of the Malagasy or the fact that their language and culture were cast in an Indonesian mold. To be sure, there were also some Negroid Malagasy whose ancestors came from the African mainland. All of them, however, were brought to the island as slaves, and as such contributed little or nothing to Malagasy language and culture. This did not quite obtain for the Andriana, who lost the Malay idiom but nonetheless imposed many features of their superior culture on the Vazimba. The essential formation of the Malagasy as a people concluded with the coming of Indians and Arabs who, like the Andriana, assumed the role of political and cultural elites in Madagascar.

After going over the evidence in support of the Andriana, Maroserana, and Anteony origins, I wrote a rough draft called "Alfred Grandidier and the Myth of Asian State-Builders in Old Madagascar." [11] I argued there that if the grand scholar and his devoted son Guillaume had amassed a body of documents far in excess of those usually available for preliterate societies,[12] this did not imply that Alfred's elaborate fantasies need be accepted out of awe and respect. No trained historian could tolerate either the way in which he *used* the early European sources or the juxtaposition of ethnographic and other materials taken out of contexts which would have given them completely different meanings.

Examples of the Grandidier technique are both abundant and telling. A Portuguese vessel, passing by eastern Madagascar in 1559, obtained some fresh fruit from a few Malagasy who came in outrigger canoes to trade. Writing decades later, a Portuguese chronicler added that his compatriots found these traders to be both Javanese-looking and Javanese-speaking. They concluded that the whole island must have been conquered by the Javanese. The chronicler himself, knowing that the Malagasy and Javanese languages were not identical, expressed his firm belief that the Portuguese sailors therefore could only have been in contact with some recently shipwrecked Javanese yet to be absorbed into the Malagasy. From this admixture of an unreproduced primary source and much secondary speculation, Grandidier constructed a theory. A group of Javanese shipwrecks, finding themselves in eastern Madagascar before the mid-sixteenth century, produced the Malay Andriana among the Vazimba following a migration from the coast. Later in his text, Grandidier added more incredible details, such as the exact area in which the Andriana had landed and the fact that lack of immunity from malaria was the cause that impelled them to go into the highlands where the vector—in the nineteenth century—was less deadly. It need only be pointed out that many eastern Malagasy look "Javanese" to this day, and that it would be foolhardy to expect some sixteenth-century Portuguese sailors to have known both the languages of Java and dialects of eastern Madagascar without ever having touched its *terra firma!* Yet, such was Grandidier's key document for the Andriana.

Again, from a Portuguese chronicler Grandidier extracted a reference to an Indian fleet ostensibly lost in Malagasy waters either in 1300 or 1325. The shipwrecked Indian sailors, whom he alone placed in southeastern Madagascar, became the Maroserana. As this dynastic family needed at least two centuries to manifest itself, one is hard put to understand the Indian connection, even if the original would-be event stood on grounds much stronger than two pure conjectures. Likewise, in the realm of ethnography many unfortunate *non sequiturs* could be noticed. For example, a French cattle trader from Fort-Dauphin visited the Sakalava in 1671. He was astounded to find that the wild boar roamed around, unmolested by humans. The reason for his astonishment was his familiarity with the Fort-Dauphin Malagasy, who exterminated the wild boar without eating the meat. Behind the contrasting attitudes was an eminently practical problem. The Sakalava were pastoralists, while the other Malagasy, living hundreds of miles away, were planters. Hence, one society killed the wild boar to protect its crops while the other had no similar need. In addition, the ruling aristocracy among the Fort-Dauphin Malagasy was partly Islamized and considered boar meat to be impure. Because a contemporary suggested that the Maroserana might have been "Arabs" rather than "Indians," Grandidier found his way into another secondary source to show that this could not have been the case since the Sakalava-Maroserana monarch "consumed pork," a fact never reported by the cattle trader himself.

The presumed Arab origin of the Anteimoro had at least one argument in its favor. Alone among the Malagasy, the Anteimoro had a developed scribal tradition, and although the language of their manuscripts was Malagasy, the script itself was Arabic. But, despite a number of more or less tortured contentions of Grandidier, there was no *other evidence* that either the Anteony or related aristocratic and sacerdotal clans of the Anteimoro came to Madagascar from the Arabian peninsula. Even the many Arabic loan words found by another researcher in the religious vocabulary of the Anteimoro priests attested to nothing more than the truism that Arabic is the language of the Koran capable of surviving as such in Bosnia or Java or Madagascar. Its use in religious ceremonies or in script cannot automatically transform the Bosnian, Javanese, and Anteimoro Muslims into Arabs from Arabia. Eventually, it was possible to establish that several generations had elapsed between the time when the original Anteimoro "great ancestor" left Arabia and the final arrival of his tenth descendant in Madagascar. One curious aspect may be noted in passing concerning the sanctity of written sources. In many instances of Anteimoro history, their living oral traditions proved to be actually more reliable than their manuscripts. Surprising as this may appear, the explanation is that collective memory itself cannot be changed with a stroke of the pen, but the Anteimoro manuscripts, known as the

Sora-bé, were doctored a number of times in order to conform to the "official" court versions.

The end result of many months of intensive work struck me as being still mainly negative. I had succeeded in proving that the alleged "origins" of the Andriana and Maroserana were unfounded in terms of historical evidence. Although there was no proof that the ancestral Anteimoro were in any sense—cultural or physical—"Arabs from Arabia" upon reaching Madagascar, I had little or nothing to show that they were *not* beyond mere doubt, itself engendered mainly by the gap of generations. The sum of my experiences so far had confirmed that it was infinitely easier to demolish than to build and replace. As a former student of Asian civilizations and an Indianist *manqué*,[13] Grandidier was convinced that all advances in seventeenth-century Madagascar must be attributed *only* to intruders from Asia. This gave him a coherent overview, but forced him at the same time into a strictly inductive enterprise. His massive quarto volumes, replete with thousands of footnotes to the footnotes, represented a monument to the primacy of Asia in Madagascar. For the most part, scholars who followed him into the study of the Malagasy past neither developed nor felt a need for any other overview. The Merina, who are the most Asian-looking of the Malagasy, having attained a degree of economic, technological, and political success that clearly distinguished them from other inhabitants of the island, were by then a living counterpart of Alfred Grandidier's printed edifice.

At this point, I took a course directly opposite to the one adopted by Grandidier. Instead of starting with the problem of origins, I sought to determine *how* the Merina, Sakalava, Bara, and Anteimoro kingdoms came into being according to their own internal sources or traditions with the aid of ethnographic data. This "folk" history would then be tested against whatever I could find of relevance in the earlier European accounts. With this much accomplished in four chapters, I could then proceed to discuss the question of origins and relationships, if any, involving the Andriana, Maroserana, and Anteony.

The ethnographic descriptions began to point to some curious cultural features from the outset. Alone in Madagascar, the Anteimoro had structured their society around age groups, each one defined by the number of years and set of economic and social functions. The ancestral cult is widespread in the island, but the Sakalava variant contained two unique aspects. They paid religious tribute to the defunct Maroserana rulers who were represented by royal relics encased in boxes containing bits of occiput bone and right patellae, teeth, nails, and hair of the departed monarchs. Moreover, through special mediums, an ancient Maroserana could "express his will" to the Sakalava in a public ceremony. The Bara, on the other hand, had a very special form of interregnum between a deceased king and his successor. These four features appeared curious because they were neither Malagasy nor Indonesian nor yet Arab, but distinctly African, as could be readily ascertained from African sources. None of the four could be dismissed as unimportant, and thus I had to ask whether and how such influences could have come from a continent that hardly figured in the past of Madagascar.

Having no immediate answer at hand, I assumed that the question must remain suspended in midair, as it were, until I could determine just how far these influences went. Because a comparative approach to the study of cultural features in two or more preliterate societies involves a considerable chance of error, I also looked for linguistic confirmation. For example, the Sakalava ceremony with mediums is called *tromba*. The written form, however, does not exactly reflect the way in which the term is pronounced, namely *toomb'* with barely audible *r* and terminal *a* silenced because it stresses the *b* ahead of it. A Sakalava possessed by the *tromba/toomb'* is said to be "like dead" or a "living corpse," an accurate impression of pitch-phase in the trance and statement of the meaning that the medium represents the dead by assuming his personality and voice. An identical meaning applies to *m-Tumba/ki-Tumba* in the ki-Ngwana dialect of Swahili, a major Bantu language spoken in eastern, southeastern, and central Africa. In this case, linguistic evidence reinforces the ethnographic comparison to show that one is confronted with a clear-cut instance of an African "borrowing" in Madagascar.

While examining several dictionaries and vocabularies, I noticed that the Malagasy terms for "cattle," "sheep," "dog," "spear," "bowl," "jar," "gourd," "pot," and wild animals like "bush fowl," "crocodile," and "snake" were all Bantu loans surviving either in pure or somewhat modified written and/or phonetic form to accord with Malagasy speech patterns. The same applied to two of the three most important food staples in Madagascar, namely, millet and manioc. Half of the Malagasy musical instruments not only repeated the original Bantu names in Malagasy, but were already traced to African prototypes through a detailed study by an ethnomusicologist.[14] Social institutions like the "joking relationship" (a form of insult allowed by convention to reduce built-up hostilities between individuals and groups) and tattooing (either decorative or as mark of group identification), whether by paint overlays or by piercing of the skin, bore unmodified Bantu names. Certain synonyms for "priest" and "doctor," and the most prevalent Malagasy terms for "clan, family" and "ruler, chief" were also derived from Bantu. No less significant, two of the Malagasy prefixes, I- and KI-, belonged to the Bantu linguistic family. KI, in particular, was often followed by Bantu roots in Malagasy. Of course, it was impossible to confirm *always* an African borrowing in Malagasy through linguistic comparison. For example, the Sakalava and Bara hair styles—very distinct in their tuft and braid formations achieved with the aid of lard and ochre—were not described by words of African provenance. Yet, the only real parallels for these styles are in Africa. Likewise, the practice of divination in Madagascar bears an Arabic loan word, but the pattern of divination is African, not Arabian.

All of this by no means exhausts the list of more or less distinct Africanisms in the island. But, even with a slight exercise of imagination, one would be forced to conclude—as I did—that the role of Africa in old Madagascar *must* have been far greater than anyone had hitherto suspected. There have been one or two very interesting "oddball" Europeans who perceived Africanisms in Madagascar and also conceived an Indonesian passage along the east African coast before Madagascar was reached. An African population substratum had thus somehow formed in the island before the Indonesian settlers arrived. Such hypotheses would, however, affect mainly the first millennium of our era, and I already knew them to be inadequate. My first hint came from manioc. This plant could not have been introduced into Madagascar until the Portuguese extracted it from the Tupi of Brazil and brought it to the Old World sometime in the first half of the sixteenth century. As I was able to report later,[15] manioc did not reach Madagascar directly through the Portuguese but rather through African intermediaries, since the manioc-associated terminology in Malagasy is Bantu. This suggested to me at once that the early diffusion of manioc in the island was the work of Africans. Indeed, a great deal of ethnographic and linguistic material in Madagascar pointed to a more complex hypothesis than those mentioned earlier. If one could postulate a settling "sequence" of pure Indonesian-speaking migrants, partly Africanized but still Indonesian-speaking, who brought along the Bantu loans for millet, domesticated animals, and a number of artifacts, there would still have to be another migration of pure Africans who continued to come into Madagascar at least until the end of the 1500s.

According to Grandidier and others, however, such pure Africans —whatever the period of arrival in Madagascar—were brought piecemeal by Arab traders as slaves. Thus, they could not exist in independent colonies or contribute much to the "master culture." Because of a previous study of Brazilian history, I could not accept the notion that slaves do not affect masters or that slaves cannot escape into the backlands and create their own societies. As a matter of fact, both the language and culture of the Portuguese masters in Brazil were heavily influenced by slaves from Africa.[16] Moreover, there was a very real African state in seventeenth-century Brazil which lasted nearly a hundred years and withstood many Portuguese and Dutch attempts to destroy it.[17] But I did not even need analogies with Brazil to be almost sure that an independent African colony did exist in Madagascar after 1500 and that this colony should have inhabited the western littoral. My major clue here was the linguistic monograph by Father Emil Birkeli dealing with the surviving pockets of the Vazimba in western Madagascar. In it Birkeli established the presence of a Bantu linguistic substratum in the Vazimba idiom. The oral traditions I collected in Sakalavaland told me that the *real* Sakalava no longer existed, though their name had become that of the inhabitants of the west coast. All I had to do now was find some old European account for this coastal section of the island and hope that it would provide some concrete documentary evidence.

A series of letters composed between 1614 and 1619 gave me more than I had bargained for. Two Jesuit fathers, having spent a year in western Madagascar and several in Mozambique and thus being familiar with both sides of the Mozambique Channel, sent extensive accounts of Menabé to their superior at Goa. They wrote that some 300 miles of the western littoral named *Bambala* (a Bantu name) were inhabited by an *African-speaking* population of agriculturalists who planted both millet and manioc. They described the cult of relics and the *tromba*, pointing out, however, that no paramount kings existed at the time and that the two institutions applied to chiefs, nobility, and elders. They reported two Bantu terms for local priests and also mentioned the Sakalava for the first time in print, describing them as the greatest of contemporary warriors, widely feared and in the process of expansion by 1620. My own excitement can be appreciated. There was now a truly significant intersection of ethnography, linguistics, and written documents of high quality showing that the "method" did work and that each type of source amplified others. Beyond this, I had discovered the Sakalava on the very eve of contact with the Maroserana, and I had discovered that they came from substantial and autonomous colonies of Africans in western Madagascar, being thus Africans themselves. Fifty years later, in 1671, an eyewitness would observe a military formation of some 10,000 Sakalava warriors, then under a Maroserana leader. It was during this interval that the founding of Menabé took place, and it was possible to reconstruct from oral tradition how the Sakalava handed this kingdom to the Maroserana and how, in turn, the new kings adopted the cult of relics and the *tromba* from the Sakalava.

Some nagging questions in respect to this early history, however, still remained to be dealt with. Did the Sakalava descend from the east-coast Anteisaka as Grandidier claimed? What happened to the Bambala Africans, and who replaced them? In what area of Madagascar did the Maroserana family form, and if their origin was foreign, from what part of the world did the proto-Maroserana come into the island? The easiest question to answer was the one concerning the Anteisaka. Their own traditions *and* those of all the neighboring Malagasy were in unanimous agreement that the Anteisaka had been, in effect, a branch of the Sakalava migrating from west to east after a dynastic dispute. No Sakalava tradition, on the other hand, held that the line of descent was the other way around. The very name of the Anteisaka aristocracy turned out to be the Bantu equivalent of "people of the inner court," indicating their former position in Sakalavaland. The Anteisaka also recalled the Maroserana king who founded Menabé as being from the time of their migration eastward. And even the toponymic name *Isaka*, vital to Grandidier's linguistic argument, was duplicated not in Madagascar, but on the eastern littoral of Africa itself. Two of the three remaining questions were eventually answered through an analysis of an uncommon ethnographic document—local cattle-markings.

It was an old custom in western Madagascar to carve symbols of clan property on the ears of cattle. In spite of the fact that there were some sixty-five clans in Menabé and a much greater number of individual symbol variants, most of them were eventually collected over a period of fifteen years by Father Birkeli. He reduced all of these to four key patterns: angular, open triangle, closed triangle, and the square. Since most of the clans could also recall the migratory movements that had brought them into Menabé, one could obtain a fairly good idea of migrations by correlating the key patterns with collective clan memories. Of the total sixty-five, the largest number, or twenty-four, came to Menabé (and farther south into the valley of the Fiherenana River) from the north. Ten came from the opposite direction, going north from south, while ten more could recall no migrations, eight of them in Fiherenana alone. Twenty-one came from the interior of Madagascar to the western coast, but the Maroserana had *not* been among them. Their special cattle-marking, called *tsimirango*, diffused from the southwest or land of the Mahafaly. An early eighteenth-century European account connected the Maroserana with this marking by noting that the king of Menabé had his cattle "marked with a mark called *Chemerango*." [18]

Stated as an oversimplification of the intricate and historically far more important evidence that can be deduced from Birkeli's ethnostatistical findings, the collective verdict of cattle-markings and oral tradition was that the agricultural Bantu of Menabé were replaced by Malagasy-speaking pastoralists. Some of the pastoralists—most of them using the square—penetrated Menabé from the north before this kingdom formed. Many more, coming both from the interior and from the deep southwest, arrived either with the Maroserana or after Menabé was founded with the Sakalava warriors. The Maroserana cattle-marking belonged to the closed triangles or "spearheads" mark of the "conquerors." All the spearheads came with the Maroserana from the land of the Mahafaly in the southwest, where the *tsimirango* marking must have been conceived first, since no antecedent existed elsewhere. In effect, the prevalent Sakalava tradition that the Maroserana emerged as rulers in southwestern Madagascar was thus confirmed independently through cattle-markings.

Because eastern Madagascar faces Asia and western Madagascar faces Africa, it was obvious why the Maroserana had to be landed by Grandidier on the southeastern littoral. In the absence of any reasonable evidence, such "landings" were seen as an implicit indication of Asian origin. Although I suspected that the Maroserana might indeed be from Africa, it would be no improvement to postulate such an origin simply because everything pointed to their birth in southwestern Madagascar instead. While hunting around for something more concrete, I learned from the local traditions the clear truth that the Maroserana were a *Malagasy* family. That is to say, a foreign provenance applied only to the proto-Maroserana, male ancestors who became politically important after having intermarried with local women. Without this prior *kinship base* they had no success in the realm of political authority. Still, how could I show that my suspicions in respect to the proto-Maroserana were well founded?

The name Maroserana is a compound of *maro* or "many" and *serana*, variously translated as "traces" or "paths" or yet "ports." This did not appear to be of any help as a linguistic item. But the oral tradition recalled the "great ancestor" of all the Maroserana. His name was *Andriamandazoala* or the "Noble Crusher of Trees." This was clearly a title rather than a family name or an onomastic one. Also, a captain of a vessel that visited southwestern Madagascar in 1607 reported that its inland capital was named *Rota*. I thus had two linguistic items: a royal title and a term for "capital" in the very area where tradition and cattle-markings placed the advent of the Maroserana. After a long search through African materials, I came across a monograph dealing with the southeast African kingdom of Mwene Mutapa located in the southern Rhodesia of today. One of the Mwene Mutapa's royal titles in the Bantu idiom of the area was "Crusher of Trees," while his royal scepter, symbol of authority, was called *rota*. Since titles are extremely arbitrary, the Malagasy *mandazoala*, "Crusher of Trees," was a loan translation occurring together with *rota* both in southwestern Madagascar and in Mwene Mutapa. But the clincher was yet to come. In the course of time, the name of Maroserana fell into disuse in Madagascar and was replaced by another, *Volamena*, meaning "gold," to indicate (as tradition claimed) that the Maroserana came to Madagascar with a shipload of gold. This metal, as could be determined from many European accounts, was not mined at all in Madagascar, where only small deposits have been found. The term *vola-mena*, or "red silver," reveals that the Malagasy were unfamiliar with gold, having no word for it and being able to describe it only in terms of silver which is red. On the other hand, southern Rhodesia was once the most important source for gold controlled by the "gold-bearing empire" of Mwene Mutapa. And what was the term for gold in old Mwene Mutapa? It was *mari*. If in Madagascar a foreign term for an unknown metal, namely *mari*, is followed by the same construct, one gets *mariserana*, or the "traces of gold." As time passed by, the pull of Malagasy speech patterns substituted first the *o* for the terminal *i* in *mari*, thus changing the meaning of a *foreign* term, and later abandoned a compound that made no sense to local Malagasy—a fact well noted by Guillain [19]—and used *volamena* instead. To make the case even stronger, both the Portuguese and French sources written before 1660 have revealed subsequently that an entire group of rulers in the southern interior of Madagascar, roughly the Baraland of today, had formed political alliances by dividing the so-called *marofeh* or "great heritage," which consisted of a *vast amount of gold*, thus associating *maro* with this metal again.

What these data suggest is that a number of gold-bearing migrants had left Mwene Mutapa from some point on the Mozambique coast and that—whatever their destination might have been—they ended up somehow in southwestern Madagascar. It is well known from a number of works in Portuguese and other languages that serious political convulsions took place in old Mwene Mutapa following the arrival of the Portuguese in Mozambique, and that some of them led to the departure of many assimilated "Moors" who had engaged in gold trade for centuries. What the data cannot do, however, is to give us an exact ethnicity of the proto-Maroserana, which will probably never be determined.

As is well known in the island, the Anteimoro have been the foremost disseminators of divination in Madagascar. Proliferating in their own society far above the tolerable norm, the Anteimoro religious specialists migrated to other parts of Madagascar, usually to attach themselves to some ruler other than their Anteony king, as priests, advisers, and court officials. In 1630 a factor of the English East India Company visiting the area of St. Augustine Bay in southwestern Madagascar purchased an Anteimoro *Sora-bé* containing cabalistic and divination formulas. Equally, rulers of this same area often adopted the name-title of *misara*, which derives from Arabic *isara* or "divination" and shows an Anteimoro influence. An *Andriamisara* figures prominently in the Sakalava-Maroserana genealogies and traditions either as a member of the dynasty or as its high priest. Although the sources disagree about his position, all of them hold that Andriamisara was intimately associated with the founding of Menabé as a kingdom. He discovered a way for the Maroserana to adopt the Sakalava religious institutions, and thus gave them a secure base for political authority.

Similarly, oral traditions of the Merina,[20] which are both descriptive and detailed (at times with clinical detachment), recall the adoption of divination, calendar, circumcision, royal purification rites, and the institution of public assembly. All strongly suggest an Anteimoro influence. The calendar is Arabic, as is the term for public assembly. The ceremony of royal purification among the Merina is duplicated in the same context only among the Anteimoro, and both societies use the same word for it. Many passages acknowledge borrowings from the Anteimoro, borrowings that are not of recent date. Moreover, a detailed study of how the Merina kingdom was formed revealed that the Andriana took a long time to develop as a dynasty. Partly Islamized settlers had lived among the Vazimba for several generations and were respected as "elders." Much later, the Vazimba were invaded by the *Hova*, the most Asian of the Malagasy, moving gradually into the area from the plateau regions farther south. As mediators between the Vazimba and the Hova, these elders became in turn the Andriana, casting their lot eventually with the Hova.

Thus, in the course of the sixteenth and seventeenth centuries, which saw first the advent of new Malagasy dynastic families and later of kingdoms ruled by them, the Anteimoro came to exercise a considerable influence outside their own society. They provide a thread of political and religious stimulus in old Madagascar, the only one, indeed, possessing *some* uniformity. This stimulus was clearly present among the southwestern and central highlands Malagasy, and it affected the Maroserana as well as the Andriana. Although there are many unique aspects of how the two dynasties formed and created their kingdoms, attesting to independent evolution, the Anteimoro stimulus may well account for the date of ca. 1550, when the two families formed in widely separated areas of the island. The problem of Anteimoro origins thus assumes an even greater importance. If it can be shown that they, too, came from Africa, one obtains a complete reversal of the role hitherto assigned to Africa in respect to major politico-religious changes in the island.

If one does not understand "history" as an absolutely accurate reconstruction of something that happened in the past, but rather as an endeavor in search of a high degree of probability, then the African

origin of the Anteimoro can be substantiated. First, the gap of generations in Anteimoro genealogy requires a plausible explanation of where
their ancestors "paused" for as much as a hundred years after leaving
Arabia and before reaching Madagascar. In purely geographical terms,
nowhere better suggests itself than eastern Africa. In this connection,
there are Anteimoro traditions that relate the passage to Madagascar
and mention sites that could have existed nowhere else. Next, the
Anteimoro pillar tombs must be taken into account. There are pillar
tombs both in Indonesia and eastern Africa, but the Anteimoro ones
offer much closer analogies with the East African *menhirs*. The pattern
of divination in Madagascar is an African one, with seven out of sixteen
terms for the pattern itself having been traced back to Africa. Two
Anteimoro Muslim titles, unknown elsewhere in Madagascar, were
used in eastern Africa. All these increase the degree of probability
without making it high enough. I dismissed many older European
sources, which simply asserted that the Anteimoro were "Moors from
Africa." Their value was rather in helping to establish that the Anteimoro arrived in the area where their kingdom would form between
1508 and 1512. The ancestral Anteimoro came to this area in three
separate migrations. The earliest of these, just to the north of the
future state, took place around 1490, whereas the last one must have
been completed by about 1540. But at least three other items tip the
balance in favor of very high probability, and point to a specific area of
eastern Africa as the original home of the Anteimoro.

One is their age-group system, unique in Madagascar and nonexistent in Arabia. This institution could not have been invented in the
island, and it is analogous to the age-group system among the Konos
people of southeastern Ethiopia, whose own pillar tombs are very
similar to the Anteimoro *tsangambato* (commemorative stone pillars).
Long before the 1500s, eastern Ethiopia and western Somalia had been
a kind of *cul-de-sac* collecting an admixture of Africanized Muslims
who created untold numbers of small monarchies and sultanates.
Their political structures and systems bear some striking similarities
with what the Anteimoro developed in Madagascar. They came to the
island as a cohesive group, importing an alien state and preserving
most of its essential features. Since there are no traces among the
Anteimoro of the Swahili culture of the eastern African littoral, and
given that their age groups and pillar tombs now pointed to a specific
section of Africa, I reasoned that at least their "ethnic" name might be
remembered either by eastern Ethiopians or western Somali. Although
this name is written *Anteimoro*, it is pronounced *Temuru* locally to
give us an etymon. It took a while to find it as *Temur*, but eventually it
appeared—first in the epic song of the Ethiopian *negus* Yeshak
(1414–1429) and next in the relatively recent oral traditions of the

Harari, inhabitants of eastern Ethiopia who recalled the Temur as a "vanished people."

Four years ago I began with a relatively small historical problem, derived in part from reading Guillain, to account for the first Malagasy empire. The nature of *internal* sources forced me to modify it in favor of the broader problem involving dynastic families and early kingdoms. This produced an acute awareness that much of the Malagasy past before the nineteenth century rested on the shoulders of amateur historians and was dominated by the myth that all major innovations in old Madagascar must be attributed to intruders from Asia. By contrast, I found the Sakalava to have been once a part of a large colony of Africans inhabiting western Madagascar. Equally, the new ideas about government and society introduced into Madagascar by the proto-Maroserana and the Anteimoro reflected their African origins. Despite the disappearance of pure Africans by more recent times, African influences in Madagascar were once much greater than hitherto suspected. What this means is that the scope as well as magnitude of the original problem underwent a complete transformation. On the one hand, there is now a clear need to write a new precolonial history for each of the eighteen Malagasy societies. On the other, this cannot be done by excluding the role of Africa in Madagascar. A reverse relationship must also be considered, since data from Madagascar have a direct bearing on Indonesian influences in Africa. As another historian put it recently, the study of the Malagasy past is "of the greatest importance for the history of Africa as a whole." Thus, the results of my work so far have a value far beyond anything I anticipated four years ago.

The basic findings are now in print.[21] The *Early Kingdoms* is almost complete. No doubt some interpretations will have to be refined and certain aspects made more precise, but the response obtained even in the short span of a few months is encouraging. It is safe to predict that other historians and anthropologists will soon begin to contribute to the study of Afro-Malagasy connections. A Sakalava history to 1896 will come next as part of an effort to write anew about the precolonial past of all the Malagasy. The ultimate reward of historical study can be summed up in the old saying, *toute trouvaille procure une jouissance.* Yet, history does not become meaningful only when confined to the study of *Herrenvolk* or when the past is used to explain the present. Such precepts would have gotten me literally nowhere.

If the present—as an intellectual influence—cannot be avoided by the historian, then I must end on a note of tragedy. A form of neurosis is pervading the academic environment in this country. Americans of African ancestry are increasingly substituting pigment for culture, so that remote and disconnected antecedents become a direct and revealed "heritage" excluding the white scholar and "his standards" as "irrelevant to the Black Experience." At the same time, there is disenchantment with post-independent Africa leading to attacks on those few of us who work primarily with the past of traditional African societies.[22] Thus, pigmental exclusivism and pseudohistory are wedded in a world of fantasy, justified on psychological and therapeutic grounds, while arteries are hardening among historians who never could stomach the "new history" or accept gracefully the idea that the past eighty years of African past represent simply a stage of a much longer process. As of now, I am uncertain whether this increasingly anti-intellectual environment will in some way manage to warp me or else reinforce the kind of humanism I have sought to acquire throughout most of my adult life.

NOTES

1. *From Madagascar to the Malagasy Republic* (New York, 1962); "Madagascar Emerges from Isolation," *Africa Report*, VII, 8 (1962); "Madagascar," in R. Sloan and H. Kitchen, eds., *The Educated African* (New York, 1962); "Madagascar," in *Encyclopedia Americana*, vol. XIX.
2. "Afrika i Jugosloveni," *Voice of Canadian Serbs*, XXVI, 1541–1542 (1961).
3. Charles Guillain, *Documents sur l'histoire, la géographie et le commerce de la partie occidentale de Madagascar* (Paris, 1845).
4. G. H. Smith, *Among the Menabé* (London, 1896); A. Grandidier, *Ethnographie de Madagascar*, vol. IV, tome I (Paris, 1908), pp. 215–228 and passim; H. Rusillon, *Un Culte dynastique avec evocation des morts chez les Sakalaves de Madagascar, le "Tromba"* (Paris, 1912); E. Birkeli, *Marques de boeufs et traditions de race: Documents sur l'ethnographie de la côte occidentale de Madagascar* (Oslo Etnografiske Museum, *Bulletin*, no. 2, 1926); E. Birkeli, *Les Vazimba de la côte ouest de Madagascar* (Tananarive, Académie Malgache, *Mémoires*, fasc. XXII, 1936).
5. A. and G. Grandidier, eds., *Collection des ouvrages anciens concernant Madagascar*, vols. I–IX (Paris, 1903–1920).
6. See R. K. Kent, "How France Acquired Madagascar," *Tarikh*, II, 4 (1969).
7. See A. B. Lord, *The Singer of Tales* (Cambridge, Mass., 1960). The title is an idiomatic translation of the term *guslar* (pl. *guslari*).
8. *Documents* (1845), p. 8.
9. "Recherches sur les Sakalava," *Civilisations Malgaches*, Tananarive, Université de Madagascar, I, 2 (1968). The second issue of this new journal was printed about two years after the initial publication date.
10. See O. Chr. Dahl, *Malgache et Maanjan* (Oslo, 1951).
11. Now published in French, *Bulletin de Madagascar*, Tananarive, April 1969.
12. G. Grandidier, *Bibliographie de Madagascar*, vol. I, in two tomes (Paris, 1905–1906), vol. II (Paris, 1935), and vol. III (Tananarive, 1957).

13. See A. Grandidier, *Notice sur les travaux scientifiques* (Paris, 1884).
14. C. Sachs, *Les Instruments de musique de Madagascar* (Paris, Institut d'Ethnologie, Université de Paris, *Travaux et Mémoires*, tome XXVIII, 1938).
15. "Note sur l'introduction et la propagation du manioc à Madagascar," *Terre Malgache* (Tananarive, January 1969).
16. See J. H. Rodrigues, "The Influence of Africa on Brazil and of Brazil on Africa," *Journal of African History*, III, 1 (1962).
17. See R. K. Kent, "Palmares: An African State in Brazil," *Journal of African History*, VI, 2 (1965).
18. R. Drury, *Madagascar* . . . (London, edition of 1890), p. 271. The first edition was published in London in 1729.
19. *Documents* (1845), p. 11 and note 1.
20. F. Callet, *Tantaran'ny Adriana—Histoire des Rois*, vols. I–IV (Tananarive, 1953–1958), translated into French by G. S. Chapus and E. Ratsimba. These four volumes, in 1,734 pages, bring us only up to the year 1810. The *Tantara*, as they are popularly called, were collected by the Jesuit Father François Callet in the 1860s and constitute the greatest classic of the Malagasy language. A fifth volume in French translation will appear under the auspices of the Académie Malgache.
21. "Africa and Madagascar," *Journal of African History*, IX, 3 and 4 (1968), and X, 1 (1969). The three articles are subtitled: "The Bara Problem," "The Sakalava, Maroserana, Dady, and Tromba Before 1700," and "The Anteimoro: A Theocracy in Southeastern Madagascar." See also R. K. Kent, "The Sakalava: Origins of the First Malagasy Empire," *Revue Française d'Histoire d'Outre-Mer*, LV, 199 (1968).
22. See, for example, L. H. Gann and P. Duignan, *Burden of Empire* (New York, 1967), pp. iii–ix, 119–32.

Clio
in the
New World

DONALD ROBERTSON

DONALD ROBERTSON was born on May 12, 1919, in Elizabeth, New Jersey. He graduated in 1942 from the University of New Mexico and received both his M.A. (1944) and Ph.D. (1956) from Yale University. In 1945–1946 he studied at the Institute of Fine Arts, New York University. He has taught Art History at Queens College, New York, Pomona College, the Universities of Texas and Kansas, and, since 1957, at Tulane University, where he is now Professor of Art History at Newcomb College and Associate in Art History of Tulane's Middle American Research Institute.

Robertson is a member of the Sociedad Mexicana de Antropología, the Société des Americanistes de Paris, Phi Alpha Theta, the College Art Association of America, the Society of Architectural Historians, the Conference on Latin American History, the Renaissance Society of America, the Society for American Archaeology, the Society for Historical Archaeology, and the Latin American Studies Association. He is also a member of the Consulting Committee to the National Survey of Historic Sites and Buildings of the United States Department of the Interior and is a contributing editor for Spanish-American art for the *Handbook of Latin American Studies*. Among numerous research awards received over the years are summer grants from the American Council of Learned Societies (1960, 1961), a Fulbright-Hays grant for travel (1964–1965), a Social Science Research Council grant-in-aid (1964–1965), and a Guggenheim Fellowship (1964–1965).

Author of *Mexican Manuscript Painting of the Early Colonial Period: The Metropolitan Schools* (New Haven, 1959), and *Pre-Columbian Architecture* (New York, 1963), Robertson has written a number of articles on Mexican art history for both journals and edited works. Among the latter are "The Style of the Borgia Group of Mexican Pre-Conquest Manuscripts" in Millard Meiss *et al.*, eds., *Studies in Western Art; Acts of the Twentieth International Congress of the History of Art*, Vol. III (Princeton, 1963), "The Mixtec Religious Manuscripts," in John Paddock, ed., *Ancient Oaxaca—Discoveries in Mexican Archeology and History* (Stanford, 1966), and several articles for the ethnohistory volumes of Robert Wauchope, ed., *Handbook of Middle American Indians* (Austin, in press). Robertson is also editor of the *Bulletin of Historians of Latin American Art & Architecture,* which began publication in February 1967.

He is currently at work on studies of Mixtec art of the Post-Classic period and the Techialoyan Codices of Colonial Mexico.

T he Art Historian as a Creative Artist" was the subject of a talk I gave at the Orleans Gallery in the French Quarter of New Orleans in 1960. My words were aimed at an audience composed primarily of artists and collectors, members and friends of an artists' cooperative gallery which is now, as it was then, an important center in the cultural life of New Orleans. The group that evening was predisposed to consider the painter or the sculptor as the "creative artist" in our society; the suggestion that the historian of art was equally "creative" was new to them. The thoughts I expressed were an early attempt to organize and formulate my personal philosophy as an art historian. During the following decade, these ideas have evolved in somewhat more detail. Rather than changing, they were reinforced and crystallized—most recently when I was asked to contribute to this volume, this "new departure in historiography."

In the *Historian's Workshop* I feel somewhat of the *rara avis in terris*, since my chosen field is an independent and rather specialized subdivision of history, not one of its more orthodox branches. Within the history of art itself, I am also one of a small subgroup, for my area of specialization is the native and Indo-European art of Latin America, a new field of study for art history, often disdained by colleagues trained only in the more traditional history of European art. In my own research I find myself dealing with works of art and sources previously almost entirely in the domain of historians, archeologists, linguists, and ethnohistorians rather than historians of art. Not only is my field unorthodox as an area for art history, it is by its very nature interdisciplinary. Because of this, my publications have appeared in both the literature of art history and in that of these other disciplines as well.

Looking back, I realize that many factors contributed to my taking this path. From an early age I was fascinated by the architecture of both the eighteenth and nineteenth centuries in and around Elizabeth, New Jersey, where I was born. At one time I thought seriously of becoming an architect, but I know now this interest in architecture was more historical than anything else. Books I still have, which I bought when I was in high school, include Banister Fletcher's history of architecture and the prime pioneering study of the archeology of Peru by Squier.[1]

My first real contact with the art and architecture of the Latin New World came during my undergraduate years at the University of New Mexico. Here I experienced at first hand the pre-Columbian and Spanish colonial architecture of the American Southwest. Visits to the family of a college friend and roommate, Edward Dozier, who was living in the Indian pueblo of Santa Clara, showed me the Indian way of life still surviving with vitality, for Edward and his family spoke

Tehua, Spanish, and English. From Albuquerque I made my first trip to Old Mexico one Easter vacation and clambered over the vaults of my first Baroque cathedral at Chihuahua.

I have never studied the Spanish language formally, but in New Mexico I first began to pick up this most beautiful language, and a friend taught me to conjugate an odd assortment of unusual and unorthodox verbs not found in college grammars. In this Hispanicizing environment I studied Latin American history with Dorothy Woodward, an inspiring teacher. Nibs Hill and Florence Hawley introduced me to the delights of the archeology and ethnology of the Southwest. The living pueblos of the region and the ruins of the dead ones created in me a fascination with the indigenous cultures of the New World that remains with me still.

Three days after Pearl Harbor, I left the University of New Mexico to return to New Jersey to face a variety of experiences, including uninspiring and unrewarding work in wartime industries and being drafted into the army for a period of nine months and four days. The last months of my military career saw me learning Japanese (possibly because I had asked to study Russian) in the Army Specialists Training program at Yale University. From the army, I entered directly into the Department of the History of Art at Yale, receiving an M.A. degree in 1944.

I have always regretted that I was never able to study with Henri Focillon, the great French historian of art who died in 1943 before I became a student at Yale. Since I never met him, what I know about Focillon, his ideas, and his teaching came from his writings[2] and his former students, who were my teachers at Yale: the late Carroll L. V. Meeks, George Heard Hamilton, and later George A. Kubler. Focillon's interests were primarily in the formal qualities of works of art and his influence has been an important element in my own thinking and writing. Others with whom I studied at that time were Filmer S. C. Northrop, the philosopher who attempted to reconcile East and West; Harald Ingholt, who deciphered the Palmarene script; and Nicholas Toll, an inspiring Byzantine scholar.

In 1944 I determined to go to New York to study at the Institute of Fine Arts of New York University, where Walter Cook had gathered together an imposing faculty composed in large part of European refugee scholars. Here I consciously chose courses in order to study with almost all the members of the faculty. The training at the Institute, like earlier training at Yale, was in the traditionally established fields of the history of art. I attended courses in Roman, Medieval, Northern and Italian Renaissance, and Oriental art, conducted by Karl Lehmann, Richard Offner, Alfred Salmony, Richard Krautheimer, Martin Weinberger, Guido Schönberger, Walter Friedländer, and Erwin

Panofsky. This exposure to some of the greatest figures in the history of art has led me in later years to advise students to seek out professors as scholarly personalities as much as, if not more than, specialists in particular fields. Knowledge is always, at least potentially, available in books and illustrations; personal approaches, in more subtle ways, are available only in lectures, and better, in direct contact with teachers outside of classes.

A teaching position at the University of Texas sent me once again into the American Southwest in 1947 and gave me access to that university's excellent Latin American Library. While at Austin, the crucial decision on a dissertation topic at Yale had to be made. My first idea was to study the architectural history of Spanish colonial fortifications with Carroll Meeks directing the military aspects of the study and George Kubler supervising the more specifically Latin American aspects of the subject. Instead, I investigated Mexican colonial art and regularly spent my afternoons studying manuscript paintings in the Latin American Library, then as now in the conscientious care of Dr. Nettie Lee Benson.

I devoted my attention to a group of thirty-seven watercolor or gouache paintings and drawings of landscapes and city plans, some painted in a European style, some in a native style, the largest number in a mixed Indo-European style. These paintings, with few exceptions, had never been published, although others belonging to the group kept in Madrid and Seville had been published forty years earlier. The paintings (*pinturas*) were made to supplement written answers (*relaciones geográficas*) to a royal questionnaire of 1577 inquiring about the geography and other aspects of life in the colonies. As I took detailed notes on the manuscripts, I began to isolate those traits of style deriving from European art from those preserving native or pre-Columbian elements.

It is somewhat ironic, but I presume in the life of scholars not unusual, that the time spent working on this material resulted in only a few pages in the dissertation that was to be published as a book ten years later.[3] This studying and note-taking in Austin would also become the basis of a paper published in an international congress and an article with appended catalog of the whole group of *pinturas* for one of the ethnohistory volumes of the *Handbook of Middle American Indians*.[4] The lesson of this experience is that works of art studied, research undertaken, notes made, even if not immediately used to their fullest, become part of one's intellectual capital to be drawn upon in later years, perhaps with even more profit than if they had been used earlier.

The more immediate value of this concentrated and consistent investigation of the Texas manuscripts was that I learned from it some of the rudiments of sixteenth-century Mexican paleography and taught myself how to take the notes which would subsequently supplement photographs. As I look at these notes now, some twenty years later, I realize how valuable they still are. For each painting, I recorded such things as the colors and their tones, qualities of line, and overall compositional devices, with written comments on important aspects of the paintings—the composition, rendering of three-dimensional space, or the two-dimensionality of design.

My second stay in New Haven, beginning in the fall of 1949, was quite different from the first. I now arrived with a large and reassuring folder of notes. I had at least in general terms established in my mind an area of research—Mexican colonial painting of the late sixteenth century—and I thought I had the lion's share of all the data that would be necessary to write a dissertation on the *pinturas* of the *relaciones geográficas* in the Texas collection, a dissertation that would have satisfied most students, the art history faculty at Yale, and the Yale graduate school.

However, early in the course of study at New Haven, the excellent Yale Library, the personal library and notes of George Kubler, and his Mexican manuscript seminars combined to transform my thinking and broaden my approach to the materials. I began to sense that whatever their value as an important group of paintings having a wide geographic distribution and made during a limited period of time (1579–1585), the *pinturas* of the *relaciones geográficas* did not offer a sufficient intellectual challenge. Like many historians of art before me, and I am sure many who will follow me, I realized that the beginnings held more fascination than the ends.

With these thoughts in mind, I undertook to expand the scope of my study to define the characteristics of the early colonial styles of the central valley of Mexico and pushed the time span of my work back to the Spanish Conquest (1519–1521). This early colonial style of mixed, native, and European antecedents, I discovered, lasted eighty years, dying out to all intents and purposes in the year 1600. The paintings of the *relaciones geográficas* were thus near the end of the early colonial style, but the beginnings were more difficult to determine. To do so I had to define the late pre-Hispanic style of manuscript painting in order to show how it changed and became the early colonial style under the impact of imported European art.

There was an additional problem here too, for the major Aztec manuscripts of the early colonial period which I wished to discuss came from the central valley of Mexico in or about present-day Mexico City, while the only manuscripts I could accept as truly pre-Hispanic came from other more southern Indian groups, some speaking Mixtec, a language quite different from the Náhuatl of the central valley of Mexico. Thus one had to define the pre-Columbian manuscript style in somewhat general terms, using the few extant Mixtec manuscripts as evidence for assessing their pre-Hispanic characteristics. Then one had to apply these characteristics to the more numerous early colonial manuscripts of the central valley of Mexico to establish what the early colonial Indian painter had added to his past heritage from the European art introduced with the Conquest.

In the traditional historiography of European art, this process would have been phrased in terms of the influence one style had upon the other. In the discipline of anthropology, it would have been considered part of the dynamic process of acculturation. In either case, the early colonial manuscript style represents the result of the interaction of Spanish Renaissance art and the pre-Columbian art of the neolithic peoples of the New World, each possessing a highly sophisticated and assured art style.

During this study of the early colonial manuscripts, I was able to establish relationships among manuscripts, as well as among particular schools of painting, all within the central valley of Mexico. These interrelationships were determined in part through studies of texts giving place of origin and evidence of date in particular manuscripts. Through formal analyses and comparisons, certain manuscripts were associated, and others were separated, putting them into distinct groups. From these data I formulated early, middle, and late phases in the historical development of the School of Mexico-Tenochtitlán, the characteristics of the School of Texcoco, and postulated a school associated with the Indian College of the Holy Cross in Santiago Tlatelolco, now a part of Mexico City. I was able to suggest relatively constant rates of change and even to measure the native component of the *pinturas* of the *relaciones geográficas* of the late sixteenth century against these rates of change, so as to point out relatively advanced and relatively *retardataire* styles.

Problems of date were actually of less importance than problems of the interrelationships among manuscripts, since dates for most of the manuscripts were fairly well established. However, a few key problems of dating still remained. Again I attempted to solve these problems through a study of style. For instance, I became convinced that the earliest colonial painting from the area around Mexico City was the Codex Borbonicus, now in the Palais Bourbon in Paris. This manuscript is so early in its style that most historians considered it pre-Columbian; therefore, it could be judged as the last in a series of pre-Hispanic manuscript paintings. At the same time, certain European elements, such as the way the artist allowed in his design for the later addition of European written glosses, clearly documented the early influence of European art upon an otherwise apparently native pictorial style and thus the beginning of the early colonial sequence. This study demonstrated Henri Focillon's idea that each work of art is at the same time the beginning of one hypothetical series and the end of another. No analysis of the problem other than a formal or style analysis could have given this result. In arriving at this colonial date, however, I made difficulties for myself, since the Codex Borbonicus was the only central Mexican Aztec manuscript assumed to be pre-Hispanic.

Another key manuscript, the Plano en Papel de Maguey, had been traditionally dated 1557–1562 by its written glosses and later pictorial additions to the original painting. We can now either assume the Plano belongs with the Codex Borbonicus as one of the earliest manuscripts produced in the colonial period or even postulate that the major part of the manuscript may actually be pre-Hispanic.

Using the same method and approach substantiated by documentary sources, I was able to show that a group of manuscripts known as the Techialoyan Codices came from the late seventeenth or early eighteenth centuries rather than from the period of the 1520s to the 1540s formerly ascribed on the basis of dates in their written texts. The Techialoyan group of manuscripts, painted on native, not European paper, using a distinctive printed lowercase letter for the written text, has a large number of human, architectural, and geographic forms. The human figure in this group does not belong to the sixteenth century on the basis of proportions, poses, costume, use of light and shade, and size in relation to the page, and is equally clearly indicative of a later date. The reattribution on the basis of artistic style was supported by a later critical study of the textual content of the manuscripts. The texts are written in Náhuatl, the language of the Aztecs, not in Spanish, and a study of the contents revealed gross anachronisms. As a result of the redating of the Techialoyan group, they can now be seen as important late-seventeenth- or early-eighteenth-century sources for the study of colonial and pre-Conquest ethnohistory as well as late colonial written Náhuatl.

All these reattributions of date have been based upon a method worked out early in my work, and still of value for my current investigations. This method was to study how the forms in the manuscripts were painted and drawn, ignoring the whole area of content or iconography except when it was significant for the formal study.

The Codex Florentino, one of the major works studied in my dissertation and later in my book, presented other problems and other answers. This three-volume manuscript is now in the Laurentian Library in Florence. The presence of two thousand illustrations and the evidence of as many as half a dozen individual artists' hands is not an exaggerated estimate of the richness of the manuscript. The Florentine codex and earlier versions in Madrid indicate the pictorial component was mostly the work of natives—Indian scribes working in a variety of styles, some very close to the European Renaissance conventions of Spain at the time, others closer by far to native pre-Hispanic conventions.

Like all early colonial manuscript paintings, the paintings of the Codex Florentino exist in an ambience of anonymity. Few of the painters' names are known, and little or no biographical information has survived. The Spanish-born monk Fray Bernardino de Sahagún, whose name is associated with the Codex Florentino, was the author, editor, or compiler, but not the artist or painter. Even so, a vignette in the Codex Florentino showing remarkable similarities to an illustration from a sixteenth-century Toledo edition of the encyclopedia of Bartholomaeus Anglicus was the clue that led to a reevaluation of the Sahagún text and the discovery that he was in effect drawing up the last of the late medieval encyclopedias and compiling the first modern Renaissance one. This theme, dealing with the text rather than illustrations, was developed more independently in an article I wrote for the *Journal of World History*.[5]

To systematize studies of the artistic style, I drew up a schema or profile more carefully developed than the one I had used earlier in Texas so as to establish a certain uniformity in analyzing all the manuscripts. This schema allowed me to describe systematically the formal characteristics of the manuscripts. After reviewing the pertinent literature, I analyzed the style in terms of composition of the page, representation of space, differences in the quality of the draftsman's line, his handling of color and treatment of forms—human, architectural, and geographic. In the course of this work I developed a new critical vocabulary to deal with those characteristics not present in traditional European art.

This new approach to the manuscripts derived from the basic assumption of historians of art: that the facts and data are first and foremost the works of art—the paintings, sculptures, buildings—in short, the unique man-made objects. Each work of art for the art historian has potentially several characteristics worthy of study: its formal characteristics, its meaning, and its esthetic message. These three aspects exist in chronological sequence and thus must be studied in chronological terms from which quasi-evolutionary patterns are to be defined. We postulate a cause and effect relationship linking these aspects of earlier works of art with later ones.

The formal characteristics or style of the work of art are those we analyze in terms of basic shapes and patterns, colors, lines, textures, and the presence or absence of three-dimensional illusionistic space, among others. (A Virgin and Child painted by Giotto is distinct in formal terms from the same subject painted by Raphael or El Greco.) A convenient, condensed, and valuable synopsis of the problem of style in art appears in a key study by Meyer Schapiro.[6] The writings of Focillon and the Swiss scholars Morelli and Wölfflin, each in their own way give valuable insight into the study of style.[7]

Meanings associated with works of art also change in time. In some ages the burden of meaning borne by a painting or sculpture can upon analysis turn out to be almost overwhelming; in other more direct ages, the burden of meaning will be less diversified and thus perhaps more specific. Such study of meaning on different levels is called iconography and was brought to a high point in the writings of Erwin Panofsky, one of my teachers.[8]

A question not infrequently asked of me was, "How can a whole book be written on an important series of manuscripts without one's getting involved with problems of meaning and subject matter?" My answer was and is that in the case of the early colonial manuscripts, the iconographic analysis, including the meaning of "glyphs," was rather well under control. When I entered upon my studies, much data bearing on the interpretation of the meanings of figures had already been published, because for many years the iconography of these works of art had been in the efficient hands of historians, archeologists, and linguists, where I chose to continue to leave it. At the same time, problems of chronology in most instances had also been solved.

Studies of the formal qualities of the paintings, however, simply did not exist. What remained to be done, therefore, was to define the styles of the artists working in a series of schools of painting, a path I followed, because to me the major interest in the work of an artist is in what he created; what he is saying in nonartistic terms belongs to another area of investigation, often to the fields of literature or cultural history. In her study of Maya relief sculpture, Tatiana Proskouriakoff uses this same division into the iconographic component, which she ignores, and the formal component, to which she devotes her important study.[9] In her work, the study of form is pursued with rigor, and the evolution of style is tied to a chronological framework. This is a work I recommend all my students read, for they can learn much from her method, even if they are not interested in Maya stelae.

From the formal patterns of the work of art and the intellectual meaning adhering to it comes the beholder's esthetic reaction. When the historian of art works on this aspect of the work of art, he is playing the role of critic, a role bordering on the field of esthetics more commonly studied as a branch of philosophy. In his role as critic, the historian of art differs from most other historians. Since he deals with a series of unique objects of unequal esthetic value, he ranks them in terms of higher and lower degrees of artistic quality, and thus establishes their position in a hierarchical relationship. He hopes devoutly that this hierarchy of quality will be the same as his other necessary hierarchy, the one determined by the relative historical importance of the individual works of art. Because he is a critic, he also has the additional task of presenting to the public his critical judgment of the esthetic value of older works of art so he can help the reader take pleasure from them now.

Along with these three levels of approach to the works of art, the art historian attempts to determine the role of this unique object in its social milieu. At this point, like other historians, he has recourse to surviving contemporary documents. These may take the form of letters by patrons or artists, contracts, accounts of persons closer in time to the work of art, and an intensive study of the contemporary literature. He also has recourse to the data of archeology.

In my book, chapters 2 and 3 approximate straight history, since they deal more with the historical and cultural *mise-en-scène* than the specific works of art that belong in this *mise-en-scène*. For my own work, the importance of the setting is that it must take the place of the missing biographical data on the artists, the biographical data so important to the study of European art.

Most apprentice scholars establish particular intellectual relationships with their dissertation advisors. Some are overwhelmed by advisors who, in effect, rewrite and even write their students' dissertations. Others are ignored and struggle on by their own efforts. George Kubler's approach to my work on the dissertation was more flattering than those of the "rewriters" and infinitely more helpful than that of the "go-it-aloners." He assumed me to be a young scholar of sufficient competence and skill and independence of thought with whom the advisor should not "interfere." What he did was give sage advice and wise counsel, and this only when it was sought. Actually, Kubler influenced my thought and methods of working more through his seminar classes than through criticism of my dissertation. Personal conversation with Kubler often consisted of the general rather than the specific problems bearing on the manuscript paintings.[10]

At an early stage in my career, introductions from Kubler were instrumental in establishing contacts with scholars living in Mexico. This was especially the case with Robert Barlow, with whom I had long and stimulating conversations in the summer of 1949, shortly before he died. Notes of these conversations even now remain in my files as valuable and useful sources of ideas. It was during this same summer that I attended the class of Wigberto Jiménez Moreno on the ancient history of the Aztecs at Mexico City College (now University of the Americas). As all who know him personally can attest, Professor Jiménez Moreno's presentation of the pre-Columbian history of Mexico is inspiring. I also attended some of his classes in classic Náhuatl, the language of the Aztecs. What little knowledge and feeling I have for this language now is due to him.[11]

Robert Wauchope, Director of the Middle American Research Institute at Tulane University, read my dissertation when I first joined the faculty here in the fall of 1957 and made most perceptive and valuable editorial comments, which I used as I turned it into the manuscript for a book presented to the Yale Press. From my first meeting with Bob Wauchope, I realized that at Tulane I was in a university where Latin American art was not an aberration, but rather part of a vital program in a community of scholars with Latin American interests and concerns. I soon met faculty colleagues in the Spanish language, Latin American history, economics, anthropology, law, and other disciplines who shared my enthusiasm for the Spanish-American world. Both the stimulus of informed colleagues and exposure to Tulane's excellent Latin American Library (formerly under the care of Edith B. Ricketson and Marjorie Le Doux) have had an immeasurable effect on my scholarly productivity.

During my first year at Tulane, while working hard on turning my dissertation into a book, I was invited by Dr. Doris Stone to attend the Thirty-third International Congress of Americanists in San José, Costa Rica in the summer of 1958. Dr. Stone, who was at that time living in San José, was the main impetus behind the Costa Rican congress. Her invitation resulted in my attending the congress and reading my first paper at an international conclave, where I met members of the international community of scholars who until then had been for me only bibliographic references. Doris Stone really launched me on a new course of participation in scholarly affairs on a national and international scale.

One of the persons whom I met at this congress was Dr. Howard Cline, who has been most helpful to me in subsequent years. Director of the Hispanic Foundation of the Library of Congress, Howard Cline is in many respects the unsung hero of Latin American studies in the United States. Sitting in his office in the library, he meets a steady stream of scholarly visitors day after day. Many are the informative hours I have spent with him as he freely exchanges information on both scholarly problems and personalities. For me he has acted as a catalyst, providing introductions and opening up channels of communication which, without him, might never have been, or would have taken much longer to establish. From our first meeting in Costa Rica, where he sought me out (because he shared my interests in the

relaciones geográficas) until the present, I have felt in him the stimulus one scholar can derive from another who is in addition a skilled
administrator.

My book on Mexican manuscript painting appeared in 1959. The
typescript had been treated with the lightest of all editorial hands.
Since my field is still considered unorthodox in my own discipline, I
was particularly happy to have my first major work appear in the Yale
History of Art Series. Like all authors, I eagerly read the reviews as
they came out over a period of years. The reviews pleased me greatly
then, and I still receive a sense of gratification as I reread them. Praise
from Charles Gibson, one of the foremost students of sixteenth-century
Mexican history in the United States, in the *Hispanic American Historical Review* was most appreciated.[12] The review by Dr. Alfonso Caso, the
dean of Mexican manuscript painting, in *The Americas* was also favorable and most flattering to a neophyte.[13] Certain minor disagreements
with my arguments led Dr. Caso much later to inscribe the gift copy he
sent me of his important work on pre-Hispanic calendars: *"Para* Donald Robertson, *con quien tengo una antigua y amigable controversia,
muy afectuosamente,* Alfonso Caso." We still disagree in friendly fashion on the date of the Codex Borbonicus. Through his published
writings as well as our all-too-infrequent personal conversations, Dr.
Caso has become one of the Mexican scholars whom I admire most
highly. All students of Mexican manuscript painting are enormously
indebted to him.

The old and friendly controversy that Dr. Caso mentioned concerns not only the date of the Codex Borbonicus, but also the problem
of the provenance of the Codex Borgia and, by association, the group
of pre-Columbian Mexican religious manuscripts known as the Borgia
Group. From this disagreement have stemmed two papers on the
Borgia Group. One of these papers was read at the Twentieth International Congress of the History of Art in New York in 1961, the other at
the Thirty-fifth International Congress of Americanists in Mexico City
in 1962 (published in a Spanish translation).[14] The original English text
of the Mexican paper was later published in *Ancient Oaxaca,* edited by
John Paddock.[15] This book is now a key document in the literature of a
small group of scholars who have been branded "pan-Mixtecists."
Paddock and I are more overtly pan-Mixtecists than other scholars
working with Mixtec materials (A. Caso, I. Bernal, M. E. Smith,
R. Chadwick, and R. Parmenter, among others). Fundamentally, the
pan-Mixtecists believe that the art and culture of Mexico just before the
arrival of the Spaniards derived from the art and culture of the Mixtec
Indians, then occupying what is now the state of Oaxaca in south-
central Mexico.

"Pan-Mixtecism" is a rather enlightening phenomenon. It demon-
strates the amount of vitality that can be associated with archeological, historical, ethnohistorical, and art historical scholarship of the
years immediately preceding the Spanish Conquest of Mexico by
Cortés. The literature both pro and con dealing with the question is
probably quite like the literature on similar controversies, if not polemics, in other fields of history. Some of the principals cling tena-
ciously to earlier positions despite every indication, if not proof, that
they are wrong, while their opposite numbers, with marvelous logic
and lucidity, interpret the data to prove that they are correct. Put into
such a context, an adept reader of history can enjoy the fifteenth
century and the first decade and a half of the sixteenth century of
pre-Hispanic Mexico as much as he can enjoy the conflicting statements and claims of a present-day political campaign.

My own association with pan-Mixtecism comes from my study of
Mixtec manuscripts and the so-called Borgia Group of religious manuscripts (which I consider to be Mixtec). John Paddock's approach to
pan-Mixtecism, on the other hand, derives from archeology. In a paper
read at the Thirty-eighth International Congress of Americanists in
Stuttgart in 1968 dealing with the mural paintings at Tulum in the
Maya area, I attempted to bring together in summary fashion the
evidence of archeology, manuscript painting, and monumental mural
painting supporting the pan-Mixtecist theory.[16] I proposed that an
"International Style" of painting and low relief sculpture dominated
the New World from Guatemala to as far north as the Mississippi
River Valley in the United States.

Such an all-embracing explanation is a logical development from
what I said in only a few pages in my Mexican manuscript book, and it
points to a major change in the direction my future research and
scholarship will probably take. Here we have an illuminating example
of what happens when a scholar attempts to pursue the antecedents of
a period he undertakes to study. This is for me another demonstration
of the proof of Focillon's idea that in the history of art (and by
extension all history), there is no beginning and no end, that each
object is an end and a beginning at the same time.

My later papers dealing with the Codex Borgia pushed my manuscript researches further into the pre-Columbian past, just as later,
more intensive study of the Techialoyan manuscripts pushed my investigations further into the colonial period.[17] These studies have also led
me into explorations of other visual media, so that now I am thinking
in terms of a major work on the arts of the late post-classic period,
that is, during the fifteenth and early sixteenth centuries, just before
the Conquest.

· · ·

A dissertation is written out of necessity; a first book, in a meaningful sense, is probably written out of vanity. An unfavorable reception granted to either can be a stifling experience, whereas favorable receptions can provide the necessary stimulus for a productive scholarly life. This is why I feel most strongly that these two initial efforts by young scholars should be very carefully done and very carefully considered. Perhaps it is a fault of our society that both these efforts have to be made before the scholar has reached the point where he can draw upon years of experience and research in order to produce a magnum opus with assurance. My own experience has shown me that a measure of success in either or both of these endeavors leads to important professional associations.

One example of this last point in my own career was my association with the *Handbook of Middle American Indians*. The invitation to join with the other scholars contributing to the *Handbook* came in 1959, the year my book on manuscript painting was published. The *Handbook*, when finished, will be a fourteen-volume encyclopedic compilation of information on the Indians of the regions from the Rio Grande as far south as Costa Rica. The general editor of the whole *Handbook* is Robert Wauchope of Tulane University. I am affiliated with the ethnohistory volumes 11–14 edited by Howard Cline and in particular with the "Guide to Ethnohistorical Sources." My major contribution is to the "Census of Native Pictorial Sources" (with John B. Glass and Henry B. Nicholson) and to an exhaustive critical bibliography devoted to "Sources in the Native Tradition" (with Glass, Nicholson, and Charles Gibson).[18] The articles of joint authorship relied upon the pooling of the notes of the co-authors for their success. However, I learned from this experience that I am more at ease when working unfettered by other authors and that in the future, except in rare instances, I shall try to avoid the problems arising out of and inherent in joint authorship.[19]

The importance of the *Handbook* for the history of Latin American art in both the pre-Columbian and the colonial periods resides in its all-encompassing sweep and scope. It brings together from the pre-Hispanic era data for the study of architecture, painting, sculpture, and the minor arts. For the colonial era, it is less complete, but the volumes on ethnohistory contain material on the manuscript paintings and the bibliography necessary for studying the historical sources of the other colonial arts, especially architecture. Easel painting and other aspects of Baroque art more closely affiliated with European colonial life are less well served.

Serious study of the art of Latin America at the university level in the pre-Columbian, colonial, and even modern periods is so new in the United States that it is still not accepted wholeheartedly as a proper area of study by some of the more conservative or traditionalist historians of art.[20] At this particular moment in time, scholars dealing with Latin America are supported mainly by the interest in their material coming directly from university students, collectors, and museum personnel who are influenced by the popular press, especially illustrated magazines of large circulation. It is somewhat ironic that this awakening was anticipated almost thirty years ago in the exhibition "Twenty Centuries of Mexican Art," held in the Museum of Modern Art in New York in 1940.[21] But despite the increasing tempo, the number of young scholars now being trained by universities still lags behind the need for teachers in this field.

It has been my good fortune that the growing interest in the art of the Spanish-speaking world, especially of the pre-Columbian period, has coincided with the path of my scholarly career. Had I pursued the same career twenty years earlier, I would by now have retired from teaching. Were I to begin my career today, it would be too late for my study of manuscript painting to have a similar impact, and I would have had no role to play in the *Handbook of Middle American Indians*. Because of this timing, I made my "entrance" at an early moment in the study of Latin American art, and I was thus able to play to some extent the role of innovator. Kubler uses this word in *The Shape of Time* to refer to the moment when the artist makes his *entrance,* but it is also applicable to the world of scholarly and even scientific endeavors.[22] He himself made his *entrance* into these studies earlier than I and thus became unqualifiedly an initiator.[23] Mendel, making too early an *entrance*, did not live to see "Mendel's Law" recognized as a key contribution to genetics; because it was premature, his work had to be "rediscovered" later.

In talking with or advising a student at the graduate level, one tries to encourage him to keep in mind that in shaping his career he should consider most seriously the question of *entrance.* To begin at this moment the serious study of certain areas of history is likely to put a student in the position of being an innovator, while other areas will deny him this privilege because of the relative amount of previous scholarly activity in the field. The innovator in this sense need not limit himself to an unstudied area. He can, of course, study areas already richly worked, but bring to them new methods and patterns of thought. On the other hand, study in a well-worked field using well-established methods and ideas can be a weak combination on which to launch a professional career. I would find it far more flattering as a teacher to have my students branch out into new areas, some of which I might have disdained, or to use my ways of thinking, my analyses, and my approach to the history of Latin American art merely as springboards with which to create more sophisticated and refined methodologies and ways of thinking and dealing with the material, perhaps even in friendly opposition to my own.

The graduate students I teach at Tulane come to me not only from art history, but also from other disciplines such as anthropology, Latin American history, and Spanish literature. As I look back on my relations with them, I realize that in addition to the normal influence the professor has upon his students, I receive a stimulating influence from them. For instance, my knowledge of things Mayan has increased since I have been at Tulane, and my interest in the Maya has been heightened in large measure because I have advised students working on Mayan topics. This enhances the essentially magnetic effect that sophisticated Maya art must have on anyone working in the pre-Columbian field. Good and serious undergraduate students, too, in seeking direction in the writing of papers for classes, can exert similar pressures on their teachers. As a professional scholar and historian of art, I consider this a most valuable effect of teaching, because it constitutes a projection and continuation of one's own learning.

Another aspect of my relations with students is that, like all historians, I have a wide variety of interests and carry around as intellectual baggage a relatively wide variety of topics that I would find it fascinating to investigate at some length had I sufficient time or more years of an active professional life ahead of me. In these topics, students often find useful suggestions for theses and research papers which have the effect of being extensions of one's own ideas and thoughts beyond the necessary limitations of time and the more direct pressures of immediate research.

I began my thoughts in this essay with the suggestion that writing art history is as much a "creative" activity as painting or making sculpture. "Creative" would then apply as well to the writing of any history, for the history of art is but a major subdivision of history. The Greeks made Clio the muse or goddess of the art of history. The classical world seemed to have had no individual gods or goddesses for architecture, painting, sculpture, ceramics, nor, indeed, for any of the plastic arts. We have come a long way from this idea: the historian in the twentieth century is seldom considered an artist, and the architects, painters, sculptors, and others whom the Greeks considered craftsmen with no separate muse to call their own are now rated as "creative artists."

If a painting, a piece of sculpture, a fine bowl, or a handsome building is the result of the creative activity of a painter, a sculptor, a ceramist, or an architect, is well-written perceptive historical writing not also the result of creative activity, the activity of a historian who is artist as well as scholar and writer? I firmly believe that successfully written history is as much a work of art as the "creative writing" or literature of our age, perhaps in some ways even more. The question, in reality, is only *how* is the historian an artist?

Perhaps the best way to answer this question is to examine the three main stages in the writing of history: the collection of data, the creation of a synthetic pattern, and the writing of prose. In the history of art, the data and the facts are first and foremost the works of art. To collect them as data the historian of art, in addition to the original work of art, relies upon published reproductions, kodachrome slides, black and white photographs, and well-executed copies (these last, especially if the original is lost). Other important data are the evidence from documents and archeology, those records of the past that give the work of art its setting. I do not think the creative and artistic activity of the art historian lies in collecting the facts and data. It may require a bit of ingenuity, but the label "tedious" more than anything else sums up this stage of his activity most of the time.

The second stage in the writing of art history is reached when the art historian weaves the facts and data he has collected into a connected account making a meaningful and convincing narrative. This is the synthesis, the heart of the matter. To do this, he must analyze and consider all his sources before organizing them into topics of such grand scope as "Painting of the Italian Renaissance." From these materials he draws a framework or setting for the individual works of art, a picture of the whole, imparting to it a logical unity that never really existed in the past. This synthesizing narrative is the art historian's invention, the result of his intellectual and creative activity. In reality it comes from his imagination, from his creative potentiality, as much as a painting comes from a painter's creative powers.[24]

A monumental and truly creative approach to the writing of history is Proskouriakoff's study of Maya sculpture mentioned earlier. I consider it basic to the study of the history of the art of the Maya. Her work is of special significance in the context of this essay, because it points out the differences between the historian's and the archeologist's or anthropologist's ways of presenting the material. The anthropologist almost routinely publishes graphs, charts, and diagrams when he has large numbers of facts and complex explanations of relationships in order to show in detail how he arrived at his conclusions. The historian of art, however, working in the tradition of history as a branch of *belles lettres*, is loath to present his data in this manner. He prefers to pose the question under investigation as well as the data and the conclusion in a literary rather than a numerical, schematic or graphic fashion. The history of art can never be a science; it is part of the art of history.

The third and last stage in the writing of art history is that of actually sitting down and writing, for the historian must present his subject in the proper form. In other words, the historian of art must take on the characteristics of a "creative writer," because the most interesting facts and the most fascinating historical syntheses will languish if they are presented in so dull and tedious a fashion that no one will take the time nor possess the energy to read them.

Beauty of style is the product of artistic activity. This explains why Bernard Berenson's writings on the history of art deserve to be considered literature.[25] When it comes to the actual writing, the art historian is therefore a creative artist. Clarity may be rational and born only of the intellect, but communication, in the best sense, is born of feeling. One can know something intellectually, but to feel it too is to really understand it. The historian as artist and writer tries to convey not the response, "I know what you have said," but "I understand what you have said." Understanding is born of the combined intellectual and emotional rapport established between author and reader. In reading history or the history of art, the imagination must fill in the lacunae, must set the stage, and equally essentially, provide the personal element that gives the printed page life.

One might conclude that some historians are artists in their chosen field, some are not. But it would be more precise to say that artists who are historians, like artists who are architects, painters, and sculptors, can be divided into the competent, the first-rate, and a few geniuses.

NOTES

1. Sir Banister Fletcher, *A History of Architecture on the Comparative Method* (London, 1931). E. George Squier, *Peru Illustrated, or Incidents of Travel and Exploration in the Land of the Incas* (New York, 1877). At this point I want to thank Professors France V. Scholes and Ryland Greene for reading this essay and for their helpful comments.
2. Especially his *The Life of Forms in Art* (New York, 1948).
3. Donald Robertson, *Mexican Manuscript Painting of the Early Colonial Period: The Metropolitan Schools* (Yale Historical Publications, History of Art, 12, New Haven, 1959).
4. "The Relaciones Geográficas of Mexico," *Actas del XXXIII Congreso internacional de Americanistas, San José, 20–27 julio 1958*, t. 2 (San José, Costa Rica, 1959), pp. 540–47. See also *infra*, p. 115.
5. "The Sixteenth-century Mexican Encyclopedia of Fray Bernardino de Sahagún," *Journal of World History*, 9, 3 (Neuchatel, UNESCO, 1966), 617–27.
6. Meyer Schapiro, "Style," in *Anthropology Today, an Encyclopedic Inventory* (Chicago, 1953), pp. 287–12.

7. See note 2. See also Ivan Lermolieff (pseud. of Giovanni Morelli), *Kunstkritische Studien über italienische Malerie*, 2 vols. (Leipzig, 1890–1893), and Heinrich Wölfflin, *Principles of Art History* (New York, 1932).

8. See Erwin Panofsky, *Studies in Iconology* (New York, 1939).

9. *A Study of Classic Maya Sculpture*, Carnegie Institution, Publication 593 (Washington, D.C., 1950).

10. His conversations thus encouraged broadening rather than narrowing the area of the dissertation topic. This I see now more clearly than I did at the time.

11. Two other *nahuatlatos* (translators of Náhuatl), the late Byron McAfee of Mexico City and Dr. Joaquín Galarza of the Musée de l'Homme in Paris, have subsequently helped me build on this foundation.

12. *Hispanic American Historical Review*, XL, 2 (May 1960), 282–83.

13. *The Americas*, XIX, 1 (July 1962), 100–7.

14. "The Style of the Borgia Group of Mexican Pre-Conquest Manuscripts," in Millard Meiss *et al.*, eds., *Studies in Western Art; Acts of the Twentieth International Congress of the History of Art*, Vol. III: *Latin American Art and the Baroque Period in Europe* (Princeton, 1963), pp. 148–64. "Los Manuscritos religiosos mixtecos," *XXXV Congreso internacional de Americanistas, México, 1962, Actas y Memorias*, Tomo 1 (México, 1964), pp. 425–35.

15. "The Mixtec Religious Manuscripts," in John Paddock, ed., *Ancient Oaxaca—Discoveries in Mexican Archeology and History* (Stanford, 1966), pp. 298–312.

16. "The Tulum Murals: The International Style of the Late Post-Classic," in press.

17. "The Techialoyan Codex of Tepotzotlán: Codex X (Rylands Mexican Ms. 1)," transcription and translation by Byron McAfee, *Bulletin of the John Rylands Library*, 43, 1 (Manchester, England, September 1960), 109–30.

18. My independent contributions to the ethnohistory volumes of the *Handbook* are on the *pinturas* of the *relaciones geográficas* (Vol. 11) and on the Techialoyan codices (Vol. 13). In the latter article, my wife, Martha Barton Robertson, appears as co-author of the appended catalog. This is a small recognition of her continuing participation in my scholarly activities.

19. I hope sometime in the not too distant future, for instance, to edit collections of essays on the Mixtec colonial Codex Tulane, the Techialoyan Codex of Tulane, and the Codex Tudela (an early colonial Mexican pictorial manuscript in the Museo de America in Madrid). For all three manuscripts, I envisage an editorial introduction, my own contribution in the form of an essay, and signed essays by other contributors. In this manner one has the advantages of joint authorship but none of the difficulties.

20. One criticism, which to me is a bit frivolous, is that "there are no documents for the study of pre-Columbian art." For the Mixtecs, for instance, this is simply not true—their genealogical history goes back to the seventh century. For the Maya of the classic period, interpretation of calendrical glyphs, and thus native chronology, is under control. Only correlation with the Christian calendar is questioned. Parallel study of noncalendrical Maya glyphs is advancing at such a rate that within five to ten years we will be able to know what *historical events* are recorded

in the large group of known dated stelae and others yet to be found to supplement the archeological evidences of chronology.

Feelings of isolation from our own discipline shared by those few students and aficionados of Latin American art and architecture have resulted in my editing the *Bulletin of Historians of Latin American Art and Architecture* at irregular intervals: numbers 1 and 2 have appeared.

21. Pál Kelemen, in his Foreword to the issue of *Art in America* devoted to Indian art of the Americas, gives a review of the status of the history of Latin American art in the United States as of 1961 (Vol. 49, No. 3, pp. 22-23). Kelemen's major books are *Medieval American Art* (New York, 1943, reprinted 1956 and 1969) and *Baroque and Rococo in Latin America* (New York, 1951, reprinted 1967).

22. George Kubler, *The Shape of Time: Remarks on the History of Things* (New Haven and London, 1962), p. 6.

23. See his *The Religious Architecture of New Mexico in the Colonial Period and Since the American Occupation* (Colorado Springs, 1940), and *Mexican Architecture of the Sixteenth Century*, 2 vols. (New Haven, 1948). Other pioneers are Pál Kelemen (see note 21) and Harold E. Wethey, who wrote *Colonial Architecture and Sculpture in Peru* (Cambridge, Mass., 1949).

24. For major examples in the history of Latin American art, see among others: Salvador Toscano, *Arte precolombino de México y de la América Central* (México, 1944); Manuel Toussaint, *Arte colonial en México* (México, 1948); Justino Fernández, *Arte moderno y contemporáneo de México* (Instituto de Investigaciones Estéticas, XXII, México, 1952), which follows his *El arte moderno en México, breve historia, siglos XIX y XX* (México, 1937); George A. Kubler, *The Art and Architecture of Ancient America; the Mexican, Maya, and Andean Peoples* (Baltimore, 1962); and George A. Kubler and Martin Soria, *Art and Architecture in Spain and Portugal and Their American Dominions, 1500-1800* (Baltimore, 1959).

25. Bernard Berenson, *Italian Painters of the Renaissance* (London, 1953).

Largely Without Benefit
of
Prior Conceptualization

THOMAS GARDEN BARNES

THOMAS GARDEN BARNES was born on April 29, 1930, in Pittsburgh, Pennsylvania. After receiving an A.B. degree from Harvard in 1952, he pursued his study of English history at Corpus Christi College, Oxford, receiving the D.Phil. degree in 1955. From January 1956 to 1960 Barnes taught at Lycoming College in Williamsport, Pennsylvania; he then joined the Department of History at the University of California at Berkeley, where he is now Professor of History, specializing in the Tudor-Stuart period.

Barnes is a member of the Mediaeval Academy of America and the Selden Society as well as a Fellow of the Royal Historical Society. He won the Alexander Prize of the Royal Historical Society in 1958 for his essay, "County Politics and a Puritan Cause Célèbre: Somerset Churchales, 1633." In 1962–1963 he received a fellowship from the American Council of Learned Societies and a Guggenheim Fellowship for 1970–1971.

Among his numerous extramural activities are Project Director of the American Bar Foundation's Anglo-American Legal History Project, editor of the Public Records, London, member of the editorial board of the *American Journal of Legal History,* and member of the Council of the Somerset Record Society.

Barnes is the author of *Somerset 1625–1640: A County's Government During the Personal Rule* (Cambridge, Mass., 1961), editor of *Somerset Assize Orders, 1629–1640* (Somerset Record Society, 1959), and co-author with Rondo Cameron and Jerome Blum of *The European World* (Boston, 1966). He has also written articles on English legal history in the Tudor-Stuart period. He is presently working on a history of the Star Chamber from 1596 to 1641.

Pittsburgh was hot and humid that last week of May and first week of June 1940. The family was engaged in its annual confused preparation to decamp for the family home in Nova Scotia. The news from Europe, where France was in her agony, was strangely slight. The radio told little, and at age ten I wasn't much of a newspaper reader. Now, almost three decades later, I remember vividly the day we heard the news from London that over 300,000 Allied troops had been evacuated from Dunkirk by an armada of small boats from England. My mother cried, my father was visibly moved, and something like an anthem of deliverance rose from the boys' boarding school where we lived. I was struck by the description of the armada, and wished desperately to have been there, for I already handled a fifteen-foot whaleboat with some skill and could beach on a rocky Fundy foreshore in a lightly breaking sea. The whole episode and its immediate aftermath had a formative impact on me: Dunkirk and the Battle of Britain, my parents collecting rifles and shotguns to ship to Britain and organizing the Pittsburgh chapter of the Committee to Defend America by Aiding the Allies, the eighteen-year-olds who left Shady Side Academy to join the RAF, and always the hush on those occasions when KDKA brought us the English language "mobilized" for war in the rhetoric of Winston Churchill. I could only grow up a hopeless Anglophile! And so I did, even singing "Rule Britannia" a year later in the isolationist fastness of western Ohio (we moved there in 1941), the realm of Robert McCormick and his Chicago *Tribune,* and getting beaten up for it.

In retrospect there were other influences no less potent in the making of this Anglophile. Though my maternal grandfather died when I was seven, his influence was long-lived both in the person of his widow, who lived with us for thirty years until her death last year, and my parents. He was a Canadian Anglican parson, who as a very young priest had gone, in the 1890s, to the missionary Diocese of West Texas because he was dying of tuberculosis contracted in the seminary. While awaiting his Maker's last trump, he was expected to serve several mission parishes that altogether constitute an area larger than most English dioceses. Riding from church to church in the hot sun around Cuero might have been the vehicle by which the Lord kept him for another four decades of service in the Church Militant. I remember my grandfather and my father arguing violently about the merits of Queen Victoria; my father took a professionally detached view of the lady, but his father-in-law was a confirmed idolator. Indeed, the only graven image allowed one in Holy Orders of that generation was Victoria Regina. It was in my grandfather's ancestral home in Digby County, on the Fundy coast of Nova Scotia, that I passed all my summers, became a child of the sea (a British sea of course), learned the lore of the

United Empire Loyalists—it has taken years to erase those myths—and hoisted the Union Jack, the Canadian flag, and the Stars and Stripes, all together, on both July 1 (Dominion Day) and July 4. "Anglo-Americanophilia" is, perhaps, a better way to describe the disease.

There was, too, the pervasive influence of Anglicanism, serving both to reinforce Anglophilia and to provide a continuous, subtle historical influence. My parson-grandfather was an avid believer in the essentially historical nature of Christian faith in general and Anglican observance in particular. The "historic Jesus" of the higher criticism of the nineteenth century had in his case, as in that of so many other late Victorian clerics, confirmed the historicism of doctrine, given doctrine a new dispensation and a new relevance rather than destroying it. His sermons were historical essays, and it was this dimension that I suspect attracted his son-in-law, my father, converting him from a rather arid rural Methodism to a broad and urbane Anglicanism. Throughout this period my grandfather's parish was in Pittsburgh, and the families were in weekly contact; hence the ambience that made the church so potent in my youth. My own church experience added emphasis to Anglican traditionalism, and so at one remove, to English history. For three years I was a choirboy in Pittsburgh under Dr. Harvey Gaul, the choirmaster of Calvary Church, whose intuitive passion for the Anglican musical tradition, from Byrd to Williams, was married to musicological genius and an awesome ability to handle brats. We left Pittsburgh for western Ohio before Dr. Gaul could dismiss another croaking ex-boy soprano, and I moved from chancel to sanctuary. In the summer of 1941 in the small wooden church at Weymouth North near our place in Nova Scotia, I served at Communion for the first time and sang a wobbly solo "Agnus Dei" while my grandmother played the organ. Before my translation to acolyte, I had pumped the ancient contraption with sieve-like bellows, managing to keep up wind as long as Gram's fingers moved quickly, but harkening in despair to the dying bleat of a *sostenuto*. In Lima, Ohio, I became one of an enormous corps of acolytes in a "high church" parish, trained, scrubbed, vested, scolded, praised, shushed, and doted on by the elderly daughter of a former Australian bishop who loved the Book of Common Prayer with a consuming passion that was readily communicated to her "acolyte children."

In retrospect, it was the majestic tautology of Cranmer's liturgy, the felicity of his mobilization of the English language to send it into battle against the "devil and all his works, the vain pomp and glory of the world, . . . all covetous desires of the same, and the sinful desires of the flesh," that determined that I would become a Tudor-Stuart historian. It also put me in some hazard of becoming a priest. It is likely I never adequately renounced the devil and all his works. It is certain I never heard the call to vocation which, strangely enough, became central in Anglicanism with the Puritans, only to come to rest and to be preserved entire in the Anglo-Catholic tradition. As it is, I find that much of what is called "advising" in the university is closer to hearing confession, and sometimes I am moved by enormous frustration that I cannot absolve, but only listen. Anyone who remembers Pierre Fresnay as the sexton in *God Needs Men*, pressed by a dying friend to absolve him, will know what I mean. I came closest to considering seriously entering the priesthood on the eve of college. After we returned to Pittsburgh in 1946 (my father joined the Pitt History Department in 1944), I served at a weekday 7 A.M. Communion regularly at our parish church, assisting the curate, an elderly English priest, a veteran of the Great War, and a cousin of Sir Stafford Cripps (whose politics were anathema to him). Father Cripps was a dear friend and confessor to a boy at a particularly tense time in adolescence, and if there can be visible saints, he was one of them. I think his counsel persuaded me to fight the good fight and finish the course, but without the armor of alb, chasuble, maniple, and stole.

If I was destined to be an Anglophile (an Anglican-Anglophile), I was predestined to be a historian. I was an only child, the object of too much attention and all affection. My father, twelve years my mother's senior, was thirty-seven when I was born. He was continuously busy with the multitudinous affairs of a boy's senior boarding school, teaching history by day and reading by night, unless there was some boy to see him with a problem, or some parent to see him about a problem (a boy). Yet I played in the peace of his study, as he read, almost as much as I did outside. This was just as well. Once I dug up the head matron's rock garden, another time put a small pet alligator in her pond, and regularly deflated the tires of the car of the senior French master (our mutual detestation evaporated only twenty years later when he approved my choice of a French bride, and I found a sad old man where once there had been a fierce adversary). I furnished an entirely deleterious leadership to all the other faculty brats by virtue of my seniority (a few months) and my audacity (no explanation). Dad's paperpunch, his World War I mementoes, a pair of large bronze bookends, miscellaneous pens, scissors, paperknife, etc., provided infinite delight for me and considerable anguish for him. Really he was quite uncommunicative, but when chided by my mother for his inattentiveness to us, he always replied with a note of plaintiveness, "I love you and I like to have you around when I'm working." A new generation must now bear with that same excuse!

There were the walks, though, the wonderful walks in the sylvan beauty of the large campus on the outskirts of Pittsburgh. Mr. Barnes carried an alpine stick, Mr. Craig (another French master, a gentle bachelor, "Uncle Wush") and Mr. Waldrop (the Classics master, "Uncle George") were similarly accoutred. I made a branch do, *pro hac vice.* We played Indians—not just any Indians, but Indians allied with the French, chasing Colonel Washington of the Virginia militia into Fort Necessity, massacring General Braddock's redcoats, finally being over-run at Fort Duquesne. Uncle Wush was, naturally, always the French general. Uncle George, a Kentuckian and the most solemn, patently sage, and magisterial man I have ever known, preferred to be the British general. Dad was the rustic militiaman. The Indian was fast and aggressive, but the inferior generalship of the French commander (Uncle Wush had no stomach for war) lost the Bourbon cause against the tactics of Hadrian's successor and the withering fire of an ex-sec-ond lieutenant of a machine gun company in the Fourth Infantry Division, AEF.

Dad was not ill-cast as a rustic militiaman. Our people had come over the mountains from upcountry Virginia in the early nineteenth century to settle in the hills of eastern Ohio. Scots-Irish and English by extraction, they were honest and godly, but poor, dirt farmers. Dad and I regularly attended family reunions in Ohio—at Warsaw, Coshoc-ton, Newcomerstown—where elderly clansmen good naturedly (and proudly) chided "young Demas who went to college" and embarrassed Dad (to my delight) with implausible tales of plausible boyhood esca-pades. Dad graduated as valedictorian of his class at Warsaw High School in a class of five or six (the rest were girls, I think), and by dint of his hard work and his father's savings went to Ohio Northern University in Ada. Graduating in three years with straight As, ruined for the plow, he left Ohio for the first time in his life to do graduate work at Harvard. He supported himself by waiting tables, but want took its toll, and though encouraged to continue by a remarkable streak of compassionate concern on the part of the almost-pontifical Albert Bushnell Hart, he left after taking his M.A. His lifelong regret was transmuted into a later anxiety that his son finish his doctorate before beginning to teach. A couple of years' teaching in a Massachu-setts boys' school was followed by a call to the colors in 1918, and he went back to Ohio for induction. The Great War left memories but not scars, for he never saw action. Yet in late 1918 when he arrived in France, the smell of gas still hung over the Somme, the mud of the Marne stank of putrefaction when a shovel was sunk into it, and Verdun was not yet the carefully sculptured monument to the trenches it later became, but the horror of a total wasteland. Even a year's happy study and horseplay at Montpellier erased little of the impact of those early sights. When in 1941 he attempted to volunteer again, at forty-eight, it was a mixture of a sense of duty and anger at the dreadful waste of the Western Front that moved him.

My father was my first and finest teacher. A decade after his death he remains the most persistent exemplar to me of what a teacher should be. In my youth everything was history, everywhere we were was steeped in history, never was the past allowed to remain hidden beneath the mean shadows of the present. The summers in Nova Scotia always included a visit to Port Royal (Fort Anne), one bastion of French (English) power in North America, and the winters involved awareness of another bastion, Fort Duquesne (Fort Pitt). Winter trips by car to Texas and Florida just before the war resulted in the opening of the history of the Southern colonies, the Mexican War, and the Civil War. A careening Pontiac stopped at every historical marker in every state—I spotted 'em, Mother read 'em, Dad explained 'em. I will still pit my knowledge of Phil Sheridan's ride down the Shenandoah against any colleague in American history! I could always get Dad to "talk history," even inveigling him to "give me a history test," in which I displayed such erudition as I had garnered. He was persistent in his correction, drawing from a fund of knowledge of ancient, European, and American history that was staggering. The first time I lectured was as a guest in his Reformation class at the University of Pittsburgh just after my return from Oxford. After each of the two lectures, while neither concealing his pride nor stinting his praise, he carefully and methodically corrected my factual errors and suggested alternative interpretations.

For him, as for his masters, the facts came first. I sometimes read his notes taken in lectures by Roger B. Merriman, A. B. Hart, and Frederick Jackson Turner at Harvard in 1915, and marvel at their capacity to put so many facts in fifty minutes and yet not fail to suggest what they mean. The parameters of history were narrower then —or so it seems—but there remains a contagious vigor about the history they taught. It was that same vigor which my father conveyed to me, a vigor compounded of respect for facts, belief in the centrality of chronology in the historical enterprise, and criticalness in evaluation of all the evidence (but also a sense of what is evidence, what is not, and what can never be evidence). "Old-fashioned" political history was an extraordinarily good vehicle for inculcating the fledgling historian with the importance of chronology, and if it was wanting in awareness of conceptual framework, question-posing, and models, it provided discipline in factual arrangement which today we stand in some peril of underemphasizing in graduate training. My father never wrote a book (for which reason Pitt saw fit to retire him as an associate professor), and he was not a research scholar in our well-defined professional sense of the term. He was an avid reader and a voluminous letter writer: to the relatives in Ohio, to his family when he lived in Pittsburgh for two years during the war while we lived in

Lima and mother worked in a war plant, and to me when I was at Harvard and Oxford. His weekly letters to me were full of what he had been reading and thinking: how this book fitted into the historiography of that period, where that author was wrong, how he might now approach a particular historical problem, what connection he saw between past developments and present concerns. He trained a number of graduate students in his fifteen years at Pitt; he also trained one other in his thirty years as father. There was a systematic quality in his epistles to me which I think was not consciously sought; each letter was an essay, strong in love, but providing intellectual substance as well. Perhaps after all he did write a book, published in brief weekly essays to one reader with love. *Mais les ouvrages le plus courts sont toujours les meilleurs.*

One other dimension of my youth, though at first sight having nothing to do with things of the mind or spirit, has had a marked effect on the course of my scholarship and even secured me my first job offer. In my adolescence, summers in Nova Scotia meant living with my uncle and aunt, who attempted to make the 440 acres of scrub wood pay. My uncle (my mother's younger brother) has many faults, but one great gift—extraordinary manual dexterity. Whether farming, fishing, woodcutting, or any of the other occupations he attempted to follow with too much initial enthusiasm and too little subsequent application, he could do all that was required with his own hands. In the process he trained his nephew in the same skills. Long after I discovered my idol's clay feet, I must acknowledge how much I learned from him. This has, of course, been useful (especially during my earlier years of teaching, when $4,200 a year allowed for few craft services) and remains a principal form of relaxation. But it has had two tangential results that directly affect my scholarship. First, from the age of twelve until I went to Oxford, I held a succession of unskilled, semiskilled, and skilled jobs in Ohio and Pennsylvania during the summer, and from 1944 to 1946 after school, that included shoeshining, running a Montgomery Ward service station (and assembling farm machinery), driving a pickup route for the Railway Express Agency and working the platform (in 1945, eight hours after school), waiting tables, working in a steel plant, and finally working as a machinist for the Bureau of Mines. This provided a wide range of experiences with diverse persons, affording a sense of the very distinct ethnic groups that peopled both agrarian Ohio and industrial Pittsburgh, and an awareness of how vocation influences reaction to political, economic, and social stimuli. Youthful empathy and brashness established rapport with people who are well beyond the limits of professorial acquaintance. The lesson of diversity learned then has outlived the experiences known and friendships made. It is a good legacy.

Second, a constant involvement with things and the act of making things and repairing things has provided a sensitivity to the material world that has sharpened my sensory acuity. I have a passion for the material vestiges of the past: buildings, hedges, an old lock, bridges, beams in an old barn, a bit of pavement, wooden conduits, furniture, pottery, plate, and so on—even a well-drawn indenture on a good parchment. There is nothing mystical or romantic about such things— they are just things, but things as different from our things as the society that produced them is different from our society. The visual parallelism of the material to the ethereal provides a powerful solvent of present-mindedness. In fact, one of my more original notions was spawned in this parallelism. When in early 1962 I hit upon the idea that the real element of radical thrust, both in religion and politics, in early seventeenth-century England was the artisan class (I mean class), the idea came to me during a long period of carpentry in a newly-acquired old house. There was evidence in some Star Chamber cases involving riots in Gillingham, Braydon, and Deane forest, ca. 1630, suggestive of this, but the idea struck me in the course of following a craft that was rather prominently represented in the leadership of rural unrest. In the long, almost languid, hours of sawing, planing, sanding, and ham-mering, I thought constantly of the nature of craftsmanship, its pride and its frustrations, its completeness and its insufficiencies, its value and its valuelessness in a society in which the craftsman was the man between, and in which he felt first the chill of depression and the cold of hunger. Others will explore this notion, not I, but if it proves ultimately to have any worth, it can be traced back to a brief living excursion into the seventeenth century via tools and techniques which are hardly more sophisticated than those used by Henry Alford, car-penter, of Gillingham, Dorset—"captain" of the Gillingham rioters.

As for how manual attainments obtained for me my first job offer, in January 1956, having returned from Oxford with a shiny D.Phil. and also tuberculosis, I found that the army didn't want me and that I needed a job. I wrote to colleges in the Pittsburgh area and received two replies, one from a small state college in West Virginia. The inter-view with the president and the dean (the latter an ex-superintendent of schools) was stiff and formal until the dean asked me what else I had done, and I recounted my saga of odd jobs. With an almost ecstatic smile he turned to the president and said, "Dr. _____, you see what I told you, despite the Phi Beta Kappa, Dr. Barnes is a regular fellow." I was offered an instructorship and $3,800 on the spot. A few days later I accepted the offer of an assistant professorship and $4,200 at Lycoming College; however, I never had the courage to ask the president there whether or not REA and USS counted for more than PBK.

What is most difficult to assess as youthful influence on the man is the particular personal relationship of the boy with his parents. Obviously, in the case of my father and me, the almost purely academic was so intimately blended with the personal, paternal and filial, that the two cannot be separated. The problem is not made much easier by the fact that my mother's influence has been almost entirely personal and hardly at all academic. Except for her ceramics and sculpture (a doubly liberal education, for when nudity was not so ubiquitous as it is now, Mom's female models were as much a part of that education as the more esthetic aspects normally taught in Fine Arts 1), she foreswore teaching me anything. But unlike my father, she made me *do* things; perhaps more important, she *let* me do things, when the more protective instincts of my father moved him to say no. He never lost an Ohioan's fear of water; my mother stands yet in greater danger of drowning than a heart attack (at age 62 she took up water-skiing), and it was she who turned me loose in a whaleboat. It was also she who let me work the night shift at 15, and do all the other things that made youth a joy. A veritable powerhouse of energy—noisy, vital, open-hearted and generous, with a strong social sense and a hatred of injustice, a Texan who sat-in in Pittsburgh roller rinks in 1948 to integrate them—my mother's greatest triumph was that she did not triumph over a quieter and gentler man, but herself fostered the relationship between him and his son that formed the son in a manner quite different from what it would have been had she been a less sensitive, less intelligent, and less loving woman. Abe Lincoln's hackneyed epitaph to his mother has no relevance for me, for what indeed I owe to my mother is due entirely to those qualities which are *not* angelic, but all human!

I went to Harvard in September 1948. My high school record was undistinguished, less because for the last six years of my schooling I had changed schools every two years than because I was far too interested in working, involving myself in the boisterous political and social activities of a large city high school that was thoroughly integrated and wanted to integrate everybody else, otherwise raising the devil, and taking very seriously my National Guard activities. It was my intention to become a career naval officer, via the NROTC program. But in the physical examination for the program in the spring of 1948, I found out that according to a lot of silly dots I was red-green blind. This was a hard blow—I wanted a liberal education, but I wanted to follow the sea. The Navy made a mistake, not only because I might have made a decent officer, but because I would have remained one.

History 1 at Harvard proved a determinant of my entire college career. For the first time I encountered European history laid out in a meaningful continuity. Both Charles Taylor and Michael Karpovich were stimulating lecturers, in quite different ways. My section leader, a teaching fellow, was a gorgon. He had the effrontery to give me a D on my first quiz (I didn't see what was so horrendous about defining "Vulgate" as the common language of the later Roman Empire). At the same time, he explained patiently, provoked discussion, and corrected consistently. There was beer with him and his burgeoning family in a quonset hut near the Divinity School, and good talk and friendship. And there still is, twenty years later, though I yet stand, figuratively, cap in hand to talk to my colleague Bill Bouwsma. He shepherded me through my first long paper, a study of the Reformation Parliament, in which my conclusions were, alas, too dependent on A. F. Pollard. Still this was the first, though not the last, thing I would write in Tudor-Stuart history. History 1 buoyed both my spirits and my grades, for a D and a C in Spanish were hard on both. It was a tough year, but strangely rewarding; rewarding enough to reconcile me to what appeared the inevitable, an academic career.

The Rostowian "take off"—or was it Kierkegaard's "leap into faith" —came in my sophomore year. A certain Czechophilia that had coexisted with Anglophilia (a historic yoking) put me into two courses (one a grad course) on Czech history and literature. These courses, both taught by Svatava Pirkova-Jacobson, opened new vistas. The natural progression of my history study put me into the honors program, and a gentle but very helpful tutor, Wendell Calkins, sharpened my critical faculties. In the second half of the year I had the treat of David Owen's lectures on nineteenth-century Britain, but it was in "Kitch" Jordan's Stuart England that the die of my career was cast. Jordan's first lecture was on the sources for Stuart history. I was enthralled, and in my lecture notes written in the margin against the brief description of "untouched local records" of the JPs and local officials in county record offices are the words, "This is for me!!!" underlined three times. I went up to the imposing Mr. Jordan after the lecture, told him I would have to do an honors essay and that I wanted to do it on JPs, etc., and would he help me? He invited me to his office at once, and for twenty minutes told me about the sources, what I might do with them, and advised me to pick a county and if possible get over for a few months' sortie into the archives. I made the resolution that February morning, 1950, that I would spend the summer between my junior and senior years in an English county record office. The particular office chosen was not accidental. I wrote to a number of county record offices, inquiring whether or not they had an abundance of early seventeenth-century records, how accessible were the records, and whether I could use a typewriter. I sought a county some distance from London, large, prosperous, and (hopefully) rich in seventeenth-century gentry. Ivor Collis, the Somerset archivist, indicated that Somerset's records were abundant from 1607, well-ordered and listed, and he thought a place might be found for me to type. Somerset fit all the other criteria. I made my decision and began reading everything I could get my hands on about the county. I am still a Somerset man, and if only by adoption, at least thoroughly.

Political activism took up a good deal of my time at Harvard. I was a loyal member and an officer of the Harvard Liberal Union in its heyday, as well as a founding member and first vice-president of the Harvard Society for Minority Rights–NAACP. I did battle with the Young Progressive remnants of the Wallace campaign of 1948, who mouthed the Red dogmas of the early 1930s in total disregard for their irrelevancy in the very different late 1940s. The Soviet Union could not be my New Jerusalem—not after Prague, the Greek civil war, and the Berlin blockade. In common with most of my generation, theoretical Marxism had little appeal for me. It suffered not only from its identification with the USSR, but in contrast to the idealism of the generation that came of age in the war and its immediate aftermath. We were the inheritors of the New Deal, and we greeted a brave new world convinced that with our sound democratic institutions and the application of good will we could lick injustice and cure social ills. We were never disillusioned, though perhaps we ought to have been, earlier than later, in the face of Joe McCarthy, Dick Nixon vs. Alger Hiss, and the Eisenhower era. Today we are dismissed contemptuously as "the old liberals," but the militant under-30s in this, as in so many other things, miss the point. We are not "the old liberals"; the generation of the 1930s is. We are just plain liberals. We are *not* the sires—biologically or spiritually—of the "new liberals," whose pessimism we detest as much as their tactics and their destructiveness. Unlike the "old liberals," the generation of the 1930s, we don't squirm when the enragés breathe fire and smoke at us, and we feel no compulsive need to identify with them, to stand awestruck by their "superior intellect" and "superior morality." After all, they are not our children, only our students, and it's *our* turn now to run the universities. The "movement" is in for a hard time.

My sophomore year also provided one healthy experience that had future influence. During most of my teens I had zigzagged from scrape to scrape, though staying away from booze and reefers (three for a buck in the high school lav), sticking to the speed limits, and save for a couple of punch-ups (in which I suffered more than the enemy), always avoiding actual breach of the peace. On a crisp October evening in 1949, I fell in with an exuberant crowd of Harvard rioters rocking trolleybuses in the square on the eve of the Princeton game. The cops knew bulk when they saw it, and I ended up in East Cambridge jail for the night—no sympathetic faculty came to bail the seventeen of us out, but then what we had done had absolutely no redeeming social importance whatever. Next morning in district court, we pleaded *nolo contendere,* the judge accepted the plea and fined us $5 apiece (he wanted to get to the game and had a large calendar of "the usual" still ahead of him). The experience was sobering. Dean Watson put me on one month's probation. Since then I have carefully avoided two or three gathered together for any purpose except one not likely to lead to rout and riot. The experience gave me one more push toward an interest in the law and the administration of justice. A high school classmate's father, Pittsburgh's first Negro judge, had urged me to go into the law even before I went to Harvard. Throughout my college years it became increasingly evident that I would work in some aspect of legal history, and this bent was confirmed by Mark DeWolfe Howe's course in the college on law as a social force (under the social science rubric) during my junior year. Even the theme content of that course, conspiracy, has figured prominently in my current work on the Star Chamber. Howe urged me to go to the law school after graduation. In later years of collaboration with him in the American Bar Foundation Anglo-American Legal History Project, he accepted with good grace my failure to follow his advice. His untimely death two years ago cost me a good friend and deprived legal history of a sterling practitioner.

My junior year tutor, Dick Lyman, had to tolerate my constant choice of Somerset to illustrate every point made in tutorials. I had gone through all the printed local records and had an unerring capacity to infuriate everyone with a choice (was it?) illustration from "a certain county." The great day came in the summer of 1951 when I took a twelve-day freighter-liner from Boston to Liverpool and set eyes on the sceptered isle for the first time. The weather held warm and sunny until we tied up in Bootle, when it reverted to stereotype. I took the train to Somerset, changing at Crewe Junction for the first (but not the last) time. One of the girls in the Somerset Record Office had found me digs, and I picked up a new bike my first day in Taunton. Ivor Collis did find me a place to type—the office was then in the basement of the mid-Victorian Shire Hall—and put at my disposal more documents in a mass of less decipherable hands than Jordan's lecture had led me to suspect possible. I couldn't read a thing. The same girl who had found me digs, Esmé Harris, came to the rescue, and patiently provided a course in paleography.

Some six weeks after arriving, the dawn of my capacity to read the stuff came bright and clear. I had an overwhelming sense of accomplishment when I finished my first quarter sessions order (1607) solo, drank Esmé's coffee-and-chicory with unaccustomed gusto, and settled down to play my harmonica for a couple of minutes. Unbeknown to me, the alderman chairman of the record committee of the County Council, Arthur W. Vivian-Neal, M.C., J.P., Esq., was passing by the window and was annoyed to hear "Road to the Isles" emanating from the office. He was mollified only when he learned from Collis that it was "the American." I was introduced to him (harmonica hidden), and he graciously invited me to tea at Poundisford Park.

Thus began a close friendship that was extraordinary by virtue of the dissimilarity of its components and the mutual affection bred between them by the agency of their similar love for Somerset and its past. From him came much of the stimulus to know Somerset. Vivian-Neal was the epitome of the scholar-gentleman. Listed in the county directory simply as "landowner," he was chairman of the local petty sessions, the appeals committee of the quarter sessions, and the record committee, stalwart of the church, chairman of both the Somerset Record Society and the Archaeological and Natural History Society. He was a last tie with the squirish antiquarianism that can be traced back to Cotton, Spelman, Dugdale, and Twisden in the seventeenth century, which had for centuries enriched English historiography and flourished in the summer of Victorianism and the autumn of Edwardian England. His Military Cross was earned on the Somme at the price of facial wounds evident until his death. A graduate of Cambridge, he had served without stipend as a curator of porcelain at the Victoria and Albert Museum before settling finally at the late-Elizabethan house at Poundisford, ten minutes from Taunton, there to "keep the port of a gentleman" (even for Americans), to do good and to fear no man (even from the Ministry of Housing and Local Government), and as a magistrate to do equal justice between rich and poor, without fear or favor. Outwardly stiff and diffident, in the great hall at Poundisford he was warm and open, graceful of expression, genteel in manner, and wholly without animus. He knew Somerset with an intimacy that was staggering. We differed on some aspects of the county's history; I bested him only once, and with good grace he admitted his error. One of his last articles, on the descent of the manor of Kingsdon from the eleventh century to 1952, was a brilliant essay in detection informed by learning and marked by a sensitivity to the meanings of landownership which easily escapes the nonlandowner.[1] From that first tea to this moment I have had to struggle to remember that Arthur Vivian-Neal was finer than the run of my JPs of Charles I's "personal rule," and that only some of his merits can I ascribe to any of his ancient predecessors on the Somerset bench.

If from Vivian-Neal came the spur to capture the *genius locii* of

Somerset, from Ivor Collis, the Somerset county archivist, came the method of historical attack characteristic of most of my work: the archival approach. The approach is simple, perhaps even simplistic. Largely without benefit of prior conceptualization, the searcher takes a *fonds* of documentation and mines it, extracting from it everything he can get. What he can get is derived not merely from content, but also from form; derived not merely from what the document says, but from what the document is. To understand what the document is, the searcher must learn what the institution that produced it was and why the institution produced it, as well as how it was produced. Whether or not dignified by the appelation "diplomatics," this kind of research puts a premium on careful analysis of documentation and sure comprehension of the relevant institution. Sampling is, almost by definition, discouraged—the searcher does not really know what he is after until he has found it, and if he makes a predetermination as to what proportion of documents he will search, he risks being haunted by the specter of having perhaps omitted those documents most pregnant to his search. Institutional-administrative history is always an adjunct and collateral derivative of this approach even when it is not the object and result of the research. The approach requires acquisition of the paleographic, language, editorial, and extrahistorical skills demanded of a transcriber-editor of a published collection of original documents. Consequently, the conscientious searcher must undertake scholarly transcription of some of his documentation and hopefully prepare it for publication according to accepted canons of transcription, editing, and introduction, and he should do this as long as he continues to use the archival approach.

There are two prerequisites for the archival approach, the absence of either of which makes the method unusable: (1) the documentation must be manageable in both quantity and quality; (2) the institutional context of the documentation must be clear. The second prerequisite is almost self-explanatory. The approach is not applicable to many types of historical research (history of ideas, substantive legal history, history of science, some aspects of economic and social history) for want of much if any institutional context at all. It is applicable in biography if the subject is conceived of in terms of an institution. Even if there is an institutional context, the institution must be already fairly well researched and its functions defined by previous scholarship if the archival approach is to prove feasible; otherwise the searcher will end up writing the administrative history of the institution—not an ignoble venture, but not necessarily the one he set himself. As for manageableness of documentation, in quantitative terms, this means no more documentation than can be reasonably dealt with in the research time allowed. The archival approach has been most successfully applied by medievalists primarily because their documentation is quantitatively sufficiently limited to be manageable.

The problem begins to arise with the documentation of the early modern period, roughly the Tudor-Stuart, in English history. Over the period 1500–1700, thorough mining of particular *fonds* tends to result in increasingly narrow subject definition or shorter chronological span. Much after 1700, the method is not really applicable to any but a narrow (and/or short in point of time) institutional study or biography. However, in my own research during the past decade, I have found that computerization, especially in providing for data retrieval, can extend the quantitative capacity of the historian using the archival approach—a point I will develop later. Yet, how much the historian can gain in quantitative manageableness by computerization depends entirely on the qualitative manageableness of his sources; that is, their relative uniformity within each *fonds*. Uniformity depends, in turn, on the degree of sophistication of the institution that produced the *fonds*. Perhaps the Tudor-Stuart historian is exceptionally lucky in that most of the institutions with which he is concerned gained in administrative sophistication commensurate with the increase in their business and, consequently, their documentation. Thus, for most Tudor-Stuart institutions, the bigger the corpus of documentation, the more uniform are the *fonds*. Measured by the rule of bureaucratic sophistication, much of the strength of Tudor strong government lay in its institutions. By the same measure, though, very little responsibility for the breakdown of Stuart government can be laid on its institutions. If those institutions failed with a vengeance in 1640, it was the executive, not the administrative element in them that collapsed.

The obvious advantages of the archival approach became very clear to me in that first summer in Taunton and its aftermath. Past-mindedness, the high degree of identification with the past that came from working intimately with manageable archives of an institution, was a great corrective to those strong present-day concerns which fired (if they did not burn) my generation in college. The evidential orientation of the method suppressed a priori assumptions, or at least kept them within bounds. I had accepted relatively unquestioningly the notions of local government organization and functioning conveyed by the books I had read and the teachers I had listened to. I remember being startled a year later when I compared my honors thesis with Jordan's lecture notes on the matter of the JPs to discover how far I was from his picture of them! Source-comprehensiveness also appeared an evident (and satisfying) virtue of historical research by the method. I really had done all that could be done with all the documentation extant on Somerset magistracy, from the beginning of the documents in 1607 to the arbitrarily chosen terminal date of James I's death. At least I thought I had, and in fact nothing more could have been done by one of my scholarly immaturity.

The grave dangers inherent in the archival approach have become evident to me only with maturity or only, perhaps, with aging! First, perfectionism: though apparently self-limiting because of the limited number of documents in any one *fonds* and the limited number of *fonds* relevant to any subject, in practice the process of increasing knowledgeableness of the *fonds* tends to impel the searcher back through them for a check of what might previously have been missed. A small misinterpretation of the nature of a *fonds* has the same effect. The searcher is stalked by the vision of the Oxford don whose scholarly life was devoted to the receipt of the Exchequer, 1272–1290, who faithfully bought his weekly cheap day-return to London during term and spent a sizable part of each vacation in the Public Record Office for forty years, only to be discovered dead in his rooms among sheaves of foolscap notes, each one more complete than the previous, the research done six times over, the writing never essayed. Second, antiquarianism: the archival approach, as it gains in past-mindedness, loses in the sense of the relevance of the historical past to the present, and the very comprehensiveness of the sources becomes a brutal enemy to the conceptualization that alone will make those sources part of a historical process. The past-facts take on a corrupting seductiveness, become Lorelei that have wrecked many a historian's intentions if not ultimately his scholarship. To the extent the archival approach discourages prior conceptualization, it makes eventual conceptualization more difficult. I have found the only way to overcome this problem is to strive constantly to relate the ongoing research to the broader historical context, and record these tentative observations either on special notes or even on the research notes themselves. Though ultimately most of the observations will be found to be either erroneous or banal, the cumulative effect of thinking constantly about the material in broader context sparks the process of conceptualization. Throughout, the searcher has to avoid confusing the vehicle with the destination; getting there can be half the fun, but if it becomes *all* the fun, one never gets anywhere. Third, officialism: the peril inherent in too-considerable involvement with the documentary vestiges of an institution is failure to overcome the innate bias of the records. The official nature and purpose of such *fonds* is integral to their creation, and they seldom if ever directly witness the dialectic of the interplay of official position and opposition to it. The opposition is at best inferentially retrievable, and this is usually not enough to counterweigh the official bias. I have been taxed, probably justifiably, with seeing the "lower orders" of Somerset too much through magistratical glasses. I have taxed Roman Catholic scholars of Roman Catholic recusancy with accepting too readily the Elizabethan official version of the nature of recusancy because they have relied too heavily on the Public Records. Of course, perfectionism and antiquarianism afflict a great many scholars who do not take the archival approach to the past. Even officialism in other guises can ruin intellectual history and biography. But the archival approach, not least because of the very narrowness of the research purview involved, tends to insulate the historian from the controversy that arises from the clash of differing conceptions of past reality until he has (hopefully) finished his labor—and then it can be too late. Who could—who would—take T. G. Barnes to task for his conclusions in "The Archives and Archival Problems of the Tudor-Stuart Star Chamber"![2]

A few days in London, some of them spent in the Public Record Office, a brief trip to Oxford with my parents (who joined me later in the summer), and an afternoon's door-knocking that got me admitted to Corpus Christi College for postgraduate work, and we sailed for home as I had come. A violent gale strewed my carefully sorted research notes all over the cabin. In the months ahead the same notes, well-sorted, became a source of anxiety and a terrible barrier to be overcome at any cost. The hundred-page honors thesis took almost nine months of collation and writing, on which I spent 4 to 5 hours every day. My senior year was passed in surfacing and sinking in one trough after another of terror. I did not know what to do with the data; I began to pay the price for no prior conceptualization. My senior-year tutor, Jacob Price, now at Michigan, pulled me out of one such trough at 3 A.M. on a winter's morn just as he returned from a research jaunt to Washington (he was finishing his Ph.D. thesis). A few choice words, a gruff reminder that others had lived through the process, and a great deal of sound advice and very specific help, and at 5 A.M. I let him get to bed. Since then, I have not begrudged students who call me at any hour of day or night for help. The final paper was better than I expected it would be. Its author had become, in the process, a better student than he expected he would be. I was almost lighthearted as I spent the summer in Pittsburgh making an incinerator to dispose of radioactive wastes for the Bureau of Mines. I was soaring as I headed for Oxford.

I wasted no time in getting digs (Corpus was too small and too full to allow postgrads to live in), and meeting with the interviewer of the Modern History Board, Professor R. B. Wernham. He looked at the honors thesis with interest, was gratified to know that I intended to do my D.Phil. on magistracy, shrievalty, and lieutenancy in Somerset, 1625–1640. With a kindness and modesty that is his wont, he asked me whether, if I had no one else I particularly wanted to work with, I might be willing to work with him, even though his own field was Elizabethan foreign affairs. I was delighted with the invitation. From that time throughout the two years I was actually living in Oxford, I met with him for two hours every Friday morning during term. His help was continuous, his encouragement constant, his friendship sustained (and sustaining). I still do not know how much of the thesis that became my first book was owed in conceptualization to him, but I suspect more than I could admit without chagrin.

Oxford was pure fun compared to Harvard. I rowed for my college and formed a college history club that expended most of its enthusiasm working on the early history of Corpus and which did some worthwhile heraldic research on the late seventeenth-century arms in the hall, restoring them to their original colors and tinctures and identifying their bearers, benefactors of the college. Cataloguing the seventeenth-century tracts collected by a former president of Corpus brought me closer to puritanism than I cared to be then or have found the necessity to be since. I went up to London regularly to eat dinners at Lincoln's Inn; I had decided to read the Bar, with no intention of practicing but only to sharpen my legal interest and provide knowledge of the present law. With the help of a young barrister (whose wife and two infant boys I had befriended on the long sea trip over), I was admitted to Lincoln's Inn that same fall. I even did some work on my thesis in Oxford.

My real research was done in the ample vacations, supplemented by a week taken off either end of every term. In Somerset I lived with the assistant archivist, Don Mirams, and his family in the country. He saw to it that I did my time in the office, and he let me out only to shoot rabbits of an evening! He, too, was a visible saint, who at a tragically young age was translated to the company of the saints above. A devout Methodist, he kept the local, aging congregation going as lay preacher; he was one of the best preachers I have heard, reflecting the love of God in a way which must have been the source of John Wesley's own power. In London, I almost lived in the Public Record Office, and there began that long association that has amounted to an aggregate of five years spent in that archive. Sydney Templeman, the young barrister, invited me to dinner the first time I met him in London. I fear I never left, and from then until long after he stood as best man at my wedding in Paris, I lived with the Templeman family. His friendship carried with it exposure to the keen mind of an equity lawyer, and I gained immeasurably from the exposure as well as from a friendship that has ripened with the passage of time.

The research for the thesis was completed by the summer of 1954, and I left Oxford to live in Wellington, Somerset, to write. I passed fourteen months in a late Victorian terrace house, built by the Quaker proprietor of the local woollen cloth mill, complete with semidetached WC. I shared the house with its owner, an elderly bachelor whom I had met in the Somerset Record Office while he was in pursuit of the local history of Wellington, and who offered me quarters at a very modest rent. The situation was ideal. I could write for 12 to 14 hours a day, taking breaks to think by wandering across the mill ponds and watching the Penzance-to-Paddington trains thunder down the long grade off the Blackdown Hills, a splendid sight at dusk, evocative of J. M. W. Turner's superb "Rain, Steam, and Speed." And daily I waited eagerly for the postman. In the fall of 1953 I had met a very demure French girl at a wild dance in a basement flat in Oxford and within a month we had decided to get married when the thesis was done.

A month later she returned to Paris. The *lien de dépendance* (Marc Bloch will forgive me for we have named our son after him) thus created drew me across the Channel the following March, despite the Francophobia which was the corollary of my still considerable Anglophilia. Paris, or at least the XXème Arrondissement, charmed me. For the next year and a half until Jeanne-Marie and I were married in Paris, I managed three weeks with her every few months, once working my way over on a Dutch coaster. I packed even tighter the small flat in which she, her mother (a widow) and her 6-foot 6-inch brother lived. All three of them worked, and I passed warm days in the parks of Paris, cold days in the flat or the Bibliothèque Nationale. A family home in a village along the Loire introduced me not only to the great châteaux of the tourists, but to the enduring *paysage* of the French. St. Laurent-des-Eaux had one claim to fame—Jeanne d'Arc slept there on her way to Orléans—two *boulangeries*, three bars, one *station-service*, and a farmer named Napoléon. Bonapartism is not dead, and our Napoléon had been a prisoner of the Boche during World War II, fortunately for the latter, for free, he would have wrought havoc among them. Great-uncle Aristide was an *ancien* of the *Guerre de '14;* during the second war, he was nicknamed "Pétain," a slur as a commentary on his politics, but also recognition of his fair skin and light blue eyes. Aristide, like so many of his generation, followed a victor into defeat less from cravenness than from the memory of defeat in victory. He gave a grandson to Algérie Française, and the old man died sorrowing in the knowledge that he never knew what happened to the young conscript.

I also visited Normandy, to meet the relatives living near Lisieux. I can never forget how familiar my first sight of William's dukedom seemed, as if I had never left England. That impression has grown in many months passed there since. I was moved, too, by the American cemetery on the cliff overlooking Omaha Beach, by the 9,385 graves, by that of the Coast Guard coxswain sprung from the black soil of

Indiana who died in the green water of the Rade du Havre on June 6, 1944. My adoption by France, which after all more than one American has experienced, opened up a new world, a new culture, a new dimension of interest and sentiment. I was lucky that it was in love that I came to France, not, like my father and so many others, in war.

As I completed chapters of the thesis, I sent them to Pittsburgh for my father and mother to read and criticize, and my mother to type. A boy's debts do not end with childhood. The writing was strenuous, for I am slow and the material was only slightly less intractable than that which had gone into the honors thesis. Finally, I was moderately satisfied with what I had done. I had set out to discover what if any relationship there was between the implementation of the "personal rule" of Charles I in the counties and the breakdown of his authority in England in 1640. I was prepared to submit, tentatively, that the failure of the institution of lieutenancy to make "perfect" the militia contributed much to the militia becoming the greatest threat to law and order in the kingdom just at the moment when it was charged to defend the kingdom. I was, also convinced that the firsthand experience of the local governors of the personal rule deeply conditioned their attitude toward the King, his ministers, and his policy when those same local governors came to sit in the Long Parliament. It seemed to me that I had mined an awful lot of archives, found out an enormous amount about local institutions and local politics, to come up with such small change in terms of conclusions.

I am now aware in retrospect that *Somerset 1625–1640: A County's Government During the Personal Rule* [3] and its offshoots were concerned with the central problem that has characterized all my work: the problem of authority, how it is established, how its functional operation affects its substance, how it dissolves, and how it is ultimately overthrown. This problem has an emotional dimension, for inevitably authority is stalked by high tragedy. Some of my cast are moved by the high tragedy of authority in Shakespeare; I have always preferred the tragedy that shadowed Elizabeth, James, and Charles to the tragedy that shadowed Lady Macbeth, Lear, and Hamlet. Such tragedy is no less moving, and it has timeless relevance in the whole dialectic of the waxing and waning of authority. If there is any predilection in my choice of subject and any bias in my handling of the dramatis personae of my history, it is a certain sympathy with those who conscientiously exercise authority, especially if they conceive of their role as that of a fiduciary trustee charged with the preservation of public authority. Hence, I intuitively identify with the judiciary, one source of my interest in legal institutions ranging from "right country justices" through judges to the Lord Chancellor and the Privy Councillors in Star Chamber. I find it hard to identify with the sovereign, in part in reflection of how unconscionably the head that wore the crown would offer up the heads of those who served the crown. I am sensitive to the dilemma of duty, not of power; for power is that which authority gives, while duty is that which authority exacts, and he in authority whose eye is fixed on power rather than duty is first corrupted and then destroyed. The dilemma of duty is the tension between the call of responsibility and the pull of sentiment, between that which one must do and that which one wishes to do. A crisis of authority at the level of the individual in authority is produced when that tension can no longer be lived with, when the pull of sentiment outweighs the call of responsibility, consciously and continuously.

A crisis of authority in the context of society is always at least protorevolutionary, and constitutes the multiplication of the individual crisis to the point of generalization among those in authority, especially those in the median ranks of authority. It is with these latter that I feel the greatest sympathy. They have the most to lose by the general crisis of authority—reputation, office, lands and goods, life itself—yet they have little real control over the direction that the exercise of their authority must take, that being determined from above only to be resisted from below. The Somerset local governors during the personal rule were of such a median rank; so, too, was the early Stuart judiciary, neither lions nor dogs nor sheep under the throne. In every crisis of authority that is surmounted without becoming a revolution, these executors of authority of median rank are the zinc plates of the governmental structure to be sacrificed in the process of social electrolysis in order that both the baser iron below and the nobler gold above will be left intact even if scarred. In every crisis of authority that does become revolutionary, these same zinc plates in their sacrifice galvanize the iron in its attack on the gold, with deadly effect.

After submitting the thesis and being examined on it in the summer of 1955, Jeanne-Marie and I were married in Paris in August. The first fortnight of our honeymoon was spent at Berchtesgaden with my parents, her mother, Sydney and Margaret Templeman—unconventional, but marvelous. After touring Italy (we will go back again to Ravenna), we sailed for the United States. Faced with the fact that I was not going to get into the Army (I had intended to be returned to England in the Provost Marshal's establishment for liaison with the English civil authorities), I was relieved that Lycoming College, in Williamsport, Pennsylvania, hired me. Lycoming is a Methodist college, and the president was a young ex-district superintendent who has since become a bishop. I was much beset by the dilemma of duty, especially when it came to my Frenchified drinking habits, and at one juncture this blew up into quite a row. I was not fired, and my sneaking affection for the president was only temporarily dented, my affection for the college not at all. We spent five tremendously happy years at Lycoming, productive in scholarship and teaching experience (Western Civ, U.S. survey, American government, International relations, and even English history). My immediate superior, Loring Priest, became a dear friend, and I have tried to pattern myself on him in his love for the institution in which one teaches. We have him to thank almost for survival itself during the year 1958–1959 when we spent fifteen months in London to launch Star Chamber—on $2,000 savings, $900 from the American Academy of Arts and Sciences, and a generous personal gift from Loring that came just in time to buy coal as our fires were dying and our spirits with them.

It was at Lycoming that I not only finished the revision of the thesis for a book, but also wrote the essay that won the Alexander Prize of the Royal Historical Society for 1958.[4] In fact, most of the essay was written in two nights at the AHA meeting in New York in 1957. And it was written in anger. With the exception of one or two friends, I was shunned by most of my peer group at the meeting; after all, Lycoming was no place, Q.E.D., I was nothing. My wrath was vented in a burst of energy that enabled me virtually to complete the essay before returning home. Having since had the luck to land "some place," I find no lack of company at AHA meetings—when I go, for I find our "professional conference" distasteful in all those many aspects that touch neither friendship nor scholarship.

I decided in 1956 that except for tidying up loose ends and completing a few lines opened up in the thesis, though not run down, that I would do no more work in local government. Star Chamber had intruded itself on my consciousness as it had on that of my JPs. Though I was not prepared to say that quarter sessions resembled the Privy Council, I was not prepared to deny that the Privy Council rather resembled a county quarter sessions writ large! Thirteen years, 10,000 cases, a roomful of notes, and 60,000 IBM cards later, I know that the Privy Council in Star Chamber *was* a quarter sessions, not always writ very large. Anyway, in 1956 the High Court of Star Chamber was virgin chase for an archival historian. A few theses in the late 1930s had barely scratched the surface, and their authors were all busy in other pursuits. I knew there was a spring gun set up somewhere on the pre-1558 ground, and that if I tripped it, Geoffrey Elton would give the body a decent though curt burial. My experience, knowledge, and sense of priorities all indicated that the last half-century or so of the court might be the best place to start. Thirteen years, etc., later, I have decided that it will be a grand place to end, too.

I conceived at the outset that Star Chamber would have to be studied as (1) a court of law, (2) an administrative instrument acting as the judicial arm of the Privy Council, and (3) the "notorious seat of Stuart despotism" of Whiggish ill-repute. As I have toiled through my mine, not least the extant Star Chamber proceedings in the PRO, I have begun to suspect that (2) is largely a mirage, (3) a highly important complicating factor, a reputation to be contended with rather than a fact to be perceived, in searching for the true nature of the court, which is (1). Officialism, of course, rears its head—the records of Star Chamber really are judicial records. Yet allowing for that fact, those who began to attack Star Chamber—very late in its history, for it really succumbed to the first major attack, raised in the first session of the Long Parliament—had to contend with it as a court of law and a peculiar jurisdiction for which no substitute could be readily found, though one was desperately needed. In the event, Parliament itself took over Star Chamber's extraordinary criminal jurisdiction for a season, the regular criminal courts its ordinary criminal jurisdiction, and the Chancery its preponderant civil function. If the Whig interpretation of why Star Chamber was killed is largely correct (and I think it is insofar as the contemporary notorious image of the court was a political fact), one still remarks that it was not distaste for what was done by the court but distaste for who did it to whom that brought Star Chamber down. In the meantime, it had for the last half-century of its life played a major, perhaps even preeminent, role in English civil litigation in an era when litigation was both a common business practice and a social phenomenon, carved out and modeled at least a half-dozen highly sophisticated crimes which remain today the legal frame of public order in the modern industrial state, and contributed more than any other single court to the early development of sensitivity to legal evidence and of precedent in judicial decision-making. These consequences have assumed more importance to me than the concerns with which I began.[5] They have also required an immense amount of work, more then I had contemplated with my sights narrowed principally to Star Chamber as a court of law.

My salvation has been the computer. In 1962, with the encouragement of my colleague, Larry Harper, I began forming a corpus of case cards that could be used for the retrieval of all data that I had on Star Chamber and also, in the case of specific *fonds* of Star Chamber records, for some statistical analysis. Card type 1 is the rendering of all information of a uniform nature obtainable from the Star Chamber Proceedings in the PRO; type 2, all fines estreated from the court found in Exchequer records in the PRO; type 3, orders and decrees of the court (few and scattered); type 4, reports of cases in Star Chamber (many and scattered). A number of ancillary types have been produced as well as these main types, one of the most valuable being that of the names of counsel in the court's litigation. Type 2, with nearly 4,000 parties fined, the fines ranging from 10s. to £70,000, the social status and residence of most of those fined, and by correlation the cases in which they were involved and the crimes of which they were convicted, allows for correlative analysis of crime/status/region/date. Ultimately, all cards will be distinguished by an arbitrarily assigned case number (based on type 1), so that all the materials relevant to any case will be produced together by the computer. Thus the court's litigation can be studied in detail by ready data retrieval of all the cases (some 16,000 for the period 1596–1641). As well, particular categories and subcategories of information—crimes, property involved, region, social status, procedural developments, fines, other punishment, counsel, etc.—can be retrieved, over 900 in all. The preparation of this case card corpus has taken time and been expensive, but the results have proved valuable, and I have applied the same method to the preparation of Chancery materials under the auspices of the American Bar Foundation Anglo-American Legal History Project, which I direct.

The use of the computer does not relieve me of the essentially literary function of the historian. Neither does it enable me to produce a finished study of Star Chamber from Egerton's accession as Lord Keeper (1596) to the court's abolition (1641) sooner than would have been the case without it. In fact, the computer has added at least three years to the process of writing the book. But what the book will have gained will be completeness and comprehensiveness, for without the computer large quantities of data would have been only partially (even perfunctorily) analyzed, and some of the data would have eluded analysis entirely. The computer has actually made more thorough the mining operation of the archival approach by affording both a better sifting and the handling of more raw data—to use an analogy very ready to hand on the edge of the great California gold fields of the past, the computer is to 3 × 5 cards what hydraulic mining was to panning for gold. I get not only the nuggets but the gold dust too. This refining of the historian's research process will be reflected in the final work when I mold the material into a conceptual whole.

At this moment, the molding process seems very far away. Some of this can be laid to the research I have yet to do, for there are still proceedings in the PRO to be mined. Moreover, with others at Berkeley, I lost two years in the commotion of the Free Speech Movement and its aftermath, 1964–1966. As a temporary Assistant Dean of Students in the fall of 1964, I landed in the midst of it all. The dilemma of duty was very potently felt at first, but evaporated in the face of growing disruption of the university as an intellectual forum in pursuit of the university as a political arena. What was gained in the experience was real insight into the process of revolution—my Tudor-Stuart lecture course has gained immeasurably by having passed through a revolution, not least by the instructor having found himself in a position, though not a role, not dissimilar to that of Edward Hyde. Exposure to revolution serves also to turn the scholar back to his books, for the frenzied excitation of a season cannot be sustained over a lifetime. Succeeding crises (yesterday afternoon the campus was blanketed with tear gas and a full-scale battle raged between a thousand insurrectionists and half as many police, with a hundred casualties) leave one unmoved and largely uninvolved. The interminable talk, the glut of writing, the hyperbole, rhetoric, incitement, resolutions, rallies, the constant positioning and unpositioning go on, but others do it. My own position is clear, respectful of authority, unpopular, and largely isolated. Save for occasional unrestrained sallies in faculty meetings on the side of restraint (the paradox surprises none of my colleagues), I do my work. This is hard for a political animal, but what else can be done all alone?

I am anxious to finish Star Chamber because there are other things I want to do. During the past few years, my legal history course in the Law School has opened up a new line of investigation, the development of real property settlement, 1580–1700. In a paper on Lawrence Stone's *Crisis of the Aristocracy* at a recent AHA meeting, I suggested that the aristocracy solved its financial "crisis" of the last decades of the sixteenth century not only by economic methods to increase rents, but by evolving legal devices which subtly though effectually changed the nature of both proprietorship and the landed estate. By settlement, the landed estate became a managerially dominated organism for the production of profit through rent to be preserved inviolable by the landlord, in whom it was vested almost as a corporation sole. The political implications of such a development are intriguing, for if in fact settlement arrived in the early seventeenth century (rather than the late seventeenth century), then the "Whig aristocracy" arrived well before Whiggism. All this is very tentative. I have a few hundred deed boxes and a few thousand feet of fines, enrollments of deeds, etc., to go through before I should say more. I mean to be true to my system: "Largely without benefit of prior conceptualization. . . ."

I almost titled this essay "Anglophilia Is Not Enough." It is not, indeed, and Anglophilia is no longer a compelling force in my motivation. When Star Chamber is done, I will even desert (for a time) my beloved Public Record Office for a stint in the Archives Nationales, to do a little comparative study of conciliar justice in England and France, 1590–1640. Over the years the conviction has grown that the historian is at most the sum of his experiences. The writing of history is always an essay in experience, and therefore the history of oneself as much as a history of the discrete object of the study. My Pennsylvania

National Guard experience might have been no less distorting of my picture of Somerset's militia than Gibbon's Hampshire militia experience was of his picture of Rome's legions, but both experiences were essential to the historians. Carpentry, ocean cruising and fishing, Normandy, politics, deanship, the church, one's students, one's friends, one's parents, one's children (the quick and the dead), Jeanne-Marie, one's past, one's present, and one's sure and certain hope of the future are the compound of which I am made. My history is made of the same stuff.

NOTES

1. A. W. Vivian-Neal, "Illustrations of the Manorial System Drawn from the History of Kingsdon," *Somerset Archaeological and Natural History Society Proceedings*, CIII (1958–59), 22–71.
2. T. G. Barnes, "The Archives and Archival Problems of the Tudor-Stuart Star Chamber," *Journal of the Society of Archivists*, II (October 1963), 345–60.
3. T. G. Barnes, *Somerset 1625–1640: A County's Government During the Personal Rule* (Cambridge, Mass., 1961); *Somerset Assize Orders, 1629–1640*, Somerset Record Society, LXV (1959); *The Clerk of the Peace in Caroline Somerset* (Leicester, 1961).
4. T. G. Barnes, "County Politics and a Puritan Cause Célèbre: Somerset Churchales, 1633," *Transactions of the Royal Historical Society*, 5th series, IX (1959), 103–22.
5. T. G. Barnes, "Star Chamber Mythology," *American Journal of Legal History*, 5 (1961), 1–11; "Due Process and Slow Process in the Late Elizabethan–Early Stuart Star Chamber," *ibid.*, 6 (1962), 221–49, 315–46.

Working
on
Ideas in Time

J. G. A. POCOCK

J. G. A. POCOCK was born on March 7, 1924, in London, England. After earning his M.A. at Canterbury University College, University of New Zealand (formerly Canterbury College) in 1945, he proceeded to take a Ph.D. at Cambridge University in 1952. From 1953 to 1955 he was Lecturer in History at the University of Otago in New Zealand. He returned to Cambridge as a Research Fellow of St. John's College from 1956 to 1958. In 1959 he began developing the Department of Political Science at the University of Canterbury, New Zealand, and served as chairman between 1963 and 1965. Since then, Pocock has been Professor of History and Political Science at Washington University, St. Louis.

Among the professional organizations to which he belongs are the American Historical Association, the American Political Science Association, the Conference for the Study of Political Thought, the Conference on British Studies, and the Cambridge History Society. In 1968–1969 he was a Senior Fellow of the American Council of Learned Societies, and in 1969 he spent eight months at Cambridge University as Overseas Fellow of Churchill College.

Author of *The Ancient Constitution and the Feudal Law* (Cambridge, Eng., 1957), Pocock has published numerous articles on English and European political thought, including "Burke and the Ancient Constitution: A Problem in the History of Ideas," *The Historical Journal*, III (1960), "Machiavelli, Harrington, and English Political Ideologies in the Eighteenth Century," *William and Mary Quarterly*, 3rd series, XXII (1965), and "The Role of Civic Humanism in Anglo-American Political Thought, 1500–1850," *Il Pensiero Politico*, I, 2 (1969).

Pocock is presently working on an edition of the works of James Harrington, to be published by the Cambridge University Press, as well as the study of Machiavelli and other Florentine thinkers about temporal instability in politics. He is shortly publishing a collection of essays entitled *Politics, Language and Time* (Atheneum).

I t is easier to describe a style than to isolate and examine a specific piece of work in it. If the historian's life is a continuity, it must consist of the constant shaping of a pattern of thinking and enquiring, and this is especially true when his work involves, as mine does, a high concentration of theory. But to describe either the growth of a personal style, or moments in such a growth, cannot be done without yielding in some degree to the seductions of autobiography. The only justification I can claim for this is that my work has proved, somewhat against my will and certainly to my surprise, formally historicist. For over twenty years I have been increasingly interested in the ways in which men in political societies find and explore languages for conceptualizing their lives in such structures, and in the ways in which these languages carry patterns of thought about the continuity of society and politics in time and in history.

I see that this interest has since its beginnings been intimately related to a sense of my own position first between two cultures and then vis-à-vis a third—those of New Zealand, Britain and America— each with its own distinctive sense of a past, and between two academic disciplines, history and political science, each with its way of looking at the generation of ideas by men in society. A possible formula would be: I locate others in social time—this is history; I study how others located themselves in time—the study of historiography; this is related to the way in which I locate myself in time—the element of historicism. Yet this might mislead. I have always rather disliked historicism in the sense of the romantic self-creation of an identity in the historical flux because of its irrational and illiberal potentialities, and have tried to practice it only in the sense of a self-disciplined criticism of the historically given. In current intellectual fashion, it is considered both false and reactionary to assert that one can locate oneself in time by formal academic enquiry; but Apollo is alive and living closer to his brother Dionysus than the maenads of California and New York imagine. What I wish to present, therefore, is far from being the record of another boring struggle for identity. I cannot offer any account of my work which is not an account of the long-term working out of a partly personal perspective; but the proportion between ego and cosmos has to be a proportion, and the perspective I aim to describe originates not merely in a personal and cultural problem, but in the need to practice certain self-testing intellectual disciplines. It is with the academic respectability of what I am doing that the readers of this book should be concerned.

The late Sir James Hight, under whom I studied in 1942, was a figure deserving and receiving veneration in what was then Canterbury University College in the University of New Zealand and is now (as he always held it should be) the University of Canterbury. He was not a very original teacher, but some indefinable grace of personality made it impossible to be in his presence for five minutes without knowing what scholarship was. Among his more easily identifiable achievements was the introduction, among the offerings of the department of history which he headed with one assistant, of two courses in a subject known as political science. This statement is intended to exert a certain exotic charm upon American readers, but at the same time it has some functional importance: many of the themes I wish to treat contain the idea of the traversing of wide distances, both between cultures and between disciplines, and the successful establishment of homes and settlements upon distant shores. The two courses in political science— it fell to me in after years to enlarge, not to say explode, this syllabus into a full-scale departmental offering—each lasting for an academic year, consisted of a general survey of some notable contemporary governments (fewer in those days) and a historical survey of political philosophy of the kind still prescribed in many famous universities and wearily termed "Plato to Nato" by my friends at Cambridge to this day. *In illo tempore* it consisted to all intents and purposes of a reading of the classic work of G. H. Sabine.[1]

Today, I find myself rather strongly committed to the view that Sabine's book is obsolete. His *History of Political Theory* does not seem to me to be a history at all, in the sense that it is not the history of any isolable and continuous human activity. And as a corollary, I insist, in both writing and teaching, that it is not possible to write any piece of the history of political thinking by his method of chronologically arranging philosophical systems. Nevertheless, I always urge students to read him; his book is a great American classic, an ideal among survey histories; and I see no reason why a beginner even today should not get from him the sudden sense of discovery which I had during a course of evening lectures in 1943. I spent much of my time filling a large exercise book with a conflation of Hight's lecture notes and Sabine's survey, and as I wrote on and on, I had the sensation, still recoverable, of growing into something, like a snake feeling its new skin. I was, I suppose, discovering the tradition which it was to be my business to criticize; but the stages by which I discovered the need for such criticism and the techniques of it, like so many of the crucial moments in intellectual autobiography, evade recall. In that year, however, I can say that I acquired an enduring sympathy for the phenomenon of political discourse itself, for the intellect's attempt to construct an intelligible world out of the materials of political experience. But though my approach to the study of politics has remained a humanist one, and I select for study that aspect of politics in which it can be seen as an agent transforming human consciousness, a curious fact is that I have never seen the activities of the politicized consciousness primarily as the construction of a world view, or become more than an amateur of political philosophy. What I suspect to be an incorrigibly rhetorical and verbal cast of mind has made me adhere to middle high politics, to those upper levels of political discourse where are generated many intellectual activities in addition to philosophy proper.

Four or five years later, when I was preparing to leave Canterbury to pursue a research degree at Cambridge, I had an honors degree in history and had taught it for over two years. I do not remember teaching much political thought during that time, yet when I sat down to propose a thesis subject in a letter from New Zealand to the Board of Research Studies—the Cambridge Ph.D., it should be explained, is awarded on a thesis only, and you are admitted to study largely on the strength of the thesis proposal you submit—it did not occur to me to propose one outside the history of thought. There are those for whom this is an independent subdiscipline—not long ago a publisher's representative tried in vain to sell me a new survey volume in intellectual history—but this had not figured in my work at Canterbury. I knew well enough that much in the history of political thought passed by the name of philosophy, but I had never taken a course in that subject, though I might have listened to the teaching of A. N. Prior if I had. During my honors year, I had listened with fascination to the lectures which Karl Popper, who passed the war years at Canterbury, was then developing into *The Open Society and Its Enemies;* but while these constituted a major intellectual experience, it was to be years before I saw the relevance of Popper's teaching to my own work. What I heard then seemed to me—as it was meant to—an account of disciplined enquiry which one need not be a philosopher to follow, and as for its stimulating my concern with intellectual history, I could see well enough that Popper's thought was inadequate history even if it was superb philosophy of method. If I search for other reasons why the direction of my interests was already irreversible, one other circumstance comes to mind that is relevant to what I am trying to say.

Imaginative writing in New Zealand, during the late thirties and forties, was not only more alive than it had ever been before, but a good deal more to my taste than it has ever been since. The poets and critics of the day (Allen Curnow, Rex Fairburn, Denis Glover), though they regarded themselves as a hard-drinking crew of iconoclasts, appear in retrospect somewhat Georgian, perhaps because an education at the fag-end of a transplanted English style—which I shared—had given them a concern with literary tradition and its relation to the environment that subsequent educational democratization has led many to insist presents no problem at all. Theirs was a pastoral landscape, its soil eroded by too many real sheep; and they explored the theme of the creative imagination confronting a land where human occupancy was not more than a thousand years old and English civilization with its books not more than a hundred. "The land was ours before we were the land's" tended to become a statement in the present tense, and it was possible to make distinctions among the imagination of South Pacific islanders like ourselves and those of the English, fed by a sense of tradition even when quarreling with it, the Americans, for whom settlement in a new land went with a series of revolutionary transformations and compulsive commitments, or even the Australians, with whom a populist nationalism maintained a mythology of the Outback which we did not share. New Zealand culture seemed sure to remain oceanic, transitory, looking obliquely toward its derivations, and the problem was that of making some sort of harmony and vitality for oneself in these conditions. History and myth, which we were told to consider necessities, were, irrevocably, other people's; we were not going to generate much of our own, and the fact of poetry was there to remind us that the creative imagination existed and must find ways of working.

The poetry written in this style is still very much in my bones, and since it clearly presented the problem of the historical imagination in an unhistoric land, I suspect that it had a good deal to do with shaping the interests I describe. When about this time I read Toynbee, I recall writing a juvenile essay in which I employed *yang* and *yin* to denote, respectively, the historical and poetic imagination—it is a curious fact that most of those who have written histories of New Zealand have also written poetry, though I have done neither—and the unhistoric landscape, neither humanized by cultivation nor devastated by extraction, which the plains and mountains of the South Island imprinted on the eye. A year or two later I was to find the intensely humanized landscape of southern England actually oppressive; I wanted to get back to the shingle rivers; and yet *yang*, if my construction had any meaning, was giving me an enduring interest in the intellectual, imaginative, and mythical presentations of history which were other people's. There was a solution to be found in eclecticism, if the methods of selection and study could be made strong enough to build on.

When, at any rate, I considered what to propose as a Cambridge dissertation, all that occurred to me had to do with the mythical element in historical thought. I was rash enough to toy with the notion of studying myth in the philosophy of Marx, but by great good fortune, and as the result of thought processes of which I can remember nothing at all, suggested instead that I should write about anti-Normanism in the thought of the English Levellers. I heard that I had been accepted and that Herbert Butterfield was to be my supervisor; I wrote to him from Canterbury, and he replied that a good deal had been done on anti-Normanism, but that there were some interesting manifestations of rather similar thought of a conservative and royalist kind from the seventeenth century. He thought I might be interested in studying them.

The work I then began to do was ultimately published under the title of *The Ancient Constitution and the Feudal Law*.[2] It is further described as "a study of English historical thought in the seventeenth century," but I find it important to stress that "historical thought" is not the same thing as "historiography." One of the book's heroes, Robert Brady, seems to have sensed this when he observed in the preface to his *An Introduction to the Old English History*, "Histories I know are written after another manner." He meant to differentiate between his critical and interpretative (and political and polemical) writings and the construction of formal written narratives, and though this distinction can no longer be upheld, it has been a central theme of my work that the beginnings and growth of historical consciousness are often to be found not in the writings of works formally entitled "histories," but in the modes of thought which entail an image of a past and its relation to the present.

On one level, it can be said that the work I have been doing ever since has been directed at discovering how these conceptualized "pasts" arise, and how thought about their relationship to the present attains a degree of critical autonomy which makes it what we call "history." I indeed think that Western historical consciousness has developed through the increase of this kind of critical ability, at least as much as through the formulation of Augustinian or Hegelian philosophies of history. But there are other levels. One of the most important thought modes through which images of the past and its relation to the present arise and are criticized is thought directed at political legitimation. The sources of authority in a political society may be located in the past, or they may be said to consist in its continuity. In either case, there is a sense of institutional structure and its transmission through time; in the course of political argument, argument concerning what is legitimate and what are the sources of legitimacy, there can arise a critical reconstruction so drastic that the past is discovered to have existed in its own right and not as a mere extension of the authority structure of the present. This, as Butterfield had pointed out before I began work, had happened in seventeenth-century England; and at one time I thought of calling my book, in a pastiche of the seventeenth-century manner, *Historico-politicus Anglicanus*.

In other words, I was still engaged in the study of political thought, of which historical thought might be a branch and historical consciousness a product; but this raised the further question of what is political thought? In the mode I was studying, it was neither political theory nor political philosophy, though it might be immanent in both; and what I was able to learn about the concept of ideology seemed to me no more accurate as a description of its character. Though I doubt if I knew it at this period, I was in need of new concepts and theories for defining the phenomena which occurred, the activity which went on, when men in political societies engaged in systematic discourse and debate about political society as they knew it and as part of their life in it. I was on the way to formulating such concepts when I realized, as I increasingly did, that the mode of thought with which I was mainly concerned could be characterized as a rhetoric, a universe of discourse, a language. Englishmen of the seventeenth century were litigious animals; they spent much time in the courts of common law, which regulated their property system, their social structure, and its distribution of power. They consequently spoke of all these things—and in speaking, identified and administered them—in the language of the common law. This language was more than a regulative terminology; it was heavy with assumptions, and these were applied, both consciously and unconsciously, to the social and political complex about which it was used. The central assumption was that law was custom, and custom immemorial; the social and political complex was therefore assumed to be immemorial in the same way and on the same grounds. In this way arose the concept and myth of the ancient constitution, against which the most original scholars of the seventeenth century developed their energetic criticisms. At a later date I was able to identify this language, and the consequences of using it, in the works of Edmund Burke; not only did it play a cardinal role in the formulation of some of Burke's most important thoughts, but Burke himself could be seen explicitly alluding to the existence of the common-law language of politics as a fact in the making of English history.

What I was coming to see was that the history of political ideas, the history of political thought considered as an activity, could very conveniently be treated as the history of political language or languages. Various conceptual vocabularies, styles of discourse or modes of thought exist, in varying degrees of formalization, in the structure of a political society. They are used by the inhabitants of that society to articulate the various utterances—the emphasis here is on the more highly formalized types of utterance—to which men are moved in the course of political life. These languages originate in various ways—the common-law language is a case of one formed out of the specialized vocabulary of a governing institution—and their content varies both explicitly and implicitly. It can be shown that any political language carries assumptions and implications in excess of those which can be made articulate at any one moment, and a significant part of what we call political theory consists less in attempts to erect a consistent theory of politics than in attempts to follow up and explore the implications which, under the stress of political debate, action, and choice, the language articulating a society to itself has been seen to possess. These implications may carry the mind, and specialize its workings, in many directions. The common-law language was particularly rich in implications suggesting the past of society, and clearly not all political languages will carry implications of that sort; but it also carried implications concerning the nature and limits of political action and knowledge; and it is remarkable how often political languages carry such implications, suggesting also, as these did, ideas concerning time as the dimension or continuum of action and knowledge.

My style of work, then, is one in which I identify languages of political conceptualization, select patterns of implication which they may bear, and try to trace the working out of these implications in the history of thought. It requires both historical sensitivity and sensitivity to patterns of political behavior—conceptualization, argument, and theorizing all being forms of political behavior of a rather special sort. But since the root concept of the whole proceeding as I have experienced and described its growth is that of language, it requires above all a sensitivity to language of a kind which links it to the criticism of literature on one flank, as its political character links it to sociology on the other. The beginnings of my interest in these matters, as I have attempted to depict them in the foregoing autobiographical case study —the reading of Sabine and so on—lay, it seems, in a high sensibility to language as the bearer of thought which stopped short of becoming an interest in the formalization of thought that might have made a philosopher of me.

Historians, I think with Hexter, are and should be rhetoricians rather than logicians. Needless to say, rhetoricians have to be logical. I have been helped as a historian, whatever it might have done to me as a philosopher, by exposure to that school of the fifties which held that philosophy could be no more than a working out of the possibilities of language. This, and the teachings of Popper concerning the logic of enquiry, have counterpointed, in a way perhaps confused, but to me fruitful, an earlier enthusiasm for the writings of R. G. Collingwood. It will be recalled that Collingwood was understood to say that all history was the history of thought and that the aim of the historian was to rethink the thoughts of the men he was studying. Plainly, this is easier to accept when the history one is studying *is* the history of thought as an overt and formal activity, and I am certain that a Collingwoodian adolescence helped me greatly later on in formulating the idea of effecting reentry into the linguistic universes of the past. But at the same time I was always fully aware that total recall was beyond the historian's powers, and that he "rethought" the ideas of men in the past by erecting an explanatory structure through which he could restate them in a language of his own designed to reconstruct, and in that sense to clarify, the language in which they had been stated. Popper, stressing that every scientific hypothesis entailed a statement of the conditions of its own validity, and T. D. Weldon, proclaiming that the business of the philosopher was to make statements about statements, in various ways assisted the formulation of the idea that the historian of thought aimed at finding out what had been said and restating it in language which defined the language in which it had been said. But I divert attention from the logical structure of the original statement to its rhetorical and sociolinguistic context, as I think any historian must do. That context—the linguistic universe—has to be reconstructed historically; and if any language structure consists of an indefinite number of possible meanings, implications, and consequences, of which no speaker at a given moment can be fully aware, the historian has an alarming degree of liberty as to the direction in which he will pursue the possible meanings and consequences of what the speaker said. He must not only reconstruct; he must select and assume.

At another level, I was aided throughout by the fact that as a student I had been enormously interested in acting—though happily never good enough to fail at it—and had thought a great deal about doctrines of the mask and the anti-self. The actor constructs, out of and at some distance from his own personality and that of Shakespeare's Hamlet, a Hamlet through whom he mediates and communicates between Shakespeare and his audience, while remaining himself an indestructibly original contributor to the communication. Since those days, of course, the theatre, like so much else, has gone in for the abolition of individuality, but this is a tedious if necessary interlude through which we must make our way. Apollo and Dionysus are both gods of the theatre, and the Apollonian view of acting, which I learned, has left me with an ineradicable conviction that historical reconstruction is possible through masklike structures of explanation which communicate as they conventionalize, as well as with an absolute refusal of philosophies which aver that communication is impossible and the self nonexistent. Even a bad actor knows better than that. He knows that his distinctness from the work he creates is what relates him to it, so that the cruder forms of alienation have little meaning for him; and this has considerable relevance to what goes on in the "workshop" of the kind of historian I am describing.

The historian of theory spends his time absorbing other people's theoretical language and reproducing it in a language of his own designed to reveal its historical character. The historical events he studies are events in the history of conceptualization. His characteristic workshop activity, then, is reading, thinking, and writing aimed at carrying himself and his readers back from the concept as articulated to the process of conceptualization, and at finding out what it was that happened, what events in human consciousness occurred, when and as conceptualization and articulation took place. There are not many ancillary skills to this, and their role, while at any time it may prove important, is not constant or continuous. For this reason, such a historian will not surround himself with apparatus. He needs, of course, access to the best library he can find, since the keys to what he is looking for may often be found in writings so obscure that even he has come upon them by accident (he will probably prefer open stacks to the best system of information retrieval that can be designed); but he may well end by basing his pattern of explanation on a quite limited selection of sources, and—if he knows how to do it properly—he may do no more with these sources than sit and read, sit and think, sit and write.

In the very complex process of combining abstractions so that they become a recognizable account of the process of abstraction as occurring in historic reality, it is above all the historian's use of his own language that must keep the relations between abstraction and reality clearly visible, and his account of these relations a piece of history. For this reason, the task of learning to think in this way draws very close indeed to the task of learning to write; it is in the construction of sustained explanatory prose that the Collingwoodian process of rethinking takes place. Historians, especially in America, are traditionally supposed to surround themselves with stacks and files of note cards, but I do not think I have ever used one. Instead, I read—books, microfilms, manuscripts or whatever—and as I read, I try to digest what I read into the constantly growing and changing patterns of re-presentation and explanation which I have to develop and expound. Pieces of detective work aimed at finding out who wrote it and when, or whether there was an earlier version, sometimes come my way, but they are ancillary tasks; the individuals of my story are paradigms rather than people, concepts whose changing use is best traced by constructing models of long-term change. Theory is prior to narrative —or rather, there is a constant process of devising, using, and improving such models of change that takes place in the sustained refinement of the inner rhetoric of one's teaching, writing, and thinking. This is another reason why it would be virtually impossible to write the history of an isolated piece of work from start to finish; each of them is a thread in a constantly reworked pattern.

A lesson I had to learn early—the earlier one learns it the better— was that much of the process of digestion and rearrangement of ideas,

alteration and sharpening of perspectives, takes place in the supposedly irrational subconscious. The circuits of the brain must learn to
carry great stores of highly verbalized and conceptualized information,
which can be recovered—and recovered, so to speak, with the right one
of a thousand facets uppermost—at a moment's notice. I sometimes,
though not often, spend weeks translating, or simply transcribing,
passages of an important book which is not in my permanent possession. To perturbed enquirers who want to know why I am not making
photocopies instead, I reply that I am getting the structure and movement of the book's argument into my bones, and that this is not a
process which can be mechanized. What matters is not simply what the
brain does with the information after it has been loaded into it, but the
shape in which the information is processed while it is being loaded;
and my apparently antiquated procedure may at times be the most
efficient way of processing information while on the in-channels.

"Processing the verbiage *in situ,*" as the Archfiend Belphegor calls
it in Michael Ayrton's splendid *Tittivulus,* renders the pattern of my
working life at once simple and complex. When I feel ready to begin
interpreting an author, a controversy or the history of a cluster of
modes of thought, I sit down with an untidy sufficiency of books and
notes, the beginnings of an expository pattern in my brain, and begin
writing. Like most writers, I have a number of physical fads: the paper
must be soft, the ink blue and the nib metal—I cannot construct
decent prose on a typewriter, and there has come to be an association
in my mind between the unwinding of a skein of thought and the long,
essentially unbroken, looped and twisted line of regular cursive handwriting. I must cast about once or twice for a suitable rhetorical
exordium, and then the patterns will begin to develop as the sentences
and paragraphs take shape.

This means that the units of thought, if such a term has any
meaning, are lengthy passages of expository prose. One does not—at
least I do not—revise one's written argument as one goes along, clause
by clause or sentence by sentence, filling the page with emendations
and refinements. If the work is going well, the prose comes of itself. I
go on writing until my argument seems to have lost its way or run out
of steam; to say that I know when this has happened because the pen
falls from my nerveless hand would be to exaggerate, but a strong
physical disinclination to go on writing is one of the symptoms. I now
go back to the last point at which the argument seems to me to have
been running authoritatively, and begin again from the top of that page
of the manuscript, throwing away several (sometimes many) sheets of
clearly written, carefully composed, uncorrected handwriting—to the
dismay of my wife if she happens to see them in the wastepaper
basket. If I do this several times and am still bogged down in the same

section of the argument, I am aware that there is something wrong at a level deeper than I had realized.

I was years learning to master this syndrome—it is much more that than a technique. When I wrote my first article for a professional journal, I sat every day for eight weeks in my room in a council house in an unpleasant place in the north of England, surrounded by a growing pile of discarded manuscript, none of which I dared throw away, and wondering in all seriousness whether I was heading for a nervous breakdown. I think people have suffered worse than breakdown in similar circumstances. The terrifying element in such an experience is not that you suddenly become aware that you are writing nonsense. Your prose and your thought seem as clear and as close-textured as they did before, you cannot find a logical flaw in what you have written, and yet the effort to continue creating what is, after all, an impersonal extension of your self becomes more and more intolerable until you physically cannot go on. *Es geht nicht.* If you try again and again, and each time reach the same point of self-exhausting clarity about the same stage in your argument, the experience is much more frightening than mere bewilderment or confusion can ever be. It is the contrast between the apparent clarity of your thought and its exhaustion and failure that is intolerable, and here you must—like a mystic whose meditation has gone wrong—break off altogether, and resist the first impulse to start again. I am convinced, though I cannot prove it, that scholars have driven themselves to suicide by going back for one more try at a recalcitrant piece of writing.

Once you have learned to break off and go away from the work for hours or days or longer, the unconscious processes of digestion, aided a little by carefully-timed thrusts and pressures from the conscious levels, may be left to do the rearrangement of your thoughts for you. I use the word rearrangement, though it is rather a weak term for what goes on, to indicate that it is a new pattern which is needed and must be allowed—and trusted—to emerge. There is an awareness of sudden release—accompanied sometimes, in my experience, by a physical sensation that the locus of tension has shifted from the forehead to the diaphragm—which signals the return of creativity and a strong and confident impulse to begin writing again. At this point it will usually be found that the concepts and data have rearranged themselves to form a pattern with the potential for growth in it that was lacking before. Sometimes one discovers that what was at the end should have been at the beginning, or vice versa. The order of analysis is not the order of exposition, but the transformation from thought that was clear but sterile to thought that is concrete and fertile is more radical than the foregoing words indicate. I can only compare it to the transition from negative to positive in photographic development. Each image is as clear as the other, but only one inhabits the same daylight as yourself. And this is also the moment—to resume the Collingwoodian exposition —at which another man's thought has become your own, and you have begun to expound it in a way which constitutes historical interpretation. You are both identified with and detached from it. There is a *paradoxe sur le comédien* to be used in understanding historiography, and the actor in a university theatre has not been useless to the historian of political thought.

The workshop I have described is, defiantly, that of a latter-day scribe: a man, that is, employing highly sophisticated scribal techniques to interpret the thought of men who lived and wrote in early Gutenberg cultures. I do not work on ideas or writers before 1500 or after 1800, though these limitations are in part accidental and do not seem to me rigorously dictated by my techniques. It may well be, however, that these methods would be less appropriate to study of the thought of men who were not primarily writers of books. I do not claim to know the inwardness—the almost tactile reality—of the thought revealed in newspaper editorials or the televisual techniques of African demagogues, and my friends who ask me why I do not conduct content analyses with the aid of computers may well be making a point of substance with regard to these or other structures of verbal communication.

If I can think only as I write, it is possible that I can only deal adequately with the thought of men for whom the same was true. But this would not matter very much. The Gutenberg era was a great era in the history of human thought, and in any but a totally barbarized future we shall constantly be going back to it, in search not merely of its thought patterns, but of its structures of individuality. And to study it as it was is a mode of being valid for the electronic here and now; the inhabitant of my workshop is no Luddite. The fact that men in the Gutenberg era wrote their books with their own hands before they were printed—even Franklin's philosophy was probably not set up direct from a tray of type—should remind us that in a complex culture many historical levels may be present and operative together, and the gloomiest vision possible of an electronic future does not depict a world in which books will vanish. They will survive, and methods of study not unlike my own will survive, because they are necessities for the survival of individuality. An ability to criticize tradition enabled Renaissance man to locate himself in the time flow, and the survival of individuality under electronic bombardment will depend on the development of means of holding up the incessant stream of communication and giving ourselves time to think. Books will survive, it might be said, as spanners in the networks; the printed page and the printed book are the most reliable means yet devised of ensuring that we have the chance to take a second and a third look at what someone is trying to sell us. It is for this reason that one historian in his highly unmechanized workshop is able to regard himself as a modern man and a reasonably militant one—a code-breaker.

NOTES

1. G. H. Sabine, *History of Political Theory* (New York, 1937).
2. J. G. A. Pocock, *The Ancient Constitution and the Feudal Law* (Cambridge, Eng., 1957, and New York, 1967).

The Age
of the
Democratic Revolution

ROBERT R. PALMER

ROBERT R. PALMER was born on January 11, 1909, in Chicago, Illinois. After graduating from the University of Chicago in 1931, he studied at Cornell University, taking his Ph.D. in 1934. He began his teaching career at Princeton University in 1936 and remained a member of the Department of History there until 1963, when he moved to Washington University, St. Louis, as Dean of the Faculty of Arts and Science. In 1966 he returned to Princeton as Professor of History, and from 1967 to 1968 he served as Dean of the Faculty. In 1969 he went to Yale University as Professor of History. Palmer has also taught for brief periods at the University of California, Berkeley (summer school, 1962), and the University of Michigan, Ann Arbor (winter 1969).

In 1960 Palmer was awarded one of the Special Prizes of the American Council of Learned Societies for his work to date. In that year he also received the Bancroft Prize for the first volume of his *Age of the Democratic Revolution: A Political History of Europe and America, 1760–1800, The Challenge* (Princeton, 1959). The second volume of that work appeared in 1964. Among his earlier works are *Catholics and Unbelievers in Eighteenth-century France* (Princeton, 1939), *Twelve Who Ruled: The Committee of Public Safety in the French Revolution* (Princeton, 1941, 1958), and *A History of the Modern World* (New York, 1950, with later editions in collaboration with Joel Colton), widely used as a textbook and translated for use in Scandinavia and the Middle East. In 1969 appeared his *1789: Les Révolutions de la liberté et de l'égalité* (Paris), of which publication in English is expected within the next few years. Palmer is also the translator of Georges Lefebvre's *The Coming of the French Revolution 1789* (Princeton, 1947).

He has long been a member of the American Historical Association (President, 1970) and of the Society for French Historical Studies (President, 1961).

*T*he Age of the Democratic Revolution, in two volumes, was produced over a period of fourteen years from 1950 to 1964. It was well received in this country, less so in Europe. I shall return to this matter of its reception, and begin with some account of how the book came into being. It is difficult for an author to write of his own work without a distasteful display of self. I apologize for the frequency of the first-person singular pronoun, without which, however, the genesis and development of the book cannot be explained or the perhaps questionable purposes of the present symposium adequately fulfilled.

The book has been praised for its geographical coverage, which embraces Europe and America at the time of the American and French revolutions. Less favor has been shown for its periodization, the forty-year time span from 1760 to 1800, which is quite rigidly followed. Some critics have rightly pointed out that the revolutionary period with which the book deals lasted until 1848. I knew this, of course, but the truth is that at the beginning there was no plan to present a forty-year period. The original idea was to concentrate on the years from 1792 to 1800. I would begin, that is, with the War of the French Revolution, and show the spread of revolutionary republicanism in the Cisalpine, Batavian, Helvetic, Ligurian, and other ephemeral republics. There was virtually nothing written about these republics in English, and their very names aroused the curiosity of the Latin scholar I once had been. The new republicanism of the 1790s could also be traced in Poland, Ireland, and the United States. The American Revolution, and French and other European developments before 1792, would appear as background. As for the terminal date of 1800, it seemed to me a fact that revolutionary enthusiasm and pressures from below, as distinct from reforms of an admittedly sweeping character imposed from above in the Napoleonic empire, simply subsided or disappeared for two decades after 1800. There was also a methodological reason: on the scale and with the geographical scope intended, the book could never be finished unless it was chronologically restricted. Nor should a personal or psychological element be ignored. The wars of the French Revolution, or rather the issues at stake in the wars of the First and Second Coalitions, appealed to my imagination and aroused my feelings; those after 1800 did so much less.

A fairly long background lay behind the decision to embark on a sizable work, broad yet detailed, at the age of forty. I had just finished the first edition of *A History of the Modern World*, had translated Georges Lefebvre's little book on the year 1789 in France, and had written, a decade before, two relatively specialized books on eighteenth-century France. One of these, *Twelve Who Ruled: The Committee of Public Safety in the French Revolution*, had left me with a vivid sense of what was involved in the wars of the 1790s. But the truth is that I was a little tired of the French Revolution in and of itself. This will come as a telltale admission to some of the adverse reviewers of my book. As long ago as 1933–1934 I had written a doctoral thesis on French ideas of the American Revolution. The idea had been proposed to me in 1931 by Louis Gottschalk at Chicago. It was the wise and merciful policy of Cornell at that time to accept brief and even fragmentary dissertations and to hold out no requirement or expectation of publication.

The thesis had been done with Carl Becker, and although Becker died in 1945, his influence continued. Becker had for years crossed and recrossed the barriers between European and American history; he had written nothing purely monographic since his own doctoral dissertation; and he liked to treat big themes and play with large ideas. He did not believe history to be a science, and he considered no history definitive. He tried to discover, persuade, reanimate, evoke, or suggest; he did not expect to "prove." Bibliography bored him. He was not an archival scholar, nor primarily a research scholar, nor in the most technical sense a scholar at all. He laughed at the idea of exhausting the sources, and preferred published to unpublished materials. Historical evidence was for him a means to an end; his idea was not to get all you can from a given body of documents, but to make documents, wherever found, serve your purpose by illustrating your line of thought. He looked things up, and when he knew enough, he began to write. He enjoyed writing more than researching. Naturally his work was therefore open to criticism. But I think I was encouraged in some of my own weaknesses, ambitions, and peculiarities by association with Becker; I am not sure that I would have flourished in the modern graduate school—or at Harvard or Columbia then.

In 1950, it seemed wise, all told, to become involved in a large-scale and long-term project, on which there need be no hurry. I had been somewhat tentatively reading a number of books that were then recent, including Jacques Droz on Germany during the French Revolution, Latreille on the Catholic Church throughout Europe at the time, Peroni's articles on Italy that appeared in the Italian journals, Dascalakis on Greece, E. P. Link on the Democratic-Republican societies in the United States in the 1790s, and Arthur Whitaker on the Mississippi Question from 1795 to 1803. There were older things also, such as Dixon Ryan Fox on the decline of aristocracy in New York, various treatments of British radicalism, and above all several multivolume collections of printed sources—Hansen on the Rhineland, Strickler on Switzerland, Montalcini on Italy, and Colenbrander on Holland—each precisely on the subject of its own country at the time of the French Revolution. For the most part, it was evident that none of these writers or editors had known what the others were doing, that the work was all tightly within national compartments, and that someone ought to put it all together. The Princeton University Library contained an abundance of other relevant eighteenth-century publications. The broad idea that I had in mind seemed to be feasible. It seemed appropriate also for the task of combination to be done by an American, who might be less swayed by European national preoccupations. And no library in Europe had such an international variety of materials freely accessible in open stacks.

Clearly, most of the work could be done at my own university, a matter of some personal convenience for one with small children and no money at a time when grants for years abroad were less frequent than now. I had had one grant anyway before the war. Later on, the fact that the book was based on printed sources rather than archival research became a matter for adverse comment from a few reviewers. I have never regretted it. Had I spent more time in manuscript collections, beyond the few days that I did, I would never have finished. Nor was it necessary. While I was busy with my own project, many other scholars published excellent work that fed into mine—Valjavec on Germany; Wangermann and Silagi on Austria; Ghisalberti, Renzo di Felice, Vaccarino, and others on Italy; Lesnodorski on Poland; Benda on Hungary; Shtrange on Russia; Maccoby and others on Great Britain; E. P. Douglas and others on the American Revolution. Without these works mine could never have been written. But in one way they continued in the older pattern, for each author related his theories only to his own country or to a single country not the author's own, as with Wangermann on the Austrian "Jacobins." There was only one exception, Jacques Godechot of the University of Toulouse.

Among the books I had been reading in 1950 was Godechot's *Histoire de l'Atlantique*, published in 1947. I knew of him by repute as the author of a large study, a French *thèse*, on the civilian commissioners who, under the Directory, accompanied the French armies in their occupation of Italy, Switzerland, Holland, the Rhineland, and Belgium. I was intrigued that a French scholar who had worked on Revolutionary expansion had also written a "history of the Atlantic." Much was then being said of an Atlantic Community. This idea had entered into my overall plan. Godechot accepted an invitation to come as Shreve Research Fellow to Princeton, where he spent about six months in 1954–1955. It was at Princeton, from the mass of notes he brought with him, reinforced by work in the library, that he wrote much of his book, *La Grande Nation: l'expansion révolutionnaire de la France dans le monde, 1789–1799*, published in two volumes in 1956. We were also invited to present a joint paper at the Tenth International Congress of Historical Sciences at Rome in 1955. We worked on it together during this winter of 1954–1955. I shall say more of it later.

The first public statement of ideas that went into *The Age of the Democratic Revolution* occurred in a public lecture given at the University of Missouri in 1951. This was a confused piece of work that was later published as two separate articles. The more programmatic of these two appeared in 1952 in the *Political Science Quarterly*.[1] I find also, in the back part of my dead files, the carbon copy of a prospectus for the book, dated 1951. It was drafted, so far as I can remember, as a proposal to some granting agency from which I must have received a negative answer, though I later received, under different circumstances, enough aid from the Rockefeller Foundation to give me considerable leave of absence. The prospectus of 1951 is of interest in showing how fully the ideas of the book were already formulated and how they changed thereafter.

The project called for a one-volume book of about 150,000 words to be written in five years. It set forth, as reasons for support, the fact that a good deal of monographic and source material existed that had never been exploited, that America and Europe should be considered together, and that comparative history was a good thing. It noted the resemblance between the spread of "democratic" revolutionary ideas at the end of the eighteenth century and the spread of communism and Soviet influence in the twentieth, notably since 1945. It asserted that dislike of this twentieth-century revolution need not lead to rejection of the eighteenth-century revolution. I thought, and said, in the prospectus of 1951 that from antipathy to communism we were "in danger of repudiating or minimizing one of the main common traditions of the Western world." In fact, I agreed with one of the common taunts of the socialist Left, that the "bourgeois," in his fear of revolution, was denying or disguising the revolutionary element in his own past. A dislike of the American neo-conservatism of the 1950s, with its habit of downgrading the French Revolution, representing the American Revolution as a mild and conservative movement, and eulogizing Edmund Burke, strongly infused both volumes of my book. On the other hand, I could not go very far with the Marxists either. For all their talk of the bourgeois revolution, they seemed to resent it because it was bourgeois, to wish that a socialist or working-class revolution had succeeded in 1793, and to object to the French Revolution and its accompanying disturbances in other countries for being what they were. In general, like other historians, I felt that my predecessors had misunderstood or misrepresented the issues. It seemed important to set matters straight, to remind people of what the French Revolution and the whole eighteenth-century upheaval had really been. It has been said that history is best written with a little spite, and I fear that I share this uncharitable opinion.

More specifically, this prospectus of 1951, together with a statement submitted to the Rockefeller Foundation in 1954, shows the main constructive or operative generalizations of both volumes already present before a word had been written. They account for what seems, in retrospect, a surprising unity that permeates the two finished volumes. They include the idea of an "aristocratic resurgence" before 1789, which had struck me in Lefebvre's book (which I had translated), and which I now proposed to generalize to countries other than France, and the choice of the term "democratic" (much-criticized later) to describe the various forces and ideas by which this aristocratic resurgence was opposed. These early statements likewise show intimations of other major themes: a three-cornered struggle among privileged groups, enlightened reformist monarchy, and democratic pressures from unprivileged persons; the thought that revolution broke out, not only in France but in Holland and elsewhere, as a reaction against a rigid conservatism too long persisted in; the idea that the wars which began in 1792 continued and heightened a conflict between conservative-aristocratic and reformist-democratic forces that had been developing for a long time; the belief that war led to further revolution as much as, or more than, revolution led to war; and the conviction that revolution in Europe from Holland to Naples, after 1795, was not produced by French propaganda or imposed by French armies by sheer force, but was a reflection of the developments of a generation in these several countries themselves, where the French victories provided opportunities for modern-minded local persons to take action.

With a book in which the main themes are so laid out beforehand, the suspicion naturally arises that the author seeks only to confirm his preconceived ideas. One asks whether such a historian ever learns anything new, or ever changes his mind. It is convenient at this point to take note of the International Congress of Historians at Rome in 1955, where Professor Godechot and I defended the paper we had jointly prepared.

The paper dealt with the "problem of the Atlantic" from the eighteenth to the twentieth centuries.[2] Godechot's interest had long been in the Atlantic as a theater of commercial, naval, and strategic activity, while mine was more in the existence of an Atlantic civilization. I think we learned much from each other, and the paper attracted some favorable attention. We argued, in general, that with the rise of railroads and the consequent "permeation" of continental land masses, and with the growing involvement of both Europe and the United States with all continents after about 1880, it was doubtful whether the countries bordering on the Atlantic formed much of a unit in the twentieth century. But we also held, offering evidence, that a trans-Atlantic civilization, with much interchange and many reciprocal influences, had been of importance for at least a century before about 1830.

A good deal of disagreement was expressed at the meeting. Sir Charles Webster grandly congratulated the authors on doing well with a subject that did not exist. Eric Hobsbawm somewhat excitedly hoped that no such topic would ever be heard of at any future congress. Professor Lesnodorski of Warsaw observed that such emphasis on an "Atlantic" area did less than justice to the European character of Poland and Eastern Europe west of Russia. I was impressed by Lesnodorski's arguments, and have enjoyed his acquaintance ever since. His own paper prepared for this meeting of 1955, followed by his book on the Polish Jacobins in 1960, were of the utmost value in my work.

This Rome meeting, I think, had a great influence on my book, of which, to repeat, not a word had yet been written. I gave up the use of the term "Atlantic," thinking that it only aroused unnecessary hostility, though Godechot has continued to employ it. I made more of a place in my plans for Eastern Europe. And I decided that Europeans had much to learn about the impact of the American Revolution in Europe. This led me to give more study to the American Revolution itself. Here my colleague Frank Craven was very helpful; indeed, I sat in on some of the discussion groups in his lecture course in 1956.

The big change was that what was planned as one volume now broke into two. The notes and ideas accumulated for the period after 1792 were put aside for several years. The original concept was deferred to a second volume, and I began to work on another (the first), which dealt with various European countries before the great events of 1789 and with the American Revolution and its repercussions in Europe.

The academic year 1955–1956, during which I was on leave with a grant from the Rockefeller Foundation, passed in a frenzy of composition, with half the first volume finished by June. From the beginning, I had decided on a basically narrative, chronological-geographical plan. In this way my book differs from Godechot's *Grande Nation*, which is therefore more useful on a great many topical subjects, such as the growth of the press in this period. It seemed to me that readers of English, having nowhere else to turn, simply needed to know more definitely what Switzerland, Holland, or the Po Valley were like at the time of the French Revolution. Essentially geographic chapters are thus presented in a time series reflecting the moments at which areas became important. These alternate with occasional chapters of more analytic or comparative content and with occasional summaries of what has been said or forecasts of what is to come.

Possibly, in thinking through these problems I owed something to the formulations of social science, in which I had a respectful but distant and reserved interest. Concepts of social stratification, social mobility, role assignment, occupational recruitment, integration, functional needs, and the prerequisites of a viable society run implicitly throughout the book. So do such unscientific ideas as right and justice. The book remains within the limits of conventional history. One of the great values of the abstractions of social science for the historian, I think, is that by creating a larger frame of reference, they may help him to reexamine the stereotypes in which his concrete material has become embedded. Especially in a field already well worked and familiar, they may freshen the subject.[3]

In view of the variety of areas covered and therefore of languages used, a word must be said of research assistants. From one French review,[4] one might gain the impression that the book represented a kind of invasion of Europe by American wealth and organization, backed by an American foundation, and involving huge teams of highly trained and organized data-collectors. Alas, there is more team research going on now in Paris than I have ever been involved in. The Rockefeller Foundation financed my time for two years, with Princeton University contributing matching leaves from teaching. The assistance came gratis, in the form of theses and seminar reports from my students, or financed by university student aid, or in some cases paid for by myself. Over the years, I found students—or in one case an instructor—who could read for me or make detailed digests of books and articles in Swedish, Polish, Russian, Hungarian, and Greek. I could read the Western languages myself, though in some cases laboriously. The book owes much to the young men who helped me. It could not have been written without them, because the books of Lesnodorski and Shtrange on Poland and Russia at the time of the French Revolution were not translated into French until my need of them had passed.

Of "methodology" I can say little, except that it consisted of taking notes on 4-by-6-inch pieces of paper, shuffling and reshuffling them, and sitting alone in a closed room at a desk. In my experience, the most useful and specific general concepts, if one may so call them, arise in the act of writing itself. I suspect that most of the work is done by the subconscious, and that moments of absent-mindedness, or even sleep, are not times of mental inaction. How else can one explain how an idea seems to jump or flash into the mind? In any case, ideas mulled over since 1950 now took more usable form. They became keys that unlocked many doors. The book became organized around the concepts of "constituted bodies" and "the people as constituent power" (*corps constitués* and *pouvoir constituant*), under which it became possible to subsume a wide variety of ideas and practices, ideologies and institutions, and innovative and conservative movements. In this framework, dissimilar situations in France, Britain, Ireland, Holland, Geneva, Poland, etc., after 1760 could be treated, the American Revolution given a central place, and the beginning of the French Revolution and work of the Constituent Assembly made into a logical conclusion or climax to Volume One. In this constitutional emphasis the book is somewhat old-fashioned, but it certainly is not in the usual tradition of constitutional history. Its interest undoubtedly lies in the detail with which this abstract structure is brought to life.

There is not much to say about the writing of the second volume. The idea for it had been with me for a long time. The French Revolution is central to it, as the American Revolution is in a way central to the first volume. The governing concept is the war—the polarization of conflicts, the radicalization of opposites, the nature of ideological struggle, and the shaping of ideas into actual issues involving choice, action, and consequences. There are subordinate themes on the failure of moderates in time of revolution and war, on the relations between a dominant revolutionary power and its satellites, on the difficulties of making peace even when everybody wants it, and of course on the meaning of "equality" (judged to be fundamental to the period) as seen by its various proponents and by its enemies. The phenomena of written constitutions and constitution-making, set forth in the first volume, are again noted in the second. And the significance of all this in most of Europe and America is reaffirmed.

A book projected at 150,000 words in 1951 thus grew to about 400,000. The two volumes form a unit, as indicated in their subtitles. A "challenge" described in the first is resolved in the "struggle" of the second. For so long a work to retain so much unity of concept raises a number of questions. Can a pattern be imposed on so much detail without violation of human reality? What is the relation of the parts to the whole? Is the unifying theme any more than the author's pet idea? Has the author really dealt fairly with the evidence? Has he done more, to repeat, than try to confirm his preconceived ideas?

Doubtless the original main ideas held up throughout. If so, it was not without effort; no one touched by skepticism is unaware of the force of contrary arguments, and impartiality requires attention to many conflicting voices. As I wrote in 1951, anticipating the difficulties, especially if the work should be prolonged: "The viewpoint wavers, the focus blurs, the grasp slackens. It is not a matter of subjectivity or of objectivity. It is a matter of judgment and of art. Without these no comprehensive and sustained piece of work can be confidently entered upon or brought to a successful conclusion." [5] I would add that without them—without elements of judgment and art (or artifice, or design) involving selection, emphasis and omission, the noting of resemblances, and the explanation of differences—nothing can be long held clearly in the mind by either author or reader. They are the prerequisites of communication.

But while the main concepts were adhered to, they underwent some modification in the course of the work. In a general way, as I now compare the book with the earliest articles and statements from 1951 to 1955, I seem to have shifted from an emphasis on liberty to an emphasis on equality as the main single and distinctive thought of the Revolutionary Era. But the relationship of liberty and equality has always been much on my mind. In talking of a "world revolution of the West" (to use a phrase of 1954),[6] I had never maintained, or supposed, that anything quite like the French Revolution had occurred anywhere but in France. In the process of composition, however, as I learned more of the facts, the idea of a revolution "overrunning all frontiers" became more qualified. In some cases, as for Poland, I found more genuine revolution than I expected; in others, as with the "Jacobins" of Hungary and Vienna, their revolutionary importance seemed less than I had thought. In general, the book talked less of revolution and more of revolutionary agitation, revolutionism, abortive or attempted or unsuccessful revolution, and it developed further a thought already present from the beginning, namely, that aristocratic, agrarian, anti-Enlightenment and anti-Revolutionary forces also became more powerful in the 1790s. It is one of the main organizing thoughts of the second volume that conservatism triumphed in Eastern Europe, as also in Great Britain and Ireland, over severe opposition, while the Continent from the Dutch provinces to Italy was "revolutionized" in conjunction with the French military victories in Western Europe. Of Germany, subject to the same contrary pressures, it is said that, in the absence of significant revolutionary action, the Germans, or rather certain German intellectuals, produced an ideology of revolution as a kind of soul-force or world-historic process. Other examples of modification can be mentioned. For example, not much is said in the book about Western separatism in the United States, or about George Rogers Clark, despite his commission as a general in the French army. I had originally been impressed by the Black Jacobins, Toussaint l'Ouverture, and the revolution in Haiti as highly relevant to the whole subject. I still think the same, but in the pressure of composition they got squeezed into a single paragraph, to my great regret.

Most unforeseen modifications arising in the course of the work were in matters of detail. Some led into temporary byways of relatively intensive research, from which, however, it was necessary soon to emerge to return to the main track. There is a good deal of detail in *The Age of the Democratic Revolution*, but it could be shown, I think, how every sentence is meant to relate to the work as a whole.

Some such detail is polemical. For example, to justify my use of terms, I collected a variety of examples of the use of the word "democracy" in the 1790s. These were published in 1953, and used again in the first chapter of Volume One. (R. C. Cobb called them *un verbalisme pointilliste.*)[7] I learned more later (enough to modify my thinking), for I became aware that "democracy" was a favorite word with Babeuf and his group and so was associated very early, in Europe, with the idea of equality of wealth. It is thus understandable that some Europeans, especially socialists, have found my use of the word "democracy" puzzling and inappropriate. Or again, there is polemical detail in the final appendix to Volume One on the question of whether the French Constitution of 1791 should be thought of as bourgeois or democratic. This is also one of the places in the book where quantitative arguments are employed.

Some detail can be called logical, in the sense of offering examples of generalizations or cases in point under essentially classificatory concepts. For example, there are tables in Volume One on the per capita tax burdens in various countries at the time of the American Revolution. Their purpose was to show that Americans were taxed very lightly, and more lightly before the Revolution than after it. To compile them required a good bit of work, but only in fairly obvious sources. With the purpose accomplished, it was necessary to abandon this little survey, but a big monograph could be written on this subject alone, and I wish somebody would do it. The whole book, like most books, is obviously made up largely of such illustrative or argumentative detail. The problem here is that if any unity or limits are to be preserved, amplification in one place requires reduction or elimination somewhere else. Thus, as illustrations of the general theme, the Dutch, Belgians, and Swiss are put in a single chapter in Volume One, but in Volume Two the Dutch and Swiss each receive a whole chapter, while the Belgians are somewhat subordinated to the war in 1792–1793 and thereafter, unfortunately, neglected. There is a big chapter on the Cisalpine Republic which took form around Milan, but hardly a word on the Ligurian Republic in the neighboring territory of Genoa. Scandinavia and the Iberian peninsula are hardly mentioned in the second volume at all, though the framework of the book could accommodate them, and a Norwegian reviewer, Kåre Tønnesson, has said that more attention to Scandinavia would reinforce the argument of the book.[8] Such choices are in part arbitrary. All that can be said for them is that, within given limits of time and space, if everything were treated in equal detail, the total impression would be weaker.

Some detail is in a sense artistic, designed to set up symbols or images to facilitate recollection and comprehension. Thus the first volume begins with a little scene at Versailles in which Europe and America, aristocracy and democracy, are made visible and concrete. The second begins with contrasting scenes in Paris and Frankfurt on the third anniversary of the Bastille intended to symbolize revolution and counterrevolution, the issues of the war then beginning, and the collapse of the French monarchy at the hands both of its friends and its enemies. Symbolic also, as well as illustrative or merely documentary, are the quotations used to introduce each chapter. The book ends with the symbolism of Bonaparte and Jefferson, in 1801, as two very different "men on horseback." The theme of Europe and America, sounded at the beginning, is echoed at the end. The same is true of "equality." Symmetry is observed also in that the book begins and ends with quotations from Tocqueville. Much of all this is a kind of shorthand. It is a contrivance, meant to reaffirm a unity running through two large and variegated volumes.

The first volume was published in 1959 by the Princeton University Press, the trade department of my textbook publisher having expressed little interest. It was received with a favor beyond any reasonable expectation. It contained enough on America to qualify for the Bancroft Prize, and other honors followed. It was adopted by the History Book Club. Its theme—the idea of a general Atlantic revolutionary movement in which the American Revolution was important—became the topic of a session at the Mississippi Valley Historical Association, a "problem" for students in the Heath Readings edited by Peter Amann, a matter considered by the Committee on Historical Analysis of the Social Science Research Council (chaired by Louis Gottschalk), and a subject for high school teachers at an NDEA summer institute at the University of Washington in Seattle. It has been excerpted for various pedagogical anthologies, and adapted for particular uses at New Trier High School and Harvard College. Golo Mann invited me to write an opening chapter, "The Influence of the American Revolution" for Volume VIII (on the nineteenth century) of the new *Propyläen Weltgeschichte*, which has also appeared in Italian. I was fortunate in having such excellent reviewers, many of whom gave a careful presentation of its content and arguments. Godechot did so in the *Revue historique*, Paul Kluke in the *Historische Zeitschrift*, Sten Carlsson in the Swedish *Historisk Tidskrift*, and Denis Brogan in the *Times Literary Supplement*. Alfred Cobban appraised it at length, and with serious reservations, in *History*. In the American historical journals, it received the blessing of Crane Brinton, Walter Dorn, David Thomson, and Caroline Robbins. In the general press, reviewers in the *Nation* and *Commentary* expressed satisfaction. Some younger American historians, forerunners of what became the New Left, were pleased with my insistence that the American Revolution was genuinely revolutionary, carried through by violence and the unseating of a prerevolutionary upper class.

It is worth saying all this to contrast the more adverse observations on the first volume and the more subdued reception of the second, which followed in 1964. On the first volume, some of the best and most careful reviewers of course expressed disagreement. One of the most thoughtful was by Betty Behrens of Cambridge University, who concluded that in the end the book failed to explain the developments of which it gave a good comparative survey. Jacques Godechot made the same point, finding the weakness of the book to be in failing to show any causation.[9] Both implied that socioeconomic causes were slighted. There is force to these criticisms; the book is possibly too narrative or even descriptive. Nor is it much of an answer to say that I still feel no certainty as to the deepest explanation or ultimate cause of the revolutionary movements.

The second volume, to simplify, was greeted either with high approval or with total silence. In the former category may be put Jacques Godechot again, Stuart Hughes and Geoffrey Bruun, and three British reviewers, Denis Brogan, Max Beloff, and J. H. Plumb. They were pleased with various things in the book, such as its rejection of the conspiratorial theory of revolution, its denial that the partisans of revolution were unbalanced idealists or fanatics, its assertion that respectable middle-class persons had risen throughout Europe and America against the various forms of aristocratic society. Plumb's very enthusiasm made his strictures the more severe.[10] He found the book so poorly written that a great opportunity had been missed. "Unfortunately Professor Palmer is so level-headed that he becomes flat-footed. The Himalayan grandeurs of the Revolution are reduced by his remorseless prose to the monotony of a steppe." He regretted that the book would not reach a wide enough audience to dissipate the gross misrepresentation from which the French Revolution has long suffered. "If only Garrett Mattingly had written this book, the bogeyman would be in danger." By the "bogeyman" Plumb meant the middle-class horror of all and any revolution wherever found. Although I think he exaggerated the book's defects, I do not disagree; I too had hoped to produce something less ponderous and felt on finishing it that it somehow fell short of its purpose.

In Great Britain the book is known and discussed. On the Continent, Godechot has carefully summarized both volumes in the *Revue historique*. One of the best reviews to appear anywhere was in the Norwegian *Historisk Tidsskrift*, in which Kåre Tønnesson gave a long, thoughtful, and discriminating account of both volumes together.[11] I would never have known of it had not my former student, Arnold Barton, who had helped me in Swedish, sent me a complete translation. Elsewhere on the European continent, so far as reviews known to me offer any evidence, the second volume of *The Age of the Democratic Revolution* has had little impact. Six years after its publication, it has never been reviewed in Germany, Italy, or (except by Godechot) in

France.[12] There are, indeed, signs of interest outside the most strictly professional historical circles. Plans are in progress for translation into German and into Spanish at Buenos Aires; one for an Italian edition was finally given up. The French publisher, Robert Calmann-Lévy, has just brought out a newly written work, *1789: Les Révolutions de la liberté et de l'égalité*, as part of a series entitled *Les Grandes vagues révolutionnaires*. This book, written at his invitation for translation into French, is essentially an abridgement of *The Age of the Democratic Revolution.*

The historians *de métier* have, on the Continent, paid less attention. Paul Kluke's excellent account of the first volume had no sequel in the *Historische Zeitschrift.* Neither volume has ever been considered in the Italian journals. In France, in the *Annales historiques de la Révolution française*, trade journal of specialists in the French Revolution, to which I have been a faithful subscriber for thirty years, Volume Two of *The Age of the Democratic Revolution* has never been mentioned.[13] I confess that I find this lack of interest disappointing and somewhat perplexing. In the cases of Germany and Italy there may be an element of accident. What happened with France calls for more explanation, especially since I am on amicable terms with most of the French historians who might be concerned.

In part, I suspect, this silence, especially in France, goes back to the international meeting at Rome in 1955, where Godechot and I defended our paper on the "problem of the Atlantic." We were thought to be riding a hobbyhorse. Some undoubtedly agreed with Sir Charles Webster that there was no such subject, and others with a general anti-Americanism of the Left to which Eric Hobsbawm gave expression. Godechot published his *Grande Nation* the following year. It was reviewed at length by Marcel Reinhard of the Sorbonne, Georges Lefebvre's successor in the Chair in the History of the French Revolution. He praised it, but concluded that "this thesis of an Atlantic Revolution cannot be accepted" and warned that the danger in so good a book as Godechot's was to give currency to "theses which have no foundation."[14]

In 1959, in a survey of recent work on the French Revolution, Reinhard dismissed Godechot and myself together. This was before my first volume was published; he cited the Rome meeting and two articles I had written. He believed that the position taken by the two of us "minimized" the French Revolution, making it "a slight episode in the general history of the Western world." It also "falsifies the perspectives by exaggerating common denominators and attenuating specific differences." It misrepresents varying orders of magnitude, he thought, and obscures the truly revolutionary character of the real French Revolution.[15]

In July 1960, in Paris, Godechot and I again presented our ideas, in separate papers, at a joint meeting of the (American) Society for French Historical Studies and the Société d'histoire moderne. Unfortunately, many of the French historians were too busy with examinations to attend the sessions. They could, however, read the papers. The net effect was probably again to bracket Godechot and myself as spokesmen for an untenable thesis.[16]

When my first volume appeared, Reinhard reviewed it briefly and praised it mildly, but remained unconvinced.[17] He still found the French Revolution to be "minimized." He saw no "democratic" tendency in the period, except in France in the *sans-culotte* irruption of 1792–1793. He called for more economic and social analysis. It was true of course, he said, that all countries in the West passed "from feudalism to the régime of the bourgeoisie" between the sixteenth and nineteenth centuries, but they did so at different times and under differing circumstances; they had nothing of interest in common in the generation of the French Revolution. In short, there was no such subject. It was hardly necessary to read the second volume of such a misguided effort.

With such an attitude I simply cannot agree. France and the French Revolution are not minimized in my book; they are central to its whole construction, as the most perceptive reviewers of various countries have recognized. In any case, it is odd to dismiss the main ideas of a book before it is published, and after publication to ignore the evidence and the arguments that it presents. It is strange to suggest no alternative explanation of disturbances that unquestionably troubled both Europe and America in connection with the French Revolution. It is dogmatic to insist that the word "revolution," as of the eighteenth century, can rightly apply only to the French Revolution, and "democratic" only to a popular upheaval that coincided in time, if not otherwise, with the Terror. It is somewhat as if a Soviet scholar today were to argue, lest the events of 1917 in Russia should be "minimized," that there is no twentieth-century "age of the Communist revolution" except in the minds of one or two amiable but eccentric historians. It is proper enough to ask for more social and economic analysis, but to declare that the political and constitutional are subordinate to socioeconomic development is to beg the question. The real question is whether the political and the economic (matters of power and rights on the one hand and matters of wealth and its distribution on the other) exist as separate categories except in the mind of the observer. I am inclined to share the doubts of the late Alfred Cobban, to suspect that the French Revolution was not really a stage in economic history at all.[18] This is indeed an unorthodox opinion. And few academic specialists have a more received orthodoxy than experts on the French Revolution, comfortably entrenched in their *Annales*, which still proudly carries on its cover the name of its *fondateur*, Albert Mathiez, who died thirty-eight years ago, while it busily publishes microscopic research that changes nobody's thinking and shies away from reinterpretation as from a distracting irrelevancy.

Some of the silence that greeted *The Age of the Democratic Revolution*, especially the second volume, is probably due to such irrelevancy felt by the intellectual Left. Except for some courteous remarks by George Rudé, historians of Marxist inclination—Soboul, Hobsbawm, Cobb, and others—have seen nothing of interest in it. It has never been reviewed in *Science and Society* of New York, or in the *Zeitschrift für Geschichtswissenschaft* of East Berlin, both of which take a great interest in works having to do with revolution.

It would seem, at first, that Marxists of any school would hail a book which, in effect, insists upon the reality of the "bourgeois revolution," attempts to cut across national barriers, and asserts the importance of class conflicts that overlap national differences. Yet there are understandable reasons why this is not so. One is simply that I am not known in radical circles. But there is much in the book that is indigestible in such company. The bourgeois revolution, so to speak, is presented by a bourgeois historian in a favorable light. The author accepts violence as a sometimes regrettable necessity; he does not idealize it. He does not identify democracy with social democracy or economic equalitarianism. He does not define social class in Marxist categories and does not believe class conflict to be wholesome or constructive. He does not emphatically maintain that the Revolution opened the way to modern capitalism. He respects Robespierre, now somewhat *passé* for the Left, but does not believe Babeuf to have been the most interesting end product of the French Revolution. He is not much impressed by conspiracy and insurrection. He actually argues that the Revolution continued after Thermidor and that the Directory was in a way, or potentially, a democratic form of state. He favors compromise, while showing why it could not work. His analysis is in the terms and language then used by contemporaries, not those developed by a subsequent ideology. He is interested in the Revolution for its resolution of problems of its own time, not as a seedbed of revolutions yet to come.

All this has been seldom said, but it was suggested in the *Partisan Review* in 1966.[19] The reviewer, Wallace Katz, treating both volumes together, found that they gave a distorted picture. The truth is, according to Katz, who quotes Marx, that the French Revolution was unique. To merge it with movements in other countries is to belittle it. It alone produced, in 1792–1793, the first experiment in social democracy. But it was "betrayed." After Thermidor, the bourgeoisie betrayed their own alleged principles of equality, repressing the workers in a legalistic apparatus that reflected their own class ideology. Eventually Marx appeared as the great link between the French Revolution and the Russian. There is of course something to all this, but only as an aspect of larger matters. It is, in short, a sectarian view.

Finally, the impact of *The Age of the Democratic Revolution* has been limited because it is not a very modern kind of book. It may have some standing as comparative history. But what could be more old-fashioned than a work of which the first volume turns upon constitutional issues and the second upon a war? Actually, both constitutional and military confrontations are shown as aspects of social conflict. Many well-disposed reviewers have called for more social analysis, more exact attention to "social structures," not because these are really overlooked in my book, but because they comprise the field in which so much contemporary research, now aided by computers, is going on. While I have doubts about such research, I hope it continues, both in general and in minute particulars. I hope that more refined quantitative measures can be obtained. I would only urge that such endeavors not become an end in themselves, but be made to illuminate the larger issues, the crises, the agony, aspirations and turmoil, the terrible alternatives and crushing responsibilities, the suffering and the achievement that a humane history should reveal. And exact data on the size and composition of social groups are no substitute for political science.

In summary, despite its mixed critical reception, the book has apparently had some influence. Both volumes have sold well, and if book club adoptions are omitted, about a fifth of the copies have been sold abroad. It has brought me into interesting correspondence with persons in Finland, Holland, Brazil, Australia, and New Zealand. Among reviewers, those with the broadest historical interests, who can look upon the French and American revolutions from outside, or in long perspective, have been the most favorable. Those more enclosed in their specialties have been more doubtful. This may indeed indicate that the book is unsound, but it may only reflect the trend by which specialists, notably those working in the eighteenth century, are concentrating on archival, statistical, regional, or local studies. The habit of seeing history within national compartments continues. There is no "school" of the Atlantic Revolution. I doubt if *The Age of the Democratic Revolution* has opened many new channels of research, as some friendly commentators have intimated. It is not sufficiently specialized in any one direction to have that effect. It is enough if it has broadened the frame of reference and contributed to the education not only of researchers, but of students and readers in general. It should help them to understand what Europe and America, in the great upheaval of two centuries ago, shared in common—how they differed, and wherein, despite appearances, they were alike.

NOTES

1. Robert R. Palmer, "Reflections on the French Revolution," *Political Science Quarterly*, LXVII (1952), 64–80.
2. Jacques Godechot and Robert R. Palmer, "Le problème de l'Atlantique du XVIII° au XX° siècle," *Relazioni del X Congresso Internazionale di Scienze Storiche* (Roma, 1955), vol. V, pp. 173–239.
3. On this matter, see my contribution to Louis Gottschalk, ed., *Generalization in the Writing of History: A Report of the Committee on Historical Analysis of the Social Science Research Council* (Chicago, 1964), pp. 66–76. The different application in Europe and America of abstractly similar ideas is worked out in "The Great Inversion," my contribution to Richard Herr and Harold T. Parker, eds., *Ideas in History: Essays Presented to Louis Gottschalk by His Former Students* (Durham, 1965), pp. 3–19.
4. Marcel Reinhard, in *Annales historiques de la Révolution française*, No. 160 (April–June 1960), 220–23.
5. Palmer, "Reflections . . . ," *op. cit.*, p. 79.
6. Robert R. Palmer, "The World Revolution of the West," *Political Science Quarterly*, LXIX (1954), 1–14.
7. At a meeting of the Société d'histoire moderne, March 27, 1960; see the *Bulletin* of the Society, douzième série, No. 14, p. 4.
8. Kåre Tønnesson, "Problèmes d'histoire constitutionnelle en Scandinavie à l'époque de la Révolution et de l'Empire," *Annales historiques de la Révolution française*, No. 188 (April–June 1967), 223.
9. Behrens, in *Historical Journal*, No. 1 (1961), 107–10; Godechot in *Revue historique*, CCXXIII (1960), 164–68.
10. J. H. Plumb, "The Great Revolution," in *The New York Review of Books*, September 24, 1964.
11. Kåre Tønnesson, *Historisk Tidsskrift* (Norwegian) (1966), pp. 259–72.
12. Minor exceptions are the perceptive paragraph by Fritz Wagner in the *Historisch-Politische Buch*, XIV (1966), 14, and the bare notice in the *Nuova rivista storica*, L (1966), 265. A sweeping negative statement is always dangerous, and there may indeed be European reviews of which I am unaware.
13. The exception is Tønnesson's comment in connection with Scandinavian history, cited in note 8 above.
14. Marcel Reinhard, *Revue d'histoire moderne et contemporaine*, V (April–June 1958), 154–60.
15. Marcel Reinhard, *Annales: Economies, Sociétés, Civilisations*, XIV (July–September 1959), pp. 554–55.
16. *Bulletin de la Société d'histoire moderne*, douzième série, Bulletin spécial consacré aux journées franco-américaines (1960), pp. 2–10.
17. See note 4.
18. Let me emphasize this, since I have differed with the late Professor Cobban in other matters. See his much-debated *Social Interpretation of the French Revolution* (Cambridge, Eng., 1964), and the continuing discussion summarized in my article, "Polémique américaine sur le rôle

de la bourgeoisie dans la Révolution française," in *Annales historiques de la Révolution française*, No. 189 (July–September 1967), 369–80. Professor Cobban, who held the chair in French history at the University of London, and who died in 1968, was for many years the source of refreshing ideas, maintained in a gently combative spirit, which will be sorely missed in the field of French Revolution studies.

19. Wallace Katz, "A Revolution Betrayed," *Partisan Review* (Spring 1966), pp. 307–11.

The Changing Face
of the
Crowd

GEORGE FREDERICK ELLIOT RUDÉ

GEORGE FREDERICK ELLIOT RUDÉ was born in Oslo, Norway, on February 8, 1910. He matriculated at Cambridge University, where he took his B.A. in 1931 and his M.A. in 1950. He also holds a B.A. and a Ph.D. degree from the University of London and a D.Litt. from the University of Adelaide, South Australia. Rudé taught history at the University of Adelaide from 1960 to 1967, and at the University of Stirling, Scotland, during most of 1968. He is now Professor of History at the Flinders University of South Australia in Adelaide. He is a member of the Royal Historical Society, the Australian Humanities Research Council, and the Société des Etudes Robespierristes. In 1955 he won the Alexander Prize of the Royal Historical Society for his essay, "The Gordon Riots: A Study of the Rioters and Their Victims."

Rudé has written a number of books and articles on popular protest and collective violence in France and Britain during the Revolutionary era. Among these are *The Crowd in the French Revolution* (Oxford, 1959), *Wilkes and Liberty: A Social Study of 1763 to 1774* (Oxford, 1962), *The Crowd in History, 1730–1848* (New York, 1964), and *Captain Swing* (London, 1969), with E. J. Hobsbawm. Rudé's articles on popular disturbances and riots have appeared in such journals as *The Guildhall Miscellany, Historical Studies, The Historical Journal, Past and Present, Revue Historique,* and *Annales historiques de la Révolution française.*

Forthcoming publications include *Hanoverian London, 1714–1808,* and a book on European historical interpretations from 1815 to 1848. Rudé is also pursuing his investigation into the socially protesting convicts who were transported from the British Isles to Australia and Tasmania between 1788 and 1867.

A s a historian I was, by Anglo-Saxon standards at least, a late developer. My first published article was written at the age of forty-two; I took my first full-time history post (in a secondary school) at forty-four; my first book was published when I was forty-nine; and I was already fifty when I went to my first university post at Adelaide, in South Australia. Yet I am in no way suggesting that I was a boy from the bush who, in middling years, took to the pen or discovered he had literary or academic talents. Far from it. I had graduated at Cambridge with a modern languages degree when twenty-one, and for many years had taught French and German in a variety of secondary schools before deciding, shortly after World War II, to take another "first" degree in history at London. And, as it turned out, the study of languages proved to be of considerable advantage to me in the field of history that I later chose.

Moreover, I had the further advantage, as it now seems to me, of having long been a Marxist, both in theory and in practice; it was, I believe, the reading of Marx, and probably of Lenin as well, that led me to history. Marx's historical ideas have been so long and so insistently misrepresented in certain countries that it may be a surprise to some that a professor of history should actually claim that a reading of Marx was of any solid advantage to him in his craft. What I learned from Marx was not only that history tends to progress through a conflict of social classes (a view, incidentally, that was held to be perfectly "respectable" a hundred years ago), but that it has a discoverable pattern and moves forward (not backward, in circles, or in inexplicable jerks) broadly from a lower to a higher phase of development. I learned also that the lives and actions of the common people are the very stuff of history, and though "material" rather than the institutional and ideological factors are primary, that ideas themselves become a "material force" when they pass into the active consciousness of men. Moreover, I have also learned from Engels that, whatever the excellence of historical "systems" (like his own and Marx's, for example), "all history must be studied afresh." What I never at any time learned from either of them was that history should be interpreted in terms of a narrow economic determinism.

With such antecedents, it is perhaps not remarkable that I should have been drawn to the study of revolutions. But why to the French Revolution? Partly, I suppose, because I had acquired a good knowledge of French; partly because I soon discovered that the sort of problems I became interested in could best be studied in the French records of that period; and partly, too, because I had the good fortune to find in the late Alfred Cobban, who at that time directed research in French history at London, an excellent mentor and guide, tireless in the service of his students, and one who, while by no means sharing my own social-political views, actively encouraged me to find a Ph.D. subject to my taste and to see it through to a reasonably rapid conclusion. My subject was the part played by the Paris wage earners in the insurrections of the first two years of the French Revolution. While reading for my degree, I had been struck by the fact that no historian of the period (not even Mathiez whom, at this time, I had read more widely than Lefebvre) had seriously asked such questions as: Who actually took the Bastille, stormed the Tuileries, expelled the Girondin leaders from the National Convention, or stood silently by as Robespierre was hustled to the scaffold? Not only who were they, but how did they get there? What were their motives and social aspirations, and by what means did they acquire them? I saw that historians friendly to the Revolution (at least from Michelet onward) had written about "the people" or, more specifically, about the *sans-culottes*, while others (beginning with Burke) had dismissed them as a "swinish multitude," a "rabble," a "mob," or a *"canaille."*

Although I distinctly preferred the "populists" to the "mobsters," I was not satisfied with either definition, as they both begged all the questions that I found to be of interest, and I began to think that a more precise analysis of "who," if it could be made, would throw a useful light not only on the activities, but on the outlook and motives of the common people who, as everyone conceded, had played an important part in the course and the outcome of the Revolution. I soon discovered, with Cobban's help, that it was not for lack of appropriate records that historians had dodged the issue: there was even a list in the Archives Nationales in Paris, fully described in Tuetey's sixty-year-old *Répertoire* of Parisian revolutionary manuscripts, that gave the names, addresses, ages, occupations, and militia units of every one of the 600-odd civilians who had been proved to have taken an active part in the siege of the Bastille. For the rest, I had mainly to make do with the police records of the Paris Châtelet and Prefecture of Police, which I supplemented in later work with the official lists of those receiving awards, pensions and compensation, or jail sentences (according to the event) for the part they played in the great revolutionary *journées* of August 1792, June 1793, and May 1795. These proved to be a mine of information about those who had been arrested, killed or wounded, or against whom information had been laid; but, of course, they provided only a sample—and sometimes a rather fortuitous one at that—and had, in consequence, to be used with discretion and with ample reservations. Still, while conscious of its limitations, I have made this type of record a basic part of my research equipment ever since.

I must add here that I did not approach my subject without commitment, a fact that may cause no surprise after what I have said above. This does not mean that I have ever felt *politically* involved with the wage earners, craftsmen or rioters with whom I have largely been concerned, but that I have always felt a bond of sympathy with them, whether their activities have been peaceful or rebellious. A recent reviewer, Edward T. Gargan in *The Nation* (February 13, 1967), wrote of my "nostalgia and affection for the class of artisan-craftsmen now vanished from our technological society"; and I would not wish to deny the charge. So, although my work has always had (to historians, at least) a sociological flavor, I have never felt in any way inclined to share the views of those American social scientists to whom riot and rebellion have appeared as an abnormal and distasteful deviant from "a stable, self-regulating state of perpetual equipoise." I believe, on the contrary, that conflict is both a normal and a salutary means of achieving social progress, and I have not hesitated in looking back on the past to identify myself more closely with some parties in the conflict than with others.

But I soon realized the limitations of my first subject of research. For one thing, it dealt only with the first two years of the Revolution, from 1789 to 1791; and this, it did not take long to discover, in itself made it difficult to find a publisher. More serious was the fact that having chosen to study the part played by the wage earners, my conclusions were bound to be a little negative. For, whatever the preconceptions with which I started, it gradually appeared that the wage earners, while engaged in large numbers in these events, were not yet in a position to play an independent role or substantially influence the outcome. In fact, even the common people as a whole, the urban *sans-culottes,* who included workshop masters, independent craftsmen, and shopkeepers, as well as their employees, only developed a distinctive social-political movement of their own after the fall of the monarchy in 1792. So I decided both to broaden and to extend my field of research—to broaden it by embracing all those who took part in popular disturbances; to extend it by considering all revolutionary and eve-of-revolutionary events from 1787 to 1795, even looking back to the last of the great popular outbreaks of the Ancien Régime, the so-called *guerre des farines* (or "flour war") of 1775. So, with this end in view, I took occasional leave from my teaching post in London and returned to the Paris archives for a number of visits between 1951 and 1957.

It was through these return visits to Paris that I became closely connected with Georges Lefebvre and two of the most active of his associates, Albert Soboul and Richard Cobb. I had met Lefebvre, almost by chance, on the first day I set foot in the Archives Nationales in April 1949 and had, from the first and like so many others, been struck by his simplicity, modesty, his friendly though somewhat austere approach, and his complete and utter devotion to scholarship and research. He invited me to his house at Boulogne-sur-Seine, which was as austere and as redolent of all the Jacobin-Republican virtues as the master himself. From then on, we corresponded, regularly but infrequently, and I went to see him whenever I arrived in Paris, always before my departure, and perhaps once or twice in between; occasionally I saw him in the archives. So, over a period of some ten years, I doubt if I met him more than twenty times in all; yet I probably learned as much from him in these few encounters as I did from reading his books. Since the publication in 1924 of his great work on the peasants, *Les Paysans du Nord*, he had been the acknowledged master of the study of the Revolution "from below"; but how important this contribution was I discovered only as my own work proceeded. The part of his work that had the strongest influence on me was, I believe, his pioneering studies on the behavior of revolutionary crowds and on the rumors and panics ("La Grande Peur") of 1789. Moreover, all who came under his spell took away with them valuable lessons on what he considered indispensable to "la bonne méthode" in all historical enquiry: *Sans érudition, pas d'histoire.* His mind remained extraordinarily vigorous and inventive until the day of his death in 1959. He was seventy-five when I first met him; in his eighty-sixth year, a few months before he died, he wrote me a letter expounding the benefits that the social historian, in particular, might derive from a closer association between history and the biological sciences.

I also greatly benefited from my friendship and collaboration with Soboul and Cobb. It was quite by chance, as far as I know, that we were all working, in no way prompted by Lefebvre, in complementary but distinctive fields within the French Revolution: Soboul on the Parisian sectional militants and *sans-culottes* of 1793–1794, Cobb on the "revolutionary armies" and the *sans-culottes* in the provinces, and I on the Paris revolutionary "crowd." (Lefebvre once referred to us as *les trois mousquetaires.*) Soboul is, like myself, a Marxist and has something of the rigorous disciplinary approach to records of *le vieux maître* himself: his advice and guidance have always been invaluable to me in my work. Applied to Cobb, the term "discipline" does not perhaps appear to be the most appropriate; yet no man in France—or, I would suspect, at Oxford—has been so tireless and devoted a searcher after original sources as he. In fact, on one memorable occasion, when the Paris archives were officially closed and we had been given special dispensation to attend (as *étrangers de passage à Paris*), our zeal was so great that we were locked in at night and had to scale down a drainpipe to get out of the building! Moreover, Cobb's generosity is as boundless as his zeal, and I shudder to think how slim my own *dossiers* on Paris revolutionary committees and popular societies would have been without the numerous slips of information that he passed me from his own voluminous researches. So it was not by any means with tongue in cheek when I wrote in the Preface to my first book, *The Crowd in the French Revolution,* that with the help of friends such as these, it was, in a real sense, an expression of collective, rather than of purely individual enterprise.

It was Professor Cobban who suggested that I should make a book of the articles that I had by this time written on the "crowd" in the revolutionary period. The book was based, in part, on my original work on the wage earners of 1789–1791, in part on my subsequent research and writing on the *sans-culottes* of 1789–1793, with gaps filled in for the introductory and terminal periods of 1787–1788 and 1794–1795. The method was broadly similar to that which I had used in my thesis nearly ten years before. Yet the book, as it appeared to historians and to students outside France (where several of my earlier articles had been published), had a certain freshness and originality, both insofar as it was the first scholarly work to treat the revolutionary crowd as a composite theme over so long a period and because it used new records to answer new questions concerning the groups that composed it, their motives, and their modes of behavior.

Reviewers treated the book kindly, though they tended to see it as just another book on the "mobs" and *journées* of the French Revolution, whereas I believed myself that it was the method used and the wider implications to which it pointed, rather than the historical framework itself, that were important. Some reviewers, therefore, though not ungenerous in their praise, seemed to me to have missed the point. Others, even when they were more critical, gave me greater satisfaction, as they appeared to see what the book was intended to be about. Among reviews that I particularly valued were those by Asa Briggs in *The Listener* (September 4, 1959), Eric Hobsbawm in the *New Statesman* (March 28, 1959), Samuel Bernstein in *Science and Society* (fall 1959), Crane Brinton in *The American Historical Review* (July 1959), Georges Lefebvre in *Annales Historiques de la Révolution française* (April–June 1959), and Jacques Zacher and Sophie Lotte in the Soviet journal, *Voprosy Istorii* (1959).

Hobsbawm rightly saw that the essential point of the exercise had been to get down to such simple and basic, though hitherto neglected, questions as, "Who actually stormed the Bastille?" Briggs welcomed the book as the product of a new type of social history, already well established in France, which did not stop at the conventional frontiers and lines of demarcation of the political or social historian. But he rightly saw that I had not paid sufficient attention to the mechanism of insurrection, to the apparatus of law and order, and to the "psychology" of crowd behavior in general and of violence in particular. Brinton, with equal justice, charged me with neglecting the irrational element in my analysis of motives. Lefebvre, on the other hand, commended my study of motives, in particular, and the methodology of my investigation; but, with characteristic modesty, he appeared to doubt if his own work had been of any value whatsoever to me. The Soviet reviewers subjected the book to a serious critical analysis; they praised the originality of its method and the "value" of its results, but they took me severely to task on a number of questions: in particular, they believed that I had failed to see that the eighteenth-century worker was just as interested in his wages as in the price of his daily bread; that I had underestimated the part played by the workers in the Réveillon riots of April 1789; that I had overestimated the influence of the middle classes on the political thinking of the *sans-culottes;* and that I had laid far too much emphasis on the role of tradition and "backward" thinking as a motive force in revolutionary events. The review provided an extremely useful forum for discussion and led, three years later, to an airing of views on these and related problems by my Soviet critics, Soboul, and myself in Armando Saitta's journal, the *Critica Storica.*[1] Unfortunately, the discussion petered out after this number, and we arrived at no agreed conclusions.

Meanwhile, I had become involved in the study of English popular movements of the eighteenth century, which I thought it might be useful to contrast with the French; here I attempted to apply the same methods as in my earlier researches. The results have not always been as fruitful as I had hoped, because the English judicial records before the later nineteenth century are, compared with the French, notoriously defective. But I had the good fortune to begin with the Gordon Riots of 1780, which I wanted to compare with the Réveillon riots of 1789, in which I saw a transition between the riots of the Ancien Régime and the Revolution. I was fortunate because in this case the number of prisoners up for trial was relatively large, and the information about them in the *Proceedings* of the Old Bailey in London proved to be reasonably adequate. Moreover, having been struck by the difference in social status between the rioters and their victims (which, it seemed to me, provided a useful clue to the deeper causes of the outbreak), I chanced on the idea of using the taxation records (in the first place, the registers of the Riot Tax levied to compensate house-holders for damages suffered) as a means of determining the value of the victims' properties. From this emerged a paper on "The Gordon Riots: A Study of the Rioters and Their Victims," which won the Alexander Prize of the Royal Historical Society for 1955.[2]

It was in the course of this work that I first met Albert Hollaender, now Deputy Librarian at the Guildhall Library in London; I owe to him, far more than to anyone else, what I have learned of the use of London records. He has been a wise counselor and a constant friend. He put me onto studying the "Gin" and anti-Irish riots of 1736 and the

"Wilkes and Liberty" disturbances of 1768–1769; and at his prompting and under his direction I have contributed a number of papers to *The Guildhall Miscellany*, which he edits. He has been a severe taskmaster and is, above all, a stickler for footnotes, which, he insists, must be both numerous and accurate. On one occasion, he had me called to the telephone in the middle of a school history lesson to berate me unmercifully for having failed to match a note at the foot of the page with its equivalent in the text!

I had written a couple of articles on the Wilkite movement; the second of these, which appeared in *History Today*,[3] led to a publisher's invitation (it was not from the Clarendon Press) to write a book on John Wilkes. I decided to do so, but not along the lines suggested by the publisher in question. Wilkes himself was a fascinating character and an admirably suitable subject for a new biography. But biography was not in my line, and I was far more interested in doing a full-length study of the Wilkite movement or of Wilkes' supporters ("the Devil's disciples," as Asa Briggs called them) than of John Wilkes himself. Essentially, the method of approach was similar to the one I had used before, but both the subject and the records used (as usual, the one being largely determined by the other) were very different. For one thing, Wilkes' supporters among "the inferior set" (the social equivalent of the Parisian *sans-culottes* of 1789–1795) provided only one element, perhaps not the most important, among his followers; and the records, for reasons already noted, did not make it possible to explore this side of the question as deeply as I should have wished. So the claim made later by the *Punch* reviewer that I had "Namierized the Mob" was really quite misleading. Moreover, as the activities of City of London merchants, manufacturers, gentry, clergy, and, in particular, of Middlesex freeholders (who occupied properties valued at 40s. a year and above) played an important part in the proceedings, I had to have recourse to a wider range of records than I had used before. These included the records of London livery companies, rate books and land tax registers, city directories and lists of justices of the peace, and, above all, the Middlesex poll-books and (an invaluable find) the town and county petitions of 1769. Once more, what in my view was original about the book was not so much the subject or its conclusions as the method used to arrive at the results.

The book appeared in February 1962 (three years after my first), and received once more a friendly reception from the critics. In fact, A. J. P. Taylor's review in *The Guardian* (February 9, 1962) on the day of publication was so fulsome in its praise as to be almost embarrassing. I was surprised to learn that I had produced "an innocent stick of dynamite which levels the Namier view to the ground" and that I had "put mind back into history and restored the dignity of man." But in case I should have been tempted to take this praise too literally, I would have been brought sharply to earth by Hobsbawm's review in the *New Statesman* (February 16, 1962). Hobsbawm reminded me that, though I had established the sociology of the Wilkite movement and defined its boundaries, I had done little to answer the important question of why this development took place in England just at this time? In short, contrary to Taylor, he believed that my attention to the revival of popular radicalism, which had lain dormant for close on a hundred years, had not been sufficiently probing. This was constructive criticism, and I had to admit, tempting as it was to choose the more comfortable course of basking in the sunshine of Taylor's praise, that it was fundamentally just. Some critics were rather less constructive: the reviewer in *History* (October 1962) took much of the gilt off his qualified praise by methodically cataloguing what seemed to me an alarmingly long list of errors of fact; in the *Revue Belge d'Histoire et de Philosophie* (1964), Jacques Godechot berated me for "playing down" the "revolutionary" potentialities of the English late eighteenth-century movements; and Brian Inglis, in *The Spectator* (February 9, 1962), thought I had written "the wrong book" and "should start again." And even though I received numerous and generally favorable reviews, it was evident that those critics who had reviewed both books—and I am thinking in particular of Hobsbawm and Briggs—thought the second a rather inferior successor to the first.

One reviewer, A. L. Morton, writing in *Marxism Today* (June 1962), had used the occasion to comment on my work as a whole and to establish the connection between my two books and the articles I had published on English eighteenth-century popular movements. I was anxious, when the opportunity arose, to write a synthesis of my studies on both England and France, supplemented by the similar work of others in the field. The opportunity was afforded by an invitation from Norman Cantor, then of Columbia University, to contribute a volume to a new series he was editing for Wiley in New York entitled "New Dimensions in History," in which comparative studies were to play a part. So I started work on *The Crowd in History: A Study of Popular Disturbances in France and England 1730–1848*, which was published at the end of 1964.

The book was intended to be more than just a synthesis of earlier work. For one thing, my own earlier published work had not gone beyond the eighteenth century, and it was necessary, in order to establish a reasonable claim to be dealing with the "pre-industrial" period in both countries, to extend my time span to 1848. This meant "filling in" with popular movements from the immediate post-Napoleonic era, from the 1830s, and from the transitional movements of

1848 in France and of Chartism in England. Here I was at the disadvantage of not being on such familiar ground, of only having done original preparatory work myself on patches of 1830 and 1848, and of finding myself compelled to fill in the missing pieces, where recent scholarly work was not available, by means of stop-gap measures either based on newspaper reports or on the (sometimes outdated) work of others. On the other hand, since my arrival in Australia in 1960, I had been building up from the convict records in Sydney and Hobart the case histories of transported Luddites, Chartists, Tolpuddle Martyrs, and machine-breaking laborers of 1830, and these served as useful additional materials for the English movements of the early nineteenth century. Moreover, I welcomed the opportunity the new book afforded of correcting some of the earlier omissions, misunderstandings, and mistakes that the more constructive of my critics had brought to light.

In particular, I wanted to lend more weight than I had done before to the irrational in human motivation, to the phenomenon of violence in crowd behavior, to the forces of law and order, to the relations between leaders and followers in riots and revolutions, to the survival of archaic forms of thought and action carried over from an earlier age, to the role of religion and millenarian fantasies as adjuncts of disturbances, to the coexistence in popular movements of "backward-looking" and "forward-looking" concepts, to the special characteristics of counterrevolutionary (or "church and king") movements, and to the transformation of ideas in the process of assimilation and adaptation. I learned some lessons (though too few, as the book appeared when my own was almost completed) from Edward Thompson's *The Making of the English Working Class*, and more from Hobsbawm's *Primitive Rebels*, which had been published shortly after my first book in 1959. I also took an elementary reading course in sociology, reread Gustave LeBon (though without changing my views on his basic limitations), and derived considerable profit from reading Neil Smelser's *Collective Behavior*, which had appeared in the course of the previous year. So, although I added little original work of my own, the mixture was by no means the same as before.

The reception of *The Crowd in History* was not as generally favorable as had been that of my previous work. But more attention was paid to the book—and I looked on this as a distinctive "plus"—by sociologists and social psychologists. My first book had been reviewed by *The American Sociological Review* (February 1960) and the *British Journal of Sociology* (March 1960), but, as far as I know, by no other journals in this field. The third book, in addition to these, drew reviews (or at least a mention) from *The American Behavioral Scientist* (September 1965), *The Annals of the American Academy of Political and*

Social Science (May 1965), *Sociology and Social Research* (April 1965), *Trans-Action* (September–October 1965), and *Social Forces* (September 1965), and there may have been others.

Some were friendly, others damned with faint praise, none were downright disparaging. Stephen Schafer, in *The Annals*, gave me a pat on the back for having "done so much work" and for presenting "so much substantial data," but thought the book rather an act of good will toward the importance of the crowd and the method of its study than a sociological analysis. D. C. Moore, on the other hand, in *Sociology and Social Research*, thought, somewhat charitably perhaps, that I was "well read in sociology and well aware of the relevance of [my] findings to social psychology and the theory of collective behavior." Even more laudatory were Herbert Blumer in *Trans-Action* and Charles Tilly in *The American Sociological Review* (August 1965). Blumer commended the virtues of my historical approach, though he pointed to the lack of an "analysis of the crowd as a generic group"; yet he was generous enough to blame this shortcoming not so much on me as on his fellow sociologists and social psychologists who had "done a rather miserable job in studying the crowd systematically." Charles Tilly, who is both a sociologist and a historian of France, recommended my "rich, solid work" to sociologists, but shrewdly pointed to certain drawbacks of my method and the sources on which it relies: "They concentrate on the event itself, leading to the construction of a typical natural history for each major class of events, while inhibiting analysis of negative cases, or of underlying social changes." This is a valid criticism; moreover, it is one that was also made, as will be seen, by the reviewer of *The Times Literary Supplement* in slightly different terms. Yet, by and large, as an intruder in the field of sociology, I suppose I had come out of the encounter relatively unscathed.

Among historians I had a mixed reception. In England, I received favorable comments from Peter Laslett in *The Guardian* (May 7, 1965), James Joll in *The Observer* (May 9, 1965), and J. H. Plumb in *The Sunday Times* (June 20, 1965). In a special issue of *The Times Literary Supplement* (April 7, 1966) devoted to "New Ways in History," Edward Thompson, while generally well disposed toward the book, regretted that I had departed from my "own high standards" in producing inadequate, second-hand material on English grain riots of the eighteenth century as well as on Luddites and Chartists. Gwyn Williams, in *New Society* (August 1965), was far more critical, as was R. K. Webb in the *American Historical Review* (October 1965). Yet I received good points, in admirably lucid and intelligent prose, from Edward Gargan in *The Nation* (February 13, 1967) and E. J. Hobsbawm in *The New York Review of Books* (April 22, 1965); and in a short article in the

William and Mary Quarterly (October 1966), Gordon S. Wood raised doubts about the "uniqueness" of the American revolutionary crowd of the 1760s and 1770s and recommended that, in the light of my findings for France and England, it should be looked at once again.

It was left to the anonymous reviewer in *The Times Literary Supplement* (December 30, 1965) (who was, unmistakably, my old friend Richard Cobb) to mount the longest and most comprehensive indictment of the method and theme of my book; in so doing, he revealed the deep gulf that still separates historians and sociologists on problems of this kind and the difficulties besetting the historian (or the sociologist) who attempts to bridge it. He criticized my "arbitrary" choice of dates and my equally "arbitrary" choice of countries. "It is doubtful," he wrote, "if anyone can offer any valuable new interpretations, or propose any general laws governing collective behaviour, merely by stringing together, over a period of 118 years, a series of largely unconnected riots, divided into two main groups—urban and rural—in two European countries." He went on to question the value of drawing any general conclusions from a statistical analysis of rioters' occupations, for the man who describes himself as a wine merchant when caught in a riot may, at other times of the day, be a clerk, a brothel-keeper, a horse-dealer, or a riverside worker; "such people will not stand still and stay in a single occupation over several years to oblige historical arithmetic." And even if we knew all about his occupation(s), his age, name, and place of birth, we should still have to "follow him to his home," "get into his head," and find out whether he was a first child or a younger son—in short, to trace his case history from A to Z. And why should he riot one day rather than another and in this place rather than the next? And if a riot happens to follow in the wake of a labor dispute or an agitation over the price of bread, how do we know with any degree of certainty that the one event is related to the other? Moreover, "the study of the crowd is only the preliminary stage in the exploration of the popular movement," for "riots are only a series of peaks, sticking out above the waters of a submerged, but discoverable, history of the common people"; the historian is liable to have his vision clouded and his focus blurred if he attaches "undue importance to what may well have been, at the time, an isolated, accidental and semi-lunatic outbreak." What is the significance of riots, anyway? At this time in England (he claimed), "people *lived* with a certain amount of brawling and rioting, a national habit familiar enough to be given a place in *Jonathan Wild the Great*." And finally, he chided me for a tendency to "intellectualize about collective motivation that must often defy analysis."

There was much in this review with which I found, after a preliminary bout of irritation, that I could readily agree. Of course, it would be better to study five or six countries rather than two. Of course, it would be preferable to take a longer time span (say 300 years) to study "pre-industrial" popular movements. Of course, we would have a more useful and valid picture of individual participants if we knew a great deal more about their case histories. Of course, one cannot be a hundred percent sure about the relation of one event to another if one does not know all that happened in between. Of course, to understand riots one should know more about the places where riots did *not* happen as well as the places where they did. Of course, riots are "peaks," or exceptional events, and may therefore easily give one a distorted impression about the whole life span of a popular movement and about the everyday lives of the people who take part in them. Of course, some riots are more significant than others (even if the example of eighteenth-century England is, *pace* Halévy, an extremely dubious one). And, of course, there is a great deal in the motivation of crowds, whether in their "collective mentality" or in that of the individuals that compose them, that defies the historian's or the social scientist's analysis.

But aren't these really counsels of perfection or, perhaps more properly, of despair? For even if we allow for the deficiencies in the book, which the reviewer had every right to criticize, is he not really saying that each historical event is unique and that it is useless, and even undesirable, to attempt to draw a causal link between one and another or to set them in a common conceptual framework, let alone (as in this particular case) to devise "general laws governing collective behaviour"?

Yet there is considerable truth in what the reviewer wrote. Above all, he put his finger on the dilemma of the historian who, while wishing to remain a historian, wants, in order to help him in his enquiry, to come to terms with the social sciences. Is he to abandon the safe haven of "the unique event" in order to devise general patterns and derive general conclusions from human conduct, which can never be fully documented or verified in strictly historical terms? It must be granted, for example, that it is far easier to document the "peaks" than the troughs of a popular movement and that there are therefore considerable dangers in attempting to mold them within a common framework of statistical analysis; granted, too, that my own particular mode of enquiry—*Rudéfication*, as the reviewer calls it—depends on adequate samples that are not always readily available. The more impressionistic method of building up a series of case histories or portraits is a tempting, and a safer, alternative; this becomes a possibility—and may even occasionally take care of the "troughs"—where the information is as rich as that provided by French police records of 1793–1795, some English county prison registers of the nineteenth century, the

Australian convict records of the mid-1820s to mid-1860s, or the present-day decennial census. But popular movements are not solely the expression of the individuals who compose them; they also have a collective identity, which it is equally necessary to attempt to measure and define. To do this, the historian must supplement the individual case history by such means as are available for determining the collective actions, moods, and motives of the "crowd." He must, in fact, look through his telescope at both ends.

To assemble his "case histories" and to get his closer and more personal vision, he may reasonably rely on the well-tried methods of historical research—provided he is willing and able to be flexible in his choice of questions and records. But to classify and correlate, and even to interpret, his findings, he may need (according to their nature and their volume) to have recourse to the computer and, more important, to lean heavily on the techniques and skills developed by the traditional social sciences. And here he is immediately confronted with a problem: Should he attempt to go forward alone, or should he draw not only on the experience but on the active cooperation of the anthropologist, the psychologist, the sociologist? In making his choice, he may do well to heed the warning voiced by Max Gluckman and his associates at Manchester in their book, *Closed Systems and Open Minds* (Edinburgh, 1964). All fields of enquiry in the social sciences (they tell us) are as open to the historian as to any other social scientist, whether they deal with societies, factory systems, urban development, human behavior, or the advance of an undeveloped nation; so there is virtually no field into which the historian may not enter. Each discipline, however, has its own purpose, its own focus and points of emphasis, and its own means of exploration; yet each, in the course of the enquiry, will inevitably draw on the "assumptions" and experience of others. But there is a point, which the authors term the "limits of naïveté," beyond which it is wiser for the specialist in one discipline not to venture without the close cooperation of his colleagues in the others. In theory, the historian may, in the course of his researches, assume the mantle of the economist or social anthropologist; in practice, however, both his tools and his "assumptions" are different, and he may soon reach a point where a measure of teamwork may save him from embarrassment, if not, quite literally, from disaster. On looking back, I think that some such thoughts as these may have entered the minds (no doubt with ample justification) of certain of the social scientists who reviewed *The Crowd in History.*[4]

I have, therefore, been on safer ground in my more recent cooperation with Eric Hobsbawm in an essentially "historical" treatment of the English agricultural laborers' revolt of 1830.[5] As is well known, Hobsbawm is an economic historian of distinction (as I most certainly am not). He is also a labor historian who has worked on labor problems of both the nineteenth century and earlier times. And, in his *Primitive Rebels* (Manchester, 1959), he has studied the archaic and millenarian movements that, in the agricultural communities of certain industrial countries, have spilled over into the twentieth century. So it has been possible to give our joint book a wider frame of reference, and to raise new questions of which I should have been incapable on my own. In fact, our book is not merely a study of the villagers' revolt of 1830, but also a history of the English farm laborer —his outlook, working conditions, and way of life—during the first half of the nineteenth century. Moreover, this combined operation has made it possible, I believe, to meet some of the objections to my earlier work raised by a number of historians, including the "anonymous" reviewer of *The Times Literary Supplement.*

For one thing, the subject chosen is supported by a wealth of documentation—not only by the London and provincial press, the Home Office papers, the reports of Parliamentary committees, prison registers, the proceedings of assizes and quarter sessions, but also by local county records and the voluminous convict materials in Australia. These are far more varied, detailed, and also suited to the study of the "crowd" than the equivalent sources relating to the English eighteenth century. In consequence, it has been easier to present a living picture of both the riots and rioters and of the agricultural population out of which they grew. It has been possible, too, to trace the laborers' history over a longer period from "trough" to "peak" and back to "trough" in two directions: into the aftermath of rural incendiarism and union organization, and, for those transported, into their enforced exile in the Australian colonies. It has meant, further, that we have been able to consider a far larger sample than is common in such cases. Nearly 2,000 laborers and rural craftsmen were arrested, of whom about one quarter (the largest batch of convicts ever transported for the same "crime") were shipped to Tasmania and New South Wales. This, in turn, has provided the raw materials for a number of case histories, though these are still disappointingly few in number—not surprising, perhaps, in view of our subject and in the absence of the modern, fully detailed decennial census. So, on the score of the sample, the study in depth, and the relation of "peak" to "trough," I think this present work marks an appreciable advance on what I have been able to do, largely unaided and with other records, in the past.

Rather more important perhaps—and this is essentially a contribution of Hobsbawm's—has been the attempt not only to consider the villages that actually rioted, but to pose and answer the pertinent question: Why did *these* villages rebel while others (often their neighbors) did not? Was there anything in the riotous village's structure—its size, its type of agriculture and settlement, its social relationships, its landownership, its proximity to main lines of communication, its religious affiliations, its political leadership, its degree of literacy, pauperism or criminality—which made it more prone to riot than another? Or was it merely the fact of lying in the path of a movement that had already begun elsewhere? Even if the evidence suggested (as, in fact, it did), that a riot-prone village tended to be larger than the average; to contain a higher ratio of laborers to farmers; to have a larger proportion of craftsmen, small landholders, and shopkeepers; to have an "open" or "mixed" rather than a "close" landownership; to have a larger measure of religious independence; to lie closer to markets and fairs; to have a longer history of local disputes; to have (on balance) a larger proportion of unemployed; and (more decidedly) to be engaged in tillage rather than pasture—all this could, on occasion, be made almost irrelevant by the simple fact of the powerful contagion that a concerted movement among its neighbors might exert on the most peaceful and least riot-prone village lying in its path. So the question might elicit no firm and conclusive answer. Yet the question was well worth asking; and to ask it was, at least, the beginning of a wisdom that I, for my part, had previously neglected.

Finally, I hope one day to fill in another gap in my studies of the "crowd": to trace the origins and course of the ideas that "grip the masses" (to use Marx's phrase) and play so important a part in both the "peaks" and the "troughs" of a popular movement. Whether pagan or religious, overt or submerged, such ideas are quite obviously a potent force in riots, rebellions, and revolutions. But it is useless to follow the traditional method of studying the ideas in their pristine, undiluted form without reference to the social context in which they germinate or the needs of the groups and classes that absorb them and the uses to which they put them. In this last book, we have tried to unravel some of the archaic and traditional notions underlying the laborers' movement. Yet a great deal more requires to be done, and over a far wider field. If the labor or social historian really wants to see "mind put back into history," this is one of the jobs he will have to undertake.

NOTES

1. "I Sansculotti: una discussione tra storici marxisti," *Critica Storica*, I, iv (July 1962), 369–98.
2. *Transactions of the Royal Historical Society*, 5th series, vol. 6 (1956), pp. 93–114.
3. George Rudé, "Wilkes and Liberty," *History Today*, VII, 9 (September 1957), 571–79.
4. For a "historical" sociologist's statement of the problems involved in this type of interdisciplinary cooperation, see Charles Tilly, "Clio and Minerva," in John C. McKinney and Edward A. Tiryakian, eds., *Theoretical Sociology: Perspectives and Developments* (New York, 1968).
5. E. J. Hobsbawm and George Rudé, *Captain Swing* (London and New York, 1969).

Looking Backward:
Andrew Jackson:
Symbol for an Age

JOHN WILLIAM WARD

JOHN WILLIAM WARD was born on December 21, 1922, in Boston, Massachusetts. After serving in the United States Marine Corps from 1942 to 1946, he returned to Harvard University, where he majored in American history and literature, and graduated in 1947. Ward then proceeded to the University of Minnesota, where he studied under Henry Nash Smith, taking his M.A. in 1951 and his Ph.D. in 1953. In 1952 he joined the Department of English at Princeton University, transferring in 1959 to the Department of History. From 1961 to 1964 he served as chairman of the American Civilization Program at Princeton. Since the fall of 1965, he has been teaching at Amherst, where he is Professor of History and American Studies.

Ward belongs to the American Historical Association, the American Studies Association, and the Organization of American Historians. In 1958 and 1968 he was awarded a Guggenheim Fellowship. In 1965 he was a Fellow at the Center for Advanced Studies in the Behavioral Sciences at Stanford, and in 1967–1968 he taught as a Fulbright Lecturer at the University of Reading in England.

. Author of *Andrew Jackson: Symbol for an Age* (New York, 1955) and *Red, White, and Blue: Men, Books, and Ideas in American Culture* (New York, 1969), Ward has also written numerous articles for such periodicals as *The American Scholar, The Yale Review, The Virginia Quarterly Review,* and *The American Quarterly.* In addition, he has edited the following works: Frederick Grimke, *The Nature and Tendency of Free Institutions* (Cambridge, Mass., 1968), Herbert Croly, *The Promise of American Life* (Indianapolis, 1965), and Michael Chevalier, *Society, Manners and Politics in the United States* (New York, 1961).

Ward is currently working on a study of ideals and values in American culture.

W hen Oxford University Press accepted *Andrew Jackson: Symbol for an Age* for publication, the manuscript had an introductory note that pointed briefly to the "method" of the book. At the final stage in the preparation of the typescript for the printer, a member of the Oxford editorial staff spent a day with me resolving minor questions of style and saved her question about the introduction until the last. "Why is it there?" "Because," I said, "I think the method of the book is the most interesting and most important feature of the book." "But," she pursued, "isn't the method implicit in the book? Won't a reader interested in that see it for himself?" I agreed that I hoped so, but persisted until finally, harried by her remorseless good sense, I admitted that my affection for the introduction derived from a certain pride that I had read the writings of cultural anthropology, psychology, and literary criticism, and wished to display the fact. She replied coolly, "Well, when we grow up, we have to put away our childish things." So, the introduction came out.

It was wise that it did come out. A methodological note would have stood like a roadblock in the way of the general reader, that necessary fiction for anyone who writes and hopes to find someone on the other end of the line. Whether it is wise now, after the fact, to write about the intellectual influences and assumptions that governed the writing of the book is hard to say. It may be rather childish, but I persist in thinking that the point of view which is implicit in the book is perhaps still its most important quality. But now, after the fact, another consideration seems equally important. It is, simply, that the book which was published was not the book I set out to write.

Santayana once remarked that we are condemned to live dramatically in a world which is undramatic. Among other things, Santayana's epigram points to the human necessity to make sense out of experience, to impose order upon the disorder of chance events so they may have a shape and a meaning. Historians are especially sensitive to the dangers in giving too pat an order to the contingencies of past events, in violating the brute irreducible particular in the unavoidable necessity to generalize in the attempt to make sense of the past. Some historians still seem to think they can avoid the necessity and give us the facts, eschewing any generalization or interpretation of them, thereby falling victim to their own lack of self-consciousness. But to write about a limited event out of one's personal experience (in this instance the writing of a book) makes one deeply aware how disorderly experience is and how much one violates it in the attempt to give an orderly description of it. So, in looking backward at the making of the book, *Andrew Jackson: Symbol for an Age,* I wish to do two things: first, as best I can, describe the sequence of events that led to an unforeseen conclusion; then, provide a brief formal account of the methodology of the book.

I

The book, *Andrew Jackson: Symbol for an Age*, is an attempt to discover the attitudes and values of the mass of ordinary, inarticulate men in early nineteenth-century American culture through an examination of the themes and imagery that clustered about the figure of Andrew Jackson. The book is not a study of Andrew Jackson; it is a study of popular ideology. The problem was: How does the historian get at the ideas and emotions in the minds of the great majority who leave behind no record of what they think and feel? That problem arose initially because the book was meant to be a study of the ideas of Ralph Waldo Emerson and Herman Melville in the context of the general values of their time. My intention was to write mainly on those two literary figures, with the bland assumption that one could draw upon the secondary scholarship in intellectual history in order to provide the basis for a comparison with popular attitudes. But there was nothing immediately useful for that purpose, so I turned to the study of Jackson as one way of discovering popular attitudes, with the notion at first that such work would still be only a part, and a minor part at that, of the completed book. Emerson and Melville do appear fleetingly in the book as it now stands, but I never did get back to them. The same is true generally. Despite my continuing interest in literature, my writing has been more in the direction of intellectual history—or cultural history, as I choose to call what I choose to do.

My interest in Emerson and Melville as perhaps expressive of a certain polarity or tension in American consciousness derived from a general interest in the study of American history and literature and, more particularly, from a seminar on Romanticism with the late Professor Perry Miller at Harvard. Both the general and particular motives were, however, the result of pure chance. After nearly four years in the U. S. Marine Corps in World War II, I returned to Harvard College, where previously I had been a major in biochemistry; by the time I returned to study, I knew I had no desire to continue a premedical course. With no idea what I did wish to study, I entered the Program in History and Literature for the simple, practical reason that it afforded the most intellectual elbow-room. One could take courses in history, literature, art, politics, or whatever, and count them as courses in a single major, the study of American civilization.

The negative reason had important consequences. Those years

after the war were great years in the History and Literature Program at Harvard, innocent though I was of the fact when I blundered into it. Not knowing what I wished to do, I caught for the first time a glimpse of the delight of making a life around books and ideas and good talk. The moment may be symbolized by two great teachers: F. O. Matthiessen and Perry Miller. They were remarkably different in many ways, but shared one common quality—a fierce impatience with the second-rate. Their impatience paid the student the highest possible compliment—that his ideas were actually worth being taken seriously. In one remarkable summer, I found myself allowed as an undergraduate to take Matthiessen's seminar on American poetry and Miller's seminar on Romanticism. Matthiessen had already published *American Renaissance* and Miller the first volume of *The New England Mind*, but I took their courses largely because my tutor, now Professor J. C. Levenson at the University of Virginia, told me I should (that same summer Professor Harry Levin was giving his course on Proust, Joyce, and Mann, with the requirement that one read the works of all three and either Proust or Mann in the original language, so everyone I knew audited that course).

By the standards undergraduates like to employ, Matthiessen would rank low as a teacher. His lectures were choppy and disorganized; one could never take notes from him; and one was only aware well after the fact what one had "learned." He combined a passionate moral seriousness with an intense searching intellectuality. He was a forbidding figure to the undergraduate, yet he acted out in his own life, and so made available to his students, a commitment to the life of the mind which transcended by far the subject matter of any particular course. Perry Miller was in many ways Matthiessen's antithesis. He was a magnificent, sometimes flamboyant, lecturer, but he had the capacity to dramatize the immense importance of ideas in the life of a culture, and could make forbidding material come intensely alive. In his hands, what Jonathan Edwards might say at a Thursday lecture in eighteenth-century Boston became far more exciting than the tense closing minutes of a college football game.

To name only Matthiessen and Miller is unfair to many others, especially those fellow students with whom I spent most of the time. You did not presume to drop in on professors like Matthiessen and Miller, at least not without having done three or four days of hard homework in order not to seem a fool, and it was the day-to-day give-and-take with many others that gave substance to what Matthiessen and Miller especially exemplified.

After a year in a small business, I knew what I wanted was what I had briefly tasted in those two years at Harvard. A congeries of motives led me to want to be out of the Boston area, so once again negative factors and chance determined the results. I had a degree in American history and literature; someone told me that the University of Minnesota had a good program in American Studies; so to Minnesota I went. If Harvard had seemed auspicious after the war, Minnesota around 1950 was the realization of the promise of an ideal intellectual community. At the time, though, I took it for granted and simply assumed that the group at Minnesota was a single instance of university communities everywhere. The only disappointment came after the fact, when I finally came to realize that it was a rare and perhaps not to be repeated chance. What I will shortly describe in self-conscious abstractions was first experienced as the normal and self-evident way to go about the study of American culture.

Although again it is unfair to so many, one man may stand for the whole: Professor Henry Nash Smith. His book, *Virgin Land: The American West as Symbol and Myth*, was yet to appear when, as a student, I first met him. That book is the single most important influence on my own work, but that personal measure is no measure of the book's importance. It is fair to say that in 1950 *Virgin Land* marked a major new direction in the study of the American past, but in courses and seminars with Professor Smith I was totally unconscious of being, as the pat phrase has it, on the edge of new frontiers in scholarship.

Virgin Land has brought Professor Smith great distinction, but among those fortunate enough to have come to know him, his greatest distinction will always be his capacity to arouse the minds of others. He represents that rare combination in the university: a fine scholar and superb teacher, a living instance of the best graduate education may achieve. Of his many qualities, two may suffice. First, in seminar, in the discussion of a stiff amount of assigned work, Professor Smith would also range over a considerable number of books and intellectual figures in a tone which assumed that everyone, of course, knew them. The implication was that anyone who considered himself an intellectual would surely be conversant with such staples of intellectual life. Whether the technique was conscious or not I have never known, but the result was that the student, embarrassed by the thought that he was the only one who did not know all these men and books, would scurry off to the library and spend countless hours trying to catch up with what he was sure everyone else already knew. The result was an even mix of hard work and widening horizons.

The second quality was Professor Smith's cast of mind, his capacity to bear down upon the particular, to demand exhaustive responsibility to detail, yet win his way to broad and yeasty generalizations through the particular. Over luncheon, a discussion of an item in the daily press would often lead ultimately to an enlarged view of the shape and meaning of experience and history. Those who know Professor Smith will instantly recognize the quality; those who do not may experience it at second hand in many places, but perhaps especially in his article, " 'That Hideous Mistake of Poor Clemens's.' "[1] At the start, that article seems to promise a parody of the precise, meticulous, factual method of the historian, an account, down even to the menu, of the formal public celebration of John Greenleaf Whittier's seventieth birthday, a dinner at which Mark Twain was one of the speakers. But as the article proceeds, playing off what happened against what those present later thought happened, the range of meaning widens until, finally, one is involved in speculation about the ambivalent role of the writer in American culture and about the tension between the values of the official "public" culture and popular "vernacular" culture. That splendid article may stand as an example of the direction of a seminar by Professor Smith, although since it is a finished product, it affords little evidence of the give-and-take and sparkling play of mind that I experienced at first hand.

More directly, though, it was as a student under Professor Smith's direction that I decided to pursue the relation of literature to history in early American democratic culture which led finally, by a series of accidents, to *Andrew Jackson: Symbol for an Age.* I was at that stage of muddled confusion every writer knows when he is hard at work on something but is not quite sure what he is at work upon, when I came upon a review of *Virgin Land* by Professor Ralph Henry Gabriel in the *Yale Review.* In that review, commenting upon the difference in attitudes toward the frontier between the old Northwest and the South, Professor Gabriel suggested that a study of the national appeal of Andrew Jackson might reveal a pattern of attitudes common to the general society. I suspected the casual suggestion of the reviewer might mean that Professor Gabriel (whose own excellent book, *The Course of American Democratic Thought,* is important in the history of the study of American culture) had such a work in hand or had a graduate student at work on such a study. I wrote Professor Gabriel at Yale and asked; he said no, it was a passing thought. So, I began the study of Jackson as a way to explore the popular values of his time, but still with the intention of making that no more than a third of a larger project.

In other words, the book evolved in a distinctly haphazard fashion, the result finally of personal accident, chance encounters, and casual suggestion. It would be pleasant to take a finalist view of that evolutionary history and pretend that everything tended toward a predetermined end. But, like Henry James' hero in "The Jolly Corner," I know it all could have been remarkably different.

Finally, before some formal discussion of what did result, a few words about the process of writing the book itself. Following Professor

Gabriel's lead, I had the obviously simple task—at least so it seemed—of reading everything I could find of what Jackson's contemporaries said about him. At first, this task was made somewhat feasible because of the splendid collection of early American newspapers at the Wisconsin Historical Society; then later, material support from the American Council of Learned Societies allowed me to travel to the American Antiquarian Society in Worcester, to Widener and the Boston Athenaeum, to the Library of Congress and the Nashville area. All too quickly the result was an enormous and ungovernable mass of notes I had no idea what to do with. For months, I spent evenings at the desk in what my wife calls the "shuffle, cut, and deal" stage of scholarship, sorting and resorting, trying to find some pattern, some lines of relationship around which to organize what one thinks one knows. This still seems to me the most important moment in the act of writing, the willingness to suffer the anxiety of having no clear sense of direction, confident that if only one soaks oneself in the material, one will find the way. In this instance, the way came from the conjunction of two of the least promising sources, a collection of funeral orations on the death of Andrew Jackson and Martin Van Buren's *Autobiography.*

I had collected some eulogies on the death of Andrew Jackson from newspapers. Then I came upon Benjamin Dusenbery's printed collection of twenty-five of them. I dutifully took the book home and spent an evening reading those declamatory tributes, taking still more notes, of course. The next day remains the clearest memory I have of the composition of the book. Seated in a dusty carrel in the University of Minnesota Library, listlessly reading what must be one of the dullest testaments of a political leader in American history, Van Buren's cautious reminiscences, in a passage which had nothing much of interest in it, I came to the word "civilization." With it, the design of the entire book was given to me, "given" in the sense that I was the passive recipient of a detailed plan and outline. After those months of stumbling in the dark, it was as if my unconscious mind had worked the whole thing out and laid it before my conscious eye. I remember pushing Van Buren to one side and hastily, for fear I would lose it, scribbling for hours a detailed outline of the plan of the book I was yet to write, an outline which stood up remarkably well, with only one major and a few minor, particular changes.

In the rush of that moment, two things came together. First, I realized what I should have when I bored my way through Dusenbery's collection. I had in my hands a priceless resource for what I was after. The eulogy on the death of a fallen public hero is a mass ritual act in which the speaker takes upon himself the role of dramatizing, giving voice to, what everyone is supposed to feel. At the same time, the circumstances surrounding the delivery of the eulogies allowed me to test the assumption that these were the ritualistic utterances of public, and not idiosyncratic, sentiment on the meaning of Jackson's career. The crucial circumstance was that no one eulogist could have read what another one had said.

When Andrew Jackson died in 1845, the technology of communication was more primitive than when Lincoln's funeral cortege moved slowly by rail from Washington to Springfield, Illinois, or when a nation listened over the radio to the muffled drums of the procession carrying Franklin D. Roosevelt to his grave, or when television brought the brutal assassination as well as the healing ceremony of John F. Kennedy's death into every home. When Jackson died at the Hermitage, mock funeral ceremonies, complete with flag-draped casket, processional, and eulogy, were held a week later in nearly every major city of the country. From New England to the South, from the old Northwest to New Orleans, people paid vicarious homage to Jackson's memory. All these ceremonies took place within a short space of time at points so distant from each other that, given the speed of communications, each speaker was innocent of what others had chosen to say. What I realized suddenly was that all the eulogies I had read, however different their anecdotes, however different their emphases, could be gathered under three major headings, the headings which now provide the three divisions of the book: "Nature, Providence, and Will." Not all three concepts were present in every eulogy; some focused on one, some two, and some had all three. But those three words defined an ideal pattern in which all the eulogies participated.

At the same moment, the word "civilization" made me conscious that Jackson's public meaning lay in the fact that he dramatized the tension between opposites in the public mind. To take the immediate instance, "Nature" was to be understood in relation to its opposite, "civilization." The concept of "Will" was divided between Promethean self-reliance and a humane regard for others; "Providence" between the fatalism of acquiescence and the necessity for personal striving.

In one sense, I suppose I knew all this all along. Certainly no student of Henry Nash Smith's could be innocent of the antithesis between nature and civilization in American consciousness. But as in the old Transcendental joke when Elizabeth Peabody walked into a tree and said, "I saw it but I didn't realize it," I did not realize what was there before me in the material until that day in the library. From then on, it was just hard work, largely a matter of testing what I was in my heart of hearts sure about, of subjecting major moments in Jackson's career to a careful scrutiny to see if the public interpretation of their meaning was to be understood as part of the pattern defined by my three major concepts. Actually, in the order of composition, what now stands first came last. I came upon Congressman Troup's speech about the Battle of New Orleans, which now provides the introduction to the book, after the book was completely drafted. I doubt if I (or anyone else) would have been able to see what is implicit in Troup's speech until I had written all the rest. Originally, I had a final sentence to that introductory chapter suggesting that one test of the argument of the book would be for the reader to suspend his disbelief about what I say about Troup's words and return after reading the entire book to see if he then agreed. But the editor took that out too.

II

An account of the background of the book may have some interest for students of the psychology of the act of writing, or perhaps of the theory of probability, but there is still the foreground, the book itself. However capricious the history, the result was the book, *Andrew Jackson: Symbol for an Age*. It must stand independent of its origins. How well it stands is surely not for me to say. Yet, although I have an inevitable personal stake in thinking it a decent book, I have criticisms of it which I am always surprised others have not made. But to make them requires, at last, some comment on the method of the book. "Method" is perhaps too strict a word; "a point of view" would be better, a point of view implicit in the use of the word "symbol."

To put a complicated subject baldly, a symbol is an object that embodies an idea. The role of the symbol may best be understood, perhaps, by reference to one's private experience in the world of dreams. In the dream, symbol and idea are fused; that is, it is the object, the image we envision, which seems to engage our attention and inspire our hopes or fears. Because of Freud, we now understand somewhat better that the image is a metaphor, that it is actually the idea embodied in the object, not the object itself, which is the cause of our affective reaction. But until we have been brought to "see" the meaning, and not just the figurative image that embodies it, the idea and its symbolic incarnation are inseparably fused. On a somewhat less riotous level than that of the dream, my purpose in the book on Jackson was to distinguish the concepts that were embodied in and dramatized by the symbol "Andrew Jackson," and to reveal them as the source of the emotional appeal of the historical person Andrew Jackson, the seventh President of the United States.

Such a way of looking at a historical figure derived, in my own case, from an avocational interest in Freud, as I have already suggested, together with a concern for the connotations of language and imagery by way of the study of literature.[2]

But the dream and the literary work of art are the products of a single mind. For the relation of the symbol to society, for a view of the symbol as a collective rather than an individual product, the writings of students in the field of cultural anthropology were most important. One book, especially, may stand for a considerable literature: Bronislaw Malinowski's slender but richly suggestive book, *Myth in Primitive Psychology* (New York, 1926). One quotation from Malinowski describes, perhaps better than my own words, the point of view implicit in *Andrew Jackson: Symbol for an Age:*

> *Myth is an indispensable ingredient of all culture. It is . . . constantly regenerated; every historical change creates its mythology, which is, however, but indirectly related to historical fact. Myth is a constant by-product of living faith, which is in need of miracles; of sociological status, which demands precedent; of moral rule, which requires sanction.*

Malinowski taught me to see that the myth-making process in which symbols arise is an integral part of culture, vital to the life of society, and not merely sportive by-play. One could put aside the vulgar sense of myth as a mistake, an unfounded belief, and perceive the symbols and myths of a society as an expression of those values and attitudes by which society comprehends the meaning of its world. The chief function of the celebration of Andrew Jackson was to project upon the man, Andrew Jackson, concepts that defined the values of the American society of his time; not to describe Andrew Jackson, so much as to affirm the validity and efficacy of the values themselves. Jackson's success was used to provide sanctions for continuing belief in the values he was understood to embody. If there was a discrepancy between the facts of Jackson's personal life and the prevalent interpretation of the meaning of his life, the point was not to pounce gleefully in a debunking mood on the mistaken belief, but to see the reality that was being expressed, the values of early American democratic culture, not objective statements about the man. The symbol served a social need; it was only secondarily historical. Its prime function was, in Malinowski's splendid phrase, to provide a "dogmatic backbone" for the culture.

Malinowski was concerned, of course, with primitive culture. For the Western world, the eighteenth century has intervened, and we are restricted to what T. S. Eliot called the lower order of myth-making, in which historical actuality is attributed to ideas instead of allowing them to inhabit a self-sufficient world of their own. Yet the imagination that once peopled the world with gods and heroes still carries on and, under the guise of reality, the process of externalizing ideals and values is still indispensable for the cohesion of culture, any culture.

Such, briefly, are the particular assumptions that lie behind the writing of the book. Beyond the particular, though, there is a larger general assumption; it, too, derives from the discipline of cultural anthropology. That general assumption is that the many forms of action in a culture (that is, literature, politics, economics, and popular thought) are, in their different idioms, related one to another as expressions of a generally shared pattern of values.[3] It is that pattern of values which defines the meaning of culture. An example may help.

As I said, I had begun the work that led finally to *Andrew Jackson: Symbol for an Age* as a study of the relation of Emerson and Melville to their time. In other words, out of a general interest in history and literature, I wished to see how one might place literature in the context of its historical moment. Emerson saw the self-reliant, autonomous man as the way to the health and benefit of all mankind; for Emerson, the man free from involvement in society, free from institutions (at least, the Emerson of the years of Jackson's public life), free from the traditions of the past and the conventional wisdom of the present, was the hero of a millennial vision of the possibilities of history. Melville looked at that same hero and saw the darker side of Emerson's sanguine trust in the hero who recognized no limits beyond the demands of his own self. In Ahab, that hero brings disaster to the world; he destroys society in his monomaniac obsession with the truth of his own particular angle of vision on the meaning of it all.

In the public celebration of Andrew Jackson, one sees Emerson's and Melville's contemporaries grappling with the same problem. In the public mind, however, there is an uneasy tension between affirmation and rejection that is resolved dramatically in the writings of such representatives of the "high" culture as Emerson and Melville. Just as Emerson's ideal hero, the symbolic Jackson represented an affirmation of the spontaneous, intuitive, self-determining self. But, at the same time, the iron will of this self-reliant hero was not allowed, as in Melville's fiction, to proceed to its logical conclusion and present a threat to society. He had to be made amenable to the moral law and the good of society, even though it required the hand of God finally to do so. Which is only to say that, when arrayed against the popular symbol of Andrew Jackson, writers like Emerson and Melville may be seen as articulating (though that is an uncomfortably abstract word for what they do) the ambivalences implicated in the system of values which defines their culture.

My fond hope is that the reader of my book on Jackson need not appreciate the particular and general assumptions, the point of view, which made it possible to write it. As I have said elsewhere, I agree with the remark of that fine historian, Mr. Robert R. Palmer, when he says that history should be written in the ordinary language. I have come to agree with that lady editor at Oxford: one should leave one's intellectual baggage in the desk drawer and not obtrude it upon the reader who may be interested in the book, but not in the intellectual ambience from which it derives. The latter belongs properly, as in this instance, in books for those who are interested in the methods and assumptions of the historian at work in his shop before he puts out what he hopes is a finished product.

III

At this point, having described its history and its methodological background, I would like finally to make a few criticisms of the book. I suspect that most people who write are deeply dissatisfied with what they write, that they are probably the best critics of the inadequacies of what they have done. Not at the first moment, of course; ego is too much involved in its extension to allow that. But, after time has made possible a certain esthetic distance, a piece of writing becomes detached, self-existent, even alien; it becomes easy to see its faults. To say so is not to affect a pose of modest self-depreciation. Even now, many years later, if someone were to say that *Andrew Jackson: Symbol for an Age* is a wretched and stupid book, it would hurt. Yet it has always bothered me that critics have never pointed out what seem to me real problems, if not inadequacies, in the book. To be candid, I recognize that to say so is to demand that critics take your work as seriously as you do yourself, an outrageously egotistic demand, of course. However, I enjoy the chance now to say three things which, so far as I know, have not been said, at least in public.

The first criticism I would make of the book is that it is static. That is, the book presents a pattern of meaning which is abstracted from the development of the symbol. It concentrates on the meaning of the three major concepts and avoids the problem implicit in the short opening chapter, which uses Congressman Troup's speech to suggest that in 1815 at the Battle of New Orleans one may see in embryo the three concepts—Nature, Providence, and Will—which characterize the fully developed symbol. To use words like "embryo" and "developed" suggests a process, and the process is nowhere present in the book. Another way to put the matter is to point out that the book (as written although not as thought out), treats all its evidence as if the material constituted a single moment in time. There is not, except in the concluding "Coda," a single quotation outside the limits set by the years 1815 and 1845. Having worried about the problem, I decided to take the plunge and write about the period as a single slice of time, to abstract the pattern I had discovered from its history, that is, from its development. The risk was calculated, but it has always surprised me that professional historians who so often insist on the sequence of events as somehow the essence of history should not have jumped on the strategy I had, with misgivings, settled upon.

The second criticism I would make of the book concerns a matter of logic. The point is simple, and may be stated baldly. The argument goes: First, Jackson was a popular hero; second, certain things were said about him; third, the historian may understand why he was a hero by examining what was said about him. But there is no necessary relation between the first and third assertions. One need only consider one's own experience to see why. A public figure may be chosen for the highest office a democratic people have in their gift. Many speeches, editorials, cartoons, songs, and reasons may be presented that argue why the people should give him their support. But the people may follow or vote for their hero for reasons quite different from the reasons that are given to them to do so. That is, the argument that the public statements which surround the figure of Andrew Jackson were the reasons for the popular worship of Andrew Jackson is no more than plausible. It is in no way necessary. If the purpose of the book was, as I have already said, to get at the emotions and attitudes of the inarticulate masses of men who leave no written record behind them, clearly the evidence of the book is derived from people, however articulate, who did leave a record behind them. The assumption is that people did respond to Jackson because of what was said about him. But they may not have. They may have responded to him for reasons that did not find their way into the record the historian has at his disposal.

Neither of these criticisms; that is, the static quality of the ideal pattern of the meaning of Jackson as a symbol of the culture's values, or the logical force of the argument in saying that he was, bothered me very much. The first was accepted simply as a necessity of organization. The second was accepted pragmatically; that is, in the opening chapter I pointed to the fact that Jackson was simply *one* symbol for the values of his age, with the further suggestion in the concluding chapter that "any student of American culture will quickly be able to point to other manifestations at the time of the three ideas [Nature, Providence, and Will], either singly or in conjunction with one another." I was conscious that the evidence was no more than persuasive. It did not have the force of a syllogism.

But there is a third question one might direct at the book, the question "why?" Why did American culture in the years of the early nineteenth century hold up the symbolic Andrew Jackson as a type for emulation? Beyond the intellectual influences I have named so far, there was one more, one very important, then and still: Karl Mannheim's *Ideology and Utopia* (London, 1936). What kind of society was it that celebrated the values one finds in an examination of the symbol of Andrew Jackson? What function did the symbol serve? Or, in Mannheim's language, what was the sociology of the pattern of ideal values of American democratic culture in the early nineteenth century?

Originally, I had a final chapter I called "Symbol for What?" that was an attempt to engage such questions. I took it out for two reasons, one esthetic, the other practical. The esthetic reason was simply that to answer those questions was to start another book. The book as it now stands seemed to me to have a certain self-contained unity, and—whatever my doubts about it—a wholeness that further questions could only damage. The practical reason was ignorance. I did not know enough at the time to answer the question that I recognized as important, perhaps crucial. The answer to that question had to be left to another book which is still in the works.

NOTES

1. *Harvard Library Bulletin*, IX (Spring 1955), 145–80.
2. My personal predilections were, of course, reinforced and clarified by books, especially Ernst Cassirer, *An Essay on Man: An Introduction to a Philosophy of Human Culture* (New Haven, 1944) and *Language and Myth* (New York, 1946), whose work I came to by way of Suzanne Langer's *Philosophy in a New Key* (Cambridge, Mass., 1942). Equally important, so far as I can reconstruct the moment, were Edward Sapir's essays, especially "Culture, Genuine and Spurious"; Lord Raglan, *The Hero: A Study in Tradition, Myth, and Drama* (London, 1936); Hans Vaihinger's theory of "fictive forms" in *The Philosophy of "As If"* (London, 1935); and Clyde Kluckhohn, "Myths and Rituals: A General Theory," *Harvard Theological Review*, XXXV (January 1942), 45–79.
3. For a fuller discussion, see my opening essay, "History and the Concept of Culture," in *Red, White, and Blue: Men, Books, and Ideas in American Culture* (New York, 1969).

How the Kingdom
of the
Great Makoko
and
Certain Clapperless Bells
Became
Topics for Research

JAN VANSINA

JAN VANSINA was born on September 14, 1929, in Antwerp, Belgium. He studied history and law at the University of Louvain, from which he earned his Licenciate in 1951 and Doctorate in 1957. At the University College, London, he also passed the qualifying exam for the Ph.D. degree in anthropology in 1952. From 1957 to 1959 and in 1966–1967 he was Visiting Professor at the University of Lovanium, Kinshasa, Congo. From 1952 to 1960, he worked as Research Officer and then Director of the Institut pour la Recherche Scientifique en Afrique Centrale (I.R.S.A.C.). Since 1960, he has been Professor of History and Anthropology at the University of Wisconsin, Madison. He has also taught as Visiting Professor at the University of Louvain (1968–1969) and Northwestern University (1962–1963).

Among the numerous professional organizations to which he belongs are the American Historical Association, the African Studies Association, the Royal Academy for Overseas Sciences (Belgium), and the International African Institute. Vansina won a research award from the Social Science Research Council in 1963 and the Herskovits Prize of the African Studies Association in 1967. In addition, he was awarded the Quinquennial History Prize of Belgium in 1967, for the period 1961–1966, and a Guggenheim Fellowship in 1969–1970.

Vansina's prolific publications include *De la Tradition Orale: Essai de Methode Historique* (Tervuren, 1961, translated into English [Chicago, 1965] and into Spanish [Barcelona, 1966]); *L'Evolution du Royaume Rwanda des Origines à 1900* (Tervuren, 1962); *De Geschiedenis van de Kuba van ongeveer 1500 tot 1904* (History of the Kuba, Tervuren, 1963); *Kingdoms of the Savanna* (Madison, Wisc., 1966, Herskovits Prize); *Introduction à l'Ethnographie du Congo* (Kinshasa, 1966); and such widely noted articles as "A Comparison of African Kingdoms," *Africa* (London), XXXII, 4 (1962); "Long-distance Trade Routes in Central Africa," *Journal of African History* (London), III, 3 (1962); "The Foundation of the Kingdom of Kasanje," *ibid.*, IV, 3 (1963); and "The Use of Process-Models in African History," in J. Vansina, R. Mauny, and L. Thomas, eds., *The Historian in Tropical Africa* (London, 1964).

I n a file close at hand to the working table lies a stack of documentation about the Tio, a people only a few thousand members strong, who live north of Brazzaville in the Republic of the Congo in Equatorial Africa. It consists of a set of notebooks that contain observations, mainly of an anthropological nature, collected during a spell of field work there in 1963–1964. Most of the observations deal with what life was like in 1963, but some purport to tell what life was like around the turn of the century and a little before. There are almost no certain dates in this supposedly historical material because people may remember how they lived, but do not remember dates in that part of the world. In addition, the files contain a few copies of manuscripts starting around 1880 and petering out by 1886, with an occasional piece from the 1930s and the 1940s. There is also a little box with cards on which words have been recorded for different languages in and around Tio country, along with lists of cultural features both similar to and different from those of the Tio. Out of that and with the help of published accounts about the Tio since 1880, and there are pitifully few of these, is supposed to grow a book about Tio life around 1880 and a history of their kingdom since its inception. And it is an old one, for in 1491 it was already known to Europe as the kingdom of the great Makoko.

So far the title of the book is known: *The Lion's Court*. And some of the mass of data has been summarized in an impressionistic form. It will be necessary to collate the summary with the original data and improve it to the point that it really contains all the data, but in a more orderly fashion. The format chosen, or if you wish, the implicit model, is the one of all ethnographic surveys: ecology, economics, social structure, political structure, religion—a rich fund this—and the arts. This exercise should refresh my memory of the culture. It should then be possible to see how to arrange the materials for the writing of the book. To make things even more difficult, at each point in this first ordering of the data, distinctions must be made carefully between what applied in 1963 and what applied earlier, say around 1900. And all data referring to earlier times should be docketed separately. Then the book can be written. The major goal is not only to give a substantive view of Tio culture around 1880, at the eve of the arrival of Brazza himself (the first Frenchman to enter the area), but to tackle the question of what is known as "the ethnographic present" as well. A present that most, if not all, anthropologists have used, but one that must be anathema to historians, since it cannot be pinned down exactly to one day, one particular moment in history. What the solution to this problem will be, I don't know yet. I can only outline the problem clearly in the knowledge that the necessary data are in my hands.

Right now I am trying to prevent dust from accumulating on the file, and I feel guilty about being a year behind schedule at this point. And nothing is being done about it, although later this summer the quarry may be reopened. At this moment, there are articles to be written for general histories of Africa and also this essay. But that is not all. On the table there lies a smaller mass of notes, this time typed out on cards. They deal with bells. To be precise, they deal with the single and double clapperless flangewelded iron bells of a certain shape which are found in West and Equatorial Africa. The notes on which I am working all come from published references, and the aim of the exercise is to find out where these bells originated and how they spread throughout such vast areas of the continent. Why bells and not beads or hairstyles? As it happens, these artifacts can teach us something about the spread of a certain virtuosity in ironworking, and they are also linked to political structures. The spread of the bells tells us something not only about connections among cultures, but about links among political organizations in different parts of Africa. Odd perhaps, but rational.

And of course it is now summer and there is no teaching. Otherwise, most of my time would be spent in lecturing, preparing for it, going to meetings, advising students, and sharing some of the rather dusty gossip and the concomitant indignations that flourish in every grove of Academe. The one rule about research all of us know, even if we do not voice it too often, is that most of it comes during the summer, during leaves, and otherwise as overtime.

How did this research take form? How did the author find himself in the position he is in now? That is the object of this story, and it all starts with my own training. In the late 1940s I was a student in medieval history at the University of Louvain. The highlight of the training given to me was the seminar then directed by the late Professor De Meyer. It was, in fact, a seminar very close in method to the famous German model of the late nineteenth century. Our professor's professor had been at the feet of Bernheim and had imported the seminar. I liked it because it gave one the comfortable impression that what was distinctive about history was its method, and because the more one learned about the method, the more logical and complete it appeared to be. History's task was to find out what had happened (*wie es gewesen war*), and with proper application of the critique to the documents, this could be done. Now certainly there was much positivism in this approach, but on the other hand, it did not claim to be entirely objective. The example of Seignobos' work, where the mere arrangement of documents already represented subjective appraisal, stared at us from the bookshelves on the wall of the seminar room. We also learned, without fully realizing it, how to apply some practical psychology to our sources. For hidden behind the logic of the method lies an appreciation of motives and aims as well as unconscious distortions. Still, history had no special goal beyond the reconstruction of the past—any bit of it that appealed to any practitioner. Bernheim, Feder, and Bauer had the most marked influence on me at this time.[1]

On the other hand, because of various external influences, I was also interested in European and foreign ways of life. This led me to London and thence to Africa. At University College, London, I studied social anthropology for one year (1951–1952) and came under the influence of Professor D. Forde and Dr. Mary Douglas. Again, anthropology appealed to me because it looked so logical. It started out from many different cases and then showed the operation of the principles hidden behind the diversity of it all. These generalizations were the "explanations" of social science. They illuminated because they brought together practices from different areas within a single culture or practices of the same nature in different cultures. And with my previous training, I took these generalizations also as "real" in a positivistic sense. It was there that I discovered Radcliffe-Brown, Malinowski, and Lévi-Strauss.[2]

Historical anthropology seemed messy. I had liked Kroeber's *Anthropology*,[3] but it did not seem to "explain" anything. And another point was painfully clear to me. Anthropologists worked with a synchronic framework. To bring history into a paper usually provoked the anthropologist to write "History!" in an accusing way on the margin. And this in red ink. For history was diachronic and did not enable one to see the relation between the parts. Social anthropology, on the other hand, was so helpful in showing this relationship for a given moment in time. Out of this grew a concern with the relation between the "ethnographic present," the one-moment-in-time analysis, and the study of culture through time: history. In 1952, however, the methods of social anthropology did not seem to me to be capable of application to historical problems.

The scholarship for anthropology came from the Institut pour la Recherche Scientifique en Afrique Centrale (IRSAC), which sent me to the Congo in 1952 to investigate the social and political structures of the Kuba. I have described elsewhere how interest in their oral history suddenly presented me with a challenge.[4] Oral traditions were not altogether new to me. Indeed, Bernheim had discussed them, and my own M.A. thesis on the value of certain types of dirges in medieval Latin had relied on a few cases of oral tradition, sometimes preserved as a *probatio pennae* in the margin of a manuscript. Now it struck me that some texts were learned by heart and thus transmitted. Therefore, one dealt with texts in much the same way as with written data. Although it was very tempting to collect all the data one could find

about Kuba history, most of these being oral, I faced the major problem of establishing a reliable method of assessing their value. It was
not unknown to me that many amateur historians working in Africa
had relied on oral traditions, but I could find none who had really
justified the value they attached to that data.

During my period of field work among a people so conscious of
their history, it became clear to me that an anthropological analysis
that did not take change into account would be incomplete. This
awareness also prompted me to collect oral data. First came praise
names and poetry, then the stories told by the king and the royalty,
then the popular traditions, however humble they might be, about the
origins of families and clan sections. Eventually, such family histories
were assembled for all the clan sections in the whole kingdom. The
more familiar I became with the culture and its language, the more
historical data were found about it.

In these years I had occasion to attend meetings of colleagues at
IRSAC, and in 1954, I spent four months at an IRSAC center. Common
seminars as well as communal living proved to be a great intellectual
stimulus. I learned most of all from the linguist, but then I was already
enamored of languages and even more so of descriptive linguistics. The
rigorous logic of linguistics was so beautiful that social anthropology
faded away in contrast! In 1954 a Bushang arrived at the center and we
were able to work intensively on a grammar of the language, following
a model provided by the works of Professor Meeussen and with the
on-the-spot advice of Professor Coupez. It was a small, modest grammar, intended simply to record some of the major outlines of a
language I had learned to speak a little, and which was, in fact, the
language of the historical oral documents. From other colleagues I
learned bits and pieces, perhaps most from Professor Hiernaux, who
was on his way to becoming one of the foremost physical anthropologists of our generation. He drew my attention to the help archeology
could give to the historian. A joint field project of three or four weeks
with him helped me to begin plugging a gap in my anthropological
education, which had included little or no archeology and physical
anthropology. Finally, my colleagues in rural sociology and economics
introduced me to simple statistics, and more important, to the problems of sampling procedures, which my former training had not included at all. And all this was done not so much in terms of abstract
disciplines, as *de visu*. We saw each other working on particular
problems, we knew each other's areas and peoples by visits, and we
discussed progress in the social science seminars held every six
months.

At that time, and especially later, I was exposed to natural scientists who taught me something about ecology as well as the research

problems and procedures in these fields. Even though these influences have been diffuse, I have nevertheless learned to pay attention to physical geography and microclimate, and to ask questions about the interrelations of man and nature. For the Tio case, where malnutrition, low density of population, and scarcity of water are major factors, this diffuse learning has been most helpful. What I learned from these experiences was that in the natural sciences progress did not assume the form of establishing firm absolute "laws," but that one had to face the same sorts of approximations and uncertainties and indeterminisms as one did in the social sciences and, indeed, the humanities.

From October 1954 to March 1956 military service prevented me from doing research, but I still found some time to begin writing a rough draft about Kuba traditions. This draft included all the traditions of the capital and an analysis of the different versions of each tradition. In 1956 the opportunity arose to go back to the Kuba for three months and to plug most of the gaps in my study. At the same time, the theoretical problems concerning versions, interdependence of traditions, and the like were being tackled. Finally, I decided to try for a Ph.D. in history rather than in anthropology, and the first contacts were made.

Upon my return to Europe in the summer of 1956, I started to write up my research. But first, the classical German writers on method were reread; then comparative data on oral traditions were gathered from Africa and other areas of the world. The bibliographical research needed to be systematic, and in retrospect I am still amazed at how much was retrieved. In fact, some major sources were missed. The Muslim theory about the chain of tradition or *isnad* is a prime instance. It turned out to be identical with mine (*vive la logique*). In the African literature, works such as those by Callet and Guillain [5] did escape me. By and large, many materials were amassed; the Kuba data were compared with them; and a general method to deal with oral traditions was devised. It may not have been so original, since the historical method already existed; but I was convinced of its logic, and if it applied to written data, it should apply to oral data too. And so it did. The only special features were the chain of tradition (not one witness and many copyists, but many witnesses . . .) and the verbal character of the tradition itself, which might have a content and no text. Putting this material into written form, however, proved to be much more difficult. Here my major professor, Dr. De Smet, was the touchstone for experiment. He rejected certain proposed outlines because they followed the theory well enough but did not really fit with the data to be discussed. In other outlines, separations were introduced where there should have been none, and in general it seemed that one had to write about everything at once and that any way of cutting the cake in order to present the questions step by step was highly artificial. One outline finally seemed a little less outrageous than the rest, and it was adopted. The general theory became the first part, constituting a good hundred pages of the thesis.

The next six or seven hundred pages dealing with Kuba history were written in less time than the first part. The plan was simple: presentation of the culture; presentation of the ethnic traditions, one after another; presentation of village and clan history; and a discussion of the origin of the Kuba. After this came the history of the kingdom, king by king, preceded by a discussion of the chronology. The positive results were then set forth in a last short section. The whole second part was later published in Flemish because a translation had bogged down in the tediousness of variants and versions.[6] If the work had been done now instead of then, I would have stressed more that it was the record only of traditions, for the passage of time along with the addition of more linguistic and ethnographic data has shown that, especially with regard to origins, the role of certain groups has been greater than had been adumbrated.

During this same period, I audited several courses in African languages and linguistics so that I could understand what linguists talked about, even if I was not really one of the crowd myself. It was important for anthropologists to learn as much about the language of the cultures they studied as possible. Certainly for a historian not to know the culture he was writing about was a capital sin. So he too had to have some linguistics, and indeed the historians who had to sit in judgment on this Ph.D. candidate (being good medievalists) felt this too. For they did check the candidate's competence in the local language, and they inquired if he had lived with the people concerned, what he had done, and how much he understood about the culture. It is a banal truth that those who write history must know the people they write about. Yet banal as it is, much of the present writing about African history manages to forget this rule. In recent years, we have seen cases where "the oral traditions" of a people were reported after two or three weeks of research in the field. One formal proposal I know of recommends the following formula for dealing with traditions in a language unknown to the researcher: tape the traditions, then tape a translation on the spot, made by an interpreter who listened to the original, and presto! the trick is done. Think of the degree of misunderstanding of what it is all about. This and similar schemes for "espresso-oral traditions" are not only appalling, but a sad comment on scholarship in general.

On leaving Belgium again late in 1957, I had hoped to go and live among a neighbor group of the Kuba and to proceed there with the same type of work, while going back from time to time to the Kuba to acquire a deeper knowledge of their culture. But I was put in charge of administration in the center at Butare (Rwanda). Since my duties took me only a day or two each week to fulfill, I could spend the rest of my time on research. And topics for research abounded. The historical traditions of Burundi presented a true challenge. They were spotty, lacking in time depth, and as heterogeneous as could be. In Rwanda I thought it best to concentrate on two major genres, the historical tale and one category of historical poetry. Abbé Kagame was already quite active in the collection of other genres. No time span for completion of these projects had been set, but as it turned out, the project was cut short after almost three years.

The situation for the oral historian there was almost ideal. IRSAC had a staff trained in the transcription and the translation of languages, and for both Rwanda and Rundi (the speech of Burundi) not only were there excellent grammars available, but also linguists to whom I could turn when needed. The irony is that I never really learned to speak either of the two languages at all. My administrative duties prevented me from settling among the folk on the hills, and the facilities did not help me to acquire much beyond a philological knowledge of either language.

Again, much was learned from the study of these traditions. For Burundi, it turned out that there were no specialists at all. Everybody there knew some history, and some people knew more than others. This presented a rather challenging problem in sampling. Obviously it was not possible to interview 3 million Rundi! So, first a number of pilot areas were combed for any storyteller and any adult who knew traditions. Then I realized that it was essential to know all the variants of a given tradition and that the variants would be conditioned by distance and presence near historical sites. So a sample could be constructed which would make certain that all the variants would be recorded. As it turned out, the study could be completed before July 1960, even though some data were lost afterward. But the analysis of the data and the writing of a book on Rundi oral tradition would take until 1967. It was only when writing up and systematically comparing hundreds of variants that it turned out that in one tiny border corner of the country, there were some precious special traditions which did tell us something about a much earlier period of history. In that corner, one check alone was not enough; a systematic hill-by-hill examination should have been made, overlapping into two non-Rundi areas across the border. Judging by the results, however, I believe the sample was sufficient.[7]

In Rwanda, dynastic poems were collected with the help of a Rwandese who made provisional translations and comments about them. These poems are highly allusive and cannot be understood without explanations from the informant. The only trouble was that many of the informants did not know the explanations. So my assistant began to build up a comparative knowledge of both the genre and the allusions, and I did not. I went with him to tape the poem, recorded the relevant biographical and genealogical data, and promised to sit down and work intensively at the material once I had found the time for it. But late in 1959 a revolution broke out, and my assistant became involved in the struggle. He was promptly jailed and exiled, so no one remained to make sense out of the poems. A salutary lesson and a painful one.

The other Rwanda project did go forward and was almost completed when I left in 1960. By 1962 all the taped texts had been transcribed and translated by competently trained people, and the corpus then consisted of more than ten thousand pages of text. My original plan was to produce a text edition along the lines already laid out by a previous text published with the help of Rwandese colleagues and linguists at IRSAC.[8] This still remains to be done, and it will take two or three years of full-time work to complete the task. The upshot of all this work so far is a slim booklet on the historiography of Rwanda and the major evolution of its past.[9]

These projects in oral traditions were useful in the sense that they helped me to revise the original text of the method book, so that when I left the area, the manuscript of De la tradition orale was ready and had benefited from all the practical work done there. If I were to write this now, some examples could be bettered by adducing other cases. The bibliography, moreover, could be extended to include the distinction between free and fixed texts. Nevertheless, it would not be rewritten as it stands now. Readers have tended to use it too much as a book of necessary recipes and to read into it an inflexibility which the author disavows. Besides the field work, Marrou's influence had permeated the book. I also read, reread, and worked over Bloch's handbook,[10] so that the notion of the probability of any historical reconstruction came to dominate and to provide the basis for the assessment of any given source.

And then suddenly in 1960 I found myself in the United States. In the beginning it was a very fruitful experience. Half my time was devoted to teaching, and since the teacher was new, few people needed him, and he had plenty of time to write. It was then that I discovered American anthropology; the archeological theories, especially those of J. Steward on evolution, proved fascinating.[11] Archeology was of much greater interest now, in part because I had helped excavate sites in Rwanda and localized many more for future excavation by specialists, and in part because it had become clear in Congo history that early iron age sites were indeed adding important chapters to the known history. Besides the theories of evolution, I came to appreciate the way archeologists used diffusion as a fact of history; and the concept of seriation also impressed me as a useful tool for the historian.

Culture history was also read more widely than before, but it seemed to be a maze of separate paths with very little order and often with little historical sense. Gradually I discovered that Kroeber was not really a cultural historian at all: he would dismiss evidence simply because it did not come from an anthropologist, yet he would make reconstructions which were of a relatively low degree of probability.[12] Murdock's historical method of reconstructing former social structures from present kinship terminologies also had to be rejected as naïve.[13] Certainly the German schools of culture historians had been much more stringent, even if I had thought all along that their methods were off the mark. In the New World literature on the topic, one work alone stood out—Sapir's *Time Perspective in Aboriginal American Culture*. It was clearly a methodological statement which ranked alongside Graebner's contribution,[14] and the sad truth was that these works dated from 1911 and 1916, respectively. Since then, not much progress with methods had been made, and it was tempting to see if any further progress could be made. Because some social analysis had been already made by comparing synchronic levels in the same society, I thought that this might be an avenue for utilizing ethnographic data for historical purposes. In fact, I wrote an article on these lines which was finished by December 1961.[15]

In reality, the major work done during the previous year included the completion of a monograph on Kuba society and political structure, in which one diachronic, that is, historical model, had been presented, and the writing of a small volume on Rwanda historiography, which also attempted to extend social anthropology into the past.[16] Ironically enough, I feel now that the Kuba work suffered seriously from the use of the undated ethnographic present. For although it did take history into account, it assumed that the situation in 1880 was roughly the same one obtaining in 1953, minus the colonial administration and a few obvious omissions. Only gradually, with the discovery of a previously unknown account about the Kuba dating from 1892 and a few more documents that indicated or hinted at change in the society, has this flaw come to light. By the time I went to the Tio, I was aware of this and decided to examine the question of the "ethnographic present." Since then, J. Goody (1967) has seen the same problem and decided that one could not work with the ethnographic present.[17] For myself, I will not know the answer until I have written the Tio book.

In 1962 and 1963 very little research work was done. Lecturing took more time, and students were constantly being advised. Somehow there were talks to give, papers to write, and there was much less time to talk to colleagues or to get ahead with one's own work. The single-ness of purpose was still there; and I still had to forge the methodol-ogy for recovering all sorts of data that could help explain the past. During this period some of my concepts gradually underwent change. E. H. Carr showed what happened when the masses of data were so great that one could not use them all and advocated how to go about it.[18] Popper went much further and attacked the whole concept of history. And all the time the evolutionists in anthropology argued that there had to be laws too, that models would show what these laws were, and that we historians had not looked systematically enough at the past.[19] But I kept working at a survey of the history of the Central African states from about 1500 to 1900, which was intended to be a reference book and to provide the background for one or two generali-zations about the evolution of political systems expressed in an anthro-pological way. This was just about done when the opportunity for new field work arose.

Now I wanted to go to the Congo Brazzaville and study either the Lwango or the Tio, because both these areas had once been important kingdoms in Central Africa. My plan was to use a first field trip for learning the language and studying the basic cultural anthropology, and then devote a second trip to the collecting of all the relevant traditions. As it turned out, we chose to settle in the Tio village of Mbe. The field work went very smoothly indeed, and to my own amazement it was possible to gather a relatively in-depth view of Tio culture in the space of six and a half months. Although my previous field experience helped, I soon discovered that there were no real traditions at all in this society. The reasons for this soon emerged. At that time Lévi-Strauss' *La Pensée sauvage* fell into my hands, and sure enough the Tio came right out of the book.[20] They had imprisoned time in a three-gen-eration capsule, and Adam was the grandfather! There were only two things left to do. First, I had to ask all the old men and women how life had been in their youth and to check their careers up to the present. The technique of collecting these oral witness accounts gradually im-proved as time went by, and the recollections became more vivid as well as more accurate and could be checked from one to the other (and later with written materials). Then it turned out that the key political and religious institution among the Tio was called a *nkobi* and that these *nkobi* had some history in the beliefs associated with them. So, second, I had to collect data about each of them. It was then I realized that here was a case for diffusion and one where the data yielded not a vague probability but a very strong one illuminating a good bit of eighteenth-century history.

Nobody had come across archeological sites on the Tio plateau before, but by asking the women, who are the farmers, about strange pottery and former habitation sites, we found quite a number of village sites and discovered by accident a few late stone age places as well. This was reported to the scientific authorities in Brazzaville, and one site was excavated by an archeologist, while we were happy enough to make a few trial pits in other places. The data recovered from these pits turned out to be very revealing, again in relation to eighteenth- and early nineteenth-century changes. Finally, evidence for loan words as well began to reinforce the data. When I left Mbe, I had very little in the way of archives, because it had not been possible to work on them and I could only describe Tio society in the ethnographic present (1963?) or from the statements of informants at least partially dating from 1870. And the object was to write about Tio life in 1880. In addition, some history since 1880 was well known, and fragments of the earlier history had also been recovered.

Then followed a stroke of luck. Not only was another anthropologist at work in the cultural area closest to the Tio, but Brazza's papers had found their way into the French National Archives, where Professor Brunschwig and his pupils, especially Mme Coquery-Vidrovich, were analyzing them.[21] We corresponded. I was able to help on some minor points, and was helped in return by a certain amount of fresh new data about the Tio from 1880 to 1886 or so. This further strengthened my resolve to write about the way of life in 1880 rather than in 1963. Yet it is clear that I cannot take facts from 1963, project them back to 1880, and then rediscover them with great glee, as has frequently been done. Obviously this magician's trick of extrapolation will not do, nor can a coherent account of Tio society and culture for 1880 be given by the oral or written data from that period. So I will have to start out with 1963 and then explain 1880 and show how this and that must have been present in 1880 as it was in 1963 and how that and the other may not have been. How artificial this will turn out to be is the great question.

In the years since 1964, more and more time has been consumed by writing survey books or chapters in textbooks, not to mention teaching, going to meetings, and supervising students. Only two research jobs have been done in almost four years. The first consisted of culling ethnographic archives about parts of the Congo close to the Tio to see if the linguistic and ethnographic materials recovered would help to make process models of related societies and show their evolution for perhaps the last thousand years or so. If the data were not quite good enough, the evidence did show that many cultural events had not only happened, but had left their traces in the area. Much of the data could be used when writing about the proper methodology for exploiting linguistic (especially loan words) and ethnographic sources. The summer ended with a paper, now published, "The Use of Ethnographic Data as Sources for History." [22] The same paper has now reached a third version which grew out of converting it into a full graduate course, and it will probably never be published. For the situations can be so different, the evidence so diverse, that what is needed now is not a rigid methodological corset nor a presentation such as D. McCall has given with small chapters for each sort of discipline,[23] but a casebook. "Do what you preach" may be better than "Do as I say."

During the same years I also wrote an article primarily intended for anthropologists stemming from my concern about fusing history and anthropology. And here the new structuralism in anthropology was very influential, because it proved to me conclusively that one cannot compare two societies or two cultures except by first making abstract models of each of them and then constructing a model which covers certain features of both. In other words, one had to generalize and abstract for the whole of a culture, not just for one feature or another, as some of the social anthropologists such as Murdock in his ethnographic atlas [24] had done. It seemed to me that one could also build a diachronic model taking history into account. If one did this for two related cultures, the beginning stage would be the same, and one model could encompass the whole of both cultures, including their common origin. There would be an element of generalization left in much of the reconstructions, but the generalization would be more than fiction: it would correspond to something that had really existed. The same article also argued that historians did in fact use models and did so in a more artistic way. The argument ran that this could be done provided the historian tried to be as aware as possible of the model he was actually using.[25]

Since 1964 I have accomplished only one other major effort in history, namely, the writing up and preparation for publication of the Rundi data. The pace of this project has been very slow indeed, considering that all the basic materials were ready as of 1960. It took a whole summer just to recapture a little of the spirit of Burundi, to find the places again on maps and recall them before my eyes, to hear the Rundi sentences again, and to find my way in the maze of notes. Without this effort, it was simply impossible to do any meaningful work. After that it took an entire school year and a summer for the comparatively short manuscript to emerge. The planning stage progressed more or less haphazardly, things being classified chronologically or by type of source, and the final plan emerged only after most of the work had been done and when it became clear that the book would tell as much about literature as about history. The analysis of the oral tale itself took up a large part of it. I am convinced that if enough time had been granted in 1960, this book would probably have been finished in three to four months. During the writing up, I could not help thinking about the Tio, and, in fact, I wrote three articles about them. Now at last the field is clear for the Tio, and again I begin to feel the hardening effects of time over my impressions, my knowledge of some of the language, and my notes. And I cannot help thinking about something else: the bells. The best time to write the Tio book has almost passed as well.

But how did the bells enter into the picture? Really I don't know. It started some time ago. There had been a discussion for years about the development of states in the savanna south of the equatorial forest in the Congo. It had been my contention that the states of the Lower Congo and those of Katanga had developed separately, at least before 1500. But others believed that there had been links between them at an earlier stage, and that all the African states south of the Sahara had originated in the state of Kush on the Nile upstream of Egypt. The idea and the structures of kingship spread from there as a "Sudanic kingdom" west and south to the rest of Africa. More to the point, scholars had held that the states of the Lower Congo were founded by influences from Katanga and those in Katanga had arisen perhaps as the result of influence from the interlacustrine area. Or perhaps the Lower Congo states owed their existence to influences from the Cameroons and Nigeria, and those from Katanga were influenced by people from the Lower Congo.[26]

Whatever the reasoning, the difficulty was that none of these hypotheses could be established authoritatively because the data were missing. Before 1500 there are no oral traditions, and archeological investigation has just begun. In addition, it was far from certain that archeology could settle a matter like this. Then one day I read in Fagan's account of Southern Africa that a new iron age of Katanga origin had arrived at Zimbabwe in Rhodesia around A.D. 1450. It was characterized among other things by the presence of double bells. Now these existed everywhere in the southern Congo and also in the Cameroons. Suddenly the idea took form. If one studied the distribution of bells from West Africa to Rhodesia, one might be able to show that all those bells had a common origin, at least for the single bell. Knowing the diffusion and the way it spread, one would know at the same time how this superior technique of ironworking spread. And since the same technique was needed to produce effective spears or swords, it was clear that this might have value for military history. Now other historians had argued that all these states arose in the Bantu area because the Bantu arrived with this knowledge of ironworking and by force of superior arms subjected the aborigines.[27] Granted that it is easy to show this to be incorrect, nevertheless when improved arms became available later, would they not have an effect on state building? Furthermore, these bells were apparently tied everywhere to political status. They were emblems of state, albeit minor ones. So that if a diffusion, especially of the double bells, could be shown, one would prove beyond reasonable doubt that different areas of Africa borrowed from each other certain features related to political systems. If they borrowed the bell, they might also have borrowed other things, such as ideas about political roles or some other feature of government.

If one could then present an argument for diffusion from a single center, it could be checked by observing the linguistic situation. Did the word for the bell spread with the bell or not? Was this word a loan word? If the ethnographic and the linguistic evidence tallied, obviously the lines of independent evidence would agree, and the resulting hypothesis would become much stronger. Better still, any hypothesis would be worth expounding, since it could always be checked. Future archeology could confirm or correct it according to the finds, since there is a good chance that such large iron masses can survive many centuries. And indeed they did, since the oldest bells known so far date from the eighth century. This hypothesis is being worked out now both as an exercise in diffusion and as a study of a concrete problem. The resulting publication should solve certain problems of method and presentation of data, while the research itself has already taught me a great deal about the difficulties encountered with laconic glosses in dictionaries, casual mentions in ethnographies, and vague indications attached to the labels of artifacts in museums. Now the material can be brought together and organized, and the first stage of the project is nearing fruition in the form of an article, "The Bells of Kings," scheduled for publication in the *Journal of African History*, X, 2 (April 1969). This first statement of the problem provides the general picture and includes the overall results of my researches, but it does not enter into either ethnographic detail or linguistic analysis. If the major results of the enquiry are ready for publication, the final version has yet to be written. It will take much more time to find the exact distribution as well as the full amount of information available, and it will take much more space to present the data as they ought to be presented.

So I have decided to include a full version of the "bells" in a book of essays dealing with particular oral traditions, smaller studies about the use of loan words, the relevance of archeological sites to the history of the Tio, an essay on chronology in Rwanda and Burundi, and another on Kuba iconographic sources. In other words, instead of moving toward a treatise on historical method applied to ethnographic sources, I trust that concrete examples will tell the tale far better.

Up to this point I have tried to describe when and how research was done and how it was channeled by chance and changing intellectual influences. Something must now be said about barriers to research. The first of these is teaching. From experience, it seems to me that the slogan "Teaching is good for you" is mostly opium for the people! This is not the place to enter into a discussion of what teaching could be or of its merits and demerits, but a paper about research can only record that teaching takes most of our time and induces in us either a dulling of the senses, leading to a lack of curiosity, or sends us off in so many directions at once that no real research can grow out of all the leads scented.

But the worst enemy of research may be found in the other duties expected from an academic. High on my list is the demand for vulgarization and occasional papers. Vulgarization is necessary: the general public does indeed have a right to learn about the current state of the art. But the older one grows, the more the demands of presses and symposia mount. In the last few years I have written two small books and almost a score of articles in this vein. For there must be textbooks, surveys, contributed papers, and what have you. In addition to this pressure, there are the professional meetings, which still put on airs of being scientific and therefore require papers and articles, usually on the most superficial of levels. The necessity to attend these meetings for the good of one's students and the weal of the school is but one of the hidden duties of the academician. Each week has its dreary succession of departmental or faculty meetings, its hours lost on this and on that, all connected with administration. Again this sort of commitment grows with time no matter how hard one tries to resist it. Often I feel that if Haydn was in bondage to the Prince of Esterhazy, so are researchers to their institution.

The inescapable fact is that research cannot be done as part of a normal working week during the academic year. Constant interruptions, as the Rundi case has shown, mean that it will take a great deal of energy and more time to find one's way back to the task. For ultimately the process of research is similar to the creation of a work of art. And which work of art, done in installments of time, really has a seamless unity? Under such circumstances it all too often becomes mere patchwork.

One question worth posing here is: Why do the research that I did? Ultimately, the answer to this hinges on the beliefs one holds about history. To me, history is the history of all the people in a culture. It is and always will be culture history, and I cannot see any basic difference between anthropology and history on this point. In most cases, few of those people knew how to write, and therefore other methods of investigation must be developed to find out more about them. This of course is true for nonliterate societies, but it is also true for literate cultures. One of the most impressive achievements with this kind of methodology may be seen in Lynn White's *Medieval Technology and Social Change*,[23] in which linguistics, iconography, and ethnography are all used to illuminate the development of agricultural technology in Europe.

One of my basic assumptions is that all the data relevant to a given problem should ultimately be used in considering that problem. This often means in practice that publications will have to be based on limited sets of documents, either because the mass of data available is so great, as in the case of contemporary history, or because the data are so disparate that it would take years and years to find them all. Consider the case of the Tio, where years of research could undoubtedly turn up considerably more archival material than is available now. But it is dangerous to delay publication too long for fear that there will never be a publication. There are always some more data to collect. So the solution is to base studies on different types of evidence and to make this quite clear: X as worked out from the archives of the Foreign Office, or Y according to oral tradition, etc. Later research can then build on the earlier publication, and with the addition of other classes of data, correct and improve interpretations. In this way historians can avoid not only the difficulties Carr mentions about the masses of data, but also his solution, which is simply to sanction success.

A more recent danger is the way some historians use their data merely as illustrations to prove a model. For many years this has been the practice of sociologists and even more of anthropologists. Indeed, one of the most respected anthropologists, E. E. Evans Pritchard, tells us in his Nuer study that "facts can only be selected and arranged in the light of theory." After complaining about "confusing documentation with illustration," he concludes, "but in case it be said that we have only described the facts in relation to a theory of them and *as exemplifications* [my italics] and have subordinated description to analysis, we reply that this was our intention."[29] One may understand the problem, but one cannot agree. For all the facts are relevant, and a writer of history owes it to his readers to give them all the facts so that they can judge whether the writer's theory is really adequate and relevant and complete. The writer cannot only "illustrate" and leave the rest in the dark. This, however, is becoming more and more the trend.

Our first task, then, is to find data and set them forth. We must work in the long perspective and with proper modesty. After two thousand years, we are no longer interested in the theories of Lucretius because they are so hopelessly antiquated—but we still read what Tacitus had to say about the Germans,[30] for that is based on evidence.

In our own work we historians lay some bricks in a building that will be completed generations and generations hence. Ultimately the history of the Kuba according to their oral traditions addresses itself to the next historian, perhaps a generation hence, who will be interested in this topic.

Another question has to do with the significance of it all. Are there not some events and data that are important and others that are trifling? Philosophers of history make much out of this to show that historians have built-in biases, and that they vary from generation to generation. More recently some have argued that only the significant is worthy of study, and the significant happens to be the successful. A mob that succeeds creates a revolution; one that fails has created what can at best be labeled an "insurrection." As I see it, there really are no data without significance. Even such a trifle as the knowledge that Mrs. Tuppence threw her cat out of the window on June 5, 1853, may turn out to be of interest to the student of the history of the Society for the Prevention of Cruelty to Animals. The historian chooses data because they are relevant to a topic. All research starts with a question, not really with the discovery of a batch of archives. And the one work that never ages is the publication of primary sources.

It can be said that the same questions will never be asked again, because the questions we ask are a product of our age, and every age differs. So there is no real continuity in historiography. It sounds nice, but a look at the actual historiography of the past shows that this view is unreal. Some things are significant now and later, and others may lose their significance for a generation or two and then find their way back into circulation.

Much more menacing than passing fashions in history are those critics who want to corral the historian and keep him in the model cage. Significance for them is an absolute, deriving from the theory propounded and the model expounded. History is social science. It should be concerned with the discovery of those famous laws, and that can only be done if a body of theory is built which shows recurrence in events and generalizes from that. Some of the extremists in this school complain that facts merely clutter up the record. My own belief is that sociology and related disciplines can help to interpret historical data, but that their task is to generalize, while that of the historian is primarily to record and to reconstruct the most faithful picture possible of the past as it happened. And that assignment is enough to keep his hands full.

Also, as it happens, history is not just a social science. It deals with man as part of society and with the individual. But then psychology really has become a social science too, and social science is generalizing and therefore inhuman. History is also the smoke of battle, the haze of dust, the glint on the pitchfork, and this is not just romanticism, because history is for people and about people. It cannot be dehumanized and sanitized. Social science does just this. It must abstract in order to find its regularities. But every abstraction must be put back into reality. An analogy with chemistry makes it clear: at first the discipline was not concerned with the fragrance of roses or the taste of wine. But now enough is known about the basic properties of matter to begin to study smells, tastes, and odors and reach a level of much more complex understanding. Social science still works only with a few crude variables; perhaps in later centuries it will be able to tackle the more subtle ones and be grateful to see the documentation available that some social scientists of our day want to suppress as irrelevant.

There is another limit to social scientific analysis. Poetry is not merely clever syntax or a play on semantics. It also has a powerful emotional appeal. The relation between the object of art and the beholder is similar to the relation between a situation at a given moment in the past and ourselves. And this too is an essential part of reality, a part which the historian must try his best to preserve.

Finally, one may ask what historical research is for. We may not believe in history as destiny or as astrology. But history does teach. Many of our statesmen or leaders in other fields read history in order to learn from the past. Yet this is not really why I do historical research. I do it first because I like it, and ultimately because I want to preserve the record of the things man has done so that mankind or some man in the future can behold it. Culture to me is like a flower, and the hundreds of cultures which have flourished in the past are the garden of mankind, a garden to wander in, to enjoy, and to learn from, with some humility and modesty at the sight of one's own cultural achievement compared with the others. This is why the collection and presentation of data and the emphasis on proper methods for finding data have been so dominant in my own endeavors.

NOTES

1. E. Bernheim, *Lehrbuch der historischen Methode und der Geschichts-philosophie* (Leipzig, 1908); W. Bauer, *Einführung in das Studium der Geschichte* (Tübingen, 1928); A. Feder, *Lehrbuch der geschichtlichen Methodik* (Regensburg, 1924).
2. See A. R. Radcliffe-Brown, *Structure and Function in Primitive Society* (London, 1952); C. Lévi-Strauss, *Les Structures elementaires de la parenté* (Paris, 1949); and most of the works of Malinowski. The influ-

ence of both Radcliffe-Brown and Lévi-Strauss grew more and more, until after 1960 or so I decidedly went over to the side of structuralists like Lévi-Strauss.

3. A. Kroeber, *Anthropology* (New York, 1948), a storehouse of information, but a very jumbled attic!

4. J. Vansina, "History in the Field," in D. G. Jongmans and P. C. W. Gutkind, eds., *Anthropologists in the Field* (Assen, 1967).

5. P. Callet recorded the royal Merina traditions of Madagascar and published them in five volumes as *Tantaran'ny Andriana* (Tananarive, 1873–1902). Ch. Guillain, in *Documents sur l'histoire, la géographie et le commerce de la partie occidentale de Madagascar* (Paris, 1845), did discuss specifically the historical value that oral traditions could have. These two examples of omissions were brought forcibly to my attention by Dr. R. K. Kent, to whom I am grateful.

6. *Geschiedenis van de Kuba, Annalen Koninklijk Museum voor Midden Afrika, Wetenschappen van de Mens*, No. 44 (Tervuren, 1963).

7. The sample is explained in *La Légende du passé: Traditions orales du Burundi*, in press.

8. A. Coupez and Th. Kamanzi, *Récits historiques Rwanda: Annales du musée royal de l'Afrique centrale, Sciences de l'Homme*, No. 43 (Tervuren, 1962). I would have added a study of variants, which was not necessary in this volume since it contained the texts of one informant only at one sitting.

9. *L'évolution du royaume Rwanda des origines à 1900—Classe des sciences morales et politiques*, No. XXVI (NS) 2, Academie Royale des Sciences d'Outre-mer (Brussels, 1962).

10. M. Bloch, *Apologie de l'histoire ou le métier d'historien* (Paris, 1952). Later, I. Marrou's contributions to Samaran, *L'Histoire et ses méthodes* (Paris, 1961), reinforced this influence.

11. J. Steward, *Theory of Culture Change* (Urbana, Ill., 1955).

12. A. Kroeber, *Cultural and Natural Areas of Native North America* (New York, 1939), opens with the argument that the missionary records for the history of the California Indians are useless because the Fathers were no anthropologists. The anthropologist will reconstruct what the situation was in the eighteenth century by himself. This is not an isolated reaction. See G. Balandier, *La Vie quotidienne au royaume de Kongo du XVIIIme siècle* (Paris, 1965), p. 53, where he dismisses a vast amount of concrete evidence from the sixteenth to the eighteenth centuries about the succession to the kingship by claiming that the Kongo are matrilineal and that the authors of the documents have confused sons and nephews and legitimate with illegitimate sons. Again, twentieth-century anthropology takes precedence over contemporary documents. For reconstructions with a low degree of probability, see A. Kroeber, *Anthropology*, pp. 564–68, about the reconstruction of the growth of some religious rites in California. Performances of this kind antagonized Boas ("the 40% probability reconstruction!") and led to the jibes of British anthropologists against "conjectural history."

13. G. P. Murdock, *Social Structure* (New York, 1949). The whole second half of the book tries to show that kinship terminologies must be logically derived in certain fixed sequences from others. This is highly doubtful, especially since Murdock did work with only two features of a kinship system (naming of blood relatives in the generation above the

speaker and terminology for cousins) and then extrapolated from there to the whole social system.

14. Fritz Graebner, *Methode der Ethnologie* (Hamburg, 1911). Graebner was driven underground by Boas, but much of his book is valuable. His discussion of the need to establish critically the value of anthropological reports is now being revived under the up-to-date name of "data control analysis."

15. "The Use of Process-models in African History," in J. Vansina, R. Mauny, and L. V. Thomas, eds., *The Historian in Tropical Africa* (London, 1964), pp. 375-98. Note the jargon in the title. The influence of American sociology does indeed show up there!

16. *Le Royaume Kuba—Annales du musée royal de l'Afrique centrale, Sciences humaines,* No. 49 (Tervuren, 1964).

17. J. Goody, *The Social Organization of the LoWiili* (London, 1967), preface to the second edition. In 1957 he thought he still could disentangle the past from the present in the study of the political structure of the LoWiili, but in 1967 he was no longer satisfied that it was possible (iv).

18. E. H. Carr, *What Is History?* (New York, 1962).

19. K. Popper, in *The Poverty of Historicism* (London, 1957), certainly is right when attacking the belief in historical destiny. But in going much further, he errs. On the same side, one will find Lévi-Strauss arguing in *La Pensée sauvage* (Paris, 1964), chap. ix, "Histoire et dialectique," that history cannot hold a choice place among the other forms of knowledge (p. 348), as Sartre and the "Dialecticians" would have it. Still, Lévi-Strauss does not deny that history can show causation through time, which no other social science can do, since the latter can show causation by correlation only.

20. Lévi-Strauss, *op. cit.*, chap. viii, "Le Temps retrouvé." I have found his discussion of the different cultural attitudes toward time very thoughtful.

21. See H. Brunschwig, *Brazza Explorateur* (Paris, 1966), and especially his "La Négociation du traité Makoko," *Cahiers d'Etudes Africaines,* XVII (1965), 5-56. See also C. Coquery-Vidrovitch, *Brazza et la prise de possession du Congo* (Paris, 1969).

22. T. O. Ranger, *Emerging Themes of African History* (Dar es Salaam, 1968), pp. 97-124.

23. D. McCall, *Africa in Time Perspective* (Boston, 1964).

24. G. P. Murdock, "Ethnographic Atlas of Africa," *Ethnology,* VI (1967).

25. Jan Vansina, "Cultures Through Time," in R. Narroll and R. Cohen, eds., *A Handbook of Method in Cultural Anthropology* (New York, 1968).

26. For the "Sudanese state," see R. Oliver and J. D. Fage, *A Short History of Africa* (London, 1962), chap. iv. The idea has been current since the later nineteenth century. For the debate about the Lower Congo, see D. Birmingham, *Trade and Conflict in Angola* (London, 1966), pp. 8-10, wherein he contends that the founders came from Katanga.

27. The thesis is most ably stated by C. Wrigley, "Speculations on the Economic Pre-history of Africa," *Journal of African History,* I, 2 (1960), 189-203, especially 201-3. The more extreme view that the iron age made for a complete break with the past can be found in Basil Davidson, *Old Africa Rediscovered* (London, 1960), and in other works by the same author. (Indeed, he has now earned the sobriquet "Iron-man Davidson.")

28. Lynn White, *Medieval Technology and Social Change* (London, 1960).

29. E. E. Evans Pritchard, *The Nuer* (Oxford, 1940), p. 261. Nevertheless, this author is one of the more wide-ranging and cautious of anthropologists. He recorded masses of data and made them available. The simile which follows about Tacitus and Lucretius may be attributed to him.

30. C. Tacitus, *De origine situ moribus ac populis Germanorum.* Most of the evidence here comes from hearsay, and it has been shown that Tacitus' interest in the matter was to contrast "decadent" Rome with a "vigorous" Germania. The quality of the evidence is thus much less than that of most modern works based on field work. Even so, it is a testimonial to the value of setting forth the available evidence.

Of Images
and
Imagination
in History

L. P. CURTIS, JR.

LEWIS PERRY CURTIS, JR., was born on June 7, 1932, in London, England. He was raised in the ambience of Yale University, from which he received his B.A. in 1953. After two years in the U. S. Army, he went to Oxford on the G.I. Bill, matriculating at Christ Church in 1955. In 1957 he became a student at Nuffield College, where he completed his D.Phil. dissertation in 1959. From 1959 to 1963 he worked as an Instructor in History at Princeton University; and in September 1963 he joined the Department of History at the University of California at Berkeley, where he is now an Associate Professor, specializing in modern British and Irish history.

Curtis is a member of the Conference on British Studies, the Irish Historical Society, the American Committee of Irish Studies, and the American Historical Association. He has received fellowships from the American Council of Learned Societies (1965–1966) and the Guggenheim Foundation (1969–1970).

He has written two books on Anglo-Irish relations: *Coercion and Conciliation in Ireland, A Study in Conservative Unionism, 1880–1892* (Princeton, 1963) and *Anglo-Saxons and Celts, A Study of Anti-Irish Prejudice in Victorian England* (Conference on British Studies, Bridgeport, Conn., 1968). A sequel to the latter work, entitled *Apes, Angels, and Irishmen,* is due to be published this year by the Smithsonian Institution Press.

Current research includes a book on the decline of the landlord class in Ireland from 1870 to 1922, and an abridged edition of William Lecky's *History of Ireland.*

W here should an apprentice in the "historian's workshop" begin a retrospective, if not introspective, account of his work
and working assumptions during the past few years? How
much or how little should he tell? For most men of prudence, restraint,
and, of course, continence, the answer would be a firm admonition: do
not begin at all. At the very least, the sober and mature professional
historian would advise the apprentice to wait for ten, twenty, perhaps
even thirty years on the assumption that by then one might have
something worth writing about. But suppose he is addressing a "sor-
cerer's apprentice" who prefers to ignore this advice and decides to
explore in print some of the more printable features of his work and
working methods? What then? Should he start with his first weeks in
graduate school and mete out praise to those few teachers who
thought well of his work in seminars, cajoled him into working in the
distinguished professor's own field, or showed him a touch of compas-
sion amid all the erudition? Should he concentrate, instead, on the
research and writing stages of the least objectionable work he has
done, eschewing all apologias and confessions, and overcoming the
almost irresistible temptation to settle old scores with a mixture of
irony and expertise? Should he not seize this golden opportunity to
exhort his fellow historians to stop writing the "old" history and start
writing the "new"—whatever that may be? Or implore them to stop
writing altogether? If the options seem endless, so they are, and the
risks of overexposure, not to mention charges of indecent exposure,
are even greater. But then, some risks are better than others, or more
fun, and the only risk I would like to avoid here is the misconception
that may arise in some readers' minds that I have lost sight altogether
of the distinction between taking oneself and one's work too
seriously.

For someone like myself, who was born the son of a professional
historian as well as a brilliant teacher of English history, but who
cannot pretend on that count to be a "born historian," it is rather
pointless to explain just when, how, and why he decided upon the
career of historian. Whenever possible I try to distinguish between the
act or art of professing history and the lifelong process of becoming a
historian, and I often wonder when some people I know and read
think they are historians rather than mere professors of history. But
that is a churlish point, and one that need not detain us here. It is
hard, as I say, to be precise about the motives that impelled me to
make history, especially modern British history, my profession, if only
because I cannot recall a time during my childhood and youth when I
lived outside an environment resonant with history. This may sound a
trifle sanctimonious. What I mean by resonance is that I grew up
slowly in a house full of first editions, grand pianos, Georgian artifacts,

and allusive as well as irreverent conversation. This unusual household provided the setting for my father's eminently Victorian pronouncements about both the eighteenth and twentieth centuries—their contents and his discontents. He introduced his children too soon, perhaps too often, to Burke, Gibbon, Lord Chesterfield, Chatham, the Duke of Newcastle, Dr. Johnson, and, of course, Laurence Sterne, who stared down at us in his shrewd, slightly wicked way from more than one wall. Admittedly, Hobbes and Locke hovered constantly in the background, but their combined voices never quite drowned out my father's favorite text, which he had distilled from Gibbon: Power guided by Virtue and Wisdom equals English civilization. Winston Churchill was, of course, the supreme embodiment of that formula, and since I was just old enough to follow e details of the Battle of Britain in the newspapers, I could not disagree with that verdict. My own acute Anglophilia of the 1940s was accentuated by the knowledge that because I had been born in London I would have the choice of opting for either British or American citizenship when I reached twenty-one. It amuses me now to recall how eagerly my boyish imagination seized upon this mere technicality to make my cause one with the British people during their "finest hour."

Of all my father's roles, that of Lord Chesterfield sticks most firmly in my mind, no doubt because of the extraordinarily rich and learned letters he sent to me intermittently over a period of some twenty years. This was a unique correspondence course laden with scholarly allusions, magisterial advice, and mordant wit. Most of the character-forming properties of those letters were, of course, completely lost on me, just as Lord Chesterfield wasted a good deal of his wisdom on Philip Stanhope, who never realized or achieved the brilliant diplomatic career his father had in mind for him. During my undergraduate years at Yale I failed to become the eccentric my father wanted me to be, although I did continue my neo-Augustan education by learning some Greek from that rugged humanist, Bernard Knox, and by majoring in modern European and British history. The only science course to leave a lasting impression on me was Professor Richard Flint's fine introduction to geology. As for the social sciences, I avoided like the plague any work in either sociology or psychology. Apart from the fact that these "disciplines" were anathema in my humanistic household, most of the courses in these two fields had the deserved reputation of being "guts" designed for athletes in academic difficulties. In my senior year I began to take intellectual matters more seriously, and after laboring mightily, I produced a rather dull and respectable senior thesis on the political career of the 14th Earl of Derby, the most readable and original chapter of which dealt with Derby's translation of Homer.

Upon my graduation from Yale in 1953 I had neither a clear nor a blurred vision that some day I would become a "professor of history." Indeed, my thoughts about a career were subordinated to apprehensions about the decision to volunteer my services to the U. S. Army for two years. Although the Korean War loomed ominously close to my class, I could have fallen back upon a student deferment in order to continue my education at graduate school. Given my background and sensibilities, I knew almost instinctively that graduate school was a matter of predestination. But for that very reason I wanted to postpone my fate until I had come to terms with some of the imperatives at work in my own mind. Apart from considerations of what used to be called civic duty, I let the draft take its course because I suspected that unless I broke out of the snug, not to say smug, mold of Yale in particular and Academe in general in which I had been reared, the chances were distinctly against my ever surviving the privileged ordeal of being a professor's son. Since the army offered the most complete as well as cheapest escape route from Academe, I found myself in the autumn of 1953 a shorn buck private at Fort Dix, determined like my hero in those days, T. E. Lawrence, to test myself against the anonymity and barbarism of barracks life.

Basic and advanced infantry training at Fort Dix for five interminable months gave me some occasion to wonder if the rigors of graduate school were not preferable to sadistic sergeants, forced marches, and the thousand and one petty and absurd acts that make up an ordinary day in any military camp. Most of my barrack mates turned out to be tragicomic, and, fortunately for me, all my army experiences turned out to be more comic than tragic. This is not the place to try to write my version of *From Here to Eternity*, but I must admit, with Gibbon's remark about the Hampshire Grenadiers in mind, that I learned more about human nature in general and America in particular from my six months at Fort Dix than I have from all the years spent in Academe. The Army was good enough to teach me how to play war games with blunt bayonets and blank cartridges, and I even learned how to shoot inaccurately by moonlight as well as daylight. But once the Korean War had ended, orders came to send me out west to Fort Carson, Colorado, where I talked my way into the splendid duty of learning how to ski and climb in the Rocky Mountains at government expense. The only dangerous part of my assignment as an instructor in the Mountain and Cold Weather Training Command was the obligation to pass on my recently acquired inexpertise to classes of regular infantrymen, most of whom were "flatlanders" who did not take kindly to winter maneuvers in four or five feet of snow with thin air and heavy rucksacks. In the summer months we taught nervous recruits the joys of "exposure" on the rock faces of South Cheyenne Canyon near

Colorado Springs. Those of us who preferred climbing to skiing devoted weekends to the real mountains in the back country, where we did our best to push the margin of safety down to the thinness of a Vibram sole or the looseness of a piton. In more ways than I can recount, I have never quite recovered from that year and a half in the Rockies with the serenity of the high mountains only a pair of skis or climbing boots away. History, I later learned, was a good deal safer than climbing, but at least twice as demanding on oneself and family. In any event, the army impressed upon me the meaning of personal liberty by taking it away completely for two years, and it proved easy to exaggerate the attractions of a teacher's life while sweating out a long day on K.P. duty. Reluctantly I gave up my daydream of becoming a carpenter *cum* skier in Aspen, not being expert enough at either pursuit, and made plans to do graduate work in England. Following my discharge in the summer of 1955, I embarked for Oxford, and my hopes soared at the thought that I could start picking up the scattered fragments of my education in as painless a manner as possible.

Those hopes were dashed soon after arriving in Oxford. The contrast between Aspen and Oxford was about as traumatic as the transition from Yale to Fort Dix, if not more so. I had survived sub-zero temperatures and lashing winds above timber line, but nothing had prepared me for the penetrating cold of Oxford college rooms. And then there were the Oxford people, so hopelessly different from my wild and unsophisticated friends in Leadville and Aspen. It took a long time for the ex-corporal to adjust to the aristocratic tone and ritual of the House (*Aedes Christi*), not the least difficult decision being whether or not to call my solicitous scout by his first or last name. In one of my weaker or more American moments I settled for "Bob," knowing perfectly well that it was a craven compromise, if not actually a subversive act in the eyes of my Public School contemporaries at Christ Church. Nevertheless, I have Oxford to thank for teaching me in its discreet, unobtrusive way over a period of four years the difference between being a civilian and being civilized. Although I can now say with a straight face that some of my best friends are dons, I never quite learned to cope with their formidable and fastidious defenses. How delicately they tried to teach us by philosophy as well as example the arts of gentlemanly intellectual discourse and conduct, and how completely foreign to their instincts were such ungentlemanly fields as sociology, psychology, and political science. But then, in the presence of Hugh Trevor-Roper, Isaiah Berlin, A. P. d'Entrèves, and other members of Oxford's humanistic aristocracy, the so-called social sciences seemed to pale in significance.

Oxford was bound to influence the kind of history I thought about and wrote, and the way I wrote, just as Princeton, where I taught history to undergraduates for four years, and, later, Berkeley have left their mark, if not their scars, on my work. At Oxford I was allowed to get on with the job of becoming a "narrow specialist" at my own pace and without any formal training in advanced historical research and writing.

Perhaps I am less of an environmentalist than I like to think, but I have found that the kind of history I do tends to reflect my surroundings, both intellectual and architectural, as much as it embodies any enduring personal or private concerns. Take the buildings and grounds of Christ Church. How could I possibly have written labor or working class history—bloody-minded or otherwise—in the sumptuous library which broods over the quintessential elegance of Peckwater Quad? The aristocratic trappings of the House made it difficult for me not to identify with the 3rd Marquess of Salisbury instead of the inarticulate peasant Irish Land Leaguers and Moonlighters whose names I encountered in the State Paper Office in Dublin Castle. At Nuffield College, on the other hand, where I spent my last two years in Oxford, I experienced something more than the shock of moving from a bastion of Latitudinarian Toryism to one of Nonconformist Labour. It so happened that the construction of the college, stone by stone, proceeded apace with the laborious task of writing my dissertation, and from my window I often watched the walls rise behind the primitive wooden scaffolding. Like the design of the college, my dissertation had a certain compromising, functional, and graceless quality. But there is one important difference: Nuffield College was built to last some seven hundred years, and my dissertation was not. The architectural hodge-podge of the Princeton campus contained just enough examples of American "girder-Gothic" to perpetuate the cloistered atmosphere of Oxford, and although I much preferred the original product, my work began to show more girder than Gothic as the trials and tribulations of junior faculty life at Princeton gradually undermined my morale. The less said about the campus architecture at Berkeley the better. But that is just the point. The absence of any dominant design, the existence of many ugly or ungainly buildings, and the overwhelming presence of San Francisco poised on the edge of the Pacific Ocean seemed to open up new vistas in my work. It was in the permissive, impersonal, curiously compelling, and deeply politicized climate of Berkeley, so far removed from the traditional centers of learning to which I had been exposed since childhood, that I found some of the answers to the Irish Question for which I was looking.

Enough ruminating about the interaction of architecture, environment, and institutional personality in my work. What I hope to accomplish here is to describe the way I moved from the reasonably safe and respectable kind of "Cabinet history" of my Oxford years, of which ministerial correspondence and Westminster ritual form the core, to something more eclectic, speculative, and, I trust, provocative which is embodied in my recent attempt to understand the course of Anglo-Irish relations in the Victorian period, namely *Anglo-Saxons and Celts*, hereafter abbreviated as *ASC*.[1]

When in the early 1960s I began to overhaul my dissertation with an eye to publication, I was still working within the Oxonian tradition of heavily documented Cabinet history. Not that my first book, *Coercion and Conciliation in Ireland, 1880–1892*,[2] turned out to be all ministerial narrative or descriptive history. But there was nothing either new or Namierite about the approach and the way evidence was handled. Indeed, Namier's name was rarely heard among the history dons whom I encountered. The Oxford I knew did not so much repudiate as ignore Sir Lewis; and I recall one prominent historian telling me that Keith Feiling had anticipated most of Namier's methods and conclusions several years before the publication of *The Structure of Politics*. Because Oxford left me more or less to my own devices, I spent many months immersing myself in the Salisbury Papers, which had been deposited in Christ Church Library. I had hoped in 1955 that the germ of a viable dissertation on the domestic politics of Lord Salisbury's administrations would emerge by some spontaneous process out of my reading and note-taking on every topic from local licensing and party patronage to the annexation of Upper Burma. In the long run my constant exposure to Salisbury's correspondents as well as his own replies, marginal notes, and queries in red ink proved not to be an utter waste of time. But it was no easy matter to convince myself, not to mention one or two interested dons, that something significant was being accomplished by this period of groping and wandering among the Salisbury Papers in that small, musty room overlooking the limpid beauty of the Dean's garden.

So far as formal historical methods were concerned, I imbibed little beyond what the kindly, low-key lectures of Professor R. B. Wernham taught me about how to survive the ordeal of the D.Phil. degree. This is not to deny the enormous debt I owe to the astuteness of Charles Stuart, my tutor for a term at Christ Church, to the shrewd advice of John Mason, now librarian and then custodian of the Salisbury Papers, and also to the unfailingly acute comments of my supervisor, Herbert Nicholas of New College, who cheered me through the last arduous chapters with the remark that my footnotes made much more interesting reading than the text. And how right he was. But few of us doing advanced research in history had the slightest idea of just how "original" a D.Phil. dissertation had to be. Most of us lived in a state of mild to severe anxiety for three or four years wondering what our fates would be at the hands of unknown examiners who had the power to humiliate us with a B.Litt. after all our labors. Not being either a quantifier or model-builder by training, I stuck to the traditional theme of ministerial politics and policies on the Westminster-Dublin axis, which had little to do with the internal or agrarian and rural history of Ireland. Too much English political history is made up of long paragraphs based on short letters from Lord X to Sir Y, written at some apparently critical juncture in the affairs of state. And two of the essential working assumptions of the political historian are that his documents are sufficient unto the day of publication and that the unknown circumstances leading up to the writing of any given letter as well as the thoughts left out or censored by the writer of that letter have no significant bearing on his story. There is, of course, something to be said for doing this kind of history at least once in a lifetime, provided that one has a good collection of documents, some imagination, a sense of humor, and a prose style that does not provoke English reviewers into using their favorite word of abuse, namely, "pedestrian."

Now it might have helped had I known some of these facts of historiographical life when I decided to write a dissertation on the Irish policies of the Salisbury ministries from 1885 to 1892. *Coercion and Conciliation* really owed its existence to Charles Stuart's suggestion in 1956 that I convert my intended chapter on the Irish Question into a dissertation instead of trying to cover every aspect of Conservative domestic policy during the Salisbury era. Among other things, this suggestion saved me from becoming bogged down in the Salisbury Papers, and encouraged me instead to get completely bogged down in the Irish Question.

Since my mother was born a Sullivan (in New York, not County Kerry) and was considered by my father to be of good "bog-trotting" stock, I suppose it would be neat and psycho-logical to assume that sooner or later I was bound to rebel against the Anglo-Saxon overlord by turning toward Ireland and Irish history. But neatness and logic seldom characterize human behavior or motives, and, as we all know, rebellions, least of all student rebellions, are never complete. The fact is that I did not abandon Westminster for Dublin, Cork, or Galway. (Belfast was out of the question.) My new focus was fixed on the policy of Lord Salisbury and his cabinet colleagues toward Ireland; and this ministerial perspective with its concomitant emphasis on the administrative process in Dublin Castle was and still is a far cry from Irish history as construed by genuine Irish scholars. In the summer of 1956 I traveled around Eire as a tourist and found much in the way of terrain and temperament that appealed to me. But the decision to switch my attention from the struggle between Lord Salisbury, Sir Stafford Northcote, and Lord Randolph Churchill over "Elijah's Mantle" to the struggle of the British political parties over Irish Home Rule had a good deal more to do with the sheer quantity of correspondence and memoranda relating to Ireland which I found in the archives. In other words, it took me more than a year at Oxford to find the "right" subject, one that offered me something more nourishing than speculation about the reasons for ministerial wrangles in the 1880s.

Working in Oxford without benefit of Irish clergy—there being no *bona fide* Irish historian at Oxford then or now—I ended up writing a D.Phil. dissertation which was neither Irish nor English history but something in between, and therefore likely to displease experts in both camps. My version of Oxford Cabinet history was, of course, entirely innocent of sociological, not to mention psychological, models of behavior. It seemed to me in those distant days when history belonged unquestionably to the humanities and when historians were not constantly worrying about ways of defining History, that I had quite enough of an assignment on my hands trying to complete the third leg of the triangle of the Irish Question in the 1880s, of which two monumental, if unequal, sides had already been built by John L. Hammond in his *Gladstone and the Irish Nation* (1938) and Conor Cruise O'Brien in *Parnell and His Party* (1957). Had I been asked to learn a new language like Parsonian sociologese, which was so much more foreign to my ear than Greek or Latin, I would gladly have settled for a B.Litt. degree.

Looking back on those probationary years spent steeping myself in the papers of Lord Salisbury, Balfour, and their colleagues in London and Dublin, I now realize that this overexposure to the documents gave me a certain "feel" for the subject. I gained a sense, or possibly it was only an illusion, that I knew something about the ways some of my protagonists thought as well as wrote and spoke. Perhaps I deluded myself into thinking that I had built a private line of communication back to certain segments of the Tory political elite. But my immersion in the primary sources before finally deciding on a dissertation topic still seems to me to have been an effective baptism in historical research. And by research I really mean the ways some historians reach back with both their imaginations and their techniques and try to grasp the times and the cultures, however remote, which dominate their working day.

Graduate research in England soon exposed me to the phenomenon of archival territoriality in Academe. Having had no previous experience of the workings of the "territorial imperative" among historians, I was naïve enough to assume that the spirit of free trade and open markets prevailed where manuscript materials were concerned. Imagine my consternation, then, when shortly after arriving at Oxford in 1955, I received a letter from a rising, now fully risen, political historian who had been the first to penetrate and dominate the arena of the Salisbury Papers. Replying to a letter of inquiry I had written to him asking for some advice about the contents of the uncatalogued collection, this historian not only sent me a short outline of his forthcoming book on Victorian politics, but added for good measure that he doubted if the collection would be of much value to my own project. When I showed this letter to my supervisor, who happened to be an expert on academic man as well as Stubbs, he smiled and assured me that the writer was trying to exercise some kind of absentee proprietarial right over the papers. So I ignored the boundary markers and soon had ample evidence to prove that the Salisbury collection was indispensable to my dissertation needs. This was only the first of many encounters with territorial behavior among historians in my *field* (the very word suggests territoriality), and I experienced the sensations of territoriality myself, once I gained entry to the Balfour Papers at the British Museum after months of badgering officials. Years later, when I started to read Robert Ardrey's effusive prose describing territoriality and arena behavior in animals and human beings, it dawned on me that political, diplomatic, and other categories of historians who defend their archival and topical boundaries from intruders are acting on much the same compulsion that drives the rabbit, the Arctic wolf, and the ring-tailed lemur to mark their boundaries respectively with fecal pellets, urine, and a special scent from the perineal gland.[3] The often silent but always intense scramble for archival territory which I witnessed in England among eminent professors as well as obscure graduate students, equally "up-tight" about boundary markers, forced me to conclude that resentments rising out of these territorial disputes accounted for far more nasty digs and hostile reviewing in the journals than any genuine ideological or methodological differences.

Although the most original portions of *Coercion and Conciliation* were based on the hitherto inaccessible Irish Letter Books in the Balfour Papers, which covered almost four years of Irish government in some two thousand pages, the book was not all administrative history. There was a thesis running through the work like an underground river and surfacing in the conclusion which had to do with the primacy of real property in Unionist thinking—in itself, a form of territoriality. The overriding concern of Unionists for the rights and privileges of landowners, I argued, made them extremely fearful lest the land war in Ireland spread across the Irish Sea to Great Britain, where Radicals and Socialists were poised and anxious to renew their agitation against "unearned increment," landlords' rights, and even private property. The tendency of this predominantly landowning and big business party to see radical or socialist agitation behind most popular demands for reform explained why so many Unionists dismissed the Home Rule movement as a mélange of "hollow, sentimental follies." At Hatfield and other great country houses, Home Rule was regarded as a "very hollow affair" masking the struggle between the masses and the classes.[4] The Unionists' efforts to "kill Home Rule with kindness," their conviction that the Irish peasantry would repudiate Parnellism once they owned their holdings by means of land purchase measures, revealed the full extent of their preoccupation with property. Salisbury and his colleagues thus looked to the pacifying effects of converting thousands of Irish tenants into small proprietors as the only way to undermine Irish nationalism.

Such was my conclusion in *Coercion and Conciliation,* and to my chagrin only a few of the numerous reviewers who tackled the book bothered to acknowledge, let alone discuss, that thesis. But once I had survived the ordeal of being reviewed for the first time, I began to realize that concern for landlords' rights did not explain every feature of the English response to the Irish Question in the 1880s. The property argument did not help me to understand why many Victorians of varying background, education, occupation, and religious belief were so quick to impugn the motives of Irish nationalists, many of whom were moderates and constitutionalists in both theory and practice. The more I thought about the way Salisbury and most of his colleagues dismissed the Home Rule agitation as a "hollow affair," the more I realized that these men were not just worried about the prosperity of their estates or even the "integrity of the empire," once Parnell had managed to wring certain concessions from Westminster. They were also blinded by prejudice against the Irish for being Irish; otherwise they might have taken greater pains, as did Lord Carnarvon and a few other more tolerant Tories, to separate the land question from the nationality question and to distinguish between land hunger and socialism or anarchism. There had to be some force or some compulsion which prevented so many Victorians from understanding not only the issues underlying the land war, but the reasons why the Parnellites won 85 out of 103 Irish seats in the general election of 1885. Besides the political elite at Westminster, there were the voters to consider. Why was it that so many Englishmen who were neither aristocratic nor wealthy opposed Home Rule in the decades before World War I? Why should respectable and comfortable middle class and professional men worry about the consequences of giving the Parnellites a modest amount of Home Rule, when they themselves had no estates in Ireland and, on the surface at least, had no good reason for regarding a semi-autonomous Ireland as a threat to their lives, liberties, and properties?

My curiosity about the real, as distinct from the rhetorical, bases of Unionist opposition to Home Rule grew steadily the more I read and thought about the ways Englishmen regarded Irishmen in those decades. Gradually and at times quite contrary to my original intentions, my interests began to shift away from "official" policy to the "unofficial" attitudes and assumptions which seemed to me to underlie and inform government policies in Ireland. The greater my distance from *Coercion and Conciliation*, and from the intellectual milieu to which it belonged, the clearer it became that I had not come to grips with all the realities and fantasies of Anglo-Irish relations. What continued to perplex or elude me were the reasons for the failure of Englishmen to understand, let alone solve, the so-called Irish Question when so much information about Ireland and the Irish lay close at hand.

From 1959 to 1963 my formal course work at Princeton forced me to learn some European history, and while my dissertation gathered much-needed dust, I began to read further afield in the literature of British imperialism as well as Irish history. The upshot of my attempts to place the English "conquest" of Ireland in a more international—the French would say "universal"—framework of European expansion overseas was my decision to embark on an interpretive study of the relationship between the Irish Question and the "new imperialism" of the later nineteenth century. The central theme was to be the nature of the challenge posed by Parnellism to what was then called "the integrity of empire." Assuming that certain irrational fears had an important role to play in the "forward policy" of British politicians and administrators, I wanted to explore the possibility that the directors of British foreign and imperial policy may have favored joining in the competition for empire in Africa, Asia, and the Pacific in order to prove to their rivals in Paris, Berlin, and other European capitals that their failure to solve the Irish Question did not signify the beginning of the decline and fall of the British Empire. While I was turning over in my mind these and other thoughts about the underlying causes of imperial consolidation and expansion, a passage kept running through my mind which seemed to have nothing to do with this project. The sentence in question had been written in 1885 by the then Irish Chief Secretary, Sir William Hart Dyke, to the Irish Viceroy, Lord Carnarvon, and the burden of his letter explained why he had failed utterly to promote the cause of conciliation for Ireland among his Conservative colleagues at Westminster. "I find the same hopeless indifference and ignorance in every quarter," he wrote, "plus an amount of prejudice, which would drive John Bright wild with envy." [5]

Now I had not made much of this observation in *Coercion and Conciliation*, but for some reason I kept hearing that sentence as though the needle were stuck on the proverbial record. Why the "indifference and ignorance"? What kind of "prejudice"? Like most students of Anglo-Irish relations, I had taken the prejudice for granted, knowing full well that Englishmen did not regard Irishmen in quite the same light or class as themselves. Just possibly this prejudice deserved a closer look. Perhaps what had been taken for granted ought to be taken apart and analyzed. Having already worked my way through some of the thickets of government policy in Ireland during the Home Rule agitation of the 1880s, and having come up with no entirely satisfactory answers to those "why" questions, I realized that I would have to go beyond the official documents, Cabinet memos, parliamentary debates, and *Times'* leaders in order to find evidence as to what this prejudice was all about. Once I had decided to explore Hart Dyke's "prejudice," I began to veer away from the "new imperialism" project and to move toward the study of stereotypes and images of the Irish in Victorian England. Just as in my Oxford days, I found that as soon as I had brought the vague outline of the subject into focus, the material began to accumulate with surprising speed. Turning aside from the more obvious political and polemical tracts dealing with the Irish Question, I soon discovered both subtle and blatant forms of anti-Irish prejudice in Victorian history books, novels, cartoons and caricatures, ethnological papers, private diaries, and so on.

The evidence I gathered during 1964–1966 convinced me that the belief was widespread among Victorians that Irish Celts and English Saxons were antithetical in physical and mental characteristics, and that these differences were assumed to be not only hereditary, but also as black and white as any two ostensibly white peoples could be. This belief went beyond anti-Catholic sentiment and was essentially an anti-Irish and anti-Celtic phenomenon. To the more familiar problem of religious and class prejudice, one had to add ethnic and racial prejudice against the Irish; and the notable feature of the latter was that it transformed the popular belief that the Irish were currently inferior into the conviction that they were permanently inferior.

Anti-Irish prejudice, as I came to learn, did not stop with ethnicity. There was also the troublesome question of color. Here and there I found traces of pigmental prejudice in the Anglo-Saxonist image of the Irish; and since I had never encountered any suggestion of this in the secondary literature on Anglo-Irish relations, I suppose my reaction should have been one of surprise. But given my suspicions about some of the springs that fed English ethnocentrism—which I later labeled Anglo-Saxonism—I was not so much surprised as enthralled by the evidence. Needless to say, the question as to whether the Irish were in fact darker or more melanous than Englishmen had not been conclusively answered by the primitive sampling techniques and morphological methods used by John Beddoe to compile his Index of Nigrescence. for the British Isles.[8] But the crucial question for me was epitomized by the loaded nature of his formula and by his choice of the term "nigrescence" rather than "xanthosity," "sanguinescence," or some other neologism connoting blondeness or fairness. The relative percentages of melanous and xanthous types in England and Ireland were not all that important, even assuming that such a precise measurement could ever be obtained. What mattered far more were the implications that swirled about in the minds of Englishmen when they faced the "fact" that Celts were darker, swarthier, more prognathous, and melancholic than Anglo-Saxons. What was the connection between melanosity and prognathism on the one hand and savagery or barbarism on the other? Beddoe had, after all, relied on his Index to speculate about the African genesis of the darker, wilder Celts of Munster and Connaught. Why did some Victorians call Irishmen "white niggers" and "white chimpanzees," and make mutually pejorative comparisons between Irishmen and Hottentots? As I read, reread, and then listened, as G. M. Young had urged us, to the Victorians discuss such problems as race deterioration, the deliberate limitation of family size by the upper classes—which they called, revealingly enough, "race suicide"— and the gradual darkening of the hair and eyes of urban Englishmen, the psychological significance of these images of the melanous, melancholic Celt gradually began to emerge.

How old, I wondered, was the equation in English minds between Irish Celts and Caliban? Whether or not Shakespeare thought of Ireland (rather than the Bermudas) in all its verdure and ordure when he wrote the *Tempest* and created Caliban whose "vile race . . . had that in't which good natures could not abide to be with," the dominant Victorian image of the Irish in the 1860s looked much more like that monstrous and deformed slave than the rollicking, carousing stage Irishman, Teague, or Paddy of earlier generations. The reasons for this "sea change" puzzled me just enough to stimulate further research into the nature of stereotypes in general and stereotypes of Paddy in particular. Once I had a clear idea of the perimeter of my field, I turned to Victorian history books, novels, ethnic slurs and anecdotes, and caricature in my search for the parameters of Anglo-Irish incompatibility.

At some dimly recollected point in my researches, I realized that I would never get beyond the stage of mere description of the changing image in question and would therefore never dig down to the roots of the Irish Question so long as I stuck to the conventional methods of historical reconstruction. To venture beyond the usual "image study" with the equipment I then possessed would have meant sharing my guesses or conjectures with readers whose own guesses might be equally valid or invalid. Something more than the familiar game of "blind historian's bluff" was required in order to bring me nearer my goal of understanding the Irish problem. The nature of my inquiry virtually dictated that I consult what may be loosely labeled the literature of clinical psychology. Since I was working on anti-Irish prejudice, I could hardly avoid coming to terms with the dynamics of prejudice itself. And ignorance of psychology, not to mention my own prejudice against psychology and sociology during my college years, provided no excuse for not trying to learn what this "foreign field" had to offer in the way of answers to my questions. It did not take me long to find out that some of those questions loomed large in the minds of modern social scientists. Granted that my search for clues about the workings of prejudice was both amateurish and eclectic, nevertheless my readings went beyond the Freud-Reich-Allport-Erikson stage and into such journals as *Human Relations*, the *Journal of Abnormal and Social Psychology*, and the *Psychoanalytic Review*. These suggestive readings enabled me to fill in some of the background and collect the analogies needed to buttress my argument about the nature of ethnic and race prejudice in Victorian England. I came away from that excursion into an unfamiliar field with more questions than answers about the nature of psychology. But that was not all. I learned something too about human nature, regardless of time, place, race, nationality, class, and religion.

It is possible that I might not have moved as deliberately as I did from political to attitudinal history had it not been for two books encountered in the early 1960s. And since I still regard these works as formative influences on my thinking—in two very different ways—I would like to discuss each one briefly. Sometime in 1962 the notable book by Messrs. R. Robinson and J. Gallagher, *Africa and the Victorians* (1961), came my way. I began to read that work with an enthusiasm that rapidly dwindled to doubt. As I understood their thesis, Robinson and Gallagher were arguing that something they called "the official mind" of the Victorian governing classes was a necessary, if not sufficient, cause of British imperial expansion and consolidation in the later decades of the nineteenth century. Leaving aside the merits of their contention that European competition for control or suzerainty in the Nilotic area worked as the triggering mechanism of the "scramble" for Africa, I balked at their suggestion that a model or concept so vague, intangible, and, above all, antiseptic as the "official mind" could have played the crucial role assigned to it by these historians in the advancement and protection of British imperial interests. Robinson and Gallagher had underlined the importance of this concept by choosing as their subtitle "The Official Mind of Imperialism." Echoing and embellishing Schumpeter's thesis about the class and caste basis of imperialism, the authors relied heavily on the "official" documents in the Public Record Office and the "official" correspondence of cabinet ministers to show how the professional "detachment" of policy-makers in Whitehall affected the decision to annex or not to annex in Africa and elsewhere.

For various reasons, I resisted the thesis that ministers and civil servants were in the habit of deciding imperial policy in a partial vacuum, that is, in some remote office, "insulated from pressures at Home," and free from the contaminating influences of their own formal and informal education, daily social contacts, exposure to newspapers as well as lobbyists, elections, financial concerns, economic interests, and persistent fantasies. I could hardly deny the existence of "official policy," but I was not convinced the authors understood all the ingredients that went into such decisions as the occupation of Egypt. When, for example, did the "official mind" become official, and when did it stop being official? When it left office? Could all the disagreement and controversy within the Foreign Office, Whitehall, and the Cabinet over the "right" policy at home and abroad be subsumed under the umbrella term "official"? If certain members of the general public shared the same convictions as those in Whitehall or Westminster responsible for deciding policy, were they too part of the "official mind"? And so on. Robinson and Gallagher did indeed admit that certain "unconscious assumptions" influenced ministers and their advisers from time to time, but these unofficial ingredients were left undefined and unexplained. The authors' virtual denial of any confusion of interests and roles between aristocrats and civil servants on the one hand and traders and empire builders on the other seemed to me to reinforce the very orthodoxies and platitudes about the Victorian governing classes that I was trying to undermine. Much as I admired the verve and dash of their prose, and envied their knack of turning a fine phrase about Gladstone and Salisbury, I had to endorse the remark of a reviewer who wrote that the book "smells of the Public Record Office (a nice but limited smell), not at all of Africa." [7]

Since I could not accept the "official mind" as the causal force of British imperialism, *Africa and the Victorians* spurred me to go beyond or behind the speeches, Cabinet memoranda, and official correspondence of the political elite in search of the bases of the prejudice that Hart Dyke had found among his colleagues at Westminster. And this search for clues about the workings of the "unofficial mind" led me to O. Mannoni's *Prospero and Caliban* (1956) in the winter of 1963. [8] For all its structural flaws and conceptual weaknesses, many of them deriving from the author's deep personal involvement in the events he was seeking to explain, this book fascinated me as few other accounts of the imperial-colonial relationship had done. No doubt my ignorance of the history of Madagascar accounted in part for my enthusiasm, even excitement, over this work. Mannoni had dared to go far beyond my own cautious notions of the proper way to explore the workings of European minds caught up in the "colonial situation." Even now, it is difficult to assess the full influence of *Prospero and Caliban* on my own work. Although there were few direct borrowings from that book in *ASC*, Mannoni's interpretation of the collision between French and Malagasy fears and fantasies, especially during and after the revolt of 1947, informed a great deal of my thinking about the British "colonial situation" around the world. If I could not accept all of Mannoni's thesis, I did find it necessary to rethink Anglo-Irish relations in the light of the Prospero-Caliban polarity, granted the existence of countless differences between the histories of Madagascar and Ireland. Robinson and Gallagher had advanced an argument that seemed to me to lead nowhere, because every decision made by ministers and colonial administrators could be explained away as symptomatic of the "official mind." Mannoni, on the other hand, had suggested the presence of a dynamic relationship between ruler and ruled that raised a number of fascinating questions.

In the following months I read various works on imperialism and colonialism, including some studies by the French imperial historians Brunschwig and Deschamps. But my thoughts kept returning to *Prospero and Caliban*, as though there were lessons still to be learned from that work. Occasionally I heard the tocsin striking, warning me not to impose the Mannoni model on Ireland, but I found that many passages appreciated in value as I returned to them for second and third visits. As both a participant and observer entangled in his own "colonial situation," Mannoni was bound to personalize issues and events in a most unhistorical manner. Nevertheless, the very involvement of the man in his subject and, indeed, his awareness of that involvement, afforded insights into the imperial-colonial relationship denied to most of us earnest and worthy Ph.D.'s writing away fast and furiously in the hothouse atmosphere of the P.R.O. Quite against my will and ingrained caution as a documentary historian, I found analogies between the colonial elite and the colonized in Madagascar and Ireland. But even more fruitful than analogies was the way Mannoni made me think again about the endless collisions of peoples, cultures, and fantasies in Ireland since the earliest times. Was there an island, I wondered then and wonder now, with quite as many candidates for the roles of Prospero, Caliban, Ariel, Miranda, Ferdinand, Stephano, Trinculo and so on as Ireland? The more I thought about it, the more certain it seemed that Shakespeare had a scruffy, lustful Irish woodkern in mind when he created the unforgettable Caliban.

This encounter with Mannoni helped to steer me away from my study of the domestic politics of British imperialism and toward the more congenial task of trying to disentangle Anglo-Irish relations. No matter how specious the dichotomy between dependent and independent personalities in *Prospero and Caliban*, no matter how little "hard" history about Madagascar Mannoni gave his readers, I wanted to test the *Tempest* thesis on Ireland and Anglo-Irish relations, even though it was clear that the two situations were by no means identical. From Mannoni I moved on to Philip Mason's derivative but suggestive lectures on the psychology of British imperial and colonial experiences, published in 1962 as *Prospero's Magic*. Although the historical sections of this work made thin reading, Mason's interpretation of the unconscious motivations of a governing class at home and abroad also contained insights and posed some disturbing because almost unanswerable questions.

Both Mannoni and Mason had had personal experience of the twilight of Prospero's rule in Madagascar and India, respectively, and both had chosen to write about the psychological relations between European conquerors with their "white man's magic" and nonwhite subjects living in tropical, libidinous climes. Ireland's climate, I hasten to add, could hardly be called tropical, not to mention libidinous, and I found it hard to conceive of Englishmen acting out their sexual fantasies quite so effectively in Ireland as they did in India. But other comparisons beckoned. Never having played the part of Prospero in a colonial setting full of Calibans, I wandered some distance away from the Mannoni-Mason line in order to explore the image of Caliban in the minds of Prospero's compatriots, namely the governing classes of Naples and Milan. In the hopes of understanding why some Victorians persisted in regarding Irishmen as Caliban—assuming that the original Caliban was in fact half-monster and half-man—I tried to cast as wide a net as possible, hauling in novels, cartoons, ethnographical and anthropometric works, as well as history books. Slowly and unsystematically a picture—or image—began to emerge of what Hart Dyke had meant by "prejudice" in 1885.

Any historian who has tried to work with such intangibles as feelings, sentiments, opinions, attitudes, ideas, and beliefs will know something about the obstacles that lie between the conception and execution of his project. At countless points in both the research and writing stages I had to contend with formidable problems of definition, especially where such "loaded" words as "race," "racism," "image," and "ethnocentrism" were involved. At a time when the term "racist" was being indiscriminately and polemically applied in America, it was all the more important to treat that highly charged label with care, if not to avoid it altogether. The definition of Anglo-Saxonism and Celticism also posed some awkward problems, because both words invited the criticism that in seeking to explain everything, they explained nothing.

Such then were some of the steps, many of them halting and not a few blind, which occupied my attention over a number of months that somehow stretched into years and which culminated in the appearance of *ASC* as a slim volume in a new monographic series, the existence of which was virtually unknown outside the genteel confines of the Conference of British Studies. *ASC* was designed as an essay, by which I mean that its argument was set forth with a mixture of hesitancy and boldness, supported by evidence that was not only selective but allusive. Part thesis and part hypothesis, *ASC* hovers in an intellectual limbo between book and article as well as between English and Irish history, belonging to neither but taking something from each. Owing to the vast expanse of the territory in which I was wandering and because I had to learn some new techniques along the way, there seemed to be a strong case in favor of not trying to write a "definitive" account of the phenomena in question. Since any serious scholar could devote a lifetime to reading and reflecting about all the primary and secondary sources germane to the subject, I decided that a short summary of my researches and thinking to date might elicit or provoke some constructive criticism from experts working in related fields. It is too early to tell just how helpful or futile this anticipated scholarly criticism will be, but I am still waiting to read something more substantial than the loud damns and undue praise I have heard so far.

Like all historians of my acquaintance, I prefer to think of this production as constituting a fresh look at some old as well as new evidence. Such originality as it may have, however, lies not in methodology, but in the use of evidence rarely encountered in orthodox political history and also in the interpretation of that evidence. For those readers who are unfamiliar with this work, I should point out that *ASC* was not only a good deal shorter than *Coercion and Conciliation*, but covered a much longer period of time: some sixty years as compared with six or seven years of Conservative Unionist rule in Ireland. I would go further and describe *ASC*—with the usual disclaimers of false immodesty—as a more thoughtful study precisely because it lacked the ponderous documentation and circumspection of the earlier work.

I wrote the original version or kernel of what became *ASC* in the spring of 1966 while I was in Oxford, profiting from my first leave of absence from professional or academic duties. The results of that writing were presented to the Irish Historical Society in June under the title "The Anglo-Saxon Image of Celtic Ireland in the Age of Home Rule." Encouraged by the comments and suggestions made at that meeting, I read more and then started to revise the paper with the object of producing a preliminary, even tentative, statement of what would some day become a full-length and comprehensive study of ethnocentric thought in Greater Britain as well as Greater Ireland during the nineteenth and early twentieth centuries.

However soft or speculative some of the argumentation may appear to me in several years' time, I found that putting the essay together gave me an excuse to learn something about Victorian caricature, fiction, ethnology, criminal anthropology, anthropometry, and other more mundane subjects. Indeed, I came away from this investigation with those mildly manic symptoms familiar to historians who like to think that they have finally broken out of the orthodoxies dominating their special fields. Instead of leaning so heavily on Cabinet memoranda, ministerial correspondence, and the reports of civil servants and police inspectors received in Dublin Castle, as I had done in *Coercion and Conciliation*, I turned to the writings of Victorian historians, ethnologists, publicists, novelists, and other persons connected in some way with Ireland, the Irish, and image-making about the two. Conceived as a study of educated opinion about the Irish rather than an inquiry into that profound abstraction called Public Opinion, *ASC* became a case study of ethnic prejudice toward an allegedly inferior people, known as the Celtic Irish, who seemed to many Victorians to possess none of those virtues and talents most highly prized by the Englishmen who determined the criteria of superiority and inferiority.

ASC thus had something to say, albeit in an abbreviated manner, about the intangibles and irrationalities underlying the official relations between England and Ireland in the Victorian era. It inhabited that twilight zone between political, economic, social, and demographic realities on the one hand and the uncharted, fathomless, largely irrecoverable world of Victorian fears and fantasies on the other.

Without being fully aware of the fact, I gradually crossed over the disputed, perhaps vanishing, frontier between history and the social and behavioral sciences in my search for keys to unlock the closets where Victorian Anglo-Saxonists stored their skeletons. In *ASC* I refrained from dragging out all those skeletons, having too little space in which to display them. Even now, much reading and thinking about human behavior and personality structure remains to be done before I can pretend to something more than passing knowledge of the phenomena in question. Indeed, throughout the research and writing stages of *ASC* I carried in my mind a road sign that said in effect: "Danger: Work on the Prejudices of Dead Men in Progress." In other words, I tried to anticipate the objections of potential readers to this attempt to interpret and explain the habits of thought, unstated assumptions, and fantasies of eminent and obscure Victorians. It seemed to me then —long ago in 1965—that historians who aspire to deal with the motives of men, living or dead, and including their own, and who do not avail themselves of the abundant "scientific" literature on human behavior and emotions, taking care, of course, to distinguish between the proven and the not proven, are simply imposing their own subjective opinions, views, or guesses on their readers. Knowing how vulnerable almost any study of prejudice is to the simplistic charge of "prejudice" by offended readers, I decided it was essential to base my study on something more objective than vague feelings, impressions, and hunches. That attempt cannot be called entirely successful. Already, *ASC* has provoked one Englishman to call me prejudiced in favor of the Irish, and, even more serious, one Celtic reviewer has described me as an Englishman.[9] So I have few illusions about the perils of fishing in the troubled waters that separate England and Ireland to this day.

The process just described of moving toward a more (but not exclusively) psychological interpretation of the Irish Question should not be taken as a smooth and steady progression from darkness to light. There was, of course, the usual groping and grasping at straws and the familiar sensation of following an idea or clue into a *cul de sac*. Since I was working on other projects at the same time, there were endless interruptions and diversions away from my reconstruction of Victorian image-making. But my interest in this inquiry grew by leaps and bounds as I neared the completion of the first of numerous drafts.

ASC was a short work on a long and involved subject. The deeper I got into the subject, the more complicated it became, and the longer it took me to answer the newer questions that kept crowding in upon the original ones. My first task was to find out how the dominant Victorian image of Paddy differed from previous images of Irishmen as well as from English self-images. Second, I had to identify the relationship between and among those competing images. Third, I sought to compare the image of the Irish entertained by Anglo-Saxonists in England and America in the later nineteenth century. Fourth, there was the problem of trying to fit the debates on the Home Rule Bills of 1886 and 1893 into the context of Anglo-Saxonist thinking, a task complicated by the efforts of most Unionist spokesmen to conceal their prejudicial feelings behind the formal rhetoric of parliamentary debate. Fifth, there was the question of the Irish antidote to Anglo-Saxonism, which I called Celticism, with roots deep in the past. All these themes were treated cursorily in *ASC* because I had chosen the essay form and was working under such severe space restrictions that I used no more than one quarter of all the notes I had taken. *ASC* was indeed the distillation of much reading and note-taking: instead of serving a gallon of watered-down whiskey, I decided to produce a pint of poteen for the delectation of a few.

In more respects than I can recount here, *ASC* became a case of "on the job training," compelling me to investigate not only Victorian ethnology and anthropology, physiognomy and caricature, but also American intellectual and social history during the 1870s and 1880s. Little by little my own insular prejudices about American historiography began to crumble and soon gave way to qualified admiration, as it became clear that some American historians had been dealing for years with questions of ethnic, religious, and class prejudice, popular religion, social mobility, status anxiety, and immigration. Important questions like these, not to mention ways of finding plausible answers to them, seemed to me to lie beyond the intellectual pale of most English students of Victorian history whose work I knew.

While putting *ASC* together I often imagined myself as an amateur archeologist working away on a remote dig and finding that every trench exposed some portion of a huge palace buried under layers of neglect. Too often I had to leave the dig and rush to the library in order to educate myself about some artifact found during the day. And then I would hasten back to the dig with renewed enthusiasm, confident that I would some day be able to fit all the discrete pieces into place. No doubt my digging methods belonged in the category of early T. E. Lawrence or Gertrude Bell, but I took the precaution of reading well beyond the immediate boundaries of the subject. And by not rushing into print with the first few objects brought to the surface, I saved myself from a number of blunders and oversimplifications.

The actual writing of *ASC* from the first to the fifth version tended to confirm my belief that something strange and inexplicable happens to my ideas and material once I become involved in the process of putting pen to paper. No sooner had I found the "right" beginning and abandoned most of my original outline than the words began to tumble out in profusion as though a small dam had given way. The pages of illegible verbiage began to accumulate far more rapidly than I expected, even though there were moments, hours, and days when a particularly awkward passage refused to unravel itself, and the words had to be dragged out under protest. I need hardly add that most of the first and more spontaneous drafts ended up in the wastepaper basket (G. M. Young preferred the fire), just as most of this essay has done. There are always moments of nagging doubt when I wonder if I have not thrown the better parts away. But the dynamic process of writing and rewriting forced me to think anew about the structure of sentences and the logic or illogic of the argument. During the long, tedious, and indispensable period of rewriting, some inner judge kept telling me that the passage in question simply would not do, and I would scrap most or all of it and start all over again. Once the almost final draft was finished, there began the laborious but rewarding operation of stylistic improvement which I like to compare to sanding wood with coarse, medium, and fine grades of sandpaper in order to eliminate the rugosities in my prose. Rewriting and rethinking are inseparable operations for me, and some of my "best" ideas have emerged or surfaced only after the verbal underbrush of the first draft has been cleared away, thereby allowing me to see what I had failed to articulate at the outset.

Among other problems, ASC raised the perennially difficult question of distinguishing between images and realities in human affairs. How close or how far removed from the Irish reality was the "stage Irishman," Paddy, and the Celtic Caliban? I recall with mixed emotions a remark overheard in Dublin after I had read my paper on English images of the Irish to the Irish Historical Society. One well-known Irish historian turned to a friend on the way out and said: "You know, the Irish are still just like that today." By "that" he meant Paddy in all his Victorian stereotypical splendor. Although I had some reason to believe that the Victorian image of the Irish was not one hundred percent fantasy, ASC did not deal directly with the realities of Irish life and character, but tried instead to expose the logical fallacies and inconsistencies of the stereotyping process. It is a legitimate criticism of the work to point out that I did not measure and compare such things as convictions for crimes of violence, as well as theft, sexual offenses, suicide, and drunkenness in England and Ireland during the period in question. No doubt there were enough violent, lazy, drunken, and dirty Irishmen with black hair, dark blue eyes, and some mid-facial prognathism in the mid-century to supply the Victorians with the necessary ingredients of the Paddy stereotype. But this was only part of the problem. How many Irishmen, not to mention Englishmen, Welshmen, Scots, and so on, actually possessed the physical and mental traits of the dominant stereotype? Surely, Irish Celts did not monopolize all the violence, indolence, and drunkenness as well as prognathism and dark complexions of the British peoples in the Victorian era. Knowing no precise way of measuring that dubious entity "national character," I turned to the question of what associations and connotations such features as dark hair and eyes, swarthy skin, and prognathous faces had for certain educated and scientifically sensitized Victorians.

Closely connected to the problem of ascribed Irish national and racial character was the question of what Irishmen actually looked like—not to mention how they behaved—in the nineteenth century. Here I was forced to rely to some extent on *The Physical Anthropology of Ireland*, compiled by the inimitable Earnest Hooton and some of his colleagues at Harvard's Peabody Museum. Based on extensive research in Ireland during the late 1930s, this treatise proved to me that the Irish people were not only heterogeneous in terms of "subracial" origins, but bore only the faintest traces of the facial features and other characteristics attributed to them by the dominant Victorian stereotype. The Harvard anthropological team found in their sample of over 10,000 Irish males, representatives of eight major European subracial groups, of which the Keltic category, as they defined it, constituted no more than 25.3 percent.[10] In view of the propensity of some later Victorians for making invidious comparisons among Irishmen, Negroes, and anthropoid apes, I wondered what bases there were in morphological fact as well as fantasy for the simianizing of Paddy. Since the popular term "Anglo-Saxon" had no ethnological or anthropological (as distinct from philological) foundation, and seemed to serve the important function of disguising the "subracial" heterogeneity of the British people, I could hardly avoid the conclusion that the English or Anglo-Saxonist pot was too fond of calling the Irish Celtic kettle black, or melanous, or nigrescent.

Now, one may well ask, where does a study like *ASC* lead if not down a blind alley? I could give a number of answers to this question posed by an Anglo-Irish historian now teaching in England, but I would rather supply one concrete answer than a host of fashionable proposals for further research. Apart from my growing awareness that it mattered a great deal more than I had thought possible what the Victorians looked like and thought they and their neighbors looked like, I ventured to write an essay in which I enlarged or magnified one of the themes in *ASC* that had to do with Victorian face, as distinct from race prejudice. Entitled *Apes, Angels, and Irishmen: A Study in Victorian Physiognomy and Caricature,* this work illustrates—with the help of some striking photographs—one of the vistas opened up for me by my initial exploration of anti-Irish prejudice in England.[11]

Research into the meaning of Paddy had brought me up against the problem of the recognizability of so-called Irish Celts. Ethnic and racial prejudice tends to function more effectively when the "outgroup" can be recognized without too much trouble on the street, in the marketplace, or at the factory. I kept wondering how distinctive Irish features really were in the nineteenth century. Could Englishmen spot an Irish Celt so readily at fifty paces without hearing his brogue or seeing his stereotypical shillelagh and clay pipe? Perhaps they could, but I still needed proof. Suppose an Irish laborer had lived in England long enough to afford the clothes worn by English laborers: were Irish facial features so distinctive as to be recognized at once by the keen Anglo-Saxonist? Since most of the Victorian literature I had read seemed to take Irish identifiableness for granted, I began to look for connections between English caricatures of Irish faces, contemporary theories about the way facial features revealed character, and the always elusive reality.

The axiomatic assumption that facial features revealed not only character and temperament but ethnicity kept cropping up in many of the novels, tourists' journals, and diaries that came my way. After taking a closer look at the Index of Nigrescence formulated by the noted ethnologist and ethnogenist, John Beddoe, I realized that what I called "face prejudice" really belonged to the ancient science *cum* art of physiognomy, as formulated by the Hippocratic and Aristotelian schools of humoral physiology. From Hippocrates I pursued the thread of this popular "scientific" lore to Galen and thence in one giant surveyish leap to Johann Kaspar Lavater, the Swiss student and master of modern physiognomy. My reading of Lavater's *Essays on Physiognomy* led me to Pieter Camper's *On the Connection Between the Science of Anatomy and the Arts of Drawing*, and from there I moved on to Anders Retzius on skull types, Francis Galton on composite photography, and Darwin on the expression of the emotions in animals and man. My reading of these and more idiosyncratic works on noses, ears, and other facial features convinced me that Victorian cartoonists and ethnologists who tried to epitomize Irish features and character had not purged themselves of the ancient physiognomical equation between physical and mental traits. Both Beddoe and Tenniel were relying on physiognomy to perpetuate the belief that Irish character was revealed by the color of hair and eyes, the shape of nose, jaw, and so on. This discovery of the conceptual ties between ethnology and caricature in England spurred me to look for similar patterns in Ireland and America. And my search was soon rewarded with numerous cartoons similar in their way to the work of Tenniel.

Although I was prepared to admit that *some* Irishmen did have relatively swarthy countenances and some degree of mid-facial prognathism, it was impossible to tell how many Irishmen fit this description. Census takers did not, of course, include morphological data in their reports, and close-up photographs of Irish faces in nineteenth-century Ireland, apart from political heroes and martyrs, are scarce. After many months, I finally came across one photograph taken in Donegal in 1867 which proved that the caricature of the Calibanized or simianized Celt was not *wholly* fantastic.[12] But the five or six distinctly prognathous faces in this rare photograph of an outdoor Mass could hardly be taken as an adequate, let alone random, sample of the adult male population of Ireland.

Looking for cartoons of ape-like and simianized Irishmen introduced me to the riches of later Victorian illustrated magazines and comic weeklies, which should become required reading for all students of Anglo-American nativism and ethnocentrism. That search almost tempted me to embark on a study of the international fraternity of cartoonists and illustrators, many of whom made a precarious living from the popular but ephemeral periodicals which began to appear in Dublin, London, Paris, New York, and other large cities in the 1860s and 1870s. Barely managing to resist that temptation, I returned to my homework on the four humors and temperaments of classical antiquity with an eye to learning more about the meaning of melancholy (black bile) in both Athenian and Victorian times. Fortified with some modern literature about the psychology and sociology of caricature, I started to rewrite an earlier version of this article in terms of the dichotomy between sanguine, orthognathous, and xanthous Anglo-Saxons on the one hand and melancholic, prognathous, and melanous Celts on the other. Often I regretted not having fully explored physiognomy and caricature before sending *ASC* off to the publishers. Here was additional proof, if any was needed, that *ASC* was only the beginning of a continuing process of rethinking and revising my original assumptions and even some of my conclusions.

In at least one respect, this study of physiognomy represented the completion of a cycle in my life. My interest in cartoons as something more than amusing or frivolous ephemera goes back to adolescence if not to childhood. Two of the principal figures in this study were Sir John Tenniel, whose work I had seen as a child in *Alice's Adventures in Wonderland,* and Thomas Nast, whom I had encountered as a schoolboy doing my first piece of historical research on Boss Tweed and Tammany Hall. How distinctly I recall even now the excitement of my first visit to the newspaper room of the New York Public Library in search of material bearing on the Tweed ring. And what a lasting impression Nast's caricatures of Tweed's corpulent figure made on my mind. The irony was that Nast had receded into the background when I set to work on images of Irish Celts, and it was not until I happened to notice a Nast drawing in the *Atlantic Monthly,* in which the unmistakable jaw of Paddy loomed large, that I realized just how trans-Atlantic the Tenniel stereotype was. A day later I was in the stacks working through *Harper's Weekly* in the 1870s, turning up one prognathous Irish-American after another, and smiling inwardly at the tortuous route taken from Nast on Tweed in 1946 to Nast on Irish-American mid-facial prognathism in 1968.

Historians may indeed repeat each other as well as themselves, especially when they have nothing more remunerative to do. But there are times when historians can say something old in a new way. In *Apes, Angels, and Irishmen* I tried out an idea that came to me in what some of my Irish friends would call a moment of Celtic inspiration. Unlike some innovations, mine was quite uncomplicated and capable of being repeated by anyone with a protractor, tracing paper, and curiosity. What I did was to apply Camper's famous facial angle to a number of cartoons and caricatures (where the two could be differentiated) in *Punch, Tomahawk, Puck* and other illustrated periodicals. Knowing something about the connections between anatomy, physiognomy, and portraiture, and mindful of the ways most artists tried to capture not only character but the expression of the emotions in the faces of their subjects, I decided to look for some measurable or quantifiable evidence that Tenniel, Nast, and other illustrators had relied on the traditional equation of primitive and brutish behavior with a low facial angle, meaning proximity to the anthropoid apes. Virtue, talent, intelligence, on the other hand, were usually rewarded by a high facial angle connoting proximity to the ideal form of Greek and Roman beauty. Prognathism was, after all, a technical term dating from the 1860s, denoting a low facial angle, which in turn meant a receding forehead (or frontal bone) and a protruding mouth and jaw. Since Camper had given his readers and students a fairly simple if not always consistently applied set of criteria for measuring facial lines or angles, it was quite easy to establish the facial angles in cartoons so long as a good, clear profile was available.

With protractor in hand, I began to accumulate evidence indicating that Camper's equation of high facial angles with European beauty and intelligence and low facial angles with monkeys, apes, Kalmucks, and Negroes was being repeated by most Victorian cartoonists. Tenniel thus awarded angles of 85 to 87 degrees to the likes of J. S. Mill, Gladstone, and Lord John Russell, while he condemned his Irish stereotypes to angles in the mid-60s and even lower. From Tenniel I moved to other artists in England, Ireland, and America, and finally ended my investigation by measuring the famous profiles of Sherlock Holmes (that Anglo-Saxon figment of a powerful Celtic imagination), as rendered by Sidney Paget in England and F. D. Steele in America. Last but not least, I borrowed my son's two comic books in order to measure the facial angles of Superman, Superboy, and their deadly enemies. The Camper formula, it seemed, had survived almost intact up to the present day.[13] What had started as a slightly frivolous exercise ended by becoming a serious pastime or adjunct to my research, one that provided me with the quantitative evidence I needed to connect physical anthropology and physiognomy to caricature in the nineteenth century. The application of Camper's angle in this way meant that I did not have to rely exclusively on subjective impressions of the cartoons in question. Paddy not only looked like an anthropoid ape in these cartoons but had a facial angle akin to that of some stereotypical chimpanzees and orang-utans. Indeed, one of the lessons learned from my reading about apes and ape lore was that anthropoids could be stereotyped just as easily and crudely as men. Given a larger sample of Celtic and Anglo-Saxon profiles in cartoons, it should be possible to measure the changing image of Paddy by comparing the gap between Irish and English facial angles in the 1820s and 1830s with that in subsequent decades when Cruikshank, Tenniel, Morgan, Nast, Keppler, Wales, and other illustrators began to produce their simianized and Calibanized versions of Paddy.

To some, this study of fact and fancy in Victorian cartoons may seem a long way from Tipperary and the Plan of Campaign. But looking back on that odyssey, I like to think that my researches helped me to understand the sources of those attitudes and prejudices which informed the policies of the political elite toward Ireland. Surprisingly enough, the more diversified my interests became, the greater the sense of unity and coherence I experienced from this study of a transoceanic phenomenon. At the same time, my search for connecting links between ethnology, caricature, and physiognomy took me further away from the Cabinet history of my Oxford years than I had thought possible. However, I never completely abandoned my original interest in Victorian politics and the ideology of the British governing classes. Indeed, most of the sabbatical year 1965–1966 was devoted to collecting material on the Irish devolution crisis of 1904–1905, the decline of the landlord class, and the failure of political moderation in Ireland before World War I. Hopefully I shall never have to choose between doing "attitudinal" and political history, simply because I must do both; the more I learn about each of these dimensions, the more obvious and fascinating the connections between them become. Some day, perhaps, I shall be able to fuse the two in a single work that will defy such simplistic labels as "political" or "social" history.

Just how fortuitous and unsystematic my historical itinerary has been may be judged from my recent discovery that working simultaneously on two projects, which seemed at first to be unrelated even though they belonged roughly to the same time and place, has produced a number of rewards. The search for evidence of Victorian ethnocentrism went on while I was gathering material for a book about the Irish landowning class in the late Victorian period, and it soon became evident that a number of the same documents, including cartoons and comic weeklies, could serve two purposes. Irish political cartoons, for example, were full of stereotypical landlords as well as stereotypical Anglo-Saxons and Celts. In reading the memoirs and reminiscences of Anglo-Irish landlords, moreover, I learned something about their thoughts on race, ethnicity, and nationality as well as how they dealt with land agents and tenants. For several years now there has been a stimulating interaction between these two projects, each one informing the other in countless ways. Some people would attribute this form of serendipity to good luck; others would blame it on bad planning. But in California, or at least in the more pagan parts of that strange land, there can be only one explanation, namely the fateful fact of my having been born under the sign of Gemini.

ASC and its offspring have taught me never to use the phrase "in the last analysis" in dealing with the affairs of men. It is presumptuous enough to explain all the motives of the living, but it is downright foolish to argue dogmatically about the motives of the dead. I need no one to remind me that much work remains to be done on the antithesis of Anglo-Saxon and Celt, and much of that future work will require both the ability and the courage to experiment. What may give me some of the necessary courage, if not the ability, is Marc Bloch's admission that "Historical facts are, in essence, psychological facts." [14]

Perhaps the burden of an ostensibly neoclassical education weighs too heavily on my soul in this age of academic behaviorists, functionalists, structuralists, interactionists, and computerists, but I remain convinced that the surest guide to the past is not *Method*, which includes the monastic and monistic faith in model-building to which some historians and most social scientists cling with a grimness or ferocity that often masks some abiding insecurity. Rather, it is imagination that interests me, by which I mean, among other indefinable things, a sensitivity to the nuances, eddies, whims, shades, and moods of the past. Imagination at its best should prompt the historian to try different techniques and even different models, provided they are judiciously used, on different subjects, just as the complete mountaineer learns how to cope with different kinds of rock, snow, and ice as well as weather conditions and climbing companions. Above all, imagination requires style, and there can be no real style without unceasing cultivation of one's dictionary and constant vigilance against the barbarizing excesses of social scientific jargon. The combination of refined thinking and finished prose style in the works of the historians I most admire cannot be dismissed as accidental or coincidental.

Beyond style there is instinct, or what might be called the historian's sixth sense about the proper order of things in his own field. Never infallible, this instinct is no substitute for the careful study of every document, but it helps to ensure that one's mind is tuned to the right historical frequency. The antennae with which good historians pick up the faintest of signals from the past are worth more in the long run than most of the models built by social scientists working in an ahistorical and, on occasion, an antihistorical frame of mind. This is not to say that all models are useless, whether or not they are conscious or unconscious, explicit or implicit. Some models are not only fashionable but heuristic; others are not only plausible but indispensable.

Enough: I begin to moralize. Within every historian, I suspect, lurks the preacher, usually a Calvinist at heart, who yearns to proclaim to the world what history is and should be all about and what it is not.

All that need be said at this point can be summed up in the Hippocratic aphorism that hangs over my workshop:

Life is short, the Art long, opportunity fleeting,
experiment treacherous, judgment difficult.

But what historian, serious or whimsical, Saxon or Celtic, radical or moderate, would want to have it any other way?

NOTES

1. *Studies in British History and Culture*, Vol. II, *Anglo-Saxons and Celts, A Study of Anti-Irish Prejudice in Victorian England* (Bridgeport, Conn., 1968).
2. Subtitled *A Study in Conservative Unionism* (Princeton, 1963).
3. Robert Ardrey, *The Territorial Imperative* (London, 1967), pp. 9–10.
4. *Coercion and Conciliation in Ireland, 1880–1892*, pp. 408, 427.
5. *Ibid.*, p. 61.
6. Beddoe devised the Index of Nigrescence in the 1870s in order to measure the amount of residual melanin in the population of the British Isles and Western Europe. Darkness of hair, eyes, and complexion were for Beddoe the most reliable means of identifying the racial and subracial strains in question. Seeking some prehistoric ties between Africa and the Celtic Fringe in the British Isles, he described the darker, swarthier, more prognathous Celts as "Africanoid." See John Beddoe, *The Races of Britain* (Bristol and London, 1885), pp. 1–5, 9–12, 143 f., 244–247, 260–271.
7. Christopher Fyfe writing in *Irish Historical Studies*, XIII, 49 (March 1962), 94. I would add to this remark that *Africa and the Victorians* does not smell enough of the Stock Exchange, bondholders' sensibilities, the mass media, and the private conversations of the political elite at Hughenden, Hatfield, Hawarden, Highbury, Highclere, and so on. But then this combination of smells might put off even the hardiest of readers.
8. O. Mannoni, *Prospero and Caliban, The Psychology of Colonization*, trans. P. Powesland (New York, 1956). First published in Paris in 1950 under the title *Psychologie de la colonisation*.
9. The anonymous reader for the University of London Press, to whom the book was referred, took one look at my comparison of anti-Irish prejudice with the attitudes of many Victorians toward "men of darker skin and more primitive cultures" (p. 121), and pronounced the following judgment: "This page, with this grossly irrelevant extension, is surely an unfortunate note upon which to end! On the other hand, by concentrating upon harmless Celtic mythology, the author lets down the Irish much more lightly."
   In his book review, "The Myth of a Superior Race" (*Irish Echo*, July

27, 1968), Patrick Campbell not only described me as an "Englishman," but twisted a good deal of my argument to suit his own predilections.

10. E. A. Hooton and C. W. Dupertuis, *The Physical Anthropology of Ireland,* Papers of the Peabody Museum of Archaeology and Ethnology, Harvard University, Vol. XXX, Nos. 1–2 (Cambridge, Mass., 1955). According to the authors, the largest single category, comprising 28.9 percent of their sample, was the Nordic Mediterranean. Hooton and Dupertuis found relatively few cases of either medium or pronounced mid-facial prognathism in Irish males, and they concluded that "the earlier population zones in Ireland have the least mid-facial projection." Almost 80 percent of their sample, on the other hand, had chins of medium projection. *Ibid.,* p. 66, and Table IV–43–44. Their morphological criteria and typology may be found on pp. 141–43.

11. *Apes, Angels, and Irishmen, A Study in Victorian Physiognomy and Caricature* (Washington, D.C., 1970).

12. "A Mass in the Mountains of Donegal," in *Sights and Scenes in Ireland* (London: Cassell and Co., n.d. [1900?]), p. 173. This photograph has been reproduced in T. W. Moody and F. X. Martin, eds., *The Course of Irish History* (New York, 1967), p. 225.

13. Cartoon readers familiar with the formidable jaw of Dick Tracy may well wonder if that Celtic super-detective (who is now, alas, completely enslaved by his electronic hardware) does not represent one of the last vestiges of nineteenth-century Irish-American prognathism in caricature.

14. "Normally, therefore, they find their antecedents in other psychological facts. . . . However, there can be no psychology which confines itself to pure consciousness. To read certain books of history, one might think mankind made up entirely of logical wills whose reasons for acting would never hold the slightest mystery for them." Marc Bloch, *The Historian's Craft* (New York, 1962), p. 194.

The Genesis * of
Confucian China
and
Its Modern Fate

JOSEPH RICHMOND LEVENSON

* or Deuteronomy, a second telling, since much of what follows derives from the work itself.

JOSEPH RICHMOND LEVENSON was born on June 10, 1920, in Boston, Massachusetts. He attended Harvard University where he received his B.A. in 1941, his M.A. in 1947, and his Ph.D. in 1949. In 1951 he joined the Department of History, University of California at Berkeley, where he taught until the time of his tragic death on April 6, 1969. Levenson had held the Sather Professorship of History at Berkeley since 1965.

Member of the American Historical Association, the Association for Asian Studies, and the Society of Fellows at Harvard (1948-1951), Levenson was the recipient of various awards and prizes. He won a Fulbright Fellowship for 1954-1955, a Guggenheim Fellowship for 1962-1963, and an American Council of Learned Societies Fellowship for 1966-1967. In addition, he spent the year 1958-1959 at the Center for Advanced Studies in the Behavioral Sciences at Stanford.

Levenson's writings on Chinese intellectual and cultural history earned him a truly international reputation, and he was one of the most respected as well as beloved figures in both his own field and in the department to which he belonged. Author of the widely acclaimed trilogy, *Confucian China and Its Modern Fate:* Vol. I, *The Problem of Intellectual Continuity;* Vol. II, *The Problem of Monarchical Decay;* Vol. III, *The Problem of Historical Significance* (Berkeley and Los Angeles, 1958, 1964, 1965; paperback, three volumes in one, 1968), Levenson also wrote *Liang Ch'i-ch'ao and the Mind of Modern China* (Cambridge, Mass., 1953, 1959; paperback, Berkeley, 1967). With Franz Schurmann as co-author, he wrote *China: An Interpretive History,* the first volume of which was published in the fall of 1969 by the University of California Press. At the time of his death, he was working on a new trilogy entitled *Cosmopolitanism,* one short volume of which will be published as *Revolution and Cosmopolitanism: The Western Stage and Chinese Stages* by the University of California Press.

Who does not know Frazer's beginning of *The Golden Bough?* I met it as an undergraduate, and the device of the single, vivid, puzzling image, leading one behind it to a complex condition of mind, led me on, from king of the wood to king of France and a juvenile senior thesis, "The Coronation of Charles X: A Study of the Cult of the Medieval in Early Nineteenth-century France." And on—the appetite whetted, morbidly, for malaise—to modern China. Malaise (alas) is a universal state. I began looking at China for ties that bind a world.

For a long time now, people have pondered the ambiguity, at least in English, of "history": the records men make, the records men write. In modern Chinese history, these seemed to be beginning to correspond. Revolutionary spirits like the famous writer Lu Hsün (1881–1936) felt that the old high culture was dead, and they resented being instructed, as it seemed, to rest quietly, uttering platitudes in silk-fan attitudes. The revolution they helped to foster in a cosmopolitan spirit—against the world to join the world, against their past to keep it theirs, but past—I came to interpret, in cultural terms, as a long striving to make their museums themselves; it was to escape being exhibits themselves, antiques preserved for foreign delectation. It amounted to this: let foreigners not be cosmopolitan *at Chinese expense* (as Japanese who prefer Brecht to *kabuki*—"for foreigners"—hold that the Western taste which the national must resist is the Western *schwärmerei* about the national traditional arts).

I wanted to match this situation in my work. Instead of painting China as a still life for a connoisseur's collection, I saw it as an action painter on a world canvas. This was not merely a matter of giving modern China its due, after the sinologues' long attention to antiquity. Such rich works on early themes as *The Golden Peaches of Samarkand: A Study of T'ang Exotics* [1] and *The Vermilion Bird: T'ang Images of the South,* [2] by my Berkeley colleague, Edward Schafer, illustrate what has happened. There is all the difference in the world between thinking about China as exotic—an old way of annexing China to the domain of Western consciousness—and thinking about exoticism in China, which (like malaise) is a universal theme.

The universal theme is particularly appropriate to our age, the age of "museums without walls," when the seals are broken and histories flow together. My universal themes, or problems, in the trilogy *Confucian China and Its Modern Fate* are suggested in the subtitles, "The Problem of Intellectual Continuity," "The Problem of Monarchical Decay," "The Problem of Historical Significance." The whole makes a "web" book, not a "thread" book. It is mainly novelists, I suppose, who have brought out works meant to be integral, with a central core of characters and an over-arching design, though offered in several volumes "complete in themselves." I have in mind not the *roman fleuve*, which may take a family, for example, down through the years, but the broad panoramas, the novels of shifting context, where the same characters, at the same time, appear in different lights and situations. At least some historical themes, I think, can be treated like that. Some, indeed, demand it. A theme like "Confucian China and its modern fate," if it is not to seem, under such a title, just a Wagnerian *pastiche*, windy and portentous, has to be scored more than once.

The first version of this Confucian death and transfiguration, Volume One, is about the tensions of intellectual choice, the hard choice between the conflicting values of two civilizations. In the nineteenth century, Chinese began to be torn between the appeal of their own traditions and the challenges of the West. Social stability and the Confucian passion for it were blighted. For a stable society is one whose members would choose, on universal principles, the particular culture they inherited; history and value should coincide. (Here, Morris Raphael Cohen's *Reason and Nature* was most suggestive.) But now these seemed to be more and more estranged, as social forces made China, once "the world," into a nation in the world, and its civilization *a* civilization (and a deeply disturbed one), not civilization in the abstract. Describing the transition from "culturalism" to nationalism (including its Communist variant) in China, and the search for continuity, for an identity as modern man and modern Chinese together, I tried to catch the process and pathos of modern Chinese history in the interweaving of many themes—science, art, philosophy, religion, and economic, political, and social change. I hoped to capture the sense of the whole, to feel the force of the environment of statements. "A traveller, who has lost his way, should not ask, 'Where am I?' What he really wants to know is, where are the other places? He has got his own body, but he has lost them." This cryptic remark of Whitehead's (*Process and Reality*), suggesting his "fallacy of simple location," became the principle of inquiry.

In this first volume, I posed the problem of Confucian China's modern fate in intellectual terms: how and why, during so much of Chinese history, have new ideas, to be acceptable, had to seem compatible with tradition, while in more recent times tradition, to be retainable, has had to seem compatible with independently persuasive new ideas? The next volume posed the problem—the same problem—in institutional terms: how and why have the institutions of monarchy and bureaucracy been so intimately involved in the Confucian view of culture that the modern abolition of the first, monarchy, and transformation of the second, bureaucracy, have rendered the partisans of the third, Confucianism, more *traditionalistic* than *traditional*? I divined and tried to analyze the tension between monarchy and bureaucracy in

Confucian China; the significance of that tension for the very definition of Confucian China, and (with a hint from Nietzsche) for its long survival; and the relaxing of that tension, and the reduction, accordingly, of Confucianism to a vestige. I felt it essential here to treat the basic political issues of the long past of China as the basis of modern history, not just to string them together as perfunctory "background." And I tried to relate the experience of other peoples and civilizations to the Chinese experience—not as forced analogy, not as decoration, not simply as "contact," and not as an aggregation making instant world history—but to reveal Chinese history as a universal subject.

Some lines of Robert Graves gave me the key to Volume Three:

"Time," he said, "is the best Censor:
Secret movements of troops and guns, even,
Become historical, cease to concern."

Cold water on the historians? But (not to break all our rice bowls), my own contention is this: this "becoming historical," this "ceasing to concern," is of the greatest human concern. In my concluding volume, I felt, if I could grasp what it means to say that the historical lacks significance, I could attribute to that stubbornly phenomenal human record the significance which the classic (western) poetry/history idealist condescension would strip from it. And so I wrote the history of how something *became* history, as modern men became modern in making their past *past*, while keeping it, or restoring it, as theirs. Values rejected for the present, as *"historically* significant,"came to be accepted for a past that was "historically *significant."* Historical relativism, conservative and revolutionary historicism, the very different ways (Confucian and Marxist, for example) in which men can be historically-minded—these began to come through to me as not only attitudes toward history. They were the very stuff of the history toward which I was conceiving an attitude.

Throughout the work, my principal tool of analysis was not the social science "model," but metaphor. "The Problem of Intellectual Continuity" concluded with the metaphor of "language and vocabulary," to capture the sense of attrition: change in the language of Chinese culture, not just enrichment of its traditional vocabulary. "The Problem of Historical Significance" suggested a connection between this and another metaphor, that of "the museum." "Language and vocabulary" applies to innovation; "the museum" applies to preservation. Museum keepers "restore." I wanted to show how restoration was not a counter-revolutionary prerogative, nor iconoclasm a revolutionary prerequisite. And I discovered literalness-to-metaphor (in the changing force of many terms like "mandate of Heaven") as a deeply significant process in the history itself.

"Confucianism" is an amorphous term. I have taken it seriously, and my "Confucian China" is not just a careless loose equivalent of "traditional China." Of course, there was more to China, much more, than Confucianism. In Volume One I gave some attention to the Buddhist side of things, and, in the next volume, to Legalism—not that these are all. Yet, the aim was not just to present a many-sided picture of China; it was still necessary, I thought, to lean to one side. Certainly we should realize that a thoroughly Confucian China is an unhistorical abstraction. But we should retain the Confucian abstraction in our minds, instead of dismissing it under the weight of evidence of Legalist qualification. We have to retain it in our minds just because out there, in history, the abstraction is surely blurred. Then we can ask, what blurs it? If Confucius was revered as the Chinese sage (to put it at its simplest), what interfered with his influence? If a moving body ought to continue to move with its first speed and direction, what forces slow it down and redirect it?

Confucianism, besides sharing space in a system, had a place in time, in a history. How large a place may we allot it? There can be just as much a question of the length as of the breadth of its existence. How can a book that purports to be about "Confucian China" spend many pages on the nineteenth century, when Confucius lived about twenty-five centuries earlier?

I had to ask myself this question, since it warned, rightly, against smearing Chinese eras together. Individualities must be respected and the sense of change never dulled. But the question could not be allowed, by putting a case for nominalism, to intimidate the study. The very truth which the question vindicates, that China has a history, would be obscured by the suggestion that discrete atoms fill it. There was not just one Confucianism over twenty-five hundred years; and there was not just one Confucianism, a school in the age of the "Warring States." There have been, instead, Confucianisms—plural, changing, but still with some real persistence. I tried in this book to give full weight to process, not stasis, and to show what *happened* to Confucianism. But Confucianism was a feature of many landscapes in time, and I felt it relevant at many moments to refer to the glimpses in many others.

Indeed, the question of generality did not stop there. Along with lines stretching down between such eras as Han, Sung, Ming, and Ch'ing, the lines went out to France, Germany, Russia, and Japan, among others. Here, too, I meant not to force identities, but to recognize relevancies. These were comparisons, not analogies—one of my methods throughout was to isolate comparable entities, then probe them for failure in analogy—and they seemed to me to throw light not only on Chinese history, but on the purpose of history-writing, on this subject, in this day.

From at least the late nineteenth century, men in all parts of the world have looked, with hope or alarm but with more and more conviction, to an impending unification of the world. This has provided the theme for much profound speculation and many banalities. People everywhere wonder about the cultural implications of a universal science and technology, and various intellectual imperatives have been suggested. Some speak of the need to construct a culture out of selected values from particular histories, so that a cultural Esperanto will accord with the new technological universe. Others speak rather of essentially parallel histories, whose cultural destinations will be essentially the same. However, I do not consider that history can ever be made in the first way, as though by cultural selection boards, taking the best from East and West for a nice synthetic balance (see Volume One); and I do not think it has been made in the second way, following some universal paradigm, Marxist or Toynbeean or any other.

As a matter of fact, just such assumptions as these are in the record I wished to study in *Confucian China*. But while I studied them as historical subjects that needed explaining, not as valid explanations of the course that history takes, I share something of the premise behind them. For (as I suggested in the beginning of this "genesis"), something is emerging that really can be called world history, not just the sum of histories of separate civilizations. Historians of China can help to make this history as they write of the past. Far removed from any fact or fancy of cultural "aggression" or cultural apologetics, an historian, bringing China into a universal world of discourse, helps to unify the world on more than a technological level. I hoped to exemplify this in *Confucian China* without contriving syntheses or warping Chinese history to fit some western model. Instead, I saw a world made when an understanding of Chinese history, without violence to its integrity and individuality, and an understanding of western history reinforced each other. The two histories belong together not because they reproduce each other (which is false), and not because economic expansion or political embroilments or intellectual influences bring them in touch (though this is true), but because minds of observers can transpose the problems (not *transplant* the problems) of one into the other.

Chinese bureaucracy is not analogous to Prussian, but it is comparable (see Volume Two). When Burckhardt too hastily believed the rumor of the burning of the Louvre by the Communards, he could have had no notion of an Imperial Palace Museum; but one who thinks of this museum in Peking and the fall of Chinese principalities and

powers must think of Burckhardt's attitude, for the issue of revolution
and culture, "high" and otherwise, is a universal issue (see Volume
Three). And Chinese history, then, should be studied because—without
making the same designs—it can be seen to make sense in the same
world of discourse in which we try to make sense of the West. If we
can make this kind of sense, perhaps we help to make this kind of
world. The act of writing history can be an historic act itself.

That ought to prove my qualifications for speaking of the windy
and portentous. I had better get back to origins, and find the point of
departure for *Confucian China and Its Modern Fate* in *Liang Ch'i-ch'ao
and the Mind of Modern China*, my first stop in China on the road from
"Charles X." In the middle and end of *Liang*, I related the early Jesuit
to the later Reformist Confucian-Western syncretism. These syncretis-
tic efforts (the first in the seventeenth century, the second in the
1890's) were comparable, but not analogous:

> *The intervening centuries of decline and fall had made the differ-
> ence. In the Jesuit episode, a syncretism was necessary to western
> thought to effect its entrance into the Chinese mind; when Liang
> wrote, a syncretism was necessary to the Chinese mind to soften
> the blow of the irresistible entrance of western thought. In the first
> case, the Chinese tradition was standing firm, and the western in-
> truders sought admission by cloaking themselves in the trappings
> of that tradition; in the second case, the Chinese tradition was dis-
> integrating, and its heirs, to save the fragments, had to interpret
> them in the spirit of the western intrusion. . . .*
> *When orthodox Confucianists of the nineties saw the Reform
> Movement simply as a new phase of a traditional battle between the
> Confucian "rule of virtue" and the Legalist "rule of law," when they
> identified western invasions with the earlier, "traditional," barbar-
> ian invasions, their wisdom was but the knowledge of dead secrets.
> A new civilization was flooding into China, and Liang had known,
> in his early years, that Confucius must either preside over the proc-
> ess or be drowned in it.*
> *But the Jesuits had known that, as for their intrusion, Con-
> fucius would either preside over it or block it. Somewhere, then,
> in the course of the years between Matteo Ricci and Liang Ch'i-ch'ao,
> Confucianism had lost the initiative. The orthodox Confucianists,
> standing still, had been moving towards oblivion. In the beginning,
> their idea was a force, the product and the intellectual prop of a
> living society. In the end it was a shade, living only in the minds of
> many, treasured in the mind for its own sake after the society which
> had produced it and which needed it had begun to dissolve
> away. . . .*[3]

That was a way of putting it—not very satisfactory. We could sum
it up (moving from *Liang* to *Confucian China*) in a dull old pair of
words: Confucianism moving from "objective" to "subjective" significance. As the world changed, the world view lost its wholeness and
contemporary relevance. Confucianists had always been historically-
minded; now they became historical themselves. Modern men could

still voice Confucian thoughts, but the complexity of a Confucian system was gone.

At the end of Volume One, I speak of intellectual history as the history not of thought, but of men thinking. Thought and thinking, rational and reasonable, satisfactory and satisfying: the possible fission between them, between philosophy and history, proved to be the subject of my work—and sensitivity to this subject was the method of my work. "Thought" is constant, ideas or systems of ideas forever meaning what they mean in themselves, as logical constructions. But "thinking," a psychological act, implies context (changing), not disembodiment, and men mean different things when they think thoughts in different total environments. Therefore, as studies of intellectual history, these volumes, even when they seem most rarefied, at least imply the social context. *Monarchical Decay*, with its "institutional" theme, is properly the centerpiece. The "amateur ideal," so prominent a motif in Confucian China and in *Intellectual Continuity*, was institutionalized as well as conceptualized. Indeed, paying respect to the good Confucian "one-ness of knowledge and action," I could not separate the one from the other. It is no use doing what so many "perennial China" theorists do, celebrating "history"—the persistence of an "essential past"—by obliterating history-as-process. They wave a cheerful good-bye to Imperial China and imply that Confucianism is essentially undisturbed, as though the bureaucratic monarchy were inessential (or the Communist regime were preserving its essence). A set of Confucian attitudes, even if one could deem them uncorroded, does not sum up the *gestalt*. Intellectual history, after all, is only a type of the history men write, only a method, an avenue of entry, not an end. "Out there," in the history men make, the web is never rent, and intellectual, social, political, economic, cultural threads are interwoven. In the specialized approach, one tampers with the unity of nature; but the end is to restore the whole in comprehensible form.

Accordingly, when I conjured up dichotomies—objective/ subjective, intellectual/emotional, history/value, traditional/modern, culturalism/nationalism, Confucianist/Legalist, and the like—these were offered, not as stark confrontations really "there" in history, but as heuristic devices for explaining (not conforming to) the life-situation. Only categories clash, categories of explanation. What they are used to explain is the overlapping, intermingling, noncategorical quality of minds, situations, and events. Antitheses are abstractions, proposed only to let us see how, and why, their starkness in definition is mitigated in history.

Thus, when the early Jesuits faced those early modern Confucianists who still retained the initiative and "objective significance," Confucianists repelled them, I observed, with "value" objections, anti-Christian ideas that might have come from Descartes or the Enlightenment. Certainly these were universalistic ideas, not just particular, "historical" reactions. But there were psychological satisfactions in wielding these weapons of logic. A tradition can always be attacked or defended on intellectual grounds. Yet, the emotional feeling for native ground is always there. "History" and "value" (as an example of antithesis) are always—together—there.

I did not suggest, then, that some (emotional) Chinese minds were attached purely to history, as against some (intellectual) minds attached purely to value: "traditionalists" with the first attachment, "iconoclasts" with the second. Wherever men stood on the traditionalist-iconoclast spectrum, concern for history and concern for value suffused their formulations.

Even when the world was upside down, and attacks on Christianity helped Chinese to desert Confucianism, not to defend it, the history/value dichotomy was relevant. I saw that Chinese intellectual disenchantment with the great Chinese tradition had emotional repercussions; and the emotional drive was translated into intellectual terms (was Darwin the answer? Dewey? Kropotkin? Marx?). *Some* alternative had to attract Chinese if Confucianism repelled them. For the rejection of what had once been defended in a cool Cartesian spirit could not be cool. Even when clearing the ground, Chinese wanted desperately to own the ground they stood on. They wanted to continue making *Chinese* history even when—or rather, by—making the products of Chinese history *history*.

Professor Gerhard Masur has taken historical consciousness as the most significant method of western self-understanding.[4] For me, he raised a Chinese question as well as a European one. First, the generalization holds true for approximately two thousand years of Confucian history, down to the twentieth century—perhaps truer for China than for Europe. The study of history was always the most characteristic Confucian intellectual activity, and historical consciousness, changing with change in civilization, has indeed been the "form in which the Chinese render account of their own civilization." Second, the great modern change in Chinese civilization, the attrition of Confucianism, which I described in *Confucian China* as a change in historical consciousness, coincided with a growing awareness of the specter announced by Ranke, the "spirit of the Occident subduing the world." Professor Masur restates Ranke when he concludes that "only the occidental civilization has gained for itself a position from which world history and European history could be considered as a corporate unity." There is a correlative statement that one could make about Chinese civilization: it lost the position from which it could consider world history and Chinese history as a corporate unity, the

T'ien-hsia, all-under-Heaven, signifying both "the Empire" and the world. This suggests the universal matrix in which I wished to locate my study. We gain more understanding of the Western position in world historical thinking by confronting it with the Confucian, where the emphasis was typically *not* on process (as in so many of the western examples) but on permanence, on the illustration of the fixed ideals of the Confucian moral universe. It was by trying to refine my own ideas about "history" in general that I was able to make my own reading of the course of Chinese history.

For Confucius, "Heaven does not speak," but rather reflects a cosmic harmony as a model to society, and a model once clothed in ancient historical fact. Thus, against the Christian transcendental sense of divinity and evolutionary sense of history, I set Confucian immanence and orientation to the past. Nothing repels the normative Confucianist more than messianic goals and eschatological structures, Christian, Buddhist (Maitreya cult) or popular Taoist. The meaning of history is not in the end-stage of culture (as so prominently in the west), but in sage-antiquity. The Chinese classical past provides man's good examples.

It also provides his bad examples. History, indeed (and history becomes the core of Confucianists' intellectual life), is conceived largely as a record of right and wrong conduct and their respective consequences. The historical emphasis is not on process, but on incident; the *pastness* of the past (the sense, with all its potentialities for relativism, that the past is not present) and the *becomingness* of the past (the sense that it is constantly dissolving into the present) are not prominently savored. Confucius establishes this feeling for the paradigm in history, beyond time, since his genius is for moral judgment, a type of absolute, and it resists the relativities of passing time and change in the human condition.

The importance of history to Confucianists was epitomized in the orthodox conviction that "the six Classics are all history." But "history" here was regarded without ambiguity; it was the form in which absolute wisdom was cast, not yet the clothing of relativism. Before the twentieth century, to call the Classics history was never construed as a limitation on the Classics, but as philosophical description. The Classics were made of historical material, but the Classics themselves were not simply materials for the history of an age; they were texts for the ages.

Syncretisms of western with Chinese classical ideas finally yielded to the full force of the western ecumenical drive, and there came to be readiness, in radical circles, to listen to foreign voices without concern for their legitimacy by any Confucian standards. I had described this already in *Liang*; it was in *Confucian China* that I went on to describe the Classics-history equation, and to see it assuming an ominous ambiguity. If the Classics were not supreme arbiters in modern times, they were not for the ages. To say, now, that the Classics were history was not to fix their character in eternity, since their title to eternity was spurious. It was, instead, to pin the Classics to the age of their composition, that age alone, and to read them as documentation of a stage of a history in process of change, rather than as final truths which were anciently established and immanent in events, and which thereby divested the idea of history of the very connotation of process.

It was the contraction of China from a world to a nation in the world that changed the Chinese historical consciousness. Not only iconoclasts but traditionalists were moving into a situation which forbade the traditional absolutes. Men who resisted the new as foreign were traditionalistic, not traditional—adhering to the old in a new way, advancing essentially romantic (relativist) arguments from "national essence," rather than rationalistic arguments from universal validity. These were no longer plain Confucian arguments for conservatism, but conservative arguments for Confucianism; the change was the measure of Confucian moribundity. And it was just this moribundity, this death-in-life, that imparted such passion to Confucianism's assailants.

I saw latter-day Confucianists and their hostile contemporaries as equally modern, symbiotically fitting together. Together, traditionalistic Confucianists and anti-traditional iconoclasts violated the traditional assumptions of Confucianism, which were anti-relativist in the extreme. Orthodox Confucianists had always studied the past, but were convinced of its eternal contemporaneity and world associations, and the absolute applicability of the fixed standards and sequential patterns of classical Chinese antiquity. Now, however, modern Confucianists relativized Confucianism to Chinese history alone, and modern anti-Confucianists relativized it to early history alone. The traditional feeling for history, as philosophy teaching by example, was dissipated equally by the traditionalistic "history" as organic life and the iconoclastic "history" as a nightmare from which men should be trying to awake.

But by this same token, the traditionalistic Confucianists and the anti-Confucianists, equally modern, had a genuine confrontation of their own. The radicals, trying to break the grip of the old ideas and institutions, began by thinking in terms of the "merely" historically significant, and thus devalued history; history, however, was far from being devalued by the romantic conservatives, for whom reason or pragmatism were "mere." The evolution of a diffuse, rationalistic Chinese radicalism to Marxism, in my interpretation, appeared a transition of "historical significance" from normative to relativist usage, in the historicism (hardly a devaluation of history) of the Marxist way of thinking. And this transition came about when the hated traditionalistic opposition could be seen as "merely" historically significant itself; that is, broken so completely that living, indeed dominant, champions of the old order existed no longer. Iconoclasts in power could do what iconoclasts struggling for power could not do: adopt the relativism of their bested opponents, and turn from blasting the old with hatred to explaining it coolly away, or to making selections from a past so truly laid, as *history* (in the sense of "superseded"), that it could hardly resist dissection.

The new Chinese "historical consciousness," in its ravaging of Confucianism, menaced the sense of Chinese historical continuity: and this was the menace that China faced while *western* historical continuity seemed to offer the world its modern intellectual constructs. But this historical consciousness, in all its disruptiveness—its assumptions of "process" tearing across the Confucian historical "reality"—repaired in its way the fractured continuity; for it laid down lines to the Chinese past through a supposedly universal (not exclusively western) sequence of historical stages. This new, ultimately Marxist intelligence was a self-sealing wound in the Chinese consciousness, at once an exemplification of breach in Chinese history and an exorcism (by redefinition of history itself) of the pain involved in suffering the breach.

What I saw, then, in twentieth-century China, was a complicated response to a situation of European expansion and expansiveness. The response to new foreign ideas took place in a new matrix for intellectual controversy. For to say that modern Chinese traditionalists and iconoclasts are all new men, both bound together and both severed from the old predominant Confucianism by their relativism, is to see them (it appeared to me) in Herder's categories: one, as Herder's vision was one in its anti-rationalism—but bifurcated, like Herder's historicism, which had forked out into conservative and revolutionary branches.

The centrality of Herder is established in his contention that every nation and every age holds the center of its happiness within itself. What Herder combines, *nation* and *age* as having their individual geniuses, romantic conservatives and Marxist revolutionaries put asunder. The former emphasize the genius of the nation and thus confirm their own traditionalism; this would be impossible if they granted equal title to the genius of the age, for then moderns could not be committed (as the Chinese modern traditionalists were) to defense of the "national essence," something distilled from the history of the past. Marxists, for their part, acknowledge the genius (or the "mode of production") of the age, and hence their mode of historical thinking is evolutionary, anti-traditionalist. Appropriately, they reject in its fullest romantic flavor the genius of the nation; nations are assumed to share the prospects of passing time.

Herder lives in both these camps of related antagonists, now Chinese as well as European. The Confucianists, anti-relativist to the core, were alien to both. When the world (as seen from China) was a Chinese world, Confucian civilization was all the civilization there was. No relativistic cultural anthropology could issue from or get through to China. But when the world (even as seen from China) seemed a European world (for which read "modern": that is, Europe as histori- cally *progressive*), then Confucianism's chances lay with the Chinese "national essence," a romantic, relativistic, non-Confucian conception.

Why should Confucianism have withered into this anomaly? Why should it be Europe and not a Confucian China that has been able to sustain its self-image as a cultural history-maker coterminous with the world, regardless of political recession? By the time I was ready to finish the book, I knew this was the "modern fate" that had been brooding in my original questioning. The answer that I developed in the book (mainly by working out from the principles of Chinese painting) is that Confucian civilization was the apotheosis of the amateur, while the genius of the modern age (evil or not) is for specialization. Confucian education, perhaps supreme in the world for anti-vocational classicism, sought to create a non-professional free man (*pace* Hegel) of high culture, free of impersonal involvement in a merely manipulative system. Accordingly, the mandarin bureaucracy, taking its special luster as a reflection from the essentially esthetic, ends-not-means, cultural content of the literati-official examinations, in- hibited development in the direction of expertise. Under these circum- stances, the Confucian deprecation of specialization implied a depre- cation (and deprivation) of science, rationalized and abstractly legalistic economic networks, and the idea of historical progress, all of these bound in the West to specialization in a subtle web, and bringing the West subversively to China. For the distinctive traits of Confucian civilization demand a classicist interpretation. No authentic Confucian- ist ever had to fight precisely Jonathan Swift's battle of the ancient against the modern books. When the issue arose in China, it was post-Confucian, forced in China at last because it had come to the test in Europe first, and Swift had lost.

By the nineteen-twenties in China, "scientism" had won. This assumption that all aspects of the universe are knowable through the methods of natural science, while bitterly contested, became widely held by men depressed at the weak state of modern China. But what was weak about modern China (as my concepts led me to see, or think I saw) was not just the paucity of science that the scientism coterie detected. It was what the scientism reflected, as something ostensibly universal, but merely historically significant in the end: too banal as disembodied *thought* to be anything more than an index to Chinese *thinking*. Anyone interested in Chinese history can profit from an account of the 1923 debate on "Science and Metaphysics." Anyone interested in science and metaphysics need not give it another glance.

Yet, one's interest in Chinese history now is of a universal order— the interest of cosmopolitans in a burgeoning cosmopolitanism, which was rising (like *The Vermilion Bird*) from the ashes of an older cosmopolitanism. The very iconoclasm of scientism, its dismissal of Confucian "spirit," was a ticket-of-leave from the Chinese world to a China *in* the world. The Chinese world had had its own provincials within it while Confucian sophisticates ruled. It was when this world faded, and a nation began to emerge, that the old sophistication began to fail. Cosmopolitan in the Chinese imperial world, Confucianists struck a provincial note in the wider world of the nations, and they passed out of history, into history. In the manner of their passing they bequeathed their particular world (universal, to them), where they had been historians in particular, to historians in general. And as one of the latter I am moving now, with a feeling of continuity of my own, to that cosmopolitan theme, the theme of cosmopolitanism itself. Beyond Confucian China and its modern fate (both that history on the stage and my history on the page), *Provincialism and Cosmopolitanism: Chinese History and the Meaning of "Modern Times"* is sputtering, and may sometime come alive.

NOTES

1. Edward Schafer, *The Golden Peaches of Samarkand: A Study of T'ang Exotics* (Berkeley and Los Angeles, 1963).
2. Edward Schafer, *The Vermilion Bird: T'ang Images of the South* (Berkeley and Los Angeles, 1967).
3. Joseph R. Levenson, *Liang Ch'i-ch'ao and the Mind of Modern China* (Berkeley and Los Angeles, 1967), pp. 218–19.
4. Gerhard Masur, "Distinctive Traits of Western Civilization: Through the Eyes of Western Historians," *American Historical Review*, LXVII, 3 (April 1962).

My Life

with

Frau Lou

RUDOLPH BINION

RUDOLPH BINION was born on January 18, 1927, in New York City. He received his B.A. from Columbia University in 1945, and then studied at the University of Paris, where he earned a Diplôme from the Institut d'Etudes Politiques. He spent several years in Paris working for UNESCO before returning to Columbia for his Ph.D. (1958). Binion has taught at Rutgers University (1955–1956), the Massachusetts Institute of Technology (1956–1959), Columbia (1959–1967), and Brandeis (since 1967), where he is now Professor of History. His special field of interest is modern European intellectual history.

While studying at Columbia, Binion won the Clarke F. Ansley award (1958), and in 1960 he won the George Louis Beer prize of the American Historical Association for his first book, *Defeated Leaders: The Political Fate of Caillaux, Jouvenel, and Tardieu* (New York, 1960). He held a fellowship from the American Council of Learned Societies in 1961–1962.

Binion's most recent book is *Frau Lou: Nietzsche's Wayward Disciple* (Princeton, 1968). Among his published articles are "What *The Metamorphosis* Means," *Symposium*, XV, 3 (Fall 1961), and "Repeat Performance: A Psychohistorical Study of Leopold III and Belgian Neutrality," *History and Theory*, VIII, 2 (Spring 1969).

At present he is completing a comparative study of the hapless Habsburg heirs, Rudolf and Franz Ferdinand, and starting research into the psychology of Hitlerite Germany.

The idea of writing a book about Lou Salomé came to me through a reading course that a student persuaded me to conduct during my third year of teaching the humanities at the Massachusetts Institute of Technology. At his suggestion, we pored over Freud during the first semester, then Symbolist poetry, including Rilke's, during the second. I already knew of Lou Salomé as Nietzsche's coveted disciple who had brought him close to suicide in 1882 and ten years later rendered a clinical account of his philosophy. Now I glimpsed her successively in Freud's lines as his esteemed co-worker beginning in 1912 and in Rilke's as "you" until *The Book of Hours* was "laid in Lou's hands" in 1901. An intimate intellectual and personal experience of three so diverse cultural heroes in turn—here, I thought, was a privileged medium for a study of culture in the making. "I am tempted to do research on Lou Salomé," I announced to my student. "What for?" he asked. I dropped the subject, wondering whether he even suspected that, in the first place, a scholar must do research on *something*.

That was the spring of 1959: I was thirty-two years old. I had studied sociology and history at Columbia University, then political science at the University of Paris; later I had worked in statistics at the United Nations Educational, Scientific and Cultural Organization for three years, then completed a doctorate in history at Columbia and taught one year at Rutgers. My dissertation[1] was just being published —it dealt with three mavericks of the Third French Republic—and I was due to take up an appointment at Columbia the following fall. My summer went in editing my dissertation, with time out for an article on Franz Kafka.[2] Lou Salomé came back to mind when, in October, Columbia invited applications from its faculty for summer research grants. I proposed to explore her suitability as a biographic subject— and, Columbia willing, did just that in Boston from June through August 1960.

Then it was that I first took a straight look at Lou herself. I was captivated—by her wide-ranging, celebrity-packed outer life to begin with, then more and more by the grand inner life that showed through her essays on art and letters, on religion, philosophy, and psychology, on woman and love; her novels and stories and dramatic verse; her published letters and diaries; and finally, that seeming last word in self-disclosure, her autobiography. I now saw in her not just a mirror of cultural development from Nietzsche to Freud, but primarily an exemplar of it in her own right. She was, then, not merely a suitable, but an irresistible, biographic subject, the more since she had recorded her personal history already and had psychoanalyzed herself in print to boot. Accordingly, I envisaged a book in which I would first reconstruct her childhood following her own Freudian leads, then show how she lived out of that childhood thereafter even while interacting with her vast cultural milieu until, in her mature years, she achieved full self-awareness and turned her past into (in her words) "a present possession." It never crossed my mind that this scheme was in any way vulnerable to further research: by then, I was an out-and-out Freudian, I was sold on her introspective prowess and reminiscent candor, and I viewed her traffic with Europe's cultural élite as just the busiest manifestation of her traffic with the *Zeitgeist.*

That winter I won a fellowship from the American Council of Learned Societies for a year's research on Lou, wherewith I proceeded to Göttingen in June 1961. Göttingen was Lou's residence from 1903, when she was forty-two, until her death in 1937. More, Göttingen is the residence of Ernst Pfeiffer, who had received Lou's papers from her failing hands and had somewhat tentatively and uncertainly granted my request to use them in preparing a history of her mind (*"Geistesbiographie"*). I got on famously with Mr. Pfeiffer, given our common enthusiasm for Lou, so long as I did not press him regarding her papers—and this I did not do until, after several weeks at the university library, I had completed all other relevant readings. By then he had developed a dramatic suspicion as to whether my ends were not biographic in the usual sense: Lou's life, he declaimed, had been written once and for all—by *herself.* I protested quite truthfully that I was interested in her mental development alone as against her personal experiences in adulthood, which were indeed available in her autobiography and which I consequently meant to ignore as far as my literary devices would permit. It occurred to me that he might be concealing some skeleton in Lou's closet of no conceivable concern to me, so I thought my troubles over when I learned by chance that her maid and heiress was her husband's illegitimate daughter; this, however, came as news to Mr. Pfeiffer and left him all the warier of my scholarly purpose. He yielded only when I told him that, unless I might use all of the documentation concerned without further ado, I would confine my inquiry to published sources. And at that he did not follow through graciously, reliably, or completely:[5] after a hapless showdown with him late in October, I retreated to the Black Forest to work through my materials.

There I remained for six months, except for a brief holiday in Paris and for research jaunts to Basel, to Zurich, and to Lou's long-time confidante Ellen Delp on an island in Lake Constance. At first I expected to see, or at least foresee, the end of my labors after such a long stretch of time; but in fact, with all the progress I made, the prospect of completion receded to the vanishing point. I proceeded by preparing "writing notes" on half-sized scrap paper, using a separate sheet for each distinct point of information or interpretation that I considered potentially useful as I leafed through my holdings. These included notes on, or in some cases copies of, Lou's fictional and theoretical writings, which I converted into so many tight résumés. The rest comprised her more personal formal writings and my records of correspondence, diaries, and other memorabilia in her literary estate. This rest fast proved treacherous, and I well remember how the proof began. When I took up the documentation on Lou's encounter with Nietzsche, I recollected that in her book on Nietzsche she had reproduced two letters from him to herself, with in each case a brief passage conspicuously deleted from an affectionate context. Out of idle curiosity—idle because I felt no call whatever to rehash that stale Nietzsche–Lou story in my book-to-be—I sought out the two presumably indecorous passages. Lo! they were decorum itself. Why then, I wondered, had she deleted them? Clearly in order to suggest greater liberty on Nietzsche's part and greater delicacy on hers than was the case. But how could *she* have done such a thing? I can still hear myself explaining how to friends in Paris shortly afterwards: "She was too discreet to tell the big truth about Nietzsche and herself: that he had proposed to her. So she compensated by this—*somme toute*—harmless device." "How charming of her!" was our conjoint verdict.

And so I labored from one undeceiving to another, and from one pseudoexplanation to another, until that big truth itself was revealed as a big lie, and I perforce concluded that nothing Lou ever said about herself could be trusted. This was, of course, a new beginning: her life story would have to be reconstructed on the basis of incontrovertible outside evidence, and then her reminiscent distortions might themselves be chronicled and their sense explored. The chief difficulty lay not in the enormity of this task, but in the refractory mind that undertook it. Again and again I had to contend against the inertial force of my prior conceptions of Lou originating in her own testimony —had indeed to strain my inner sights in order to spot them in their cerebral hiding places. And over and over I found, in ironing out some contradiction in my writing notes, that I had lately relapsed into taking her beguiling word for this or that. Rectifying her successive, inconsistent accounts of her early childhood was a special, tricky operation because direct evidence was wanting: here the key was the hard-won insight that her basic attachment was not to the "all," as she rapturously professed in her mature years, but to her father, as she casually denied in those same years—that her father was not a mere substitute for the "all" in her infantile love life, as she claimed, but that the "all" was a postinfantile conceptual disguise for her father.

I did not come this far until the summer of 1962, which I spent, following a trip to the Hauptmann archive near Locarno, in northern Germany, first in Friesland and then in Holstein. Here, in a gorgeous natural setting, with time off for a single visit to nearby Kiel to see the

Tönnies papers, I completed my writing notes. They numbered gro-
tesque thousands upon thousands in their helter-skelter heaps, and
they raised as many questions as they answered. In particular, I had
no considered notion of how they added up concerning Lou's reminiscent madness, let alone how they would ever add up to a book. And I
was fretful lest they fade away—lest the urgent uncertainties surrounding each and all of them expire in me—before I could immerse
myself in them anew for months on end. So, even as I resumed my
campus duties that fall, I began petitioning with devilish pertinacity
for a new leave of absence the following year, despite a hard and fast
university rule that precluded one.

I wound up with a one-third teaching load and in June 1963 betook
myself to the tranquillity of Concord, Massachusetts, within easy reach
of the Harvard libraries, for fifteen months less the twenty-two days on
which I commuted to Columbia for an M.A. seminar, reading thesis
outlines and drafts in the train both ways. I had meanwhile enriched
my documentation and writing notes in New York with the generous
cooperation of Lou's kinsman Franz Schoenberner and of Mirjam
Beer-Hofmann Lens, whose father, Richard Beer-Hofmann, figured
inconspicuously in Lou's annals and turned out to be the last and
tenderest love of her maidenhood. And I had decided to arrange my
writing notes in a basically chronological sequence straight off (using
marked duplicates for alternatives in placing such facts as the color of
Lou's eyes or hair), then fuse them all into a wieldy manuscript,
however huge, which would serve as groundwork for the book to come.
The arranging took an unexpectedly brief six weeks, but the fusing
lasted the remainder of my stay in Concord.

Actually, while I fused my preexisting notes, I also thrashed out
discrepancies and chased insights back and forth. And I ran into
exhilarating psychoanalytical trouble for literary reasons, and depressing literary trouble for psychoanalytical reasons, as follows. In a short
first section I retraced Lou's psychosexual development with strict
Freudian orthodoxy—from penis envy, through cravings for her father,
through fantasies about a private god, to a flame for a preacher who
brought her down to earth—indicating at the close how she thence-
forth pursued her childish purposes in letters and love for all her days
(except that I treated her sex life proper this way only later, at the
point where it began). To follow up my own lead, I would have had to
go on pointing out the same old infantile motives behind each of her
writings and amours in turn, even behind all her thinking and doing—
but what could be more tiresome? My plight was the worse for her
fiction, because there was so unconscionably much of it; yet her very
first piece of fiction, being a semi-autobiographical novel, afforded me a
recourse. To a relevant footnote on her adulthood as a derivative of

her childhood I added: "As a rule, my explications of Lou's fiction will deal only with proximate latent identities of character and situation, the deeper-lying ones having been monotonously Oedipal." This recourse was only too productive, with the result that, as I advanced, I came to wonder whether *everything* in her fiction was not adapted from her adult experience. I finally tested this possibility on a story she wrote in her late fifties: what emerged between her lines was not just one complex of adult biographic referents for everything in them, but two such complexes, a Freud complex of a few years' and a Nietzsche complex of a few decades' anteriority, with, moreover, a whole mess of lesser adult complexes mixed in.

Beneath all these, the discernible infantile material was swamped. More surprisingly still, it transpired that this story had served Lou in unconsciously aligning her Freud complex on her Nietzsche complex, and, in the first instance, a shock recently received from Freud on her great shock at Nietzsche's telling her off; that she had already aligned lesser complexes on the Nietzsche one in previous stories without my having realized it before; that in fact the experiences behind those complexes, involving her men after Nietzsche, had themselves been patterned on her Nietzsche experience to the end of absorbing that great shock, which in her earliest fiction she had unconsciously aligned on her sentimental casualties with her preacher, her god, and her father to the same end. All this opened up enticing new trans-Freudian perspectives. But by the same token, it undermined the whole Freudian structure of my rough working draft, which was even then being typed (triple-space, with capacious margins) for piecemeal revising. Besides, it ruled out hacking the cluttered, sprawling draft down to size: so many of the seeming trivia of her life now loomed gigantic that my finished account of it, to be consistent, would have to be comprehensive. Ordinarily, I might have fretted at that juncture; however, as it was high summer already, I fused my last writing notes instead and interred Lou's ashes beside her husband's bones just in time to meet my first class of 1964–1965.

During that busy academic year I was able, altogether unexpectedly, to cope with the problems I had brought home from Concord. I first took up interpretative threads left dangling. Did Lou's essays front for the same complexes as her stories? Hardly: The seamy side of her essays proved obstinately infantile—although I had already recognized Nietzsche's and Freud's new theoretical departures following their respective encounters with Lou as unwitting commentaries on those encounters. What, then, was her ego's unconscious stake in her essays? It eluded me—though often she prescribed conduct in them that she afterwards adopted. And what was her ego's stake in her stories? They helped her to assimilate past disappointments in love,

and, at bottom, the blow Nietzsche had dealt her. Where did her
autobiographic fables come from? Most suggestively, from her fiction
—and in such cases I always found that the fiction behind the fables
amounted to a literal abuse of some statement that figured among the
facts behind the fiction. What was the composite unconscious sense of
her misrememberings? To heal her rift with Nietzsche, or with her
father before him. Where did her ideas come from? From persons she
loved; or else from herself, and then they would shape up in the same
way that mental symptoms do: as distorted avowals. Where, then, did
the Zeitgeist enter into her development? Nowhere. And so forth—with
each answer raising further questions. By spring, my manuscript was
thick with discrete revisions all cutting across the lines along which it
had been drafted. My inclination was to redo it altogether during my
coming sabbatical, but there was no telling where that could lead. So I
decided instead to inventory the loose ends in a conclusion and move
on to another historical case that would be both dissimilar and comparable.

That inconclusive conclusion was composed during my spring
vacation; and only then, in retrospect, did I notice that my subject
proper was not Lou Salomé, but a mind at work throughout a lifetime.

The manuscript was typed that summer. I trimmed the text page
by page in advance of my typist, an alert student of mine who queried
it continually, with the result that it was late August by the time we
ran off our last dittos. Three copies went to prospective trade publishers, one went to a senior colleague who had requested it, two went to
my departmental chairman to support his bid for my promotion, six
went to friends for critical readings, six were packed away by my
amanuensis, and two flew with me to Europe. There, after vacationing
for a few weeks, I set up in Vienna till the approach of the year-end
holidays. By then, two of the publishers had rejected my opus as too
good to be marketed; the third never even bothered to reject it after
consulting my senior colleague, who on his side had written me that it
was fit only to scrap; a fourth, contacted by a lone enthused colleague,
had rejected it uncomplimentarily, while in my department, my promotion had been shelved. My morale had meanwhile been sustained by
my private readers, whose marginalia had assisted me as I emended
my text that whole autumn through—enriching it, incidentally, with
some nifty excerpts from Schnitzler's diary as provided by his son. "A
university press it must be, then," I told myself toward mid-December.
I chose one reputed for liberality, sent it a painstakingly fair description of the work while preparing a neatly corrected copy, received an
eager reply, and dispatched my wares by air. In Zurich ten days later,
just after Christmas, word reached me that, following a unanimous
editors' decision, my wares were being returned. (But one of the then

editors recently related to me how she had been excluded from the others' counsels because of her dissenting opinion. "They went just plain hysterical," she said.)

After brooding out the old year, I met 1966 with a double resolution. I would submit *Frau Lou* as was to press after press until one finally accepted it, and meanwhile I would plunge into my next historical case.

This resolution took me straight to Brussels, for the case I chose was that of Leopold III of Belgium. An M.A. student of mine at Columbia had done excellent research the previous year on Leopold's neutrality policy of 1936–1940. However, neither he nor I could discover sufficient political, diplomatic, or military cause for that policy, especially as Leopold himself foresaw the disaster to which it exposed Belgium. The missing sufficient cause was psychological, and it struck me all at once as the school year was ending. In 1935 Leopold's wife, Astrid, had been accidentally hurled to her death in Switzerland from a roadster which Leopold was driving with his chauffeur in the rumble seat. Leopold relived this traumatic experience in disguise as, beginning a year later, he took the control of foreign affairs away from his government and drove Belgium, alias Astrid, to the catastrophe of May 1940.

Strictly speaking, this was only a working hypothesis at the outset, based on the irrationality of Leopold's policy, the sameness of the mournful figure he cut after Astrid's death and after Belgium's defeat, the neat dreamlike equivalence between the two happenings as seen from his vantage, and the enticing parallel with Lou's reenactments of her Nietzsche trauma. In fact, the evidence that I then gathered in Brussels during the first four months of 1966 was merely presumptive—the strongest being Leopold's recorded statements of 1936–1940 predicting Belgium's defeat in terms strikingly applicable *mutatis mutandis* to Astrid's death—except perhaps for an affirmation deriving indirectly from the Royal Household that throughout those years he was "haunted by the presentiment that Belgium might one day share the fate of Astrid and perish also in some terrible catastrophe." Conclusive evidence that he himself associated the two events came only ages later (in June 1968, when I tapped some final sources before sending the piece to press) in the form of a diplomatic dispatch quoting Leopold during the Munich crisis on how a peaceable nation ran the same risk of sudden catastrophe as a motorist driving with all due caution. Yet I was so sure of my working hypothesis from the beginning that for me there was really nothing hypothetical about it. Indeed, I was half loath beforehand to bother substantiating it, and have been half sorry ever since that I did bother. Between times, while toiling in Brussels, I thought out why. In Lou's case, I realized, I had discovered what I had only after overcoming my interpretative preconceptions, which had then been Freudian. But now I had approached Leopold's case with a preconception of my own devising—in fact, with a foregone conclusion. I should rather have approached a new biographic subject without any manner of working hypothesis, however tentative; with, instead, an open mind, asking only how that person's experience hung together psychologically. The time for comparisons with Lou should have been afterwards.

If I did nonetheless investigate Leopold's case, that was primarily for purposes of comparison on two points. The first was the psychoanalytical one of how an adult trauma is abreacted short of neurosis. By both Lou and Leopold, it turned out, the traumatic experience was repeated in disguise—straight, yet at the same time with variants departing from the original in three disparate ways: the roles of the principals were reversed; the guilt involved was expiated; the traumatic finale was undone. And by neither Lou nor Leopold was the traumatic shock finally absorbed. But Leopold also imitated his father, Albert, while reliving his Astrid trauma, and here I could not match his case against Lou's or, for that matter, elucidate it to my own satisfaction. The second point of comparison was historical. In Lou's case I had concluded against the *Zeitgeist*, indeed against all superpersonal or impersonal influences on her highly cultured mental life. At the same time, I had conceived the wild hope of founding a new science of history on subpersonal rules of necessitation (like the one about the misconstrued phrases behind her autobiographic fables mediated by her fiction)—a microphysics of the mind, as it were. Leopold's case bore out my negative conclusion all too well. For it disposed of large-scale causes for Belgium's neutrality of 1936–1940, which came of a motor accident. But that left history accident-prone, like Leopold, and thus ruled out a science of history.[4]

After hours, in Brussels, I prepared fresh corrected copies of *Frau Lou* for submission. One more trade publisher and one more university press turned it down. And the Princeton University Press was about to follow suit when, as I learned in due course, a discerning young editor salvaged it and began soliciting outside readings. At the same time, my enthused colleague at Columbia submitted it on his side to another university press, which sent it for approval to a professor at Princeton to whom my discerning editor then mentioned it one day: had he not been more devoted to it than to the publishers' code, it would have been thrown back at me in duplicate all the way to Venice. For Venice is where, that summer, I wrote up the Leopold story, after having organized it in Trent during May and June. It was ready for typing—as a mammoth lecture—when I returned to Columbia in September.

That fall I broke with the alternative press over its demand for drastic revisions, only to find myself confronted by Princeton with the requirement that I expand my preface into a full-scale, alluring introduction at my editor's discretion. I capitulated at the year's end, but then by springtime I was able to produce only a single supplementary paragraph (on Lou's Europe). By my hard lights, I could add nothing further, except either advertisement or apology for my opus, unless I were to give the plot of it away in advance. However, my editor, after finally clearing his desk for *Frau Lou*, resigned. Technically this released me from my obligation, so publisher and author bickered until Walter Kaufmann interceded with a foreword that gratified both.

The rest of that spring of 1967 I defended my Freudian first chapter sentence by sentence against my new editor's red pencil. And between times I resigned from Columbia chiefly because of *Frau Lou*: enough said. Over that summer I pursued a hunch that Leopold's seeming father complex was really only a predecessor complex, for Leopold succeeded to the throne upon Albert's untimely, grisly death. With this in mind I toured archives across Europe searching into Archduke Franz Ferdinand's reactions to the untimely, grisly death of his cousin Rudolf, whom he succeeded as Habsburg heir. Hardly had I begun searching, however, when I noticed that Rudolf's weird death at Mayerling was a disguised reenactment of his Bavarian cousin Ludwig II's weird death at Starnberg. This macabre reenactment inverted my Lou-Leopold formula, since Rudolf did not relive his shock at Ludwig's death, but reenacted that death itself. As for Franz Ferdinand—well, *Frau Lou* interrupted my labors with him in Vienna when it was decided that, to reduce the footnotes, straight reference matter should be excerpted from them and relegated to the rear of the book. This laudable decision entailed indescribable difficulties that were not all surmounted until the page proofs were behind me after my first year at Brandeis University.

The book appeared in September 1968. It sold rapidly, and has brought me high public and private tribute with no little derogation mixed in. A single reviewer accentuated the negative, which came to the estimate that, "even if there is anything to be found out" from demonstrations of how Lou's writings transformed her personal experience, "Binion makes its cost in complexity and involution prohibitively high," and to the question: "Why on earth should Binion devote such prodigies of skill, learning, and energy to the microscopic study of an eccentric Russian woman . . . ?"[5] Actually, I sweated more down the years to express the relations between Lou's works and her experience exactly than I did even to discover them. It was those relations themselves that were complex and involuted—as when, in my reviewer's example, a given fictional character and incident represented, indeed misrepresented, several real persons and occurrences in her prior experience at differing removes from her conscious thoughts at the time of writing. When such relations do not admit of felicitous expression, should they be left unexpressed? The scholar in me shouted "No!" at the rest of me not once and for all, but time and time again, while *Frau Lou* was under way. And why should I have taken the pains I did with my devious lady of letters? Precisely in order to discover and express such relations between reality and fantasy and between past and present—running relations that are human history itself. In this, minutiae proved to be of the essence: thence my microscopy. A microscopic study, *Frau Lou* is no portrait. Seen as a portrait, it is oversized and out of focus. Yet it has been most praised to date as a portrait—which baffles me twice over.

Less bafflingly, no critic has yet noticed the big theoretical and literary trouble with *Frau Lou*, which is that it derives Lou's adult thought and conduct all in all from her father complex, but then also refers them back for the most part to her Nietzsche complex as their first cause. This trouble hits me on its literary side straight off when now I look on *Frau Lou* with contrived detachment on top of inside knowledge. Obviously, the aftereffects of Lou's Nietzsche trauma should have been delineated in general terms before the myriad particulars were supplied, and those particulars should have been supplied accordingly. The account of Lou's Nietzsche affair itself should have been recast in the perspective of the trauma that ensued. And so too should even the account of her childhood, insofar as she romanced with her father, her god, and her preacher only retroactively and only for love of Nietzsche. The catch was that "insofar," that theoretical side of the trouble: I *could* not have reworked my manuscript in its entirety, pursuant to however judicious an adjustment of Nietzsche trauma to father fixation, without turning up in the process some new principle binding enough of her experience together to subvert the reworked manuscript in its turn. This much my earlier misadventures with Lou had taught me for certain. And the reason lay not in me, nor in Lou, but in my method: psychoanalysis. For psychoanalysis is as yet in its very uncertain beginnings even in its native consulting rooms. So whenever it is now applied independently in the historian's workshop —against the going tendency to read pregiven clinical findings into the historical data, or at best to try pregiven clinical findings against the historical data—the results are bound to be unexpected.

My own unexpected results confronted me recently in flesh and blood outside the historian's workshop, when a young lady of my close acquaintance reenacted a traumatically unfulfilled love after five years of brooding over it. Despite those results, I saw her trouble for what it was only some weeks after she went to pieces this second time round. Then I psychoanalyzed her at her urgent request—and in the process solved, until further notice, my Lou–Leopold problem left outstanding. For she had relived a sorry father romance with one nonlover after another, until once her routine frustration took a drastic new form in which she could not assimilate it. She then relived that traumatic experience alone in its specific, unassimilable newness—all appropriately disguised, of course, and frequently modified in the same three ways as in Lou's case and Leopold's. From her I was able to ascertain what I could not from documents: that the traumatic experience was undistortedly remembered throughout (though for a long time she distorted it in the telling as Lou did hers) and that the feelings remained consciously fixed on it throughout. This double point about consciousness quelled my curiosity, though it made no discernible difference as far as history goes.

Or does the whole stream of experience (including that obscure living girl's) belong to history? Not if human history is human performance alone—yet even then, what actuates the performance must actuate the performers first, and what actuates the performers must show in their inner lives. More, what actuates them will differ haphazardly from case to case for practical purposes unless it involves some collective determination operating through them. Regular social occurrences do argue the existence of a collective consciousness with its own compelling force: here Émile Durkheim is, I think, conclusive. Nonetheless, search as I might, I could not detect its operation on or in Lou. Lou plied people and things, ideas and words, all to her very own uses, even though as emancipated woman, or perfect Ibsenite, or Rilke's muse, or what have you, she was preeminently of her times. Thus she "went the Zeitgeist's way with no guidance from the Zeitgeist." [6] So here again, Frau Lou is the reverse of definitive. And here again, had I rewritten it to adjust Nietzsche trauma to father complex, as now I could, and realized bit by bit in the bargain how Lou was guided impersonally in the pursuit of her inmost ends, it would have wound up the ungainlier for my achievement. The next time I relive my Frau Lou trauma, I shall aim to undo its outcome on this score specifically and reconcile private with public history, whatever new literary hazards that may entail.

In sum, Frau Lou was irremediably deformed in the making by the very dynamics of its approach to its subject: the psychoanalytic approach to a historic personality through whom culture ran its course.

NOTES

1. Rudolph Binion, *Defeated Leaders: The Political Fate of Caillaux, Jouvenel, and Tardieu* (New York, 1960).
2. Rudolph Binion, "What *The Metamorphosis* Means," *Symposium*, XV, 3 (Fall 1961).
3. See further *Frau Lou: Nietzsche's Wayward Disciple* (Princeton, 1968), pp. 557–60. While I could not ascertain what portions of Lou's estate Mr. Pfeiffer withheld, my guess is that I saw all of the manuscripts, roughly half of the letters, and practically all of the other papers.
4. See Rudolph Binion, "Repeat Performance: A Psychohistorical Study of Leopold III and Belgian Neutrality," *History and Theory*, VIII, 2 (Spring 1969).
5. Anthony Quinton, "Salomé Unveiled," *The New York Review of Books*, February 13, 1969, pp. 8, 9.
6. *Frau Lou*, p. 508.

The Historian
and the
Culture Gap

LAWRENCE W. LEVINE

LAWRENCE W. LEVINE was born on February 27, 1933, in New York City. He received his B.A. from the City College of New York in 1955 and then attended Columbia University where he took his M.A. in 1957 and his Ph.D. in 1962. After teaching history at C.C.N.Y. from 1959 to 1961 and at Princeton from 1961 to 1962, he joined the Department of History at the University of California, Berkeley, where he is now Associate Professor of History, specializing in modern American history. During 1967-1968 Levine was Visiting Professor of American Studies at the University of East Anglia in Norwich, England.

A member of the American Historical Association and the Organization of American Historians, Levine was the recipient of a Social Science Research Council grant for 1965-1966 and a Guggenheim Fellowship for 1970-1971. He is the author of *Defender of the Faith: William Jennings Bryan, The Last Decade, 1915-1925* (New York, 1965), co-editor with Richard Abrams of *The Shaping of 20th Century America* (Boston, 1965), and co-editor with Robert Middlekauff of *The National Temper* (New York, 1968). Among his articles are "The Future of Academic Freedom," *California Monthly* (January-February 1967), and "The Diaries of Hiram Johnson," *American Heritage* (August 1969). In addition, he was one of the contributors to Kenneth Stampp *et al., The Negro in American History Textbooks* (California State Department of Education, 1964).

He is now working on a book dealing with patterns of Negro culture in twentieth-century America.

A t some point in his studies (for many historians at *all* points), the historian is faced with a situation where there is little continuity or connection between his own cultural conditioning and expectations and that of his subjects. He is faced with a culture gap that must be bridged both by painstaking historical reconstruction and by a series of imaginative leaps that allow him to perform the central act of empathy—figuratively, to crawl into the skins of his subjects. This situation is a familiar one, which any good historian has had to face and overcome. It is, in fact, the primary function of the historian and gives the study of history much of its excitement and importance.

Less familiar is the assertion, made increasingly of late, that some historians, regardless of their talents or determination, cannot bridge the culture gap. I first heard this charge in 1962, six months after my dissertation on William Jennings Bryan had been completed and accepted by Columbia University and while I was revising it—stylistically more than substantively—into a book.[1] In December of that year, Professor Carl Bridenbaugh of Brown University, in his presidential address to the American Historical Association, delivered a long lament on the future of the historical profession in the United States. Professor Bridenbaugh's main point is worth quoting at some length:

> *In former days, the ablest historians were educated amateurs, or perhaps a better term would be amateur scholars. They were men who had previously been men of action: Herodotus, Thucydides, Caesar, Comines, Macaulay, the Americans Bancroft and Adams, and today, Churchill. These great writers knew life at first hand, life which they described critically and interpreted reflectively for their readers. Historians of our Recent Past shared a common culture, a body of literary knowledge to which allusion could be usefully made. . . .*
> *Today we must face the discouraging prospect that we all, teachers and pupils alike, have lost much of what this earlier generation possessed, the priceless asset of a shared culture. Today imaginations have become starved or stunted. . . . Furthermore, many of the younger practitioners of our craft, and those who are still apprentices, are products of lower middle-class or foreign origins, and their emotions not infrequently get in the way of historical reconstructions. They find themselves in a very real sense outsiders on our past and feel themselves shut out. This is certainly not their fault, but it is true. They have no experience to assist them, and the chasm between them and the Remote Past widens every hour. . . . What I fear is that the changes observant in the background and training of the present generation will make it impossible for them to communicate to and reconstruct the past for future generations.[2]*

In part, Bridenbaugh was indulging in historical mythology. As if such historians as Herodotus, Macaulay, Bancroft, and Adams were a golden race of men whose emotions never got in *their* way. Insofar as they were important historians, they recognized their emotions and either overcame them or channeled them constructively. Not infrequently, they failed to do either.

In part, Bridenbaugh was repeating a warning which historians have long recognized. As E. H. Carr put it in his George Macaulay Trevelyan Lectures in 1961: "Before you study the history, study the historian. . . . Before you study the historian, study his historical and social environment." This was necessary because, as Carr also noted, "The historian, being an individual, is also a product of history and of society; and it is in this twofold light that the student of history must learn to regard him."[3] This is a fair enough warning, the validity of which most historians would admit. But Ernest Nagel has indicated some of the dangers of taking it too literally. To do so would mean that before one could study a work of history, it would be necessary to re-create the environment in which the historian lived, which would mean going to the work of other historians whose own histories could not be relied upon until one had in turn studied their environments, which would entail going to the work of still other historians whose work again could not be trusted until their backgrounds were researched, which would mean going to the work of other historians and so on and on until one was mired in the quicksands of infinite regression.[4]

Professor Bridenbaugh, of course, went beyond Carr's caveat. It was not merely that all historical creations were affected by the environment in which the historian lived and matured, but also that certain environments literally made it impossible for historians to understand and re-create the American past. I found it difficult to take Bridenbaugh's lament impersonally since it would have been hard to find a better example of the incongruity he seemed to be warning against than the spectacle of the historian Lawrence Levine and the historical figure William Jennings Bryan enlisted in a joint endeavor to throw new light on the American past. Indeed, what connections had I with that America for which Bryan was such a crucial and central figure? My paternal grandfather was a butcher in a Jewish *shtetl* in Lithuania buying cattle from neighboring farmers, slaughtering them according to Jewish ritual, selling the rear half to the town's Gentiles and the rest to his own people. He died in 1904 leaving his wife with eight young children, all of whom gradually wandered from their birthplace and came eventually to America. My own father followed his older brothers and sisters here just a year before World War I engulfed Europe. My maternal grandfather deserted from the Russian army during the Russo-Japanese War of 1904–1905, wandered across a vast expanse of Russia to tell his teen-age future wife he would send for her, and then made his way over the border and ultimately to America where he both sustained himself and saved enough to send for my grandmother by working as a house painter in the halls and classrooms of the College of the City of New York. My mother was born in 1907 and spent her youth in the Jewish and Italian immigrant neighborhood of East Harlem, living with her parents and her siblings in a small apartment behind the hand laundry my grandfather maintained until he was in his seventies. I was born and raised in a lower-middle-class area of Manhattan in which my father kept a tiny fruit and vegetable store and where almost everyone I knew was either an immigrant or the child of immigrants—mostly Jews, but with a strong sprinkling of Greeks. For me "Americans" meant the Irish Catholic kids who lived on the other side of the trolley tracks, crossing them occasionally to engage us in battle.

My upbringing was filled with the cultural confusion so common to the lives of second-generation Americans. Among my oldest childhood memories of my father are those of him wearing a stained white apron, lugging heavy crates of fruits and vegetables, rushing to wait on customers, skillfully stacking high rows of fruit which would need to be repacked almost as soon as he had finished. The amazing amount of labor and attention demanded by that small, dark store where one froze in the winter and sweated in the summer and where my father worked fourteen hours a day, six and one-half days a week, drove both my parents to want their children to "succeed," which in their terms meant simply to be able to live an easier life with more material rewards than they had known—especially if this could be done as a "professional" of one sort or another who relied upon his mind rather than his hands. Since the route to this "better" life lay in that semimysterious world outside the confines of the subculture in which I was raised, I was encouraged to venture forth away from the familiar world of my childhood. At the same time, I was expected to remain at home spiritually, to retain the values so carefully inculcated in me for so long. The result of this dual mandate was a cultural ambivalence which I retain to this day.

My schooling, right through the City College of New York, whose walls my grandfather had once painted, may have introduced me to strange worlds and new concepts, but my teachers and classmates were more often than not people very much like myself whose roots in America were just as tenuous, whose ambivalence was as profound, and whose English would have sounded equally alien to a William Jennings Bryan. Even in my graduate school days at Columbia University, half my fellow students of history came from backgrounds almost identical to my own. It was in this environment that I first began to come to grips with Bryan. More than two years after I had begun work on Bryan, I finally crossed the Alleghenies and the Mississippi and saw the America in which he grew to maturity and for which he spoke for so long and with such fervor. What I saw, of course, was primarily the geographical reality of Bryan's America. Culturally, the America that had nurtured and formed Bryan had begun to fade at the turn of the century. His people were the farmers and townsfolk, his politics the agrarian democracy, his religion the Presbyterian fundamentalism, his speech the full-blown rhetoric, his moral universe the simple world in which one took it for granted that good was rewarded, evil punished, and progress assured, which had flourished during the nineteenth century.

Here then was I—the epitome of Bridenbaugh's lower-middle-class "outsider" of foreign origins, and Bryan—the personification of that America from which I was supposed to feel myself shut out. It was little wonder that I took Professor Bridenbaugh's address very seriously indeed. But no matter how closely I pondered it, I simply could not see its relationship to my own experience in studying Bryan's final years. I was willing to admit that unconsciously I might well have been led to study Bryan originally in order to catch up with a past that had become my own through adoption rather than experience or direct heritage, though even here I remain unconvinced. (It might be much truer to say that this was why I gravitated into the study of *American* history in the first place.)

Settling upon this topic seemed more accident than design. As a first-year student in Richard Hofstadter's graduate seminar, I knew too little American history to devise with any confidence the master's thesis topic that would occupy me for the next year or so. After several timorous attempts to come up with a subject (each one of which was rejected by Hofstadter and my fellow students as either unimportant or not feasible), I vaguely suggested the possibility of studying the social and political philosophy of William Jennings Bryan. I knew little enough about Bryan at the time, except that he was an important figure whom I tended to admire because he had been a force for reform. At this point Hofstadter, who had just finished his *Age of Reform* (in which Bryan and his world played an important role), suggested that if I were really interested in Bryan, I might look at his final years, during which he went through a metamorphosis from reform to reaction. At Hofstadter's suggestion, I read C. Vann Woodward's *Tom Watson*, the latter part of which examined a similar transformation. Before finishing Woodward, I knew I had a topic that thoroughly engaged me—a condition Hofstadter insisted upon before he encouraged his students to begin their theses. Without a day's research, I even had a title: "The Decline of William Jennings Bryan as a Progressive." Years of research may have made my premature title inappropriate, but only deepened my sense of engagement. When my master's thesis did not begin to exhaust the potentialities of the problem, I continued to explore it in my doctoral dissertation and book.

In retrospect, then, my subject seems to have been born out of a combination of my own inexperience and timidity and my professor's interests. Even if my ethnicity had a relationship to my choice of a subject, that connection ended once my research began. The forces that threatened from the very beginning to cut me off from Bryan and his universe had less to do with my ethnic and environmental background than with my choice of a profession. In deciding to spend my life as a historian and teacher, I had taken my place in a milieu in which, ideally, the life of the mind was paramount, in which there was a commitment to thought in general rather than to any one set of ideas, in which there was a dedication to the dissection and understanding of institutions rather than to their perpetuation or alteration, in which comprehension of the past took precedence over the task of keeping its values alive. These goals in themselves, of course, constituted a set of ideals that potentially weakened the ability of the historian to understand a populist figure like Bryan. Even at the height of his reformist glory, Bryan's militant egalitarianism, his tendency to *use* ideas rather than to value them, the simplistic lines of his moral and spiritual universe, were enough to make even the most sympathetic historian shudder. When, during his last years, these qualities no longer seemed tied to a dedication to social, political, and economic reform, the scholar's inward misgivings were transformed into overt anger and ridicule. Bryan became more a target than a subject.

I still remember vividly the anger and incredulity with which I read of Bryan's failure to oppose the activities of the Ku Klux Klan in the 1920s, his anti-urban proclivities, his defense of the Southern attitude toward Negroes, his "fanatical" campaign for prohibition, and, above all, his crusade to drive the teaching of evolution out of the public schools. Ironically, my Eastern European, Jewish family would have understood Bryan instinctively far better than I at first could. If they had been more politically conscious in the 1920s, they undoubtedly would have opposed many of his activities, especially those aimed at rendering the new urban, immigrant wing of the Democratic party impotent and thwarting the rising power of the new polyglot cities. Nevertheless, they would have *understood* the Bryan who insisted that "it is better to trust in the Rock of Ages than to know the ages of rocks," who urged his audiences to remember that "man is infinitely more than science; science, as well as the Sabbath, was made for man," who admitted that "the objection to evolution, however . . . is not, primarily, that it is not true. . . . The principal objection to evolution is that it is highly harmful to those who accept it," who put faith above reason, who spent his final days on this earth protecting a culture and a way of life from the erosions of the outside world. If I had trouble understanding the meaning of these things initially, it was not because I had come from a particular cultural and ethnic milieu, but to a certain extent because I had strayed—had been encouraged to stray—from it.

Professor Bridenbaugh was correct in maintaining that there is a culture gap separating the mid-twentieth-century historian from the American past. His error was in identifying the nature of that gap. The problem the historian faces in confronting Bryan and those he represented is not primarily whether the historian is urban or rural, immigrant or native-born, Jewish or Protestant, white or black; the problem often is his intellectuality and the complex of values attached to it. For all the differences in the cultural background of Bridenbaugh and myself, as professional historians we share values that transcend our upbringing. I doubt that he would have found the Tennessee anti-evolution law of 1925 and the resultant Scopes trial any less repugnant than I, or have been any more detached from the issues involved in these events than I was. Nor should either of us necessarily have been detached. Objectivity does not necessitate detachment; it does not entail the abandonment of passion or the emasculation of ideals. It means simply and profoundly the ability to keep one's mind open and to allow one's powers of empathy to range widely. It means, above all, the desire to understand. It means perceiving the truth of John Higham's observation, "The serious historian may not wrap himself in judicial robes and pass judgment from on high; he is too much involved in both the prosecution and the defense. He is not a judge of the dead, but rather a participant in their affairs, and their only trustworthy intermediary." [5]

These qualities of mind may come instinctively, but more often than not I suspect they have to be sought after and learned. What enables one individual to assimilate these lessons and approach these goals more successfully than another is, for me, still wrapped in mystery. It is at this precise point that my own teaching often breaks down. I can tell my students what it is they have to strive for, but I have yet to learn to show them concretely how to accomplish what they must accomplish if they are to be good at what they want to do. All I can say with any certainty is that in studying the careers of my predecessors, my peers, and my students, I have not discovered any cultural preconditions that allow some of us to be more successful than others. Certainly by now we have sufficient evidence that a sense of social and cultural marginality can be as conducive to the development of historical skills and insights as the feeling of a shared culture—that "priceless asset" which Professor Bridenbaugh argues contemporary historians are the worse off for having lost. Both, of course, can also constitute impediments to historical understanding. It is not the mere existence of marginality or cultural sameness, but the way they act upon the historian, and the manner in which he reacts to them that is crucial. Becoming a sensitive and perceptive historian still remains an individual process, the meaning of which demands more study and thought than we have devoted to it.

All these lessons still lay before me when I began my research into Bryan's final years. At that point, I had no reason to challenge the prevalent image of Bryan drawn so indelibly by H. L. Mencken in his famous eulogy: "He came into life a hero, a Galahad, in bright and shining armor. He was passing out a poor mountebank." The assumption that Bryan had passed through the relatively familiar evolutionary pattern from angry idealism to angry conservatism was useful in the initial stages, since it provided a focus for my research and thought. It enabled me to concentrate on that phase of Bryan's long career in which the change I set out to understand appeared to have taken place. And it allowed me to winnow from his prolific writings those materials that seemed relevant to the problem with which I was concerned. As I worked my way carefully through Bryan's invaluable periodical *The Commoner*, however, I began to discover evidence that simply did not fit the traditional image. Even as Bryan was stumping the country on behalf of prohibition and fundamentalism, even as he became increasingly interested in the moral and religious purity of his countrymen, even as his ideological constituency became narrower and narrower, his efforts to secure political, economic, and social reform not only continued but broadened, and his interest in wielding political power within the Democratic party remained as great as ever.

At first this evidence was only mildly troubling. Not even neophyte historians should expect too much in the way of perfect symmetry. I had little hope of finding a clear point at which Bryan dropped his reform proclivities and became an intractable anachronism. Even then I realized that no man was ever totally one thing or another, and I fully anticipated discovering ambivalence and contradiction. But as I continued working through Bryan's speeches, his personal correspondence, the press of the period, the private papers of his contemporaries, the evidence mounted well beyond these contingencies. My research was making clear what no other historian, a number of whom had been through the identical materials, had so much as indicated: that in the decade between his resignation from Woodrow Wilson's Cabinet in 1915 and his death at the close of the Scopes trial in 1925, Bryan had moved to the Left on political and economic questions. He now advocated more government ownership, development, and regulation than at any previous point in his career; his relatively narrow reform program of 1896 was by 1925 far more comprehensive and bold.

It was becoming clear, even to so reluctant a revisionist as I was at that stage of my career, that I had been asking the wrong questions. The problem was not why Bryan had abandoned reform, for clearly he had not, nor why he had deserted the area of political activity for the hazier regions of religious and moralistic panaceas, for again he had not, but rather why he supplemented his traditional reform endeavors with new activities in the 1920s. How could he continue to espouse political and economic innovations while at the same time forging alliances with the antiurban, xenophobic, backward-looking Ku Klux Klan, and participating actively in the militant fundamentalist and antievolution movements? And what implications did all this have for our understanding of the decline of progressivism in America after World War I? Merely by posing these and similar questions, I was forced to rethink and challenge the accepted picture of Bryan in his later years and perhaps that of his followers as well. This was not in itself an easy task, for, my evidence aside, the traditional interpretation seemed so firmly based.

First of all, Bryan had reasons for abandoning reform and becoming "the bitter and malignant old man of the Scopes trial" whom Richard Hofstadter had portrayed in his influential essay on Bryan.[6] His tenure as Secretary of State from 1913 to 1915 saw the frustration of his efforts to bring about world peace, and his failure to convince Wilson and his fellow cabinet officers of the correctness of his course forced him to resign the only important official position he ever held (with the exception of his four years as a Congressman from Nebraska in the 1890s). His resignation during a time of heightened international tension brought him more criticism and ridicule than he had known at any time during his career. His efforts to secure prohibition further divided his old followers and clouded his reputation. His attempts to hold on to his power within the Democratic party and continue his crusade for reform were constantly thwarted. Although he was treated with respect and even affection during the Democratic National Convention of 1920, every one of his reform proposals was voted down, and a man he considered reactionary was nominated for the Presidency. Four years later, even the respect and affection were gone, and he could scarcely get his fellow Democrats gathered at the New York convention to listen to him. Postwar America was in general a strange and difficult place for Bryan.

The reasons for Bryan's apostasy were certainly present, and there even appeared to be a confession of that apostasy in a widely quoted letter Bryan wrote in 1923:

... my power in politics is not what it used to be and, therefore, my responsibility is not so great. While my power in politics has waned, I think it has increased in religious matters and I have invitations from preachers in all the churches. An evidence of the change is found in the fact that my correspondence in religious subjects is much larger than my correspondence in political subjects. My interest is deeper in religious subjects. . . .

Yet in spite of all the alleged reasons for his transformation, and in spite of what Bryan himself seemed to be saying, I had uncovered massive evidence to show that during these very years Bryan was spending much of his time and energy going before political rallies to plead for progressive labor legislation, liberal tax laws, government aid to farmers, public ownership of railroads, telegraph, and telephone, federal development of water resources, minimum wages for labor, minimum prices for agriculture, maximum profits for middlemen, and government guarantee of bank deposits, while maneuvering endlessly and always optimistically to regain power within his party.

At this point I reached an impasse in my work. I spent day after day rereading my notes, reshuffling my cards, rethinking my evidence. The conundrum posed by the letter was easy enough to resolve: Although historians had quoted it widely, none of them had discussed the context in which it was written. In 1923, in an effort to strengthen his antievolution crusade within the churches, Bryan decided to run for the position of Moderator of the Presbyterian Church. Accordingly, he wrote a series of letters to prominent Presbyterian ministers asking their support. One of them, the Reverend John A. Marquis of New York, responded by warning Bryan that should he be elected to the position, his chances of attaining high political office would be ruined. Bryan's answer was the letter quoted above, and it clearly was intended as an argument in favor of his increased activity in the religious sphere rather than as a serious admission of a diminished interest in politics. In 1922 Bryan had been far more accurate when he told a New York political rally, "I am not yet out of politics," and he meant just that, as his numerous political activities throughout the 1920s showed. (Significantly, statements such as this—and there were many of them —were never quoted by his biographers and historians.)

As satisfying as this explanation may have been, the fact remained that Bryan, after all, *had* attempted to be elected to his church's highest position, *had* enlisted in the crusade against evolution in the schools and modernism in the pulpit, and *had* placed himself in opposition to such newly emerging urban reformers as Al Smith and Fiorello LaGuardia. I had by now convinced myself that these activities supplemented rather than replaced his traditional reformist efforts, but I still had the obligation of explaining them, of understanding why he had chosen to engage himself in these new areas in his final years. The explanation lay in those copious notes I continued to ponder, although I could not see it at first. My dilemma remained until I began to reconceive the entire nature of my work.

Since Bryan was a political figure, I thought of my study as the reconstruction of the activities of a politician. That is, I saw it as primarily political history. In another essay in this volume, my late colleague Joseph Levenson defines intellectual history as the history not of thought, but of men thinking. Sitting there before my notes, I reached a similar conclusion. I came to the realization that I was engaged fundamentally in the study of Bryan's mind, of his world view. Bryan, after all, was a prolific writer. In his last ten years alone he had written five books, dozens of pamphlets, hundreds of editorials, and uncounted speeches. The problem was that most historians had merely used this large body of work to document Bryan's essential "vulgarity" and show the ludicrous nature of his mind. They had quoted ad nauseam Bryan's indictment of Darwin for having men descend "not even from American monkeys but from Old World monkeys," and his own version of the evolution of the leg:

> The leg, according to evolutionists, developed also by chance. One guess is that a little animal without legs one day discovered a wart on the belly, it had come without notice or premonitory symptoms; if it had come on the back instead of the belly the whole history of the world might have been different. But fortunately this wart came on the belly, and the little animal finding that it could use the wart to work itself along, used it until it developed into a leg. And then another wart and another leg. Why did man stop at two legs while the centipede kept on until it got a hundred?

But aside from having great fun with selected quotations from Bryan's writings, they really had not studied or come to terms with the thought of his later years. It was only when I realized that if Bryan was not an intellectual, he was nevertheless a "man thinking," and that as such, his thought, *as thought,* was worthy of study, that I was able to become, in John Higham's phrase, a "participant" in his affairs. It was then that the pieces in my puzzle began to fall into place, and I was able to understand the meaning of his last years. In short, only when I was willing to take Bryan seriously as a man and a mind, as well as a political force, was he willing to reveal himself to me.

Bryan had been a fundamentalist all his life and had objected to the religious and social implications of Darwin's work as early as 1904 in his popular speech, "The Prince of Peace." Why was it not until the 1920s that he became a *militant* fundamentalist and an *active* opponent of the promulgation of Darwinian thinking? The answers were all embodied in Bryan's writings. World War I came as a profound shock to him. At no point could he allow the spectacle of Christians slaughtering rather than loving their neighbors to stand as proof of the bankruptcy of the very Christian ideals that had always provided the basis of his reformist endeavors. Rather, he was led to search for those forces that had driven men away from the teachings of Christ. In 1916 he began to tie Nietzsche's philosophy (which he saw as the philosophical underpinning of German militarism) to Darwin's theory of the survival of the fittest. By 1920 he had become certain that Nietzsche in propounding a philosophy "that condemned democracy . . . denounced Christianity . . . denied the existence of God, over-turned all standards of morality, eulogized war . . . praised hatred . . . and endeavored to substitute the worship of the superman for the worship of Jehovah," had merely carried Darwin's teachings to their logical conclusions.

The shock of the war was intensified for Bryan in the postwar era. The significant accomplishments of the progressive years seemed threatened by what appeared to be one of the most extensive displays of political apathy and indifference in American history. No matter how hard Bryan tried, all his efforts to continue the reform spirit of the past were rebuffed. Nor was Bryan's trauma exclusively political. If the economic primacy of agrarian America had been overturned at the beginning of Bryan's long career, his writings make clear that at the end of that career he saw its cultural primacy being eroded by what Walter Lippmann called the "acids of modernity." No institution seemed safe from assault. Not the churches, not the schools, not even the reliable Democratic party. Again Bryan frantically sought to convince himself and his followers that the fault lay not in the inefficacy of his ideals but in some new force that was paralyzing the will of the people and undermining the religious, cultural, and political certainties of his past. And again the finger pointed to the new science and the new theology that were so closely tied to it.

Bryan's letters, speeches, and books make it possible to travel with him as he made his way through the country on his endless lecture tours and help us relive his experiences as he encountered, or heard of, a professor of geology at Columbia University who told his students to throw away all they had learned in Sunday school, a professor at the University of Wisconsin who taught his students that the Bible was a collection of myths, a congressman's daughter at Wellesley who glibly remarked, "Nobody believes in Bible stories now," and a teacher in a Methodist college in Ohio who taught his classes that Christ was a bastard. All of this—and there was a great deal of it—presented Bryan with an explanation of the postwar decline in progressivism. Bryan had fought plutocracy and imperialism, war and liquor, in part because he felt they dehumanized man. Now he found abroad in the land an intellectual force that he was convinced also tended to dehumanize man by supplying him with a brute heritage. The younger generation was indifferent and apathetic not because they did not care, but because the doctrines taught them in their schools caused them to lose faith in man's ability to become anything other than what he was. No longer could they believe in the ultimate triumph of righteousness or in a life after death where their virtue and patience would be rewarded.

For Bryan, morality and reform had always been inextricably bound together. At the height of his political power he had argued: "If one actually thinks that man dies as the brute dies, he will yield more easily to the temptation to do injustice to his neighbour when the circumstances are such as to promise security from detection." In his last years he repeated this message endlessly: "How can one fight for a principle unless he believes in the triumph of right? How can he believe in the triumph of right if he does not believe that God stands back of the truth and that God is able to bring victory to His side?" Science and rationality were not enough. The science that was demanding absolute freedom in the classroom was "the same science that manufactured poisonous gases to suffocate soldiers. . . . Science has no morality. Science gives us weapons and means for escape but not the means for control." Bryan presented the graphic picture of a child reared in a pious home going to college and learning that man descended from the beasts below, that his development was not part of God's plan, and that even his morality was man-made:

> And the child goes out with its faith in God shaken, and its faith in the Bible shaken, and its faith in immortality shaken, and its faith in prayer shaken.

> Oh, are you surprised that men become brutish as they deal with each other?

> That is the sentiment today. "There is no God; there is no future; we will do as we please." And doing as we please is bringing the world into dangerous ground.

If many of his former followers saw tensions between his religious and political crusades, Bryan did not: "People often ask me why I can be a progressive in politics and a fundamentalist in religion. The answer is easy. Government is man-made and therefore imperfect. It can always be improved. But religion is not a man-made affair. If Christ is the word, how can anyone be a progressive in religion? I am satisfied with the God we have, with the Bible and with Christ." He was more than satisfied; he was convinced that without them there could be no reform. Bryan saw himself wielding "a double-barreled shotgun, firing one barrel at the [Republican] elephant as he tries to enter the treasury and another at Darwinism—the monkey—as he tries to enter the school room." At the heart of all Bryan's writings and polemics one message became increasingly evident: that Bryan joined the fundamentalist and anti-evolution crusades not in order to retreat from politics, but in order to combat a force he held responsible for sapping American politics of its idealism and progressive spirit. He remained a progressive in the only way he knew how: by attempting to preserve and strengthen the values and faith of that part of America—the rural West and South—with which he had always been most closely identified.

The argument and evidence I presented in my book are, of course, more detailed and complex than I can indicate here. I want only to illustrate how taking Bryan's words seriously—entering into them rather than merely using them—allowed me a number of insights not only into Bryan, but also into the movements he was engaged in. The fundamentalist movement of the 1920s, for instance, has too easily been seen as a politically conservative force. This was certainly true of many of its leaders, who were convinced that the function of religion was to save individual souls and not society at large and who reacted against liberalism wherever they found it, in politics as well as in theology. This was never true of Bryan, who continued to espouse the social gospel and to see in Christianity a set of infallible beliefs leading to eternal salvation *and* a social movement leading to the reformation of society. Bryan's ability to combine these two aspects of Christian belief and his great influence as one of the nation's leading fundamentalist proponents in his last years force one to wonder whether he may not have been more characteristic of the mass of fundamentalist followers than his more conservative colleagues.

Bryan's last years not only reopen this question, but lead one to think again about the entire fate of progressivism in postwar America. Bryan's career in the 1920s gives evidence for supposing that the decline of progressivism as a movement was due less to economic and political factors than to the growing cultural schism that engulfed America in that decade. There were no yawning political or economic gaps that prevented Al Smith and Bryan from combining their programs and their followers into a new progressive movement. But there were cultural reasons: the Americas for which these two leaders spoke were increasingly different and threatening to each other. The progressive urge in the 1920s, then, did not disappear; it fractionalized and was rechanneled into the struggles waged over prohibition, religion, immigration restriction, evolution, the rights of Catholics and Jews. The primary issues of the twenties were not political or economic, but cultural, and over these issues the old progressive coalition disintegrated.

If I have one great regret about the book I published, it is that it does not go into these matters more fully. At the time, I thought of doing enough research to test, in some areas at least, my supposition that Bryan's urges, motives, and actions in the 1920s were representative of those of large segments of rural America, but I feared this would involve me in writing another book and would structurally and esthetically interfere with the book I had written. I may well have been right, but I allow myself the luxury of some regrets anyway.

I am sorry, too, that I did not have either the materials or the knowledge to do more with Bryan's personality structure. Bryan lacked all introspection; he left behind no truly personal revelations for any part of his life; he appeared almost incapable of having a private life. He seemed to me a particularly inappropriate subject for psychic analysis. One better versed in psychoanalytic theory than I might well have been able to make something of these very qualities, as well as such salient personality characteristics as his compulsive optimism, his inability to question any of his own actions, his propensity to see himself as a vessel carrying out God's ends, his devotion to men in the mass rather than men as individuals, his unfailing ability to rationalize all events so that they confirmed his expectations and the fundamentals of his faith. Traits such as these struck me as more indicative of a cultural than a personal syndrome and more suitable, therefore, for societal rather than individual psychoanalysis. For me, the real question was, and is, not how Bryan got this way, but why the United States produced so many leaders like him at the turn of the century and why the American people were so willing to follow them; it was a question that I was in no way qualified to answer, though I do wish I had raised it more explicitly. Nevertheless, the mere recognition and identification of Bryan's personal qualities tended to confirm my historical thesis, for this kind of personality simply did not lend itself to the traditional image of a man who became so frustrated and disillusioned that he could throw aside the work of a lifetime and end his career leading a cranky religious crusade.

At the time I published my book, I had other misgivings as well. I worried about writing what amounted to a sympathetic study of a man whose actions in the twenties I would have opposed vehemently had I been alive then. One or two friends who read my manuscript were similarly troubled by my failure to inject a sense of moral outrage into my account of many of Bryan's activities. I thought seriously of doing so and rejected the urge largely because so many previous studies of Bryan had been written in just such a manner—as dialogues between Bryan and his contemporary critics, with Bryan invariably coming out second best. I had no illusions that I could keep moral judgment out of my work; I felt only that this should not be my primary object. Bryan had been too often judged and too little understood, and I decided that comprehension, not judgment, should be my basic purpose. I decided also to get off my back, once and for all, the old dictum that to understand is to forgive. For the historian, understanding can be an end in itself with no moral goals attached. About this decision I have no regrets at all, as the earlier parts of this essay undoubtedly make clear. It was this determination that allowed me to bridge the gulf that had for so long separated Bryan from his historical interpreters.

I have written thus far as if my work on Bryan was composed in splendid isolation with no outside influences. No one who has attempted a work of history will believe this, of course. Ultimately, I had to make my own decisions and come to my own conclusions, and this *is* a lonely process. But along the way the influences upon me of other historians, of colleagues, and of friends were crucial and probably more numerous and decisive than I am aware of even now. Two men will serve to illustrate the nature of this debt. John William Ward's study of the ideology of Jacksonian America and his article on Charles Lindbergh [7] taught me both the possibilities for and the necessity of taking *all* thought seriously and provided a methodology for discovering the tensions, ambivalences, and symbolic meanings embodied in thinking. My personal friendship with him, which began while I was finishing my dissertation, has driven these lessons home and opened new vistas that have largely altered the way I look at the past. Richard Hofstadter, who first suggested my study and supervised it at every stage, played a central role. His own work on the reform ethos in America [8] taught me much about its subtleties and tensions and allowed me to understand that the past must not be viewed in absolute terms—that although we may prefer our reformers and conservatives pure, men may harbor reactionary and progressive impulses not only at the same time, but also for the same reasons. Although my study of Bryan contradicted his own essay on Bryan at several points, and although I am sure that to this day he has important reservations about my interpretations, it was he who urged me to expand my master's thesis into a doctoral dissertation and then helped me to publish it. In this respect he was instrumental in teaching me that it is possible to transcend the very human tendency to defend our own specific conclusions and engage in a truly scholarly dialogue. I have tried to incorporate this example into all my own work—especially my teaching.

Unfortunately, it is not an easy lesson to get across in today's political and social atmosphere. Professor Bridenbaugh's insistence that the products of certain cultural environments have little hope of understanding the historical products of others has won a host of new allies. I have learned this unmistakably in the past few years. Shortly after completing the Bryan book, I became engaged in a new study of Negro protest movements in twentieth-century America. I soon found that I was less interested in the organizational aspects of black protest and more concerned with the problem of to what extent the leaders of these movements were reflecting the attitudes and desires of the larger mass of Negroes in America. If my study of Bryan was a tentative attempt to understand the ethos of rural America by examining the attitudes of one of its leaders, I now wanted to reverse the process. I wanted to study the feelings and thought of a group of historically inarticulate people not by looking at their spokesmen, but by examining the cultural records they left behind. Thus, for the past few years I have been attempting to learn how to work with materials hitherto unfamiliar to me: folk music, folk tales, humor, popular culture, as well as with more traditional sources. I have found this work difficult, but illuminating and exciting. I have found it also a bit depressing, for once again I was destined to discover that I am the wrong man working in the wrong field.

Just as six years ago I was told that as the child of lower-middle-class, urban-immigrant parents, the door to the American past in all likelihood would remain closed to me, so today I am told that as the child of white parents, I have little chance of understanding the black past. This message is repeated endlessly. Negro students tend to stay away from classes in black history taught by white men. Negro intellectuals proclaim stridently that they alone are qualified to study and interpret Negro history. In the recently published critique by ten black writers of William Styron's novel, *The Confessions of Nat Turner*, a number of contributors argue not only that Styron failed to transcend his own culture to penetrate that of Nat Turner (a criticism worth making and exploring), but that no white man could be expected to do so. A few illustrations will make the point:

> . . . it is likely too much to expect a white, twentieth-century American novelist to be able to conceive of the world of a black, Old Testament-type Messiah.

> There can be no common history until we have first fleshed out the lineaments of our own, for no one else can speak out of the bittersweet bowels of our blackness.

> Just as it was impossible for the slave master to look at slavery from the point of view of the slave, it has proven impossible for the slave master's grandson to look at slavery or at the contemporary black-and-white confrontation from the perspective of Rap Brown and Stokely Carmichael or Floyd McKissick or any other black revolutionary, or black non-revolutionary, for that matter. The first mistake was for Styron to attempt the novel.

> . . . it is impossible for the slavemaster's grandson to see the revolutionary black man in the sense that Gabriel saw himself, as the "George Washington" of his people, ready to lay down his life for their liberation.

> Historical fiction about Negroes that has real characters and is true to history is almost impossible even for the most understanding white writers in the racist, separatist United States.[9]

Nor is this attitude confined to Negroes. White graduate students studying black history are too frequently sheepish not only about their ability, but about their very right to do so. A number of white scholars in one way or another have publicly or privately apologized for their own work or the work of their white colleagues on the grounds that the black man is eminently more fit to penetrate his own past than the white man. Although some of these white scholars and students are themselves doing important work in the area of Negro history, they somehow feel it necessary to put their *mea culpa* on record. More tragic is the number of young scholars capable of writing important studies who may be frightened away from this much-neglected field by the irrelevancies stressed by this rigid cultural and pigmental determinism.

The emotional and psychic content of this new argument is so strong it almost seems futile to point out that such white scholars as Roger Abrahams, Charles Keil, and Elliot Leibow have recently made important strides toward a greater understanding of Negro culture and society in the United States.[10] Yet it is necessary to do so, just as it is necessary to assert continually the truth that there are no impassable culture gaps in the realm of historical scholarship. If too many previous historians have tripped over their own cultural umbilical cords, it is because they were poor historians and not because they were tragic prisoners of an inevitable cultural myopia. The historian who cannot significantly transcend the culture of his youth, the needs of his present, and the hopes of his future in order to come to terms with the past deserves repudiation, but we must take care not to transform his failures into unbending laws governing all historians.

Historians have always had to combat what Marc Bloch called "the virus of the present" and what I would call the virus of culture-boundness. Many historians today are overcoming these handicaps. They are beginning to cast their nets wider to take in not only the articulate leadership classes, but the historically inarticulate lower and lower-middle classes. They are paying attention to the materials of folk and popular culture as well as to those of élite culture. They are finally taking seriously the lessons that cultural anthropologists, psychoanalysts, sociologists, and other social scientists have to offer them. It is ironic that at this very important and pivotal stage in the development of their discipline, historians are being asked to pay obeisance to rigid judgments which seek to tell them who is most fit to study what. I can only hope that when my own study of Negro culture in twentieth-century America is completed, it will be but one of an increasing number of serious studies of black history by scholars from every conceivable cultural background that will help to discredit this new historical obscurantism, just as I like to think that my study of Bryan helps to point out the central fallacy of Professor Bridenbaugh's lament.

NOTES

1. Lawrence W. Levine, *Defender of the Faith: William Jennings Bryan, The Last Decade, 1915–1925* (New York, 1965).
2. Carl Bridenbaugh, "The Great Mutation," *American Historical Review,* LXVIII (January 1963), 322–23.
3. Edward Hallett Carr, *What Is History?* (New York, 1962), p. 54.
4. Ernest Nagel, "Relativism and Some Problems of Working Historians," in Sidney Hook, ed., *Philosophy and History* (New York, 1963), pp. 81–82.
5. John Higham, "Beyond Consensus: The Historian as Moral Critic," *American Historical Review*, LXVII (April 1962), 620.
6. Richard Hofstadter, *The American Political Tradition* (New York, 1948), chapter VIII, "William Jennings Bryan: The Democrat as Revivalist."
7. John William Ward, *Andrew Jackson: Symbol for an Age* (New York, 1955); "The Meaning of Lindbergh's Flight," *American Quarterly,* X (Spring 1958), 3–16.
8. Richard Hofstadter, *The Age of Reform* (New York, 1955).
9. John Henrik Clarke, ed., *William Styron's Nat Turner: Ten Black Writers Respond* (Boston, 1968), pp. 29, 32, 36, 43, 50.
10. Roger D. Abrahams, *Deep Down in the Jungle . . . : Negro Narrative Folklore from the Streets of Philadelphia* (Hatboro, Pa., 1964); Charles Keil, *Urban Blues* (Chicago, 1966); Elliot Liebow, *Tally's Corner: A Study of Negro Streetcorner Men* (Boston, 1967).

ACKNOWLEDGMENTS

Every historian's workshop should be provided with typists as painstaking and tidy as Mrs. Dorothy White of the Department of History, Berkeley, and Mrs. Grace O'Connell of El Cerrito.

Before locking up this Workshop for good, I should also express my thanks to those of my departmental colleagues at Berkeley who helped me find the right combination of "hands" and minds.

A Note on the Type

The text of this book was set on the Linotype in Aster, a typeface designed by Francesco Simoncini (born 1912 in Bologna, Italy) for Ludwig and Mayer, the German type foundry. Starting out with the basic old-face letterforms that can be traced back to Francesco Griffo in 1495, Simoncini emphasized the diagonal stress by the simple device of extending diagonals to the full height of the letterforms and squaring off. By modifying the weights of the individual letters to combat this stress, he has produced a type of rare balance and vigor. Introduced in 1958, Aster has steadily grown in popularity wherever type is used.

This book was composed, printed, and bound by Kingsport Press, Inc., Kingsport, Tennessee.

TITLES IN THIS SERIES

12 G. R. Elton. *Political History: Principles and Practices.* 1970.

13 Martin Feldman, Eli Seifman, eds. *The Social Studies: Structure, Models, and Strategies.* 1969.

14 John A. Garraty. *The Nature of Biography.* 1957.

15 John Higham, Leonard Krieger, Felix Gilbert. *History.* 1965.

16 H. Stuart Hughes. *History as Art and as Science.* 1964.

17 Paul Murray Kendall. *The Art of Biography.* 1965.

18 William Leo Lucey. *History: Methods and Interpretation.* 1958.

19 Raymond G. McInnis, James W. Scott, eds. *Social Science and Research Handbook.* 1974.

20 John Madge. *The Tools of Social Science.* 1953.

21 Arthur Marwick. *The Nature of History.* 1981.

22 Hans Meyerhoff, ed. *The Philosophy of History in Our Time.* 1959.

23 A. D. Momigliano. *Studies in Historiography.* 1966.

24 Herbert J. Muller. *The Uses of the Past.* 1953.

25 Allan Nevins. *The Gateway to History.* 1938.

26 Roy Pascal. *Design and Truth in Autobiography.* 1960.

27 A. L. Rowse. *The Use of History.* 1946.

28 Robert Allen Skotheim, ed. *The Historian and the Climate of Opinion.* 1969.

29 Robert Stover. *The Nature of Historical Thinking.* 1967.

30 Pardon E. Tillinghast. *The Specious Past: Historians and Others.* 1972.

31 Ludwig von Mises. *Theory and History.* 1957.